WEALTH FOR ALL

Books by R. E. McMaster, Jr.—

Cycles of War, The Next Six Years, 1977
The Trader's Notebook, 1978
The Trader's Notebook, 1979
The Trader's Notebook, 1980
Wealth for All, 1982
(Book 1—Religion, Politics and War)
Wealth for All, 1982
(Book 2—Economics)

WEALTH FOR ALL

Religion, Politics and War

R. E. McMaster, Jr.

A. N., Inc.
P. O. Box 67
Whitefish, Montana 59937
1982

Published by
A. N., Inc.
P. O. Box 67
Whitefish, Montana 59937

This book is dedicated to my
greatest fan and most helpful critic,
my wife,
Linda E. McMaster

TABLE OF CONTENTS

Read This First!

OVERVIEW

The way the world really works is a far cry removed from the way the American public perceives it operates. Pleasant illusions are far more popular than painful facts. The normal state of affairs for each of us individually should be increasing wealth through time, natural tragedies and wars aside. Inheritance, free solar energy and cumulative technology in a *"fair play"* economic system should, in just one generation, provide each of us with such a substantial base of economic wealth, that we should then be free to pursue the development of our individual talents, which are not only in our own best self-interest but also in the best interest of society-at-large.

Cooperation should be the norm in our society, not conflict. Conflict and class warfare are harmful social mutations, stemming from a political and economic system that benefits a few special interests and exploits the masses. The age-old question of whose rights are superior, those of the individual or those of the group, is easily resolved to the benefit of both when a long-term perspective is enacted within the framework of a truly free market where individual men develop their talents, are responsible, and commodities are monetized on the local level.

Beyond question, the economic, political, social and environmental evils that exist today are a result of, and will disappear as soon as, each of us personally becomes responsible in every area of life. In truth, human misery today can be directly tracked to the failure of each of us, individually, to assume all of our personal responsibilities. Freedom, happiness, prosperity and security are all bound up in our willingness to assume our individual responsibilities. For example, the man who starts a business assumes responsibility for that business. He has accordingly also assumed risk. But he receives commensurate rewards with the assumption of responsibility and risk. He reaps the fruits of prosperity and maximizes his security also. After all, if the business fails, the owner of the business is the last one to lose his job. Thus the owner, the risk taker, has the greatest job security. So, assumption of risk and the security which Americans so desire today are one and the same. We are most vulnerable, by contrast, when we strive for security alone, as is overwhelmingly the case today.

The tremendous number of controls and programs which governments at all levels impose upon us today are an arrogant and proud
attempt to stop time, the underlying assumption being that we *"know
it all,"* that we can thus achieve security in an ever-changing world,
and that further change and growth is unnecessary. Such pride goes
before a fall. This is exactly what we should expect at the end of a
200-year national cycle and at the end of a 510-year civilization cycle.

The Great American Dream of *"rags to riches"* is a myth! The economic system is so constructed with booby traps, regulations, and in-
centives to assume debt, to be wasteful and short-term oriented, that it
is next to impossible to succeed long-term. For the most part, those
who have become wealthy today are either wealthy on paper, or have
become prosperous through debt which, as articles in this *"Wealth
For All"* series of books will show, not only contributes to inflation,
but is directly harmful to society. They have promoted conflict and
class warfare in the process. The system is so designed.

The present economic and political system is effectively, by design
or negligent accident, bankrupting, enslaving and impoverishing us
all, spiritually and materially. Americans live with the illusion of a
high standard of living. The harsh reality, however, is that when debt
obligations are considered, many, if not most of us, are in the red—
technically bankrupt. With little or no understanding of economics
and the financial curse of compound interest, Americans merrily skip
along the road to slavery, calling it all the while the road to freedom.
Unconcerned about a tax system which demands more of them than
the Vietcong does of its slaves or feudal lords did of their serfs, each
generation of Americans burdens the next with more debt as the productivity fleecing process continues ad infinitum.

There is no reason for enduring the economic burden we bear today.
The economic and political logic of the Founding Fathers who built
this great country is still applicable today. Human nature has not
changed. Cause and effect still rules supreme. It is no accident that the
United States of America became the most prosperous country on the
face of the earth. It is a by-product of the economic and political rules
under which our society operated. Those rules could just as easily be
restored today, quickly returning us to *"Wealth For All."*

Wealth is seldom destroyed. Rather, it is transferred. There is a great
deal of information in these two *"Wealth For All"* volumes about why
very few are so rich and many are so very poor. It all boils down to
special interests filling the vacuum of our personal irresponsibility, and
violation of the principle that theft is wrong at all levels, including theft
by government. This moral *"theft"* issue is a religious one.

The greatest resistance you personally will face to understanding *"Wealth For All"* and applying it in your own best self-interest **and** the best interest of society long-term will come from within you. You will be your own worst enemy. All of us like to feel secure in what we have learned, that what we have been taught is true. None of us likes to feel that we have been deceived. But Machiavelli warned us, *"One who deceives will always find those who allow themselves to be deceived."* Thus, the greatest psychological hurdle that you will face in overcoming your aversion to what follows is your natural resistance to change, and pride.

None of us likes to feel that we have been played for a sucker. The truth of the matter is, however, we all have been fooled. While our educational systems have been excellent when it comes to teaching us technical material and how to function in the factual world, by contrast, education today is a dismal failure when it comes to teaching us how to think, and in providing us with guiding abstract models about how the world really works. It is the conclusion of many who have watched the accuracy of the *"Wealth For All"* analysis through the years that too many Americans today are empty-headed, robot-like, nonthinking humanoids. Sadly, most Americans consistently act contrary to their own best interests long-term.

Why should you believe me? In addition to my track record and credibility established professionally, you need also to know that I have moved about in powerful circles. I have worked with the richest men in this country. I have interacted at the highest levels of government, all the way from the Shah of Iran to the White House. I have been able to call up and talk to any congressman or senator in the Republican Party. I've worked within the system. Sad to say, the system stinks, unless you are a willing bureaucrat or a manipulator at the top. What we suffer with today is a bad case of *"institutional constipation."* I was not able to unclog the system, working alone, within the system. But all of us, as individual plumbers, can free things up in no time at all.

Each article in each *"Wealth For All"* book is dated so that you will be able to discern the original date of publication as it appeared in THE REAPER, a newsletter. Very little editing has been done to the *"original"* piece. This is important. Why? There is an old proverb that states, *"Those who live close to the truth are seldom surprised by the future."* By leaving the *"original"* essay basically untouched and dated, you will see that the analyses and projections made have, in most applicable cases, come substantially true. There is your proof! Cling to it. You will know that what you are reading is true because the analyses and projections made at the time of *"original"* publication are, for the most part, now history. *"Those who live close to the truth are seldom surprised by the future!"*

Next, it is important that you understand my motivation behind producing this *"Wealth For All"* series of books. First of all, I'm fed up with seeing the trusting American people so totally and consistently deceived. Secondly, I want to help move our country back onto a constructive course. My intentions are in keeping with the understanding and discernment of some of the great minds who have built this country. Consider the following quotes:

> *"The minority, the ruling class at present, has the schools and press, usually the church as well, under its thumb. This enables it to organize and sway the emotions of the masses, and make its tool of them."*
> Albert Einstein

> *"I really look with commiseration over the great body of my fellow citizens, who, reading newspapers, live and die in the belief that they have known something of what has been passing in the world in their time."*
> Thomas Jefferson

> *"The press of this country is now, and always has been, so thoroughly dominated by the wealthy few of the country that it cannot be depended upon to give the great mass of the people that correct information concerning political, economic and social subjects which is necessary that they shall have in order that they shall vote and then act in the best way to protect themselves from the brutal force and chicanery of the ruling and employing class."*
> Edward W. Scripps, founder of Scripps-Howard Newspapers.

At this point, you may well recall the timeless words of Abraham Lincoln:

> *"It is true that you may fool all the people some of the time; you can even fool some of the people all the time; but you can't fool all the people all the time."*

There has been enough foolishness in American society long enough.

Finally, these *"Wealth For All"* books are an attempt to head off a violent revolution in this country, the growing probability of which is almost beyond question at this point, the culmination of which would be the fulfillment of a long-ago, patiently laid plan. When economists tell us that the only effective way to fight inflation is to throw millions of people out of work, as economists admitted in the BUSINESS WEEK of February 22, 1982, we know the economic system is bankrupt. Inflation and/or unemployment lead to revolution. When respected political analysts tell us, *"The way the country is constituted now, the road to political authority and influence is less open to those of political genius. Opportunities to move up are somehow clogged by institutions,"* as William W. Abbot did in the U.S. NEWS of February 22, 1982, we know the political system is likewise bankrupt. The American public is increasingly politically frustrated and alienated. Alienation in a democracy leads to revolution. A bankrupt economic and political system is a revolution waiting to happen! But revolutions always lead to tyranny. So, to put it quite bluntly, our personal peace and prosperity in the remaining years of our lives and our children's lives depend directly upon our individual willingness to get involved and become responsible in all areas of our lives. Misery always eventually fills the vacuum of irresponsibility. There is no other way. There never has been. There never will be. Human nature has not changed.

The answer, ultimately, is spiritual. Correct religious assumptions precede accurate principles; these lead to clear thoughts and ideas, both written and verbal. These, in turn, result in productive and constructive deeds, leading to good habits, and a prosperous destiny for all of us. As Abraham Lincoln said, *"It is difficult to make a man miserable when he feels he is worthy of himself and claims kindred to the great God who made him."* In terms of our American Christian heritage, God himself solved the problem of eternal salvation for man through Jesus Christ. In terms of solutions in time, as heirs with Christ, we are responsible, and thus must be free to pursue and develop our God-given talents, not only so that His will for our lives will be fulfilled, but so that we will maximize our own best self-interest long-term. The will of God, and each of our own best self-interests, properly understood, are one and the same. Organized religion today, sad to say, has missed this basic point.

Again, under the principles of *"Wealth For All,"* increasing inheritance from generation to generation, free solar energy leading to increasing material abundance, and cumulative technology mean that economic welfare should not even be a consideration for us. Each of us, in a properly ordered economic and political system, should be so rich and secure that we're literally freed from nearly all basic economic considerations so that we can pursue the development of our individual talents from which all men will benefit. Such an encouraging economic system is practically possible today, promoting cooperation rather than conflict. Just as each snowflake is unique, so, too, are each of us uniquely created individuals who have a special contribution to make to our fellow man, promoting cooperation, harmony and peace in time.

"Wealth For All," the essay which appears at the beginning of each of these two volumes, is the summary statement. The two volumes under this *"Wealth For All"* umbrella are:

1. RELIGION, POLITICS AND WAR
2. ECONOMICS

Each book stands on its own. Yet each volume is also an integral part of *"Wealth For All."*

It is my deepest hope that the little time and effort you spend in working through both of these volumes will give you not only a clear understanding of how the world works, but also provide you with the factual and abstract basis upon which you will be able to personally prosper and make decisions that will again restore our country to the greatness which it once had, and as our ancestors intended, it deserves today.

R. E. McMaster, Jr.
August 2, 1982

WEALTH FOR ALL
(An Economic Manifesto)

10/16/81

Economics all boils down to two basic ingredients—land and labor. A well-watered, nutrient and mineral rich, humus-filled earth in a temperate climatic zone, populated by healthy, hard-working, future-oriented, free and creative individuals brings forth the best of all economic worlds.

The commodity futures market, overall, is one of the best lead indicators of future economic activity. Commodities, being the sensitive and volatile *urchins* they are, are like the tip of a whip. Their backlash carries all the way down to the whip's handle. The rural country (tip of the whip/commodities) eventually speaks to the cities (handle of the whip/mature, developed economic centers).

The laws of physics teach us that *energy* and *matter* are interchangeable, basically one and the same. As such, the *abstract* and *concrete* are one and the same in the real world in a never ending flow. This perspective is pregnant with economic truth. Economic exchange, thus, when you boil it all down, is nothing more than the exchange of goods and services, the swapping of *matter* (goods) for *energy* (services and labor) and vice versa. Money, in the sense of classical economic exchange (barter), is a real good, a commodity, *matter*, whether in the form of gold, silver, tobacco leaves, salt, barley, sea shells, wheat—all of which have historically served as money. Money is subsequently also **potential**, stored, inactive *energy*, ready to spring forth **kinetically** as the catalyst for the production of additional goods and services (*matter*), the end product of the mixture of land and labor. Quickly, we, too, see that all honest money is ultimately a product of the land, a good, a resource, a commodity, *matter*, if you will. This viewpoint is consistent with the laws of thermodynamics, the basis of physics and the concrete application of theological truth. The first and second laws of thermodynamics state simply that *energy* is neither created nor destroyed (first law), but that when *energy* is transferred or used, useful *energy* is lost in the transition process (second law). The second law is referred to as entropy—that all things move toward a state of decay.

The first and second laws of thermodynamics hold true in a **closed** system. While we appear to live in a closed system on this earth, we constantly are blessed with a new shot of *energy* each and every day, courtesy of the sun. So, in fact, we live in an **open** system. Because the sun provides us with new, real, useable *energy* each and every day, we have the opportunity to make real economic progress and create real new wealth by using working man's productive efforts to groom the earth and prevent the natural disorder which automatically occurs as the sun's *energy* creates new *matter*. The sun creates *matter* (real new wealth) on its own. But this newly created *matter* (real new wealth) will become disorderly and far less useful unless man takes dominion over it.

Real new wealth (*matter*) is created as new *energy* (solar) comes into the system. Grass, trees, and ocean vegetation grow freely. Cows, horses, sheep and fish eat the grass, leaves and algae and subsequently produce calves, foals, lambs and more fish. New *energy* creates new *matter*. Real new wealth is thus created. *Energy* in and *matter* out as the system goes. (*Matter* subsequently produces *energy*, too—wood, oil.) Solar *energy*, mixed with man's efforts, brings to harvest the fields of wheat, corn, oats, barley and soybeans—all of which are real new wealth. These grains grow randomly, utilizing just the *energy* of the sun. When hardworking productive man is added to the equation, aided by the blessing of favorable weather, production of grain protein explodes, as does meat protein. Man's dominion over animals short-circuits the *"law of the jungle."* It's a miracle. And it's ultimately free. The sun shines and also out pops the oranges, grapefruit, walnuts and pecans. Pineapples and bananas join the *"natural hit parade"* which feed man, providing him with the physical *energy* necessary to increase the bounty of new free wealth (greater agricultural production) or, for example, in the case of mining, harvest other natural resources which then create a virtual supermarket of economic goods (*matter*) for mankind.

After a lifetime of productivity, a man, if he has planned wisely, practiced deferred gratification and sexual restraint, gained wisdom and looked to the long-term, can leave a boatload of material goods to his lineage. So ever-increasing wealth should be a normal state of affairs for mankind if he will only act consistent with his long-term self-interest. Man's long-term spiritual instincts must thus rule over his short-term animalistic desires if this wealth inheritance is to occur. So, multigenerational families are crucial for individual man's, and thus collective man's, increase in wealth.

Reward is also commensurate with responsibility. Parents take care of children. When the children grow up, they take care of their elderly parents with the family's resources. Turn about is fair play. Men have the incentive to work and save for their own future (old age), as well as for their children's. The incentive to raise secure, loved, happy, productive children is apparent. As a result, there is less crime, less taxes for police forces and less welfare, and so the entire society benefits psychologically, socially and materially. The destructive inheritance and property taxes are abolished. Women are important as mothers. (The hand that rocks the cradle rules the world.) Minorities are no longer displaced by women in the work force. Social Security is unnecessary. The "throw-away" society disappears, as do drugs, abortion and illegitimacy. Property rights are thus seen as necessary for human rights.

Finally, a culture's technological advancement is cumulative. Technological advancement in a free society finds higher, better and more efficient ways to utilize natural and human resources at less cost with less labor. Technology, thus, is an additional creator of new wealth. The free market has given us the technology we enjoy today. Technology creates a shortage of labor, making people more valuable and necessary. Some day technology will provide us with a machine that creates excess energy. De Palma's, Jefimenko's or Maglich's prototypes refined?

In summary, natural catastrophes and personal tragedies aside, **wealth from the sun**, particularly when combined with man's efforts, **wealth from inheritance**, and **wealth from technology are all cumulative**. Thus, **the normal state of affairs for mankind collectively is increasing WEALTH FOR ALL through time**.

Given this perspective, doesn't it stand to reason that real money should be tied to real new wealth in order to prevent the curse of inflation, which the masses never recognize, due to their economic ignorance, until it's too late and the system is about to self-destruct (hyper-inflation) or crater into a depression (deflation). Money should be spent, not borrowed into existence, at the local level, equal to the amount of new wealth created. (Monetarist theory is thus satisfied.) Free market money, commodity money, should be allowed to co-exist with government money as a check against government and to allow for freedom of choice. It is an unethical and immoral banking and economic system, as well as a destructive one long-term, that allows a few to become filthy rich at the expense of the masses, particularly when the few become filthy rich not due to any real productive increase of goods and services on their part which would benefit all of mankind, but rather due to speculation in zero sum games, use of other people's money without their direct approval or participation, and the paying of outrageous interest to a non-productive middleman (banker). Isn't it logical that "real" money should only be created consistent with the creation of real new wealth? Wouldn't such a system provide a sound economic framework, a set of "fair rules" for the economic game, which would still stress incentive, and reward the most productive, and encourage the most capable to prosper, but only when they served the best interest of the masses long-term, consistent with their own long-term self-interest? Doesn't it make sense that debt should only be short-term (seven years), that debt should be utilized for productive purposes only, such as for producing new goods and services, that debt should never be for consumption (short-term gratification) (supply side economics satisfied), and that debt should be free of the abstract, compounding rate of interest? When monetary interest is involved in an economic system, those who put up the money (bank deposits) for the economic activity are intellectually, and often geographically, removed from the economic venture. Thus, the natural check against misuse of investment funds is removed. The feedback loop, responsibility and accountability, is reduced. More economic boondoggles, embezzlements and other marginal, fraudulent economic activities are able to occur, all of which are contrary to *"the greatest good for the greatest number"* long-term. Also, *"interest"* does no work. Neither does it show mercy on "trial and error" man. It grinds on and on. It compounds. Eventually it consumes economic man. Such is the case today.

Economic reality is that the production of goods nearly always precedes the production of services. Goods first, services second is the natural order of things. How can it be otherwise? Unless there are basic goods provided to meet man's basic needs, such as food and shelter, which provide the necessary energy and protection for mankind, no services are produced. Furthermore, without goods (*matter*) produced in excess of that needed to sustain basic life, there would be no excess potential *energy* floating around in the economic system to produce the additional goods (*matter*) and services which make life so much more enjoyable. It is these enjoyable things, these things that make life more pleasant, which is what real wealth is all about.

Again, recall that all real new goods, all real new wealth, and, therefore, all real new money originates in the rural country. This is concrete reality. Wealth ultimately comes from the natural environment. Even great ideas (abstract) and energy require some matter (concrete) to come to economic fruition. But while real new wealth (raw materials) ultimately comes from the rural country (natural environment), the highest and best use of labor through the division of labor, as well as the best abstract ideas that creatively find a way to utilize the earth's resources, are usually spawned in the cities' intellectual centers. The rural country is the resource pipeline to the city where the finished goods are usually created, where the resources are transformed for the higher satisfaction of man. Services follow. Goods and services proliferate as a result of the rural country's excess and the city's creativity and productivity combined with capital.

The city can (and usually does) become a parasite living off of the rural country, if it fails to stimulate new and better productivity within the voluntary division of labor. When the economic system gets out of balance, and there is no longer parity, no economic equality (fair play) between the rural country and the city, and when the city has devoured its country host (bankrupted the rural country through city welfare and the creation of money), the city then dies, too. This happens at the end of a civilization cycle. **This is why world cities are historically both the highest achievement, as well as the culmination, of a mature civilization.** It's *"truth in tension"* realized. We are now at the end of a 510-year cycle for Western civilization. We have some critical choices which must be made. It's either radical change for Western civilization or revolution and poverty. Take your pick. It will be one or the other. And, it will come within the next 20 years.

It's easy for the city to dominate the rural country. And it is in the city's interest, **short-term only**, to dominate the country. Intellectual power gravitates to, and expands synergistically in, the metropolitan complexes. Because thoughts precede action, because the pen is mightier than the sword, because the abstract in an ultimate sense rules the concrete, and because all these activities usually originate and take place primarily in the city, so the city rules over the rural country. On a day-to-day level, in our developed culture, we see this reality very clearly. Men in the cities, for the most part, work with their minds, getting rich, while their brothers in the country, toiling with their hands, become poor. The short-term, misguided, but historical rule of civilization's progressions is that men in the city get increasingly richer while those in the country decline into poverty, sustained only by loans, speculation, and part-time jobs in the cities. This unfavorable skewing of economic wealth (a city becoming richer and richer while the country becomes poorer and poorer) is suicidal, because ultimately the country is the resource lifeline to the city. When the country, in its economic death throes, is forced to cut the resource lifeline to the city, the city dies and the entire civilization crumbles. This is where we are now, in our civilization, at the end of the 510-year Western civilization cycle. So, events and time are *"square."*

The city's short-term perspective, that of raping the rural country, of ruthlessly gobbling up its resources at bargain prices and undercompensating its labor via the creating of money out of nothing (inflation) for short-term benefits, is a knife to the city's own jugular long-term. Long-term, the city cannot afford to bite the hand that feeds it, literally. Consistent with the laws of physical and economic reality, the city, in its own best interest **long-term**, should allow the country to be the original source of money. After all, the country produces money's true equivalent, real new wealth, which leads to real new goods and services. The sun, for now, is still the ultimate source of physical life and material wealth which is created in the rural country. Money is first and foremost a commodity, and only later a commodity substitute.

This economic subordination by the city to the country is difficult for the following reasons. Men in the city are, by and large, smarter, more intellectual, than their brothers in the country. Thus, they are more fit to lead, plan and dictate to their country brothers. Marx called farmers effectively the "rural idiocy." So, it is difficult for city men to become subordinate to their intellectual inferiors, country folk. It is contrary to man's pride. But pride, long-term, always leads to destruction. When men are proud, they do not/cannot listen, and thus do not learn, change, adapt or grow. They suffer and die in an everchanging world. Established institutions, like government, are the ultimate manifestations of pride, terribly slow to listen or change. Pride is short-term, and men today, just like throughout history, are predominantly proud and thus short-term oriented. They are just more so today, as one would expect to be the case, at the end of a 510-year civilization cycle. A short-term orientation is an animalistic character trait. All animals are short-term, fact oriented, non-thinking creatures which **react** to concrete reality, with no ability to contemplate the long-term, abstract realm. This is man's tendency, too. Greed is also a short-term orientation, in violation of the wealth-creating, long-term, economic law that *"self-interest is best served by service long-term."* (Classical economics is satisfied—the "unseen hand.") Greed is now pervasive in the cities. Cities are the home ground of the *"rat race,"* where men scramble greedily to get rich quick at all costs.

It flies in the face of human nature to believe that the cities will automatically humble themselves economically, in accordance with economic law, before their simple country brothers. After all, through the thinking genius of the cities come the abstract ideas which lead to patents, technology **and weapons**, produced from country resources, which can and do have the ability to overpower the rural country in the twinkling of an eye. Perhaps city men should earn more. Thinking, creative men are always the bosses of labor. But, city men should not, in their own short-term self-interest, be allowed to fraudulently create money. They have not created new wealth. Thus, to prevent this natural tendency toward self-destruction, a **moral** framework must be socially established (abstract separation of church and state is impossible) for the economic system to allow all members of society to prosper long-term, their individual economic achievement consistent with their individual temperaments, talents, convictions, abilities and production. In the marketplace, whoever meets the public's needs best, profits most. Race is never a significant factor.

In a way, the commodity futures market is the ultimate slap in the face to the rural country. Thinking men get rich in the cities trading paper commodities which represent real commodities produced in the country. Meanwhile, the real producers of commodities in the country go broke working with their hands. Country folks slowly, but surely, slide into poverty. Country folks are forced to buy everything they need at retail, while selling all they produce at wholesale. Thus, country people can only become increasingly impoverished, particularly as long as favorable weather for crop production exists and farm revolts do not occur. (Bad weather hastens poverty.) Eventually, the resource lifeline to the city (country excess) is effectively cut, the city disintegrates, and the whole civilization falls.

Decentralization of city industries, mixing them in with the country's real wealth production, would provide a practical, healthy balance for an economy long-term. It also should be obvious now that the creation of money out of thin air (inflation), whether by using the printing press, the Federal Reserve's monetizing of the federal deficit, credit cards, or through the creation of credit via the fractional reserve banking system—all of these economic heresies are creations of the cities. These money-creating shenanigans are foreign and antagonistic to sound, long-term, progressive economic reality.

It should come as no surprise that these economic heresies are all spawned in the cities. Cities are historically the production centers of heresies. It should be evident why banks have the nicest buildings and structures downtown, too. Bankers get rich, short-term, until economic reality comes knocking at their doors. The miracle of compound interest, while a windfall blessing for the banker short-term, is a curse for all of mankind long-term. The love of money is the root of all evil. Banks and bankers, OPM-types and governments love money. But, bankers cut their own throats with their fractional reserve banking system because, while they prosper for awhile, the system itself is ultimately inflationary. And so, in the terminal stages of inflation, bankers usually lose big as the rates they charge for money can no longer keep up with the rate of inflation, or they get whipsawed in booms or busts, or make bad loans and investments, or are subject to a bank "run." Finally, the piper is paid, and

the bankers are strung up from the lamp post, right along-side their
cohorts, the OPM-types and the politicians. What we are talking
about is a revolution. This happens in a small way at the end of every
50-year economic cycle, and in a major way at the end of the 510-year
civilization cycle. We are at the end of both. Avoid harm's way. Being
a banker, an entrepreneural OPM-type who has become undeservedly
enriched (thanks to inflation) via the use of the economic assets of ignorant others, or a cooperating politician are the most high-risk oc-
cupations going at this late stage of our civilization.

It almost goes without saying that for men to be creative, productive and responsible, they must be free, subject only to natural and
moral law. And this means free of government. When government is
the central planner, it is looked to, to be responsible for the welfare of
all the people, plan creatively for their futures, and direct productive
enterprises. But, we see that experientially government fails miserably
in the Soviet Union and its satellites such as Poland. Government is a
parasite, an overhead expense. It can only take from some first and
then redistribute to others. The larger the government, the bigger the
parasite. The bigger the parasite, the closer the civilization is to its
demise. If government bureaucrats were creative and could correctly
anticipate the future (plan), they would be risk-oriented entrepreneurs. Government is an overhead expense, which, once it has
redistributed all of society's wealth, with an ever-increasing take for
itself, breaks the economic back of the society.

A strong central government effectively enslaves its citizens through
regulations. Slaves, like children, react and are short-term oriented.
Therefore slaves and children are pretty much one and the same, both
uncreative, both unthinking, and neither free. And they are neither
productive nor responsible. So government, particularly the federal
government, must be minimized, not only so that the free division of
labor will be enhanced, consistent with each individual man's unique
talents, but so that man will also be free to become creative, productive and responsible, to succeed, **or** to suffer the pain of failure which
negatively reinforces a lack of initiative, which negatively reinforces a
lack of creativity, and which negatively reinforces laziness and
irresponsibility. Without government support, without a federal government "safety net," men are forced to grow up, to accept the
responsibility of freedom. They can no longer be children. They have
to think and grow. This is particularly enhanced in a decentralized environment. Man and men, individually and collectively, are always
better off when they accept responsibility in all areas of their lives. For
example, welfare payments (taxes) to Washington are out-of-sight and
out-of-mind. A man who is forced, however, to give his hard-earned

money to a lazy neighbor is liable to revolt, to put him to work mowing his lawn. This is why decentralized government provides *"the greatest good for the greatest number"* **long-term.** The waste, fraud, laziness and overhead of the government bureaucracy is cut in a decentralized system. Furthermore, the federal government can then concentrate on its sole priorities—national defense and internal peace and justice maintenance.

We are so blind. The same advice we give to the underdeveloped Third World countries, which, if they apply it, brings them prosperity, applies equally to us. In Third World countries, even in the cities, the jobless rate is very low. If people don't work, they starve. Unemployment is voluntary. Folks becomes responsible in a hurry. Minimum food amounts to an effective check on population growth. They are, thus, very much in touch with economic reality. They work. And the whole economy benefits. *"The greatest good for the greatest number"* kicks in. This theological truth, that if a man doesn't work, he doesn't eat, has been violated historically by mature cities, which not surprisingly, were/are, the center of religious heresies (Alexandria, Babylon, Rome, London and New York). Yes, consistent with the economic laws, truths and realities that we have discussed above, is the perspective, from the labor side of the equation, that simply, if a man doesn't work, he doesn't eat (local, decentralized charity excluded in cases of real need). It takes work, both mental and physical work, the sweat of men's brows, to prosper economically and maximize real wealth for the *"greatest good for the greatest number"* long-term.

The earth is cursed in a sense. It is miserly (disorderly) in that it does not **readily** produce all the wheat, oats, barley, sheep, cattle, fish, bananas, pineapples or coconuts we want on its own without our effort (our expended physical energy). So, abstract theological truth must be used in harmony with concrete economic reality for real wealth to increase for all of mankind. Cities, the highest and best source of abstract ideas, try to play God. That is why cities are also the centers of government. Government is a parasite which attempts to play the role of God as it creates something (money) (laws) out of nothing. Government also says that if a man doesn't work, he can still eat (food stamps). Cities are the source of these short-term, unrealistic, abstract, social welfare ideas that create social friction. The warped, abstract, short-term, theological heresies of the city produce a distorted economic fantasy land that cannot survive long-term. The laws of cause and effect, of equal and opposite action and reaction, come into play long-term. For, during tough economic times, the people in the cities suffer the most. They receive, in kind, economic retribution for their easy, parasitic, good times. For, city folk can't produce the basics of life. When the economic chickens come home to roost long-term, the people in the city suffer miserably. They can't feed themselves.

Michael Lipton, in his book, WHY POOR PEOPLE STAY POOR, observed that in the poor Third World developing countries **investment in the agricultural sector of the economy brings investment returns (real new wealth) three times higher than those in other parts of the developing economy.** Is this scientific observation consistent with the principles we have delineated previously? Of course. Reality rules long-term in all cultures. Folly can only last for a short while. The cities of mature Western civilization are growing folly centers, and unnecessarily so. When resources in Third World countries are poured into the cities (the potential parasite) rather than into the host (the rural areas), this misallocation of resources leads to overcrowding in the cities, rural stagnation and poverty, followed by general poverty in the entire nation. Isn't this exactly what we are witnessing in our own nation now? Can't we learn from the Third World's example? Can't we learn from our own history? A healthy civilization develops its rural, raw material resources, and then, next, its cities. The cities pump out productive ideas, products and services in a low-cost, efficient division of labor way, which benefits the rural country. But the city, even though it is able to economically and intellectually dominate the rural country, refuses to do so. It also refuses to be the creator of money. Instead, it returns to its roots, the rural country, and establishes its industries there in the country, thereby promoting decentralization, responsibility and freedom. Decentralization, responsibility and freedom are all linked in the vital long-term chain and perspective which promotes *"Wealth for All."*

Now let's turn and attempt to grasp the economic importance of the recent devastating decline in commodity prices. The late Carl H. Wilken, an American farm economist, proved that a definite link exists between the value of farm products and national income. Wilken's evidence suggested that **real new wealth created in the economy multiplied itself seven times as it worked its way through the economy.** (There is that *"magic"* number *"seven"* again.) Put simply, $1.00 of farm income generates $7.00 of other income. Also, a 1% increase in unemployment results from a 1% drop in farm income, according to Wilken's studies. Wilken stated that the only factor that remains consistent with the earned profits and savings of a nation as a whole is the total price paid for all the raw material production. Agriculture is the largest source of this new wealth. And, as discussed previously, this new wealth is renewable and additional thanks to the sun, when combined with the savings, creative thoughts and hard work of free men, and it generates increased wealth year after year. What we are dealing with here is the multiplier effect which works for the benefit of all mankind. What a folly it is for man to chain himself to the lazy, uncreative, multiplier effect of compound interest, which enriches only a parasitic few, unjustly so for awhile, but which causes rampant instability, encourages short-term ill-advised speculation, leads to moral corruption and the destruction of governments, and impoverishes the masses long-term.

When the price of raw materials drops, there is an exact ratio decline in terms of national income. There is also a commensurate increase in debt expansion and unemployment according to Wilken. Economic good times are multipled by abundant production of real new wealth. Economic bad times are magnified by declining raw material production and debt assumption. Again, Wilken purported that the total national income is five to seven times the annual price paid for all raw material production. Thus, real new wealth, economic parity, ties real money directly into the production of new goods. Stability and prosperity result long-term. Then, there is no need for banks in their present sense, for the purpose they exist today.

It is well documented that multinational banks today are evil, contrary to the best interests of mankind long-term. Multinational banks provide the capital, through loans, which finance the multinational corporation ventures in communist countries (the USSR, China and Angola for examples), that allows and encourages communism to survive. Furthermore, multinational banks provide loans directly to the communists so the communists can build the capital facilities necessary to produce the weapons to not only enslave their people, but also the masses of the earth, eventually destroying us. Finally, adding insult to injury, multinational banks, by providing the capital for the industrial plants built in the communist countries, eliminate American jobs. The slave labor which works in industrial plants in communist countries (or countries reconstructed after a war) can produce cheaper goods and services than those produced on the free market by free men in Western civilization. So the deposits the free working man makes in a multinational bank go to finance his own economic self-destruction, if not political destruction, long-term. And where are these multinational banks located? In the big cities!

Banks should be transformed into decentralized joint venture, partnership and stock centers, where men with land, labor, ideas and capital of all types meet in order to structure productive economic enterprises, exclusive of (void of) monetary *"interest."* If monetary capital, money, is poorly invested in a joint venture, partnership or a stock, its unproductive use is limited to this misguided venture. No monetary *"interest"* "hangover" remains to curse man in future time. In other words, the budget is balanced. The laws of thermodynamics control. An economic check and balance is created by limiting the poor use of labor, capital, money, land, etc. to a unique venture or organization on a "pay as you go" basis. This economic isolation, thus, keeps men from being cursed by the mistakes of their forefathers in generations down the line. It is no accident that it has been historically proven that debt is long-term detrimental to any enterprise. It's clear cause and effect. Furthermore, because money earns no *"interest,"* men are forced to carefully look for **productive** economic ventures in which to invest their money in in order to increase their wealth. This, too, benefits all mankind because better decision-making occurs. Men become individually responsible and thus accountable for the investment of their excess funds. No devious, indifferent, dishonest, uninformed, incompetent, undiscerning or corrupt banker or OPM-type is left to make the decision as to what economic ventures do or do not deserve an infusion of capital.

Money is power. Power corrupts. Politics is power. Power corrupts. Money and politics combined is absolute power corrupting absolutely in a ruthless, evolutionary *"king of the hill,"* *"law of the jungle"* way. This is why the connection between banking and politics in an evolutionary-biased culture, such as ours, is so apparent, and also so corrupt. Absolute power corrupts absolutely. Is this in the interest of *"the greatest good for the greatest number,"* long-term? No. Or of the individual? No way.

Finally, a man can save his money if he wishes, to spend, for his children, or until a good investment comes along. The pressure to *"earn interest,"* which leads to poor investments via deposits in banks, is thus absent. Patience, a virtue, is instead practiced. While such saving is penalized in the sense that wealth-creating opportunities are bypassed, this is a short-term perspective. Saving, and effectively stopping time in this way, allows man the time to research, reflect, and decide upon the very best economic investments. Because man, with a stable monetary system, is able to *"stop time,"* he is not moving backward short-term, financially, as a result of his failure to *"earn interest."* Again, the pressure to *"earn interest"* short-term leads to the pressure to invest money short-term. And short-term decision making is nearly always against the best interest of man long-term.

Interest on money borrowed is a treadmill working against error-prone man. Booms and busts are brought about by the expansion and contraction of credit. Most men miss the turning points. Debt is a form of slavery. An interest/debt-free economic system provides for the *"greatest good for the greatest number,"* long-term. The all too popular OPM method (Other People's Money), which has mush-roomed as never before in these inflationary times, leading to boom and bust, is strictly limited under a "non-interest"-oriented financial system. Instead, real economic return is more closely tied to an in-dividual's real productivity, involvement, assumption of responsibility and accountability. The tendency for a few to become very, very rich because they are clever, due to currency speculation, at the expense of the economically ignorant masses, by borrowing to purchase or create assets particularly during inflationary times, is thus checkmated. Thus, the probability of revolution is sharply reduced.

Revolution is spawned when there are a very few rich and many poor in a society. Such income disparity always occurs in inflationary times. This is the breeding ground of communism, too. But, we have already seen that communism is government, an overhead expense, a parasite, playing the role of God. Communism leads to mass misery and economic poverty everywhere. It has been conclusively shown that communism can only survive as long as a free market and free economy exists to support it. This is why Russia depends upon Western loans, technology and grain. If communism ever became the world's government, there would be no way of determining the value of anything, either. Price (reflecting value) is only determined in a free market between buyers and sellers. Under communism, men, with no incentive to get ahead, maximize their self-interest by being lazy and moonlighting. Furthermore, because communism, if it became the worldwide government, is a parasite, civilization would self-destruct. The parasite would have totally devoured the host. At best, a massive slave state would exist.

Using OPM, entrepreneurs get rich using other people's money. They do this with money borrowed from banks on which they pay in-terest. They are, thus, not accountable directly to the providers of the capital (money). It is a far better system, more just and equitable, as well as conducive to individual growth and responsibility, for en-trepreneurs to deal directly, by way of joint ventures, partnerships, or stock issues with those who have the capital. This is why the raising of money for projects through these methods, not by borrowing, is far more economically prudent and fair. There is more accountability, more checks and balances, against abuses which may be the modus operandi of greedy, unethical, short-term oriented entrepreneurs. Entrepreneurs still have the incentive to be productive. They can struc-ture the deal any way they wish. Banks are thus cut out, save maybe a service or finder's fee, and are not allowed to be pyramiding parasites, particularly via the fractional reserve banking system. The productive efforts of small men are thus rewarded in this way, as opposed to being penalized through the OPM system. Labor, thus, has a stake and sees a common self-interest with management and entrepreneurs. Labor unions, which fight management and discriminate against other workers, disappear. (Marx is satisfied.) Jobs are created by men with foresight, entrepreneurs, who start businesses to meet consumer's needs. Entrepreneurs cannot be "educated," because education teaches about the present and the past. Entrepreneurs deal with the future, and so are key. Entrepreneurs must be protected and encouraged.

Geographic proximity is desirable to enhance the checks and balance system. With geographic distance comes greater economic foolishness. The way that money is spent at the local and state level, as opposed to the federal level, is a good example of this.

With decentralized government, and money spent, not borrowed into existence consistent with the production of real new wealth, taxes all but disappear. A *"head tax,"* encouraging family fidelity and sexual restraint, and/or a *"flat tax"* on income encouraging saving and production (long-term benefits), are best. The nonproductive efforts of all the tax CPAs and attorneys, as well as the IRS, are eliminated. Local men, women, local churches and local civic groups meet the health, education and welfare needs of the local people. Thus, the human condition, psychologically, socially and economically, is enhanced. Real meaning in life comes from relationships with people who assume responsibility. And, the health, education and welfare needs are met more efficiently, with all the concomitant local checks and balances, on the local level. Taxes, then, on the federal level are only needed for defense against all enemies, foreign and domestic. Taxes are also for a well-run court system that settles disputes and brings criminals to justice, preferably on a local level, with equality under law.

With the decentralized, constitutional, local militia concept, foreign wars cannot be fought, young men cannot be butchered, a world empire cannot be built, the federal government is held in check, and there is no incentive for multinational banks and corporations to finance and promote wars for the purpose of the economic destruction of a foreign power so they can then finance the reconstruction effort and make tremendous profits, by lending money, earning interest and rebuilding industry. Nor is there the waste and all the expense of the outdated, expensive, unnecessary military/industrial defense systems. The military item works or it is not purchased. Esprit de corps is also enhanced when a locally-manned militia elects its own qualified officers. A dangerous professional military, which is always a coup threat, is eliminated. Wars have difficulty getting off the ground where there is free trade in open markets. Men have no reason to fight with other men who enrich them through the exchange of goods and services. Wars destroy wealth. Wars are inflationary.

At the end of 1945, banks were only lending about 17¢ of every dollar deposited. Bankers used their political clout in Washington to change this general public prosperity. A few years later, at the end of 1952, banks were lending out only approximately 37¢ of every dollar deposited. They again protested to the politicians and used their political influence to gain *"most favored status."* In 1952, when the Farm Act of 1952 was enacted, the Steagall Amendment was effectively eliminated. The Steagall Amendment had provided 90% parity for farmers. Its purpose was primarily to ensure a stable dollar, **not** to benefit basic agricultural producers. (Farmers are always behind the economic curveball because they buy at retail and sell at wholesale.) The November, 1980 issue of ACRES, U.S.A. reported:

> *"The cumulative loss to realized net farm income, small business income, rental income and corporate income from 1952 to 1979 is an incredible $2,428.8 billion with the largest loss—$977.4 billion— attributed to realized net farm income alone.*
>
> *"The dollar loss to the private sector was off-set by the increase in the public debt of the nation, from $500 billion in 1950 to an estimated $4.8 trillion in 1979. The difference between the loss of $2,428.8 billion and the public debt of $4.8 trillion can be largely accounted for in 28 years of accumulated interest."* [Emphasis added]¹

What does all this mean to us? It means that real wealth and real money can only be created first in the rural country where the real new *energy* (solar energy) is converted into *matter* and harvested, and then transferred to the city where creative, abstract ideas can be applied to transform this new *matter* into its highest and best use with a minimum of labor under the free division of labor. The illusion under which we suffer today is the false *"wealth"* created primarily by the fractional reserve banking system in the cities through debt and compound interest. Debt and compound interest is to economics what abortion is to life. Compound interest, an abstract concept, which, theoretically, can increase to infinity, is an ever-heavy anchor which pulls down and impoverishes finite, limited, economically ignorant, error-prone, common man. *" 'It may take 20 years, but we're going to see the emergence of a national banking system.' "* (THE WALL STREET JOURNAL 10/7/81) If so, we're approaching the end of the age of the financial dinosaur. Wealth and money, first created in the rural country, are true and honest on both an abstract and concrete level. Wealth and money, first created in the city, are illusions and shams which cannot last long. Reality comes home to roost for us, here and now. The 1981 net farm income, in uninflated dollars, was the lowest since The Great Depression.

The reality of life is that few men perceive, much less act, in their own best self-interest long-term (enlightened Christians, libertarians and conservatives aside). Acting in one's long-term interest in all areas is rare. Collectively, men are undisciplined. Thus, collectively, men, by acting in their own self-interest short-term (selfishness), act contrary to the best interest of those they affect and interact with long-term, as well as often short-term, in addition to acting against their own self-interest long-term. The rise and fall of nation after nation, civilization after civilization, attests to this pitiful fact. Governments always gleefully fill this destructive vacuum, created by a short-term orientation which is usually joined by irresponsibility. Governments always fill the vacuum of irresponsibility. Men who lust for power over other men are drawn to government like moths to a flame. Government power feeds their insecurities. Politicians and bureaucrats are seldom strong enough individually, much less collectively, to realize that they lead best from behind, that they lead best by serving, and that the public will adore them and give them endless power if they don't need or abuse it, and, instead, return it (power) by way of freedom and service to the people. A necessary check against power-lusting politicians is to allow only those who pay taxes and receive no government benefits to vote. Privilege is then commensurate with responsibility, and social conflict brought about by envy, brought about by wealth redistribution programs, legislated by politicians elected by the nonproductive members of society, is alleviated.

Government power fills the vacuum and assumes the responsibility of personal, and then collective, irresponsibility. Yet government is an overhead expense, a parasite, which lives off the host of productive, responsible free men until it devours them and the system comes unglued. ATLAS SHRUGGED.

What we have done in this manifesto is present a structural, moral framework whereby men are positively reinforced for acting in their own self-interest long-term and negatively reinforced for acting in their own self-interest short-term. When men collectively follow their natural, animalistic tendencies to secure the satisfaction of their own self-interests short-term, like animals, they exercise the *"law of the jungle"* and the *"survival of the fittest."* Man is pitted against man in cut-throat competition. The weak fall by the wayside. This is why neither communism (socialism) or debt capitalism works. Neither meets the criteria of providing for *"the greatest good for the greatest number"* long-term, nor for the individual. Every man is important. Every man has something to contribute. The miracle of the long-term view, and in fact the greatest achievements of civilization, are made through the voluntary cooperation by free men in the free market's division of labor, where each man does what he does best, whatever he so chooses to do, for which he is rewarded by profits if the people value his service or buy his product. The marketplace does not discriminate racially. Production is what counts. A man is rewarded because, consistent with the long-term view, a man sees that his own *"self-interest is best served by service to others."* Thus, with the long run perspective, both collective human good and self-interest are not only served, but both are maximized. The *"greatest good for the greatest number"* is resolved to the benefit of the individual, too. The individual and the group both benefit because the individual, by meeting the economic requirements of the group, profits, and thus serves his own self-interest. Competition to serve others in the marketplace thus becomes, in the long-term, cooperation within the framework of the division of labor in the free market. Monopolies, always created by government, corrupt this natural perfection. All the destructive side effects, all the regulatory, physical, psychological and sociological damage done to mankind, individually and collectively, disappear when the short-run perspective is abandoned. **Evil is men doing what they consider right in their own eyes, short-term. Good is men acting in their own self-interest long-term.** The long-term view results in a full cup overflowing, self-actualization as Maslow would call it, resulting in *"the greatest good for the greatest number"* and the maximum achievement for the individual, as wealth for *"one"* becomes a by-product of *"Wealth for All."*

"He shall lend to thee, and thou shalt not lend to him: he shall be the head, and thou shalt be the tail." Deuteronomy 28:44

Wealth for All: Added Confirmation
11/6/81

One of the critical threads of truth running throughout *"Wealth for All"* is that the economic viability of the rural country is critical for the entire civilization's economic health. Enlightened bank-dominated governments realize this and so they subsidize (enslave/feudalize) the farmers to ensure that enough food is produced to feed those in the cities. Romania and Poland are not so blessed with such *"enlightened"* governments. In September, Romanian farmers were ordered, in no uncertain terms, to increase their food production for people in the cities. Now, a few months later, an AP release from Bucharest, Romania is head-lined with the title, *"Threat of Imprisonment Calms Panic Buying by Romanians."* (typical for a tyrannical state) The AP release read,

> *"An anti-hoarding edict that threatens greedy shoppers with five years in prison is restoring calm to markets plagued by short- ages and bad food, the government says . . .*
>
> *The government restricted sales of sugar, cooking oil and butter last Friday, and warned that anyone caught with more than a month's supply of basic foodstuffs could be jailed for five years."* [2]

Two quick observations:

1. When the economic free market of a nation deteriorates, particularly agriculture, the city dies. We are seeing the proof of this pudding in Romania and Poland now. And, since the communist bloc countries are economically dependent upon Western civilization, we would expect such trouble and economic chaos in the communist parasites first, a preview of coming attractions for Western civilization.

2. The conservative, constitutionally oriented western United States are heavily populated by Mormons. Can anyone imagine the Mormons, who are asked by their religion to store up a year's supply of food, giving up their foodstuffs in an economic crisis if such an edict is issued by our federal government (ex post facto aside)? Not likely, particularly as well organized and well armed as the Mormons are.

On October 16th, Poland's government agreed to freeze food prices. The food price freeze was a result of strike alerts and wildcat strikes over food shortages in eight provinces.

Since then, there have been strikes or strike threats in 28 of Poland's 49 provinces over food shortages. A general strike was staged on October 28th over the lack of food. Poland has gone back to real money— barter with the likes of tobacco and alcohol. From the THE WALL STREET JOURNAL, quoting a Pole, *"Money no longer matters."*

Warsaw, Poland is not so pretty these days. It's disturbing to contemplate the fact that the only thing that successfully distracts hungry men and women from their biological distress, is a greater biological threat, that of death in war. Recent civil unrest in Romania and Poland is a catalyst for war.

Now let's turn to our own country. Farmers have been sustained in recent years by loans collateralized by farmland which has been increasing in value. Now that farmland values are only rising slowly, and declining in many locations, lenders are increasingly unwilling or unable to finance or refinance farmers' operating capital. Expect agricultural bankruptcies to soar, or increasing government control.

Agricultural prices, adjusted for inflation, are at Great Depression levels. A farmer receives $2.30 for a bushel of corn which costs him

$3.10 to grow; he receives $3.60 a bushel for wheat which costs him $5.30 a bushel to raise. Agriculture is a bankruptcy waiting to happen. The farmer has only been able to hang on the past few years thanks to increased credit lines supported by ever-inflating agricultural land prices. But this land strength has now run out, too.

Is the government likely to act? No, not until the crisis is as bad as it has become in Romania and Poland, when the city folks scream bloody murder, figuratively and literally, at the politicians. Governments, parasites that they are, seldom anticipate. They only react when the crisis is upon them.

Those of us who are future oriented cannot get a hearing. We're not powerful like the industrial, establishment religion, and government leaders. But these powerful folks are primarily concerned with the here and now, and so they seldom anticipate the future. Nearly all our institutions are geared toward a day-to-day, short-term view. Antagonistic to the free market, which historically is the best anticipator of future demands, and which is by nature long-term oriented, these establishment giants, by contrast, seek to effectively stop time, promote the maintenance and status quo of the organization, promote bureacracy, security, government subsidies and monopolies, limit "competition," and minimize risk. An early awakening by the general population to this problem is unlikely because, as a result of Machiavellian planning decades ago, the masses, too, are brainwashed, possessed of a short-term view.

Are food shortages on the horizon? Will there be riots in the cities? Count on it. Purchases of bulk wheat and a wheat grinding mill are highly recommended, as is food storage, the development of a garden, a greenhouse and the purchase of milk goats and chickens, both of which are very efficient protein producers and require a limited amount of space.

Wealth for All: City vs. Country Breakdown
11/6/81

"Food is rotting in rural Ghana while an estimated 4 of every 5 children in the capital, are suffering from malnutrition, according to one of the country's leading doctors.

"Herman Odoi, head pediatrician at the Princess Marie-Louis Children's Hospital, said the mortality rate for the cases of nutritional deficiencies that reach the hospital had doubled since 1977.

"Dr. Odoi says a major reason for the deterioration is the acute food shortage and rapidly rising food prices brought about by Ghana's general economic decline. Food is abundant in rural areas,

with frequent reports of produce rotting on farms rendered inaccessible by washed-out bridges and impassable roads." [Emphasis added] (Source—Daily News Digest, Box 39850, Phoenix, Arizona 85069, from Reuters)

This breakdown in the Third World may be a preview of what is coming our way. Our interstate highway distribution system is deteriorating rapidly. Now, 9% of our interstate system is in "poor" shape; over 50% of the pavement will need replacing by the end of the 1980s; only 63% of the roads are in "good" condition now; 40% of the bridges are "functionally obsolete" or "structurally deficient" at the present time. Where is the money going to come from to finance these billions of dollars of repairs when the federal government, the states, the cities and the corporations are all battling for the same limited capital supply? The money simply won't be available unless *"Wealth for All"*-type changes are made. Otherwise, we will duplicate the same downhill spiral as Ghana, with starving cities isolated from the food producing country.

Wealth for All: The Ultimate Fallout
6/18/82

Today, the only real new wealth we have still comes from the good earth. (In the future, it may come from mining other planets and higher uses of present resources.) Thanks to the sun, energy is translated into real matter, which is real new wealth (money). Thus, the supply of money can ever be increased in society because real new wealth is continuously being created through solar energy. Commodities, monetized at the local level by the free market, should be the source of all new money. This new real money, created at the local level, will lead to political decentralization, a dispersement of population from the cities, and more freedom for man.

The finer, important things in society are only realized when there is excess capital (wealth) available. For example, primitive societies do not have the capital (wealth) to attempt to solve water and air pollution problems or finance such things as medical research and development. Western civilization, by contrast, has been able to attack these issues, which greatly impact the quality of life, because the capital surplus in Western civilization has made such *"quality of life"* advancements possible. That the financing of such important areas has been cut back in recent years is not so much a result of political action, as it is a consequence of present economic necessity. We have squandered our capital base through wasteful bureaucracies, centralization, loaning (giving) of our wealth abroad, financing our enemies, etc.

The long-term solution to the *"quality of life"* desires of man is ultimately bound up with the *"Wealth for All"* concept. With the abolition of debt capitalism, and the resultant demise of alienating compound interest, the balance between *"quality of life"* priorities and economic realities will be more easily met. When *"the people,"* through stock ownership, partnerships and joint ventures (not debt), directly own and thus are directly involved with all capital intensive economic projects in this country, then economic self-interest and social issues will become one and the same for society. The free enterprise owners of factories and power plants (the people), for example, will decide more equitably the economic trade-offs between such things as air pollution and rate of return. Both of their interests will be vitally at stake. A sane, reasonable solution will be found.

Finally, by having real new wealth monetized at the local level, the inefficiencies, not to mention the corruption (inflation) of debt created out of thin air, will disappear. Excess capital will accumulate due to greater human efficiencies brought about by cooperation in the free market, stored real new wealth generated each year from solar energy, cumulative technology in the civilization, and the increased wealth generated through inheritance. This will allow man the extensive capital base necessary to more freely spend on the *"marginal"* economic areas of life, the *"quality of life"* items. Put more simply, once this wealth base is more greatly created and distributed freely throughout all of society, and the basic economic and recreational needs of man are met, man will look for some place else to spend (invest) his money. This will make capital (money) available to finance the *"quality of life"* projects to an extent never before seen in human history.

The ultimate fallout should be in the development of human potential. Under the *"Wealth for All"* system, since man's basic economic needs will be met, man will be free as never before to develop his talents, which will in turn benefit society. Cooperation will be enhanced as free men exchange the *"fruits"* of their developed talents. With the welcome death of international debt capitalism, and a return to political decentralization, international economic free trade will again be able to rapidly expand, leading to enhanced world-wide cooperation and harmony. The Third World will follow our example. They still look to us to lead. The communist systems will fail, by economic default.

THE IMPORTANCE OF ULTIMACY

New

A clear-thinking Founding Father stated, *"Men must be governed by God or they will be ruled by tyrants."* This simple truth needs to be rediscovered by 20th Century Americans. Understanding the full impact of these words is basic to turning this country around, back down the road toward real prosperity.

Throughout my writings, I have established an unstated religious foundation. That undercurrent is **not** there out of some evangelical conviction. Rather, it is established out of a love for truth and reality, and its practical necessity for maintaining liberty within a free market, and thus ensuring our social order.

All men are religious. It just boils down to where men place their ultimate faith—in themselves, money, material possessions, whatever, or God. Whatever I read, whatever I hear—the first thing I ask myself is, *"What is this individual's ultimate source of authority?" "What is his basic faith?" "What are his assumptions about the nature of reality, his presuppositions?"*

Individual sovereignty, man establishing himself as ultimate (God), is fraught with problems. (Human sovereignty today is couched in the terms *"humanism," "human potential," "human rights," "libertarianism,"* along with the collective versions—*"socialism"* and *"communism."*) The basic problem is that man is finite. Finite man cannot also be ultimate. Man's **mind** is limited, as is his **life span**.

Scientifically, the limits of man's mind have been established by Godel's theorum and Heisenberg's indeterminacy principle. Because man's mind is limited, he is only capable of one thing perfectly—error. Error is, of course, separation from total truth. Truth can be defined as an accurate conception or perception of that (whatever) under consideration and its relationship to all other things as it has always existed in the past, continues to exist without a single exception in the present, and will exist universally in the future. In other words, there can be no conflict in truth. Truth is integrated and universal. Truth is principle and fact in unity perpetually. Man, therefore, because of his finite and limited mind and time, is only capable of partial truth. Man cannot understand all relationships of all things to anything throughout all time. But **partial truth is error**. The philosophers down through the ages have recognized this to be man's fundamental problem, that of a finite mind, with limited time, which is incapable of holistic truth, unless, of course, there is a God who dictates truth to him (Special Revelation).

There is the problem with plain old time anyway. Now, there are two basic concepts of time—cyclical time and linear time. Cyclical time is subordinate to linear time. When linear time is up, the cycle dies. Here are two quick examples. First, the fertility cycle in a woman can continue until sometime in her 50s. At that time, age (linear time) takes over and terminates the fertility cycle (cyclical time). Second, we have cycles in the natural order. There is the seasonal cycle—spring, summer, fall and winter—with its shorter formative cycle, the daily cycle—the rising and setting of the sun. At some point of time (linear time), the cycle of the rising and setting of the sun, and the subsequent seasonal cycles, **stop** because the sun novas. Linear time has overruled cyclical time. When linear time is up, the cycle ceases.

This reality of cyclical time being subordinate to linear time smashes the *"eternal"* cyclical concepts of reincarnation and evolution, and therefore the **unconditional, natural** ultimacy of man. The winding down of the universe, the ultimate nova of our sun, with the accompanying laws of thermodynamics, are supportive of **devolution**, not evolution, long-term. Man is trapped in a spiral down long-term, even though, in time, he can make real progress (*"Wealth for All"*). It takes quite an imagination (and pride) for a man to promote himself as a god. (Perhaps he needs a Savior.)

I have oft stated in THE REAPER, *"Human nature is a constant."* Our day-to-day observations concur. All the old movies we view of times past reveal pride, greed, self-righteousness, fears and lusts which are **identical** to what we see in contemporary America. We also observe these human characteristics in history. Furthermore, the underlying principle (*"Human nature is a constant"*) has proven successful time and time again in the commodity futures market. This is why bar charts, moving averages, oscillators, and all the other technical and cyclical indicators, based upon historical research, are still useful. These indicators, which are based upon man's past *"tracks"* in the market, and project similar action in the future, work because human nature has not changed!

But, the concept, *"Human nature is a constant,"* is a religious concept, contrary to the theology of the *"evolution"* of man. Obviously, if man is evolving, his nature cannot remain constant. The two concepts are contradictory. (Please don't confuse evolution with progress. Progress is the result of the discovery and successful application of scientific and moral laws given by a Law Giver, passed down cumulatively in a civilization.)

The very fact that inflation has plagued mature civilizations, and has been met by such idiocy as wage and price controls time and time again through history, is additional testimony to the reality that *"Human nature is a constant"* in the economic/political realm. Perhaps, not surprisingly, it is the bureaucratic establishment that promotes aggressively the theory of evolution. Their self-interest is at stake, as the *"survival of the fittest,"* at the top of the evolutionary spiral.

The Eskimos and the *"primitives"* of Africa have devolved from more mature cultures. The Eskimos once had corrals and out-buildings. They were **not** always nomadic tribes. They were *"civilized"* at one time. Margaret Mead, the great secular anthro-pologist, has told us that the rise of occultism takes place at the peak of a civilization, just before it collapses. It follows, therefore, that oc-cultism will **increase** as the civilizatibn degenerates. At maximum degeneracy, we logically expect a saturation of occultism. And, this is exactly what we see among the aborigines and *"primitives"* of Africa, etc.—an all-encompassing occultism in a totally degenerate and devolved culture, **not** the starting point of evolution. This is what **we** have to look forward to if we continue on our present road. Notice the rampant spread of occultism in Western civilization today!

Science? The war betwen evolutionists and creationists in science rages. Both are religious. Both rely upon some ultimate religious assumptions about the nature of reality.

Men make mistakes (errors). Each of us looks at his own life and sees that obvious truth. (We train our children to hopefully make less mistakes.) Day-to-day reality tells us that we are not perfect, that we are continually in error. (Another word for error is sin.) Therefore, we, collectively, seek another source of sovereignty, if not God, usually the state—the government. The typical individual 20th Cen-tury man is all too happy to assign responsibility and sovereignty to a collection of men because he believes *"they"* are more capable, and/or because he is less responsible, for *"there is strength and wisdom in numbers?"* Yet, this is folly. Truth seldom, if ever, runs in packs. The beacons of truth who have led humanity down the road of progress are individuals. When we place sovereignty, or assign the role of God to government, we are assigning ultimate infallibility to presidents like Reagan, Ford, Carter and Nixon, to vice-presidents like Bush, Agnew and Mondale, to senators, congressmen, IRS agents, SEC bureaucrats, U.S.D.A. workers, etc. Do we really believe these people have the capability and wisdom of God just because they are bunched together? In an ever-changing world, how can a stale, status quo-oriented bureaucrat anticipate the future?

It is no accident that HEW (when it existed) had a budget larger than the combined budgets of all 50 states. The health, education and welfare needs of a people will always be met. (Conservatives beg this question.) The real question is, *"Who meets the HEW needs?"*—individuals who assume their personal responsibilities before God, or the state (government) which **always** fills the vacuum of unbelief left by the failure of individuals to assume their individual responsibilities. This failure results in a concomitant loss of freedom for the individual, for real freedom is always commensurate with responsibility. They always go hand in hand.

Just where do we find total security **and** no responsibility today? Among slaves. In hospitals. In jails. In the atheistic Soviet Union and China (slave states). People there have no freedom, and no real responsibility. The Soviet slaves are constantly entertained by cultural activities of all sorts, just like irresponsible children. This is the direction in which we, too, are moving. The entertainment of TV and professional sports dominates our culture, just like it did Rome's prior to the fall.

There is no question that the federal government today acts like a god. The government gives us laws. But, laws are ideas about morality, values and ethics. These ideas are religious concerns. Therefore, the source of law is the god of any society. And since the number of laws created since 1977 are greater than the number of laws created from the beginning of this country up until 1977, there is no question that our source of law today is the U.S. government, and therefore, our god. Furthermore, the act of creating something out of nothing is the act of a god. Governments, which inflate their money, create something out of nothing—the act of a god. Additionally, with our evolutionary legal system, we no longer have any protection under the Constitution. How could we? It is an archaic document which has not **evolved** in some 200 years. We are now subject to legal tyranny, where law is relative and no firm standard exists.

Government is, in reality, a parasite. It survives because people pay taxes to sustain it. How can a parasite be a god? An irreconcilable conflict, the maximum distortion of reality, exists. Government, a parasite, is playing the role of God. A parasite grows until it consumes (kills) its host. Therefore, the growth of government is suicidal. This is why civilizations fall when their governments are fully developed. The parasite has devoured the host (the people).

The great truth, *"Power corrupts, and absolute power corrupts absolutely,"* has foremost application to government. Today, the federal government is garnering absolute power, and is, therefore, becoming absolutely corrupt. Reagan has been unable to change the trend. Just look at our money (the dollar)! **Inflation is a corruption of money**. The federal government is the creator of money. By simple syllogistic reasoning, our government is corrupt.

The flip side of the coin of *"Power corrupts, and absolute power corrupts absolutely"* is *"The love of money is the root of all evil."* Now, money is **not** evil. Money has many useful purposes. It is the **love** of money which is the root of all evil. Who loves money the most today? Multinational fractional reserve banks and corporations in collusion with government (a trend since the U.S. Civil War). Who benefits the most from inflation? Who consumes the labor (taxes) of the people? The government and its cohorts! They are the greatest lovers of money. They are, accordingly, logically evil.

Our problem is compounded by the generally accepted concept of Social Darwinism—the evolutionary idea of the *"survival of the fittest"*—which lends justification to those in power (government), as to the correctness of their position and their ultimate authority. The *"kings of the hill,"* so to speak, have the right to be there because they have fought their way, by whatever relative means necessary, to the top. By virtue of having reached their lofty position, they have the *"right"* to tell all the rest of us what to do, because they are *"the fittest."* If we buy social evolution, we buy the concept of a slave state.

Our social evolutionary philosophy today was Hitler's philosophy. There is no philosophical difference, only a difference in application. Isn't it obvious why the statement, *"Men must be governed by God, or they will be ruled by tyrants,"* has such import? Men who assume the position of God **become** tyrants. It is a historically documented, recurring reality (e.g., Pharoah, Caesar, "divine" right of kings). And tyrants typically seize wealth, both yours and mine. Furthermore, evolutionary *"survival of the fittest"* promotes conflict, not cooperation. No small wonder everyone is at each other's throat today. Man's natural state, as spiritual creatures, is cooperation, because the very act of the free exchange of goods and services is cooperation.

Under the relative philosophical, theological, legal, social and operational framework today, we have no protection, no real rights. We are wide open to tyranny, to blatant exploitation. There is only the *"illusion"* of protection under law, because law is what the government (IRS) says it is. Government is the god. But, the government is unstable and changes its mind to serve its own interests. And it only responds to the tyranny of the emotional mob (democracy). *"Might makes right." "Numbers make right."* Additionally, while historically God's absolute law encouraged freedom and was negative in a limited sense, telling man what few things he could not do, government law is generally comprehensive, telling man what he must do, as well as what he cannot do.

Taxes and wars will increasingly continue to plague us because governments (internationally), as gods, demand tributes (tithes/taxes) and sacrifices (wars) which shed the blood of young men on the altar of government.

In our mad quest for **ultimate** security, we have insanely placed our trust for ensuring that security in a parasite—government, the ultimate distortion of reality. We have even forgotten the **ultimate** political question, *"Whose rights are superior—those of the individual or those of the group?"* The answer to this question is only found in a free market, bounded by laws which encourage individuals to pursue their self-interest by service to their fellow man. Such an environment requires limited government.

It is no small observation that the greatness of our country and its government were built upon the ultimate, universal laws of a sovereign, loving God who solved the ultimate political question. For, the Biblical God is both the individual and the group (Father, Son and Holy Spirit, separate yet united). And, in time, the rights of the individual are balanced with the rights of the group, where each man responsibly seeks his own self-interest long-term by serving his fellow man in the free market. The individual serves himself by serving the group (society) in free economic exchange.

There is not a single Biblical law laid out for man that I can find, in either the Old or New Testaments, where the long-term self-interest of the individual, the group, and God are not one and the same. Not one! If you don't believe this, for a start, just plow through the *"Great Commandment,"* the *"Golden Rule,"* and the *"Ten Commandments."* Their correct application results in a *"Win-Win-Win"* situation for the individual, the group, and God.

There is no mystery as to why this unique nation has been the greatest, most free, and most prosperous country on earth. The religious presuppositions of our forefathers were correct, which set in motion the chain of *"human action"* that has brought us the good life:

> *"Correct religious assumptions—accurate principles—clear thoughts and ideas (written and verbal)—productive and contructive deeds—good habits—prosperous destiny."* (Those of you familiar with Aristotle will recognize some parts of this sequence. Human nature hasn't changed much, has it?)

We reap what we sow; action and reaction, cause and effect—all still come home to roost in 20th Century America as tyrants, carrying chains, fill the throne room formerly occupied by God.

The importance of establishing ultimacy is the ultimate decision for man. *"Men must be governed by God or they will be ruled by tyrants."*

LIFE, LIBERTY AND THE PURSUIT OF HAPPINESS

New

The only **mandatory** thing in life is **death**. What we all have in common is our birth, physical development, old age and death. Here, indeed, we are all equal. But, for the most part, that's where equality ends. For, from this point forward, inequality, or perhaps to put it a little more succinctly, **progress** and **excellence**, become **optional**. Americans heretofore saw the individual drive for excellence (perfection) in their individual talented areas as desirable. They became, accordingly, more *"Christ-like"* in their pursuit of perfection. Individual excellence brought variety and excitement to life. Things are unfortunately different these days.

From observing a wealth of investors, speculators and businessmen, who have crossed my path in the past decade, two observations are clear-cut:

    1. **The greatest natural tendency every man has is the tendency to self-destruct,** to create one's own misery.

    2. **There is really very little difference between people,** physically and/or mentally. The differences and achievements that come are, by and large, the result of conscious decisions to achieve excellence in specific areas of talent.

Regarding the first tendency, the tendency to self-destruct, historic, constitutional, early Christian America provided us with **three institutions**, which were not only **supportive for the individual**, but also **checkmated this tendency to self-destruct**. These were/are the **local family**, the **local church**, and the **local community**, in that order. Man, by nature, being a gregarious and social animal, likes to conform, to be accepted and to go along with the crowd. He is inhibited from self-destructing when he is surrounded by family and friends, where he has genetic, religious and social ties. (It takes time and pain to build up. By contrast, destruction comes quickly and easily. Human production must be protected.)

The second area, **the achievement of excellence, the development of one's unique talent in one's self-interest,** is not so difficult once a few basic principles are recognized, embraced and applied. **I have yet to meet a man, who was successful in all areas of his life long-term, who was not marked by humility, responsibility, giving, and a long-term**

29

view. I consider these four attributes to be the *"nutshell of excellence/ success."* All four are contrary to human nature, which tends to take the *"animalistic"* short-term view. All four are *"spiritual"* in nature. All four go against the crowd. Contrary opinion, anyone?

Mankind is very proud, collectively speaking. Men are thus, accordingly, very stupid. Men who are proud think their own thoughts, demand recognition, take, and are short-term oriented. They are usually irresponsible in *"people"* areas. These characteristics are antagonistic to our *"Fearsome Foursome of Excellence/Success."* Men who are proud cannot or will not listen. Therefore, they cannot or will not learn, change or grow. Yet, success **long-term** requires adaptability to the facts which are always changing in our living environment. Thus, proud men are doomed to failure long-term. Pride does precede a fall. (Governments in a futile attempt to provide security try to inhibit change, stop time and are, accordingly, proud.) By contrast, **humble men are always listening, reading, learning, growing and are, accordingly, more open to profitable, factual changes.** They respond and flow with their environment. Their openness, in contrast to proud rigidity, allows them the flexibility to take advantage of opportunities in all areas of life. The meek in spirit do inherit the earth.

All men desire to be free and happy. *"Life, liberty and the pursuit of happiness"* are long-established, desired goals for most Americans. Freedom is doing what you want to do. Happiness is liking what you're doing. **The illusion of freedom in our society today, however, is that freedom is free.** It is and never has been so. **Freedom only flows with the river of responsibility.**

A baby has no responsibilities. He is totally dependent which is, by definition, an absence of freedom. A baby is receptive to whatever parental attention, emotional or economic, spiritual or material, is given. This dependency principle, basically economic, hopefully changes as a baby matures to a child, a teenager, and finally an adult. Slaves and convicts (adults?) have no responsibilities. They are also totally dependent and, accordingly, lack freedom.

All any of us really have in this world is time. Each of us basically chooses how we shall spend our time—responsibly or irresponsibly. If we are responsible, and grow up in the real sense of the word, **we have more freedom and flexibility in how we spend our time.** For example, the most free man in any business is the boss/owner. He has the maximum flexibility in choosing how and with whom he will spend his time. He has the maximum freedom/independence because he has assumed maximum responsibility. He is also, in a paradoxical way, the most secure. If the business goes under, the owner/boss is the last one to be *"fired."* So, ironically, in a *"truth in tension"* sort of way,

assumption of responsibility (risk) is necessary not only for freedom, but also for security. The only security which comes with dependency and irresponsibility is the security of slavery, and slavery is dependent ultimately upon some risk taker who is responsible. This is also clearly evident from the fact that the irresponsible, insecure, dependent, slave state of the Soviet Union would collapse if it were not for the subsidies provided to the U.S.S.R. by Western civilization's multinational corporations and banks. One other point: it goes almost without saying that individuals who are responsible exercise self-discipline. It takes responsible self-discipline to move from a short-term orientation to a long-term one. Self-discipline is totally lacking in a child and comes, hopefully, with responsible adult maturity, as does patience. Here is where the local family, local church, and local community exercise responsibility in the training of a child. In the growing up process, a child who is "given to" moves from "taking" as a child to "giving" as an adult. The essence of contract/covenants is giving. As a child matures, his "animal" needs hopefully become subordinate to, and disciplined by, his abstract "spiritual" values.

The proud and the irresponsible are always taking. They do not care to, or do not have the ability to give. All of their interactions are thus *"win-lose"* confrontations. They are also, accordingly, short-term oriented, *"taking,"* whether by way of conspicuous consumption, stealing time or goods from an employer, debt assumption, or such things as welching on a contract, verbal or written. All are short-term oriented actions. People do not forget the evil done them by their fellow man. Friends come and go, but enemies accumulate. Thus, *"taking,"* a *"win-lose"* situation short-term, is a *"lose-lose"* situation long-term, when the chickens come home to roost, as they almost always do.

The mature adult has moved from *"taking"* **as an infant to** *"giving."* The mature adult has grown from an *"animal"* being to a *"spiritual"* being. For, the mature adult realizes that *"giving"* **is the only way that he can** *"get"* **(take) long-term and benefit (win) (regarding both his spiritual and animal needs) in all areas of life.** Stated differently, *self-interest is best served by "giving,"* **when viewed correctly from the long-term perspective. It takes a humble and responsible, mature man to see this truth and implement it to his own best self-interest long-term.** It takes true wisdom to see that one's best self-interest is maximized by *"giving,"* not *"taking." "Giving"* is a *"win-win"* perspective long-term. It is synergistic.

In a marriage, where both husband and wife *"give,"* the blessings which accrue are compounded. By contrast, in a marriage, where both parties *"take"* selfishly, short-term, misery is likewise compounded.

(Synergy in reverse.)

A free enterprise system, a contractual system, can only exist in a free society (responsible society), where *"giving"* **is the valued way to achieve one's own best self-interest long-term.** The very nature of a contract, an agreement between two mature parties, is a *"win-win"* situation, where both parties *"give"* to each other what each party desires, so that both are satisfied. Thus, it becomes obvious that **cooperation should be the normal state between men, not competition, not** *"survival of the fittest."* Thus, the free market kicks evolution in the head. (It should come as no surprise that with the rise of evolution has come the demise of the free market, subverted by special interests.) Sure, buyers compete in a second-hand way against buyers, and sellers against sellers, but buyers and sellers cooperate to the best interest of both parties. (Actually *"buyers and buyers"* and *"sellers and sellers"* cooperate. That's what shopping centers and motor cities are all about.)

Cooperation and freedom go hand-in-hand. Both are necessary for contractual arrangements. Cooperation is, thus, antagonistic to forced communism, socialism and collectivism of all types. It follows, logically, that collectivism, like communism, is an immature, animalistic, competitive, slave-like *"win-lose"* society. *"Win-win"* situations and cooperation, by contrast, require humility, responsibility, giving and a long-term view, whereby all social/economic transactions benefit all parties concerned.

The nebulous, intangible, politically tagged categories with which we are plagued today, such as *"masses,"* *"society,"* and the *"group,"* cannot be dealt with in the real world of application because they are, in fact, intangible (spiritual). Such nebulous terms are used too often for manipulative purposes. **It is only when we boil all things down to their smallest component part, and come back to the individual, a concrete reality, that we can see that** *"the masses,"* *"society,"* **and the** *"group"* **benefit from the individual maturity that results from the application of humility, responsibility, giving and a long-term view.**

It should now be apparent why the individual should be given priority for free decision making in our political/economic system. He is the building block of society. He may hopefully learn and mature the easy way. In a free (responsible) society, in any case, maturity comes almost automatically, through checks and balances. The individual, if he does not learn the easy way, if he does not learn the importance of humility, responsibility, giving and the long-term view, will learn these lessons the hard way. He will, accordingly, fail long-term. Other members of society almost automatically penalize pride, irresponsibility, taking, and the short-term view, particularly where there is local, geographic proximity. Such unteachable members of society tend to become dependent, losing their freedom commensurate with their irresponsibility.

The long-term view ties together humility, responsibility and giving. These are *"spiritual"* concepts. **Men naturally tend to take the short-term view,** an *"animalistic"* tendency (*"survival of the fittest"*). **It is this implementation of the short-term perspective which nearly always leads to personal self-destruction and to creating one's own misery.**

Because men resist change and fear the unknown, they tend naturally to do the easy thing, the obvious thing, which is nearly always short-term in nature. Rather than dig down deep to the roots of a matter, rather than think deeply and patiently about the long-term beneficial implications of humility, responsibility, and giving, as it serves their own best self-interest long-term, **men,** in typically undisciplined fashion, **almost automatically choose the proud, irresponsible, taking, short-term perspective. This is to the detriment of their own self-interest long-term, unless the rules (laws) in a free society penalize such action. As a result of this individual and thus collective human tragedy, the** *"greatest good for the greatest number"* is shattered. For, with this proud, irresponsible, taking, short-term view, the inevitable result is tyranny of the masses, subjection under the thumb of a few elite at the top (commanding a bureaucracy) who, by stark contrast, have assumed the responsibility which the masses of individuals have rejected. Such is increasingly the case today in our progressively non-free society and world.

The long-term view always results in a *"win-win"* **situation.** It necessarily includes humility, responsibility and giving, because **the true long-term reality is that humility, responsibility and giving are in the best self-interest of each individual as well as every other member of society.** The fact that our society today is so far removed from these basic truths speaks clearly as to why, in our civilization today, little works, and much is failing fast, particularly our long-established, traditional institutions. (Rot tends to come with age in institutions.)

These timeless truths we have discussed so far are religious in nature. The very nature of a timeless truth, a *"spiritual"* **truth, is an eternal concept, and also religious.** And, because man has limited time and a limited mind, he can never know everything about anything. Thus, he is forced to make some ultimate assumptions about the nature of reality. He is required to make spiritual guesses regarding ultimacy. These are inescapably religious concepts—ultimate presuppositions about the nature of reality. Thus, to go further, it becomes obvious that **one (if not the main) reason our civilization's in-**

**stitutions today are bankrupt is our established religious institutions'
religious presuppositions are likewise, precedingly, bankrupt.**

Religion in America today misses the crux of the true religious issue.
Nearly all religion in America today has error-prone, imperfect man
either attempting to become a god (humanism), or attempting to
please God in some direct, eternal way, or be as God. Thus, God in the
American sense today is a very small god. He is dependent upon weak
men. A society can be no bigger than its concept of God. America's
God today is very puny.

As a believer in cause and effect, I went back and checked to find
out what really were the early religious presuppositions that built this
great country. My study was investigative and pragmatic, not religious
in nature. My reasoning was as follows: *"If religious presuppositions
are necessarily the basis of society, what was the nature of the religious
presuppositions of early America? What was it about the bigness of
early America's God that allowed this country, in cause and effect,
thought and action fashion, to build the greatest and most prosperous
society on the face of the earth?"* The answer was surprisingly simple:
**Early religious America believed in a sovereign, all-knowing, ever-
present, and all-powerful God who was, is, and has everything. He
was and is also just, righteous, love, unchanging, eternal and the
source of all truth.** Being the creator and possessor of everything, this
God could only **give** to man. Man could give nothing in return to a
God who had it all in the first place. All man could attempt to do in
return for God's good and perfect gifts was simply acknowledge the
blessing (gifts) received, through faith, prayer and worship.

While at first blush (short-term) it is true (and also somewhat
depressing) that it is impossible to please on an eternal level a God
who is and has everything, the long-term view, by contrast, is that
there is great peace, security, and motivation which comes with existence under the perfect law of a personal Sovereign who is love and all-
giving.

If you think about it, if there is not a sovereign God who is and has
it all, then there is no God at all because then everything is relative. If
everything is relative, there is no truth, and it really is a *"dog eat dog"*
world of total conflict and *"survival of the fittest."* If there is no sovereign God, then there is no total and ultimate source of knowledge,
or of love, or of giving. Then everyone and everything is in error and
on the *"take."* Then, truly, life is a tragedy, void of meaning, and
God is dead. If this is true (which in my opinion it is not), can our personal and collective deaths be far behind?

We now see more clearly the importance of practical, workable, successful theology upon which our early American political/economic system was based, and which was the foundation for the tremendous economic prosperity we have enjoyed.

Now, here we get to the guts of the issue, up close and personal. As we have seen earlier, every man is religious. People ask me if I'm religious and, if so, to which religion do I subscribe. I answer, *"Yes, I'm a Christian, nondenominational."* Why am I a Christian? Because the God who provided the Christ, consistent with His sovereignty and His total ownership of everything, rightfully and logically, has required nothing of me, his creation, other than my acknowledgement of His work—my faith, when it comes to the **eternal** realm. (Faith is nonmeritorious, as is prayer and worship.) I have earned nothing. I can do nothing about my eternal welfare because I am a temporal being. God has solved the eternal problem. Thank goodness. The beautiful *"truth in tension,"* however, is that as a God-chosen ambassador and individual believer/priest, in time, through prayer and my talents (spiritual gifts exercised in the free market), I have access, **in time**, to the most positive powerful force behind the creation. This gives me the ability to be successful, pursue individual excellence in keeping with my talents, and exercise dominion **in time**. Furthermore, there is not a single rule, not a single law, given by this all-giving God which is contrary to my own best self-interest long-term. **Every single God-given law operates consistent with my own best self-interest long-term and in keeping with the key pragmatic points in the nutshell of excellence/success—humility, responsibility, giving and the long-term view!** Every one of them!

Does religion today have man fruitlessly trying to please a God who already has everything? What can you and I do for a God who has and controls all? Nothing! The result is that insane asylums today are *"full up"* with religious types, who *"logically"* have gone crazy trying to achieve this impossible task. Besides, this God can and wants only to give to you and me, His creations. The sovereign God who created this universe, and provided the sacrifice of Jesus Christ for eternal salvation, only asks that each of us, in time, here on earth, as a unique, created, creative being with a unique purpose, act consistent with our own self-interest which is accomplished by obeying His law and developing our God-given talents. That is His will. This is the purpose for which we were created. The fact that we can think and act with long-term abstract concepts separates us from all other animals, making us spiritual creatures, not subject to *"the law of the jungle,"* if we pursue our spiritual interests primarily (with the help of the Holy Spirit).

God has solved the *"eternal life"* problem. That's what Jesus

Christ and the cross were all about. **This makes the issue for us what happens in time (here on earth).** All God wants to do for us in time is give, so that we will maximize our development and God-given talents and, in the process, maximize our self-interest long-term. This will benefit our fellow man and please God. What a fantastic and perfect plan. Such a God, to my mind, is a truly loving God that I can worship, give thanks to and praise; a God who has it all and yet who is humble, responsible, giving and possessed with a long-term view, so that His purpose for my life is consistent with my own best self-interest long-term, benefitting all the while society-at-large. It's a *"win-win"* contract/covenant. **He makes all the decisions in the eternal realm. I make the decisions in the temporal realm,** with His loving intervention and guidance from time to time, coupled with the ever-present helpful work of the Holy Spirit. How much better is this than government doing the planning for us (playing the role of God)? To the extent that these decisions of mine are humble, responsible, giving, and long-term oriented, everyone wins all around—Him, my fellow man, and me—everyone! And love, joy, peace, patience, kindness, goodness, faithfulness, gentleness and self-control are just a few of the naturally flowing by-products benefitting all mankind. Now, that's real freedom (grace) under law.

Look at it another way. The basic spiritual issue in time is economics. Banks, today's spiritual temples, are economic institutions. Politics today is confiscatory economics with the largest item in the budget being wealth redistribution. Trotsky declared, *"The old principle: who does not work shall not eat, has been replaced by a new one: who does not obey does not eat."* Thus, we see that the power of Russian communism, playing the role of God, is rooted in economics.

Not only is the earth the Lord's (economics), but man's spiritual growth determines how he fulfills his, and his fellow man's, economic/animal needs. Because man has biological primary needs, the economic issue is basic. How this economic need is approached spiritually, with abstract ideas, determines man's satisfaction of both his spiritual and material needs in time. We have seen clearly that economic prosperity all around is only achieved as men grow spiritually and individually in character, through a humble, responsible, giving, long-term perspective, whereby men are then free and able to contract (covenant). Covenants/contracts attempted by men without character leads to communism and resultant tyranny. Thus, individual character development must precede covenants/contracts for the covenants/contracts to be any good. Any other way of bringing men together, other than freely, through covenants/contracts, based upon the character of the individuals, is a pipe dream, leading eventually to group coercion, with a few elite at the top. The ultimate covenant/contract was made by God who, by His impeccable character, provided and accepted the sacrifice of Jesus Christ on the cross, thereby solving the problem of our eternal welfare.

This is what early religious America really understood. This is what made the U.S.A. unique among nations. The U.S. Constitution rightfully chained the federal government and made the humble, responsible, giving, long-term oriented individual supreme (*"a government of the people, by the people, for the people"*). After all, how could it be otherwise when the individual was seen as the elected heir with the *"King of kings?"* Men, as restored *"second Adams,"* saw that their eternal rewards were based upon their *"occupation"* and *"stewardship"* in time. *"Thy kingdom come, thy will be done, on earth, as it is in heaven."* *"Occupy till I come."* Men got busy and were careful and diligent in their actions because they knew they were to be judged according to their works. **Men saw clearly that the proof of their eternal salvation was the manifestation of their works in time,** pursuing their own best self-interests long-term through their God-given talents, in keeping with the principles of humility, responsibility and giving. Men will do whatever is necessary when it comes to their eternal welfare. What a fantastic long-term motivation!

We reap what we sow. Man has only one of two choices in time: either he can responsibly govern himself and develop his God-given talents with God as the master planner, or he can be irresponsible and let an oppressive, fault-finding government attempt to do the planning, creating misery for all. The rise of government as a central planner is the logical result of the savagery, chaos, and anarchy wrought by the theory of evolution applied.

Separation of church and state? Philosophically impossible, physically necessary. All governments are religious because they issue laws which are ideas about right and wrong and morality. These are religious concerns. **Physical** separation of church and state was accomplished in this country to prevent a concentration of power, like that which had occurred in Egypt, Rome and England.

Organized, centralized religion? The colonists would have none of it. One of the reasons for the American Revolution was that the Church of England was going to impose its bishops on the colonies. Nearly every colony had its own church. *"Separation of church and state"* **prevented any one Christian denomination from dominating the** *"federal"* **government.** Early Americans desired freedom to work out their individual God-given destiny. Cooperation and group harmony followed because each individual had a unique God-given talent that benefitted his fellow man. Thus, decentralization was mandatory, even in religion, to maximize the development of each believer/priest. Organized religion, by contrast, tends toward a centralized, bureaucratic, non-free hierarchy.

Early Americans wanted reality. They saw the earth as theirs to subdue and groom, not rape (as is the case under the evolutionary *"law of the jungle"*). Organized religion, by contrast, emphasizes ritual and escape from reality.

Early Americans believed in building character. Covenants/contracts are worthless without men of character making them. Organized religion, by contrast, attempts to instill guilt rather than build conscience and character.

Early Americans saw that individual and group worship were maximized on the local level, just like with local government efficiency, where *"checks and balances"* come into play.

A major issue is "How does man please God?" How does God want man to please Him? Look at it this way. Making money does not bring blessings and benefits long-term by a self-centered effort to make money. Making money is a result, a by-product, of doing things correctly, of providing a desired good or service. Pleasing God is not accomplished by trying directly to please God who is and has everything and only wants to give to His creatures. Such an effort by man leads to guilt, helplessness, and a sense of unworthiness. Pleasing God is a result, a by-product, of pursuing one's own self-interest long-term, fulfilling and using the talents which are God-given. This also benefits mankind generally. By so doing, man succeeds in time and willingly gives God the praise, glory, and worship which He deserves. God is the ultimate self-actualizer. He is the perfect Father. He can only give and love His children (even in discipline). He just wants credit, rightfully so, for what He has given.

Limited man, with limited time and a limited mind, is today still religious. Even true scientists, if they are honest about their scientific investigations, know their work depends upon the presupposition of an underlying law and order for the discovery and application of scientific laws, the real essence of scientific progress. Law and order requires a Law Giver. There are at least three reasons scientists reject acknowledging God today: 1) they are proud; 2) they rightfully scorn what passes for religion today; 3) the scientific method operates in the *"material"* realm, not the *"spiritual"* one. Scientists can't acknowledge what they don't see.

There are only two basic theories of origin—creation and evolution. Creation assumes man's spiritual nature is primary. Evolution assumes man's animal nature is primary. We have already seen that man's animal needs are best met when his spiritual nature has the upper hand. Practically speaking, thoughts precede action anyway. When evolution is assumed primary, all the human misery of conflict, the *"law of the jungle"* and *"survival of the fittest"* kick in. The weak and stupid are abused and oppressed. Wars proliferate. Such is our evolutionary world today.

Today, the religious battle is between humanists, such as those in the World Council of Churches and the National Council of Churches who support the communists all too often, **and** early American-type Christians. Organized (particularly centralized) religion, in the institutional sense, is nearly totally humanistic today. Man is attempting to be God, to be as God, or please God in some eternal sense based upon his own efforts without the preemptive work of Christ. Humanists, whether collectivists like our federal government and communists, **or** individualists like Libertarians, all claim that man is sovereign, that man is the measure of all things, the judge of good and evil. (This is identical to Satan's sin in his desire to *"be like the most High."*) Humanism, thus, is at war with the underlying principles which made this country great—with our own best economic self-interests—as well as at war with the sovereign God who is the giver of all good things and the ultimate judge of good and evil.

Humanism is correct in the sense that it recognizes man's tremendous potential to achieve and accomplish much. It is rightfully at war with oppressive, guilt-ridden, manipulative, organized, centralized religious America. But, then again, it was organized, centralized religious Israel, along with the Roman government empire, that put Christ on the cross.

Humanism is not surprisingly also at war with humanism. What humanism has achieved is technological (*"material"* realm) excellence **without** the necessary preceding moral underpinnings (*"spiritual"* realm), without the vital abstract laws which allow technology to be a blessing rather than the curse it is today. Humanistic technology today has brought us to the brink of political, nuclear, social, economic and ecological devastation. It has been proud, irresponsible, taking and short-term oriented. Yet, properly applied, we know technology now has the ability to save us. We just have to get it into the right hands, supported by the moral underpinnings discussed above.

"Collective" humanism today is bankrupt. The false, evolutionary, *"survival of the fittest"* federal government, socialists, communists, multinational corporations and banks are dying. Reality is returning to the world, as must be the case in a universe created by a reality-oriented God.

The *"individual"* humanists, like Libertarians (followers of Ayn Rand) are likewise frustrated. But, they need only see that real individual achievement, freedom and happiness comes not with the proud, selfish, irresponsible, short-term "taking" by either collective or individual humanists (both one and the same philosophically), but instead with the classic early constitutional Christian American philosophy of humility, responsibility, giving and the long-term view. Only in this environment is personal development maximized, while everyone wins. Such an approach provides man with the security and stability of an eternal anchor, which encourages him to become a risk taker and achiever in time. The support provided by the local family, local church, and local community also provide help and security, making it easier for men to take risks and progress in time. The abstract and concrete are in perfect harmony as well. Thoughts and actions are in unity. Anything else leads to tyranny and exploitation. There is no freedom without law; law is the establishment of responsibility, and responsibility, freedom and human satisfaction are maximized on the local level where man's self-destructive tendencies and power lusting ambitions are kept in check.

Man was not meant to rule over man in any area of life, except on the local level where elections and checks and balances exist, a limited national government excepted (for defense and justice). It seems, accordingly, that God hates empire builders of all types, from the Tower of Babel forward. Why? Empires lead to *"the greatest misery for the greatest number"* and *"the tyranny of a few over many."* Empires are never in our best individual or collective self-interest long-term. Ever notice how all empires are at war with God? No accident.

Political empires are built upon the backs, blood and money of *"the people."* Financial empires are built with *"other people's money"* (OPM). Religious empires are built upon the money, guilt and gullibility of a trusting, common people. All empires utilize huge, expensive, wasteful bureaucracies that squander the wealth, resources and energies of the people. Empires maximize the benefits of a few and the misery of the many. Today, we have imperial governments and world cities. The people are accordingly miserable and poor (debt considered). But there's hope. Computers and satellites today have made it possible to maximize the benefits of the city while living in the country.

God's laws are for our individual and collective long-term benefit. We see the truth of freedom only under law in our very efficient automobile traffic system. The *"rules of the road"* are absolute, limiting boundaries—laws. When they are obeyed, everyone has the freedom to travel *"freely,"* to cooperatively achieve his own best self-interest, as it were. The traffic system assumes humility to the law, the assumption of individual responsibility, *"giving"* (yielding) and a long-term view. God's laws for man in time are for the same purpose.

Every Biblical law I have investigated provides the *"greatest good for the greatest number,"* as well as maximizes the self-interest of the individual. This can only occur by (and all good *"laws"* include) the virtues of humility, responsibility, giving and a long-term view.

All societies are based upon religious assumptions about the nature of reality. The religious lie of the ages, still with us today because human nature is a constant (man has progressed under scientific and moral law, not evolved), is that man can do something to please God directly or become God or become as God. This leads to guilt, insanity, frustration, suicide and needless emphasis on the *"Great By and By,"* (God's total realm of responsibility), creating, in the process, through this temporal irresponsibility by man, hell on earth. By stark contrast, the all-loving, all-giving God of early Christian America is big enough that all He asks is that each individual in time act in his own long-term best self-interest for which he was created. Such just happens, by perfect divine planning, to be consistent with God's laws for man which require humility, responsibility, giving and a long-term view. All he requires in return is the nonmeritorious response of faith, prayer and worship.

It's all so simple. **God's will and man's best interest for time are one and the same, rightfully understood.** Only thoughtless rebellion (and an *"animalistic"* sin nature) should keep man from following this critical path of *"life, liberty and the pursuit of happiness."* In Proverbs 8:36 (Proverbs is the book of wisdom), God wrote: *"But he that sinneth against me wrongeth his own soul: all they that hate me love death."* A man who wars against God wars against his own best self-interest. A man who hates God, a God who only has man's best self-interest at heart, does love death! He self-destructs. It is, accordingly, no accident today that our world, captured by humanism, is on the verge of economic, political, social, nuclear (scientific), and ecological death (self-destruction/suicide), to the detriment of all of our best self-interests. It, thus, seems that the only real hope for this country begins with a spiritual revival, the kind that encourages men to simply accept the eternal salvation which has been **given** them by God, so they can then move out and act in their own best self-interest, in a humble, responsible, giving, long-term way **in time**.

Is our country to be worth a plug nickel—*"One nation under God?"* A country cannot long survive alienated from its spiritual roots. Spiritual roots are basic.

Where has classic Christian America missed the boat? Given that Christ's work on the cross is central to Christianity, and further given that the Gospel (*"Good News"*) about Christ's work on the cross is basic, it is this writer's thinking that Christian religious America today no longer understands the Gospel and what it truly means. In fact, religious America today may have it backwards.

The Gospel is truly the *"Good News,"* that God has saved man eternally through the work of Christ in time. This, in turn, makes man responsible in time, to exercise his talents, subdue the earth, and exercise dominion in time, as proof of his eternal salvation. *"Faith without works is dead."*

Today, Christian religion leaders humanistically make the Gospel, the *"Good News,"* and thus God, dependent upon man and man's efforts primarily for eternal life to be secured. Today Christians are told that the Gospel, the *"Good News,"* is necessary to get man saved eternally. Thus, the Gospel becomes the instrument, the means of salvation, dependent upon the whims of error-prone (sinful) man to get other men saved eternally. In other words, God has left the eternal welfare of men in men's hands. Pretty tenuous, unstable, unreliable, and insecure, wouldn't you say? An all-loving, all-powerful God did that? Not hardly. Today's perverted Gospel then is no longer the *"Good News"* announcing that God, who is all-giving, has done it all and saved man eternally, in keeping with such doctrines as election and predestination. Rather the Gospel today, as it is misunderstood and perverted, encourages men to build religious empires to *"get other men eternally saved from hell,"* using guilt, fear and manipulative techniques to draw in huge sums of money, focusing on the eternal realm (which is God's jurisdiction), leaving man irresponsible in time, just the opposite of what God intended, contrary to man's self-interest in time! And the Gospel, by the way, in this modern apostasy, no longer really becomes the *"Good News,"* that God has saved man eternally, but rather the *"Bad News,"* the instrument of damnation. Here's how.

If lost men only get saved eternally by already eternally saved men bringing them the Gospel, then what happens to those men who don't hear the Gospel? There are only two choices. These *"lost"* men are either eternally saved or eternally lost. If those who don't hear the Gospel are eternally saved, then we're better off never taking them the Gospel at all, because some of them who then hear the Gospel will reject it and as a result be eternally damned. Such a damning Gospel is not the *"Good News."* If those who don't hear the Gospel are eternally damned, then righteous American Christians should spend every cent they have for missions since there is nothing more important than saving men eternally. But rich American Christians don't do this. They have big homes, cars, fine clothes and huge churches. Is a fair, loving God, the God of the Bible, in some warped, cynical, Greek sense, going to save rich, American Christians who have satisfied their own creature comforts first, and in the process, by ignoring or not totally giving everything they own to missions, condemned their eternally lost fellow man, some poor heathen, to hell. Of course not. We have already seen that God's will is individual economic prosperity in time, the by-product of men developing their God-given talents. Thus, the Gospel is not the means to eternal salvation. The Gospel is truly the *"Good News"* that God has already saved man eternally and called him to service in time, for both man's good (individual and collective) and God's will.

Why do men reject such basic, simple, uplifting truth? Either because they cannot understand the Gospel (God's realm of responsibility), or they have been deceived, or they are proud. Men, by nature, reject grace. The best way to make an enemy of a friend is to do him a favor he cannot repay. That friend's ego (pride—the first and worst of sins) cannot handle it. This psychological truth was prevalent in the American Indian culture, too. It is true today also in American foreign aid. U.S. abundance is given to Third World countries and, in return, they despise us for it.

We all want to be equal. We all want to be as God. None of us are ever equal, however, in all areas. This inequality is a blessing because it leads to cooperation, variety, and stimulation in life. We need each other because we each have different talents. This is the division of labor. But, we can establish relative equality in economic exchange, the free trade of goods and services, contracting and covenanting with one another. From this, we derive our sense of self-worth in time as *"spiritual"* creatures with a basic *"animal"* nature and need. The problem comes with the ultimate source of all things, both spiritual and material. Here we are forced to confront our total inequality, our *"total depravity,"* before a God who is and has everything. We see clearly our inferiority and, by nature, rebel against it. Nevertheless, an all-loving God who is only capable of giving, through the eternal salvation-providing gift of Jesus Christ who died on the cross for our imperfections (sins), has made it possible for us to have fellowship with Him in time and eternally. This is truly grace. This is truly the Gospel. This is truly the *"Good News."* Biblical salvation is spoken of both eternally (God's responsibility) and temporally (man's responsibility). This is what our forefathers in this great nation fought and died for. This is the theological base which has given us our tremendous prosperity in time, the **evidence** of our eternal salvation, and the basis for harmony among all mankind.

In the economic realm, in time, our covenants/contracts with each other are only as good as our character. The strength of our character and the resultant covenants/contracts stem from the original covenant/

contract made by a perfect God, as provided in both the Old and New Testaments—the Old and New Covenants/Contracts. This spiritual truth, applied in time, inescapably leads to economic prosperity and *"Wealth for All."*

WAR ON ORIGIN

New

Down through the ages there has arisen, over and over again, a head-on conflict between the two basic theories of origin—creation and evolution. Both are intensely religious, because both involve assumptions/guesses about the ultimate nature of reality. One entails a supernatural intervention, the other natural processes. One involves cause and effect, the other chance. One is personal, the other impersonal. One is Creator initiated, the other creature initiated. One is found in the Western Christian tradition, the other in Eastern tradition and atheism. One assumes original order, the other that complex systems arose out of chaotic systems. One is time limited and historical, the other timeless. One holds to absolute truth and limits, the other to relativity—no limits and no truth. In one, life has meaning; the other, no meaning. The war is over what is true.

Because no men were actually present at the time of creation/the beginning of evolution, all men make guesses about how the origin occurred. In a scientific sense, since there were no witnesses, and neither can be experimentally duplicated, neither theory can be proven. Thus, any individual who discusses creation or evolution has assumed the role of a religious priest.

All of man's thinking is circular. Man can never be totally objective because he cannot learn all things about anything, due to the fact that he has a limited mind and limited time on this earth. The faith/belief in creation or evolution is, therefore, the ultimate presupposition/ guess concerning physical reality. Now, any of us can believe anything we like as long as the consequences of our beliefs are unimportant/ trivival. But, when our personal welfare and survival, as well as the welfare and survival of mankind, depends upon our religious beliefs (creation or evolution), our beliefs had better correspond to the real world. Beliefs precede thoughts. Thoughts precede actions. The pen is mightier than the sword in that those who think and reason, also plan and lead; those who lead have some underlying beliefs or values which are by definition religious. Here are the two origin models.

The Creation Model

Each man is made by the Creator. The Creator has designed each individual for a special, specific purpose in life, and has given each man the necessary talents to achieve that purpose. Thus, every man must be free to pursue the development and use of his unique Creator-given talents in time. Every man must have the liberty to fulfill his destiny. To facilitate the Creator's master plan for the human race collectively through men individually, the Creator gave men rules (principles) to live by in THE BIBLE, whereby each individual, by acting in his own self-interest of personal talent development long-term, serves simultaneously each other individual, thereby bringing into harmony the best interests of both the individual and the group, fulfilling the Creator's purpose.

Since each individual has been given specific talents which benefit every other individual, directly and/or indirectly, men readily cooperate in the free market. They contract and covenant with each other for various purposes, so that each party can benefit from the other's developed talents—the production of goods and services (economics).

All human production in time has economic roots because man's economic (biological/animal) needs are basic. Government is hired as a decentralized servant of free men to ensure that the Creator's laws for man are enforced for the betterment of all men, both long-term and resultingly short-term. Government is the employee, the overhead expense, paid for by free men to protect these free men from internal and external violence. Government also referees and settles disputes in the free market. Man, the *"spiritual being"* with an animal nature, is eternal. Government, man's created institution, is temporal and, therefore, inferior.

The Creator, in his wisdom, first created man as a *"spiritual being"* with a subordinate animal nature. Man *"blew it"* when Adam disobeyed the Creator in the first economic garden. Then, man's animal nature became primary. He fell from spiritual grace, so to speak. But, a loving, sovereign Creator, with a perfect plan, came seeking after man, and provided man with a perfect atoning sacrifice, Jesus Christ, which restored man to spiritual fellowship with the Creator, so that man's animal nature could again potentially be subordinate to man's spiritual nature in time, and the economic development of the earth (garden), through the development of each man's talents, could continue. The struggle back, however, is a tough one.

Knowing that since man had fallen from spiritual and material (economic) perfection in the garden (the first economic world trade center), the Creator knew that man would by nature pursue his animalistic instincts, preying on his fellow man, acting in his own selfish, short-term interests, based upon *"facts,"* just like animals do, in a *"survival of the fittest"* way. To encourage man to develop his spiritual nature, to give fallen, animalistic, fact-oriented man an incentive to pursue the development of his principled, spiritual gifts primarily, thereby better meeting his animalistic needs, the Creator, to prove to man in time that His way was the best, developed the free market.

Through this free market, men learned that the Creator's purpose for their lives, their own best self-interest, and the self-interests of their fellow man, were all wrapped up in a unified harmony when the Creator's primary, spiritual, principled methodology was pursued. (This is cooperation under the voluntary division of labor.)

By men thinking, conceiving, planning and acting creatively on *"principle"* primarily, and *"facts"* secondarily, long-term, in keeping with their spiritual nature, men best met, as well as subdued in the free market, their biological/animal needs, their economic needs.

The creation model moves from perfect economic conditions, to imperfect, fallen, cursed, natural/economic conditions, to restored man working to rebuild perfect economic conditions. Perfection, though not totally attainable, is the standard and the goal. This ensures continual human progress. Economic blessing is a result of man's principled development of his individual talents, man's subduing of his animalistic instincts, and the resultant harnessing of the *"law of the jungle."* Social harmony abounds then, because not only does man love his work and is rewarded for it economically as he develops his Creator-given talents, he, in the process, readily cooperates with other men who have complementary talents, and simultaneously provides for his family, thereby enhancing love and security, along with the fulfillment of his basic biological/economic needs.

The Evolution Model

Here, too, like in the creation model, the issue is economic. But, under the evolution model, man, the *"animal,"* and nothing more, is pitted in never-ending conflict and competition against every other man. The *"law of the jungle"* reigns supreme. The *"survival of the fittest"* is the standard and goal. Each individual is continually at war with every other individual, seeking whatever gain and advantage is possible, preying on the weak and vulnerable. The short-term view and *"facts,"* (not principles—facts are all that animals can understand) are the focus for obtaining this economic superiority. The spiritual, thinking, planning aspect of man is subordinate to, and is distorted into, scheming, plotting, self-serving and conspiring to benefit man's animalistic short-term lusts. Widows and orphans beware. It is a *"dog eat dog"* world under the evolution model.

This competition is rooted in a lack of love. There is no room for the likes of love, pity, giving and charity, only room for sex, arrogance, taking and exploitation, just like in primitive societies, which are accordingly animalistic. There are no savings, no economic capital formation, no tools produced, which would allow the development of culture, technological progress, health, medical and scientific research, as well as all other forms of social advancement. (Economic savings is a long-term concept, foreign to the short-term, evolutionary, fact-oriented world of animals.)

As animalistic evolution increasingly engulfs a social order, men's spiritual natures cry out for protection and relief from the evolutionary terror of day-to-day life. Men look to government, the collective power, the epitome of the evolutionary spiral, the ultimate in the *"survival of the fittest,"* to protect them. Government agrees to do so, but at a terrible price. Government, after all, must and will seek the short-term gratification of its own interests in the evolutionary model. (This is why big governments are continually plagued with corruption and scandals.)

Government, instead of the Creator, becomes the master planner. Individual freedom progressively dies, as government creates more and more laws and regulations in an attempt to harness and control the individualistic, animalistic, evolutionary nature of man. External discipline is substituted for internal discipline (the modus operandi of the creation model).

Government, of course, likes its exalted role as the king of the *"survival of the fittest."* Government thus finances wars, revolutions, and joins with powerful financial, business, media, educational and religious interests to further centralize wealth and power. Government also encourages the teaching (in public schools) and use of the evolutionary model to a limited extent in day-to-day life, in order to continually justify its controls over human evolutionary existence.

When this government control is maximized, commerce and politics dominate a society. Commerce and politics are both *"facts"* oriented, and so the government *"animal"* has reached the epitome of its development, backed by high economic interests. Empires and world cities dominate the landscape then at this tip of the evolutionary spiral. But eventually reality strikes, and strikes hard. The empire and emperor are found to have no clothes. Government and cities are both seen for what they are—economic parasites.

Governments do not create wealth. They can only steal it through inflation and legalized theft (taxation), and then redistribute this wealth to the people under them, who demand it in order for governments to maintain and justify their power. Likewise, the cities, historically always slave centers, parasitically draw their human and economic resources from the rural country. When the parasites, the governments and cities, are fully developed, the society dies, either from without, as government sacrifices its defense responsibility to its illicit economic function, **or** from within through revolution, as the common people pull down the government for failing at an impossible task, the production of *"Wealth for All."* Men revolt when they cannot do meaningful work and be paid honest money for it. Men revolt when they receive favors (welfare) which they cannot repay. The parasites, governments and cities, have at that time consumed the host.

The deception of an evolutionary spiral up is seen for the charade it is, a short-term, superficial, illusionary glorification, leading to long-term destruction and chaos in a spiral down. This typically occurs when the climate turns less favorable.

There are only two factors in the basic human economic equation—land and labor. Together, with savings (impossible under the evolutionary model), they produce capital (tools), which bring about the economic good life. Government centralization schemes can only last while the climate is favorable and the land's production is abundant, allowing the squandering of human resources. When the climate becomes harsh, however, human energy must take up the slack and become efficient, throwing off the wasteful human folly schemes of the centralizing planners.

In the evolution model, individual conflict leads to group coercion and slavery by government, lasting for a while to the benefit of a few at the miserable expense of the many, until the ultimate economic and following political collapse comes, resulting again in individual conflict, as the pathetic never-ending cycle continues. In the evolution model, human action, throughout time, grinds over and over again on a bloody wheel (cycle). There is no real human progress as in the linear progression of the creation model. Furthermore, the blood sacrifices and the inevitable revolutions in the evolution model are the substitutes for the blood sacrifice of Jesus Christ in the creation model. Revolutions occur when governments are seen for the lie they are—false and inept creators, who fail to solve the basic economic problems, from which all other human conditions stem.

*   *   *

Some further elaboration on creation and evolution at this point is appropriate.

The theory of evolution goes back to ancient times. It is almost as old as creation. It was prevalent in the Egyptian Empire, in Greece and Rome, and found its way into Western civilization through social theory and thought **prior** to its application on the scientific level, as Dr. Gary North's book, THE DOMINION COVENANT, so clearly pointed out. Darwin's biological evolution **followed** philosophical evolutionary thought in Western civilization.

In terms of Christian cosmology, creation, the act of a sovereign Creator, is in direct conflict with the cosmology of evolution, because evolution is humanistic and atheistic. As Gary North further pointed out, Darwinian evolutionary thought is fundamentally Greek paganism. Thomas Huxley referred to Darwinian evolution as *"the revivified thought of ancient Greece."* And, since it is Greek culture that the United States government today is attempting to emulate and reestablish, it therefore follows that the religious belief of America's ruling elite, that of humanistic evolution, is aggressively antagonistic to Christianity and creationism.

Evolution is and always has been an elitist humanistic religion, which has been found to accompany the rise and fall of world empires. Empires and humanistic pride go hand in hand. As mentioned above, the ancient empire of Egypt and Greece held to the theory of evolution. The modern world empires of Nazi Germany, the U.S.S.R., Red China and the U.S.A. also held and hold to the religious theory of evolution. Evolution is the religion of the U.S. public schools. (The Supreme Court affirmed it in the 1960s when it established humanism/evolution as a religion.)

Now, whether we look at the forced slavery of ancient Egypt, Nazi Germany, Red China or the U.S.S.R., we quickly see that the result of the working out in time of the theory of evolution is massive human misery. Because in America we still have the vestige of a Christian creationist culture, we find repugnant the mistreatment of the Israelites by the Egyptians; we are outraged at the atrocities that Hitler's Nazi Germany committed toward the Jews; we are appalled at the violations of human rights and mass murders of Mao Tse-tung in China and by Stalin and other Soviet leaders in Russia which Aleksandr Solzhenitsyn so graphically discussed in his book, THE GULAG ARCHIPELAGO. But, consistent with the theory of evolution, these actions by the pharaohs, Hitler, Chinese and Soviet leaders are justified. Evolution, the humanistic elitist religion, condones whatever actions big government may take as valid. Government is the *"survival of the fittest."*

Question: Given that the U.S. society increasingly, through indoctrination in the public schools, is captured by the religion of evolution/humanism, is it not logical that actions taken against U.S. citizens will eventually be similar to acts exercised in ancient Egypt, Nazi Germany, Red China and the Soviet Union? After all, our federal government is the *"survival of the fittest,"* too. The federal government is the highest product of the evolutionary spiral, the end result of *"natural selection."* Thus, according to the *"law of the jungle,"* *"might makes right."* Therefore, consistent with evolution, the federal government can do whatever it pleases. It is the *"god"* of our society, the evolutionary *"king of kings."* And, it is, without a doubt, elitist since the evolutionary spiral allows for only a few to ascend to the top, their ascension justifying their right to dictate to the rest of us.

These elitists are top-level government employees (civil service types), multinational corporate officers and multinational bankers, high-level decision makers in the military/industrial complex, federal judges, attorneys, scientists, social scientists and high-level elected officials. Their right to rule, is, of course, supported by the media ruling elite, which reinforces this religious, humanistic, evolutionary, indoctrination process, once the public school's years of conditioning are complete. Today in the U.S. we have voluntary slavery, debt slavery, and slavery to the state.

Now, it can be argued, and it's true, that the federal government, in an ironic twist, prevents the savagery of the *"law of the jungle"* and the *"survival of the fittest"* from being played out to its full, violent fury in society. This is the way the federal government justifies its gigantic existence. Men have never allowed anarchy, the *"law of the jungle"* and the *"survival of the fittest,"* for long. Men seek law and order. When men do not see themselves as self-governing, with the Creator as the master planner for their lives, developing their individual talents, working out their Creator-given destiny in life, then government, the substitute planner, comes in and fills this vacuum of unbelief. Government justifies its planning and control function logically by preventing the strong from always preying on the weak, a natural animalistic process under evolution. Fearful men look to government for protection. Men are insecure and live for today under evolution. Under evolution, men have no rest.

By promoting the theory of evolution (effectively humanism) in the public schools, the logical result of this religious theory, carried out in the real world, is that the strong continually **do** attempt to prey on the weak, which further justifies increasing government control and a concomitant loss of personal freedom. Either the Creator, through the creation of each individual, is the master planner, and thus has an important purpose for the life of each individual on earth, which requires freedom to be fulfilled, **or** government, the substitute god, is the master planner and increasingly dictates, controls and rules over all areas of life, thereby minimizing individual freedom. As such, government, the substitute god, is and always has been the foremost adversary of a Creator God. In Christian cosmology, this makes government Satan's most important institutional workhorse. We're never told today that in 1892 the U.S. Supreme Court declared the United States a Christian nation, and that U.S. presidents were sworn into office with their hand on Deuteronomy 28.

Under evolutionary government, we have no protection under law. We have anarchy waiting to happen. How could we have protection under law if law and lawyers (mini-gods as law givers) are evolving? The Constitution is of no value under evolution. How could it be? It is a 200-year old document which hasn't evolved. All men used to be equal under God. Nixon would have been prosecuted for Watergate 100 years ago. Then, we did not yet have a *"divine right of kings,"* so to speak. Never mind that when the Constitution was adopted, out of a population of 3½ million, there were 2 million Christians, whose religious beliefs, captured in Biblical law and the Constitution, which protected the individual, led to the greatest **economic** national prosperity in the history of the world. All this creation cause and effect is forgotten today. But, the lie of government (and its underlying religion of evolution) is the reality that government, playing the role of God, is still a parasite. Government, like fire, is a wonderful servant of free men, but a fearful all-consuming master when it becomes wrongfully involved in economics—wealth redistribution. Government is the guard, hired to protect the economic marketplace. It has no rightful role in economics, none. Government consumes all wealth eventually (hyperinflation), because it always finds work to do which consumes men's productivity. It also always creates class warfare through wealth redistribution, when it becomes wrongfully involved in economics.

The maximum distortion of reality comes at the pinnacle of the evolutionary spiral, where the false *"lord of lords"* is government, an economic parasite. For, the hard truth is that government cannot create anything (but misery). It can only steal wealth, through taxes and inflation, and then redistribute it. (Today, unfortunately, many see gun ownership by free men as the last stand of economic and human protection against a thieving, immoral, illegitimate government.) Inflation is the government's corruption of the currency. Government-created laws have choked our economic society, frustrating real progress and meaningful human advancement, not to mention the numerous laws created which favor special interest groups, creating monopolies and bureauracies, which allow a few shrewd elite to prey on the many ignorant in the masses. Evolutionary big business, for example, hates competition and the free market. Big business runs in wolf packs, fixing prices, raping the environment, seeking whomever and whatever they can devour. Labor unions do the same thing on the other side of the battle line. Conflict is the standard under evolution. Consumers, which all of us are, lose in the fight.

Under evolution, justice is sacrificed to power, just as truth is sacrificed to facts and deeds. Politics is power. Economics is power. Evolution recognizes powers as right under the *"survival of the fittest."* Politics depends upon an economic base. Evolutionary political powers go to war for economic reasons. Men's strength and power are thus drawn from external things. Money controls everything. A perfect illustration of how money rules supreme in our political process, and law is what government chooses to enforce, is the fact that Jimmy Carter, in 1978, signed into law legislation requiring a balanced federal budget. This law has been ignored.

By contrast, under the creation model, power is given to men of character who can handle power, who turn right around and give it away, granting freedom to their fellow man. These men are statesmen, unlike the economic-lusting evolutionary politicians, whose desire to control others stems from insecurity and feelings of personal inadequacy.

Laws used to be just. Under the creation model, laws and justice are one and the same, and provide a stable, unchanging, reliable standard. Government's function is to enforce the Creator's law. Law protects the family. (Under the creation model, treason is against the family, not the state.) Law protects the individual, because the individual had Creator-given rights, purpose and destiny. Law prevents men from imposing their will and ideas upon other men. Collective rights are based upon these individual rights. Individual force is justified for self-defense. Thus, collective force (government force) is only justified for self-defense. Realizing that a government ruler's only legitimate purpose was/is in this limited defense realm, in 1649, King Charles of England was brought to trial and executed for egregious violation of the Creator's law.

Under the Creator's law, all men are equally in need of a Savior. There is no natural elite, just an economic elite, who have rightfully earned their elevated status by serving their fellow man in the free market. This natural aristocracy flows from a long-term perspective. The long-term view marks the true upper class of society. Only slaves are equal economically.

The building of political empires is impossible under the creation model, just as is the building of economic empires where debt and compound interest are outlawed. Nor are religious empires possible under the creation model, where all men are seen as equal under a Creator's law.

Justice tempered with mercy in our legal system came directly from the unified Biblical harmony of Old Testament law and New Testament grace. If insanity is properly defined as a separation from reality, then it is no accident that our political lawmakers are truly crazy, as they increasingly legislate laws far removed from the legal guidance of a reality-oriented Creator. Also, all trials should be by jury (Article III, Section 2, paragraph 3, of the U.S. Constitution).

It is impossible to hold to the theory of evolution and consistently believe in the free market, development of individual human talents, family, economic rights, or even human rights. Evolution is logically and consistently antagonistic to the best interests of man individually and collectively long-term. And yet, it is willfully and consistently embraced and defended by modern man, an inconsistent action at best, and most probably an insane one if man has his own best self-interest and the interest of society both at heart long-term. How has this occurred? Why is man so willing to defend a religious theory which leads him to the slaughter? The answer can be found in the public schools, where it takes 12 years, and possibly four years more in college, to educate a man to act contrary to his own and society's own, best interest long-term, and then also passionately defend the position.

We have two religious schools in this country—the public schools and the Christian schools (which are popping up at the rate of three a day now). The public schools submissively teach the religious theory of evolution/humanism. How could it otherwise when the public schools are supported by funds (our taxes) provided by the evolutionary government. Thus, the financing of public education today, to the extent that it teaches the religious theory of evolution and promotes big government, is using taxpayers' money to ultimately finance their own suicide. Insane?

Government, the parasite, playing the role of God, as the maximum distortion of reality, can only self-destruct long-term. This is why mature civilizations fall when their governments are fully developed, just as ours is today.

As the war on origin between the public schools, teaching the religious theory of evolution, and the Christian schools, teaching the religious theory of creation, heats ups, it should come as no surprise that there is increasing federal government harassment (stemming from the states, the Justice Department and the Department of Education) of the Christian schools. The Christian schools are teaching a theory of origin which is contrary to the self-interest of big government.

Education is and always has been religious. Education teaches the young the basic values and faith of a society. This type of instruction is of its very essence religious. And because teachers, like all other men and women, have limited minds and limited time, they, too, make religious assumptions about the nature of reality. Teachers usually teach what they have been taught.

This religious split on origin is also seen in our bookstores. We have the Christian bookstores, and we have the secular bookstores. One's underlying religion is creation, the other evolution.

To the extent that man can be brainwashed into buying the theory of evolution, and thus taught to act contrary to his own self-interest, he is playing directly into the hands of those who want to manipulate him, use and abuse him, and then throw him away. Have we already become a society of human robots? We do pay taxes to a federal government which is intent upon creating social conflict through the redistribution of wealth, minimizing our freedom through bureaucratic alphabet-agencies, congressional laws and judicial decisions, thereby limiting our human rights and thus our economic rights. (Economic rights are always an extension of human rights, because it takes a mind to first think the thoughts and formulate the plans which create economic wealth.)

We also irresponsibly give our hard-earned productivity (our money) to banking institutions, which then use it to finance our own eventual unemployment, by first lending our funds abroad, where low cost foreign workers manufacture products, which are then dumped back onto U.S. markets, throwing U.S. workers (you and me) out of jobs. Not only were these foreign workers' manufacturing plants financed with our savings (economic suicide), but deposits in our financial institutions in the first place became inflationary through the fractional reserve system, and went to finance the implements of war (very profitable for the military/industrial complex) and the government-initiated war effort, which made the destruction of our present-day economic competitors (Japan and Germany) possible. Enemies are created so someone else can profit. After the war, the parasitic, financial debt capitalists (international bankers) come into the war-torn countries and buy up property cheap (using our dollars again), rebuild foreign plants and factories, and make a killing (financially and literally), all with the productivity/capital/money provided by the American working people, who naively first deposited their money in these *"banks."* U.S. taxpayers have bailed out Soviet communism twice—after the Russian Revolution and again in 1941. In

1975, 78% of Chase Manhattan's earnings came from international lending.

All this, of course, is justified under evolution. John D. Rockefeller had the nerve to tell his Sunday School class, *"The growth of a large business is merely a survival of the fittest . . . the working out of a law of nature and law of God."*

Undoubtedly, American's financial banking and debt capitalistic system today, supported by big government, is to the economic welfare of the common man what abortion is to life. It just kills it. Would the average American be far better off, and act consistent with his own best self-interest long-term, if he never used a financial institution?

Again, why do men act so insanely? They have been educated/ indoctrinated/brainwashed into doing so. They have been taught to be *"dumb"* through years and years in the public schools.

Technical *"factual"* education in the United States used to be quite good—accounting, engineering, scientific research, math, reading and the like. It has broken down as the teaching of principles has ceased. It is in the all important spiritual, thinking, abstract areas of religion, philosophy, economics, history, literature, civics and social studies, where men today are taught to be willing slaves. All of these areas to-day are clearly founded upon evolution.

It is no accident that the father of American education, John Dewey, a confirmed atheist who praised Lenin, left this country and went to attempt to work his educational *"miracles"* under Stalin in the Soviet Union. Both educational systems, in the U.S.A. and the U.S.S.R., are essentially the same—evolutionary! Under evolution, men are encouraged not to think. After all, if there is no truth and everything is relative as it evolves, why think? John Dewey was a con-firmed evolutionist who admired Thomas Henry Huxley, Darwin's staunchest defender. Dewey taught, true to evolution, that man is an *"animal,"* pragmatic, without morals or conscience, and therefore, void of evil. This is in direct contrast with the Biblical teaching of a sin (animal) nature within a *"spiritual being."* John Dewey declared, *"There is no god . . . "* The foundations established by John D. Rockefeller and Andrew Carnegie financed the textbooks touting Dewey's evolutionary perspective.

The Doobie Brothers, in their smash hit, sang, *"What a fool believes he sees no wise man has the power to reason away."* We Americans are played for real fools today. Yet, creative thinking still calls ideas into life. Think and grow rich (economics). No wonder we're held in contempt by our government. Only fools act contrary to their own best self-interest and the best interest of society long-term.

We are now a ship of fools. The educational brainwashing process has been shrewd, clever and effective. Because the ruling evolutionists really do know that human nature is a constant and does not change as the evolutionists purport, the ruling evolutionists' planners have ruthlessly used man's two foremost psychological barriers—pride and resistance to change—against him, to prevent him from seeing how his self-interest dovetails with creation.

Men are by nature proud. They hate to be wrong and in error. Stated differently, men hate, in this sense, to sin. Thus men, because they are proud, are reluctant to alter radically a position they presently hold. To do so is to admit that they were wrong and in error. This makes men feel foolish and is embarrassing. It hurts their pride.

After being taught the propaganda of the religion of evolution for 12 years in the public school system, it takes a good dose of humility for men to admit they have been played for suckers. Thus, pride is the primary barrier today to be overcome for men to reject the destructive religious theory of evolution. But this is to be expected. Pride is the worst of sins (Proverbs 6:16). It was Satan's first sin, according to Christian cosmology.

Are the public schools today Satan's workshop and playground? If creationism is excluded from the public schools because it is an expression of the Christian religion, shouldn't evolution be excluded because it is an expression of atheistic communism, socialism and Nazism, which are all anti-religious religions?

Running in the same harness with pride is man's resistance to change. Men desire security. They fear the unknown. Thus, they are reluctant to change. This security need is basic, whether stemming back to the ultimate in physical security in the womb of the mother, or to the ultimate in spiritual security, the anchor of an infinite sovereign, loving Creator. In terms of these ultimate physical and spiritual securities, men are naturally drawn to family and God. Perhaps one of the primary reasons men are so unhappy today is that these basic security needs are violated as government planners attempt to make government, the false mother and the false god, the source of security.

Men have to be educated to act against these natural security instincts. It takes awhile, but after 12 years of being taught that the religious theory of evolution is true, men, as would be expected, resist their true spiritual inclinations. They defend what they have been taught, even though it is contrary to their own self-interest and is destructive for society long-term.

To change the basic religious, evolutionary presupposition is a fearful thing, requiring men to reject and then restructure all they have learned throughout their carefully orchestrated lives. They first have to overcome their pride and resistance to change. George Orwell's *"1984"* came in 1948, the date he originally intended for the title of that book. The programming of the American public began to pick up momentum 34 years ago.

What about the churches? What about the religious leaders with all their rich, bureaucratic hierarchies, the evolutionary pinnacle of which are the National Council of Churches and the World Council of Churches? Consistent with the harmony of the elitist's theory of evolution, these organized, centralized, religious organizations have helped finance atheistic, Left Wing and/or communist, evolutionary, revolutionaries worldwide.

Organized, centralized, evolutionary, Western religion is little different today from that in the Soviet Union. There, the Russian Orthodox Church is provided limousines and the fine life by the Soviet government. In the Soviet Union, the Council for Religious Affairs has the ultimate say as to which individuals are selected as bishops and priests. Today, in this country, the IRS wields the ultimate federal government hammer over religion.

Karl Marx, the father of communism effectively observed that, *"religion is the opiate of the people."* Institutionalized human religion wherein man attempts to find or become God (evolution) and please him in some eternal sense, logically focuses on the eternal realm, the *"Great Hereafter."* This *"opium,"* this *"escape,"* mentally and thus functionally neutralizes man in time, which allows evolutionary elitists to do what they have always done best—rule and oppress (I Samuel 8). This is also the reason why all world religions have always been aggressively antagonistic to creationist Christianity. Christianity involves the Creator seeking after man, providing eternal salvation, and holding man accountable and responsible in time. This is the last thing the elitists want—involved, responsible, knowledgeable citizens. If man is individually accountable and responsible as a steward in time, he is concerned with current events. This thwarts and frustrates the purposes and plans of a ruling, evolutionary elite.

America's Christian churches are currently coffins. They are lukewarm institutions which have been spewed out by thinking men. They are effectively dead, having bowed to the sovereignty of government rather than having held to the sovereignty of the *"King of kings."* As such, it should come as no surprise that these Sunday social clubs, these whitewashed tombstones, have little purpose or meaning in society today. The all too effeminate American clergy, being most ignorant of economics, has thus missed the essence of man's Christian spiritual responsibility in time. Adam's responsibility in the garden was an economic issue. Israel's taking of the Promised Land had an economic base. The stewardship and development of talents in line with New Testament doctrines are ultimately economically based because the development and use of talents involves contracting, covenanting and personal interaction. Economics is, by definition, human action.

Governments cannot exist without an economic base—taxes. Churches cannot exist without an economic base—tithes, gifts and offerings. While the real war is being fought in the real world over the real economic issue of who rules (dominion), and the evolutionary government is stealing the church's tithe, leading to centralization rather than creationists' decentralization, the American clergy, so-called leaders of the Christian soldiers who have been given the responsibility of putting on the whole armor of God, are in fact no better than chess-playing warriors, if not the enemy. America's religious leaders have bought, in too many cases, the Greek and Manichaean idea of a separate and segregated spiritual and physical universe, thereby denying the reality of a Creator God who unified the spiritual and material realms. The American clergy, tiptoeing through the tulips of the spiritual realm, are heretics when compared to the religious leaders who helped build this great nation. Today's religious leaders' opium-type plans, conceived with a sound and fury signifying nothing, are being smashed as the evolutionary barbarians descend upon us. Sad to say, but too many ministers simply spew back out what they have been taught at seminaries which long ago became captured agents of centralization.

Evolutionary religion is a man-directed attempt to attain eternal life. Nearly all pagan religions are evolutionary, denying a Creator, and instead, assuming the ultimacy of space/time/matter. Creationist Christianity is the God-directed plan of providing eternal life through Jesus Christ's work on the cross, calling man to service in time. Christianity is the one *"religion"* in the history of the world which focuses upon the fate of a single man, Jesus Christ, at a point in time, as the central issue of the entire creation. Jesus Christ was/is the transitional bridge between man and God. He bridged heaven and earth, the infinite and the finite, eternity and time, spirit and matter, the perfect and the imperfect, the one and the many.

If, by contrast, evolution is true, there never was an original perfection. Therefore, there is no need for the restoration of that perfection made possible by Christ's work on the cross. Thus, the crucifixion of Jesus Christ was a waste. Evolution has no room for, or way of dealing with, love and self-sacrifice as epitomized by the historical act of Jesus Christ on the cross. For man, under evolution, those individuals genetically predetermined toward love and self-sacrifice, which help the human species survive, should by now have been eliminated, according to *"natural selection"* and the *"survival of the fittest."* However, their very elimination would unleash the evolutionary flood of violence which would destroy the human race, not very evolutionary.

Evolution is, in fact, a spiral down, headed today for nuclear holocaust where Satan destroys the world by fire, thereby thwarting the Creator's plan for the restoration of perfect environment, in the process proving Satan a liar. As an alternative to nuclear war, men may opt for a new elitist, economic, political and religious world order; in other words, a global slave state.

It is a timeless, proven truth that real progress in the human condition only comes through self-sacrifice, with an eye toward the future. Under evolution, it is impossible for man, the *"animal,"* to understand time or self-sacrifice. Thus, under evolution, progress is impossible. In fact, the opposite is true. A recent poll claimed that 94 percent of Americans believe in God, 80 percent in Jesus Christ, and 78 percent in the Ten Commandments. It's time for the American clergy to hit the comeback trail.

Evolution holds that man is an *"animal."* America's religious leaders have, in effect, in too many cases, bought and parroted this atheistic, evolutionary line. True, man is the highest *"animal,"* the pinnacle of the factual universe. But as an *"animal"* primarily (and exclusively), once this evolutionary assumption is bought, mankind has opened himself up to being treated like one. The idea that man is a *"spiritual being,"* with an animal nature, the highest earthly creature made by the Creator, is today hanging on by a thread in our society. It's important that we now look at the devastating implications of our having adopted this evolutionary theory that man is an *"animal,"* as opposed to a *"spiritual being"* with an animal nature. The working out of this evolutionary assumption is shocking.

The Human Evolutionary *"Animal?"*

We have seen that societies and their governments, operating under evolution, move logically toward collectivism, whether socialism, communism or fascism. Under evolution, governments, to prevent the full fury and ruthlessness of the doctrine of *"survival of the fittest"* from being manifest in society, act as master planners and regulate society. The tremendous wealth accumulated by the rapacious few, through the likes of bank loans (OPM—Other People's Money) and debt capitalism generally, is redistributed by government to the hapless, victimized masses so these poor folks can survive economically.

All the while, the parasitic government grows in size and power as it patrols the demilitarized zone between these warring classes, the producers and the consumers in the welfare state. Meanwhile, government-sanctioned bureaucrats build personal empires, based on seemingly limitless government finances, promoting the development of super egos among the scientists, social scientists, social workers, academicians and urban planners whose programs keep expanding but never function as planned.

Group action can only be accurately forecast when the individuals within the group are free. A nation is a complex system. All complex systems function best when authority and responsibility are delegated to the lowest possible level of efficiency, that of the individual in the case of a nation. The Creator appoints each man as a manager (believer/priest) who is provided with ethical guidelines (principles), impossible under evolution.

As the dependent folks, particularly those in the cities, feel increasing alienation, isolation and powerlessness in society, they either react with anger and violence (frustration externalized), or depression (frustration internalized). These folks are isolated in their *"neighborhoods."* These poor folks know little or nothing about anything. They have not been taught. They cannot reason. They are effectively the true products of evolution—*"animals,"* or, as one Eastern Establishment liberal planner put it, *"maggots in a flour sack."*

Under evolution, since everything is relative and always evolving, everything is permitted. There are no standards under evolution whereby child molestation, incest, murder, rape, homosexuality and the like can be prohibited. Nor is there any protection for following property rights. There are no morals or ethics under relative evolution. Thus, there is no personal responsibility because responsibility is moral. The inner cities truly give us the *"animals"* who are the undesirable result of evolution.

Now, the question becomes, *"What do the evolutionists at the top of the government-dominated evolutionary spiral do with their 'maggots in a flour sack' (the common people)?"* For evolutionary, socialistic government has an inescapable problem. Whatever government taxes, there is less of. There is more of whatever government subsidizes. Government taxes the productive middle class and thus eliminates them, dropping them into the lower class, where eventually they wind up as demoted members of the welfare state. Evolutionary government subsidizes the welfare class, allowing it to reproduce beyond its natural economic checkpoint, and so evolutionary government is continually plagued with overpopulation as a dominant problem in society. (Overpopulation was viewed as a problem in the dying Greek evolutionary culture, too.)

Because, under evolution, men are *"animals"* and thus cannot think, they cannot be creative, a situation which is maximized at the lower echelons of an evolutionary society. Without creative thinking and productive individuals, a society stagnates and overpopulation truly does become the issue. There is no real economic progress. Next, the government is faced with the necessary elimination of all the excess *"animals"* (people) in the society. This was true in evolutionary ancient Egypt where the Hebrew slaves were expendable. It was true in evolutionary Nazi Germany where not only did Hitler attempt to breed a super race, but also eliminate the undesirable *"animals"* (the Jews). It is and has been true in atheistic/evolutionary modern Soviet Russia, Communist China and Cambodia, ad nauseam, where millions have been slaughtered. How long until it will be true in the United States? War is traditionally the government's easy way out. Argentina versus Great Britain at the Falklands comes quickly to mind as a case in point.

Abortion is already slaughtering many of our unborn, some estimates running as high as one out of every three conceptions. If the evolutionary model is false, and the creation model is true, with rampant abortion today, how many Albert Einsteins, Albert Schweitzers, Julius Irvings, Ernest Hemingways and Abraham Lincolns have been lost to this world? Under the creation model, God has a perfect plan for each individual which benefits other members of society. Are we any better now than the decadent ancient Greeks who put their imperfect babies in clay jars to die along the side of the road? The Greeks we so admire today were an aggressive, self-destructive, unloving bunch, reflecting the cynicism of their gods. A society always reflects the character (or lack thereof) of its god(s).

If men are *"animals,"* as logically is the case under the evolution model, how long can it be until we, like Hitler, in our science-oriented, technological, *"fact"*-dominated society, *"breed"* for evolutionary perfection, simultaneously eliminating, for the *"good of mankind,"* the downtrodden, the poor, the old, the racial minorities, the criminals, the *"troublemakers,"* the defective, and the weak, particularly as economic conditions become more difficult? Isn't this what primitive societies do with their undesirables? Isn't this consistent with the evolutionary doctrine of *"survival of the fittest?"* Will our civilization instead opt for *"drug therapy,"* *"shock treatment,"* *"psychological conditioning"* and/or *"subliminal advertising?"* How many geniuses will our evolutionary government eliminate in the process? Today's geniuses are yesterday's crackpots. An evolutionary government logically eliminates a genius at the crackpot stage. And yet, it has been the so-called *"crackpots"* throughout history who have eventually been seen as the true contributors long-term to the improvement of the human condition. Will we see a world the likes of *The Boys From Brazil* or *The Island of Dr. Moreau?*

Scientists can measure IQ but they cannot measure creativity. Creativity is the product of self-discipline, of long, deep, consistent thinking, or desire, if you will, which is unrelated to IQ. How many creative individuals have been (and will be) slaughtered if evolutionary governments continue to sweep the earth? This is another good argument for decentralized, local, people-controlled government, the preferred role for government under the creation model. Local individuals can fight City Hall a whole lot more simply than they can Capitol Hill.

Here again we see the lie of government as the great benefactor in the evolution model. From a short-term perspective, government can, through the welfare state, provide for the economic necessities of the lower class. But once the surplus is consumed, as it always is, and the middle class dies, and the economic/climatic conditions become unfavorable, the parasite (government) does what it has to do—it ruthlessly eliminates those who it earlier supported economically, either directly, or indirectly through war. (One of the best ways to prevent a war is to refuse to finance it.) Governments don't redistribute wealth. They distribute poverty.

Given the God-like status of our fact-oriented, evolutionary scientists, supported by an evolutionary government, given the tremendous advances being made today in genetic research, and further given the impending collapse of our evolutionary economic and social order, how much longer will it be until the genetic techniques being applied to animals now are applied forcefully to human *"animals?"* How long until each of us has a number just like a cow at a cattle auction? SSAN? How long until we are under a required systematic breeding program, such as that which is already in operation in Red China? How long until certain men are castrated and others are held for production as human *"studs?"* Who believes, given the government's ineptitude at planning in all other areas of life, that government will be effective in the genetic area?

Under evolution, man should logically attempt to breed up, as Hitler did, to attempt to produce a higher class of men, perhaps the ultimate *"superman,"* the ultimate anti-Christ. Such would represent the epitome of the scientific/factual, genetic completion of the evolutionary spiral. Already, the scientific community is about ready to produce *"super animals,"* as we enter the age of embryo engineering. In this animalistic fashion, an Arizona woman in 1982 gave birth to a baby girl whose male seed came from a *"scientific genius."* Is this any different than the freezing of the semen of prize bulls which is later inseminated into cows? Gene manipulation, embryo transfer, and cloning are realities today in the production of animals. If man is an *"animal,"* rather than a *"spiritual being"* with an animal nature, as under the creation model, how long will it be until such genetic techniques are applied to man, particularly when push comes to shove during tough economic times? How long until women (the weaker sex in a world of *"natural selection"*) have no say in whose baby they carry or whether they can bear children at all?

Do we trust the scientists and multinational corporations who are conducting the avant-garde experiments in these genetic research fields? We have no reason to trust them since in other areas corruption has clearly come with size and power. (Men just can't seem to play the role of God without becoming corrupted.) Genetech is hooked up with Monsanto. American Cyanamid owns 27 percent of Molecular Genetics. International Minerals and Chemical Corporation has linked up with Biogen. So, just like with solar energy, the evolutionary multinational debt capitalists are swallowing up the genetic research firms.

We are now seeing groups call for equal rights for animals and plants. We have already witnessed the environmental and operant conditioning human experimentation conducted by B. F. Skinner, based upon stimulus/response, just like with Pavlov's dog. *"Natural selection"* among human *"animals"* is on the way. How many human *"animals"* will we need when robots become pervasive and computers coordinate their work? After all, truth and life itself will be what the government and its scientists say it is. Power under relative evolution will always determine truth, right and wrong, life and death. It's all relative, if evolution is true.

Animals can't know truth. Truth exists in the timeless, abstract, thinking realm. Animals can know only facts. It takes a leap of faith (religion) for man, who can only know facts as an evolutionary human *"animal,"* to become a god and operate beyond good and evil, thereby knowing truth in the abstract realm. Government has made that leap of faith today. Government believes it has all the answers. It legislates accordingly. So, here, too, evolution is seen as requiring faith, classifying evolution as a man-centered religion.

Evolution today has already polarized society into two powerful animalistic categories. One category is individual; the other, collective. The *"macho man"* epitomizes the *"individual"* at the top of an evolutionary spiral, the *"survival of the fittest."* The popularity of the likes of Charles Bronson and Clint Eastwood movies, the *"macho"* movies, as well as the heroes of professional sports (worshiped as idols), are the appropriate gods of the individualistic-oriented evolutionists.

The centralized federal government, multinational banks and corporations, religious, media and educational empires are the *"collectivist"* gods at the top of this other evolutionary spiral. The individual evolutionists, of course, are at war with the collectivist evolutionists. Confict is always present with evolution. What both camps have in common is that other men, those beneath them in the spiral, are expendable. Sensing this, the masses are escaping into drugs (in many cases provided by the collectivist's establishment, as discussed in the U.S. Labor Party's book, DOPE, INC.), or into the escapist movies such as *"Star Wars,"* or into television. The average American home watches seven hours of television a day.

Human rights and their following property (economic) rights, too, become relative under evolution. After all, if all men evolved, then all men may be brothers somewhere back down the line, and so they should logically *"share the wealth"* (communism). Another evolutionary perspective, however, is clearly racist. If there are different origins for the human race, then certain races are obviously substandard—which ones, of course, to be determined by government where government is powerful.

As economic and climatic conditions become more harsh, racial lines will be more clearly drawn as society, consistent with this evolutionary logic, further discriminates against the economically dependent in society who cannot meet their own economic needs. *"Might makes right"* under evolution, and because the Whites have the population numbers in their favor, the minority groups in this country are headed for abuse. How many George Washington Carvers and Thomas Sowells will be victimized? By contrast, under the creation model, racism is never an issue for economic advancement. Men, in the free market, pay for the best goods and services available, at the lowest price, regardless of who produces them. Just look at the American public's preference for Japanese automobiles.

The Blacks particularly, and now the Hispanics, are being played for suckers by the centralizing planners in this country. Having been freed from slavery by a wise Abraham Lincoln, too many Black minority groups have been conned into accepting the slavery of the dole, the economic dependency and slavery resulting from the government's welfare handout. Some Blacks have further been deceived into adopting the religion of the slave traders who ruthlessly abused their ancestry—the Muslim religion. For it was the Arab Muslims who composed nearly three-quarters of the world's slave trade in Black Africa.

Animals take their clothes off. Pornography has flourished.

Animals react instinctively. They cannot reason. Animals react short-term to facts. They do not think in the abstract realm, long-term. They have no sense of time, no sense of history, and no sense of values. Animals live in the present and *"do it now."* Animals cannot progress. Progress demands self-discipline and sacrifice short-term for achievement and progress long-term. Such *"animals"* can and will be controlled by the technocrats who run the machinery of the oppressive, collectivist government social order.

There is no dignity for man under evolution, only slavery. Slavery used to be personal. It was abolished. Slavery today to the state is far more prevalent and deadly than personal slavery ever was, and it's getting worse as the evolutionary/humanistic cancer grows and spreads. Communism is forced slavery. Debt capitalism is voluntary slavery. Slaves cannot develop their Creator-given talents. The accurate perspective is not, *"My country right or wrong."* The correct perspective is, *"My country when right, to be kept right; when wrong, to be put right."* It's time for this country be put right!

By glorious contrast, the future under the creation model of *"Wealth for All"* can be fabulous. Men will have the opportunity to be free and independent financially as never before, working at home. Already, the information processing and service sectors of the U.S. economy are engulfing nearly 75 percent of the work force. With advanced computer technology moving into the homes, upcoming audio/visual two-way communication, and with robots performing mindless tasks, more and more families will become autonomous, self-sustaining, creative, economic units. Men and women will be able to develop and market their complementary creative talents from the home, living wherever they choose, via computer satellite communications. No location will be remote. With the solar energy breakthroughs, families will permanently kick the utility and service station habit. The world will become one big economic supermarket, with men buying and selling freely globally via computers. World harmony will exist as men barter and exchange their productivity directly as debt capitalism, OPM, compound interest, socialism, and communism all die. Banks will become safekeeping centers, brokerage and economic centers where men establish partnerships, joint ventures, and buy and sell stock, all the recording of which activity will be available on home computer. Education will move to the home via computer audio/visual instruction. The city will finally come to live in the rural country (the garden). Governments will finally compete in the free market for the citizenship of men and women, based upon governments providing the services desired by individuals. Politicians will finally learn that the key to maintaining power is to give it away, allowing men to be free.

Catch the vision of the future? *"Animals,"* as men are under evolution, have no vision. But, *"spiritual beings"* with animal natures under the creation model do. We are on the brink of the greatest disaster **or** opportunity in history. The choice of each individual will determine our collective destiny. Men must choose whom they will serve.

Science: Evolution's Ace in the Hole?

Now we come to the great stumbling block for credibility for the creation theory in the modern world, the great unknown (to the masses) on which evolution casts its lot—science! All, or most of us, have been taught in the government-financed public schools, the government-financed and subsidized universities, and by the government-financed public television programs (PBS) that evolution is unquestionably the *"working"* basis of modern science, and thus the foundation of our wonderful technological society. But, is it really?

It's important that we distinguish between academic science and research science. It is not academic evolutionary scientists but research scientists—hard-working, practical men and women investigating the natural, scientific laws of the universe, based upon their **faith** that those laws exist—who have made our world a better place in which to live. The scientific method itself precedes from an idea assumed as true (faith), verified or disproven through experimentation.

Science, before Darwin's evolution, primarily emphasized math and chemistry. It can be well argued that all of our real material progress has been a product of chemistry. But, since Darwin and evolution, evolutionary academic science (theoretical science) has emphasized geology and biology. These academic so-called scientific pursuits operate in the evolutionary universe of chance when it comes to origin, and thus, by scientific definition, are not scientific. No research can either affirm or deny their evolutionary conjectures. There are no experimental methods in geology, paleontology, astrophysics or astronomy that are infallible. Such are impossible, in most cases. The scientific method is totally useless when it comes to proving evolutionary biology because that evolutionary experience, if it ever occurred, cannot be repeated. Besides, the scientific method itself, an experimental method, is not infallible. It is subject to the perspective of the experimenter, the conditions under which the experiment is conducted, and the way the observations and conclusions are formulated.

It is true that the natural realm above the level of the atom, based in math, gives us a reliable, mechanical, scientific language. This is the arena in which real research scientists work best, not the spiritual arena.

When scientists take a position on evolution or creation, they, too, are religious priests. In other words, they, too, are guessing about origin. And, contrary to what the general public hears today, there is a considerable war going on between scientific creationists and evolutionists, as to which origin religion is correct. Let's look at a few eye-opening comments:

"Even Einstein couldn't come to grips with it. His general theory of relativity predicted the creation, but it was years before he reluctantly accepted what his own equations showed." Robert Jastrow, Director of the Goddard Institute For Space Studies, a division of NASA.

Astronomer Sir Fred Hoyle and Chandra Wickramasinghe challenged the basic foundations of the evolutionary theory in their recent book, SPACE TRAVELERS: THE BRINGERS OF LIFE! They stated, *"Once we see that the probability of life originating at random is so utterly miniscule as to make it absurd, it becomes sensible to think that the favorable properties of physics on which life depends are in every respect, deliberate, and it is almost inevitable that our own measure of intelligence must reflect higher intelligence, even to the limit of God."*

An associate of the infamous Dr. Carl Sagan, Dr. William Provine of Cornell University, on November 17, 1981 stated, *"First, I agree with him [Mr. Sunderland] that creationism should be taught along with evolutionism from grade school through high school."*

The senior paleontologist at the British Museum of Natural History, Dr. Colin Patterson, a respected evolutionary scientist for 50 years, speaking to over 50 classification specialists on November 5, 1981 at the American Museum of Natural History in New York stated, *"Then I woke up and realized that all my life I had been duped into taking evolution as revealed truth in some way."* Dr. Patterson also referred to evolution as, *"Positively anti-knowledge,"* and *"story telling."*

Dr. Colin Patterson has also declared, *"One morning I woke up and something had happened in the night, and it struck me that I had been working with this stuff for 20 years, and there was not one thing I knew about it. It's quite a shock to learn that one can be misled for so long. Either there was something wrong with me, or there was something wrong with evolution theory."*

The scientific evidence which reveals how badly we have been deceived by the evolution theory is available for curious minds. The comments which follow will be heavily weighted to the creationist scientific perspective, to better give *"equal time."* This evidence is drawn primarily from three excellent sources: (1) One, if not the best book, discussing this creation/evolution issue is THE CREATION-EVOLUTION CONTROVERSY, by Dr. R. L. Wysong (Inquiry

Press, 4925 Jefferson Avenue, Midland, Michigan 48640, 1976). This work is, in its own way, what Josh McDowell's book, EVIDENCE THAT DEMANDS A VERDICT, is to Christian apologetics. (2) An excellent, and possibly the best monthly newsletter on the creation/evolution issue is BIBLE SCIENCE NEWSLETTER (2911 East 42nd Street, Minneapolis, Minnesota 55406). (3) One, if not the nation's leading think tank on the subject of creation, is the Institute for Creation Research (2716 Madison Avenue, San Diego, California 92116).

M. P. Schutzenberger, a computer scientist, in a speech given at the Wistar Institute of Anatomy and Biology Symposium declared, *". . . we believe there is a considerable gap in the neo-Darwinian theory of evolution, and we believe this gap to be of such a nature that it cannot be bridged within the current conception of biology."* Scientist M. Eden has computed that the probability of forming proteins and DNA for the smallest self-replicating entity, given astronomically large quantities of reagents and time, is 1/167,626. To write this number would require 150 pages of solid zeros. Thus, the probability of DNA being formulated through evolution (chance) is negligible.

How about mutations leading to evolution? Mutations, as it turns out, have been shown to be almost always harmful and are evidence of degeneration, not evolution. Most mutations are buried within the genes or are corrected by DNA repair systems. Here, too, the mathematical probability that random mutations and natural selection ultimately produced complex systems from simpler life is infinitesimal.

The renowned scientist, Lord Zuckerman, who is not a creationist, has been unable to find any fossil traces of a transformation from an ape-like creature to man. (The atheistic philosopher, Jean Jacques Rousseau pushed this ape-man theory as far back as 1754, long before Darwin came on the scene.)

The Piltdown Man and the Nebraska Man, both hailed as *"missing links,"* have both proven to be frauds. The only evidence that was used to reconstruct the entire Nebraska Man, a tooth, turned out to belong to an extinct pig. The Nebraska Man had been called an *"authentic, genuine, impeccable"* link, and aged at one million years. The Piltdown Man, even though a proven hoax, remained as the classic proof for evolution in textbooks nearly 40 years later. Along this same line, the Southwest Colorado Man was found to be a fraud when the single tooth used to construct it was discovered to belong to an extinct Eocene horse. The Neanderthal Man was found in rock formations similar to those in which modern man has been found. The Neanderthal Man is now believed to have been crippled by osteoarthritis and fully human. Cro-Magnon Man is now conceded to have been fully human, too.

In the Paluxy riverbed, on the McFall farm outside Glen Rose, Texas, 24 Tyrannosaurus footprints have been found along side four human footprints. This was verified by a certified geologist, Dr. John Morris of Oklahoma University. (Dinosaur and human footprints together have been discovered at many locations.) According to evolution theory, these particular human and Tyrannosaurus footprints should have been separated by 70 million years.

The records of man date back to only about 3,000 B.C., and they reveal highly-developed and sophisticated civilizations, just the opposite of what we are taught under evolution, that primitives evolved. In fact, in these early civilizations are found remains of highly-developed societies that degenerated into a less complicated, more primitive lifestyle.

Using standard population computation methods, man's existence is shown to be only several thousand years. If an evolutionary history of just one million years is used in these computations, the earth's population could not fit into our entire universe.

One of the best books on the fossils is Dr. Duane T. Gish's EVOLUTION: THE FOSSILS SAY NO! The fossil skeleton that was held to be a link between birds and reptiles, Archaeopteryx, was found to be a true bird. All kinds of contradictions have also been found in the so-called evolutionary horse tree, with one of the most striking being that the Eohippus is almost identical to the African Hyrax. The Seymouria, the supposed evolutionary gap between the reptiles which followed the amphibians, even using evolutionary methods, is said to have existed 20 million years after the reptiles appeared. The link between snakes and lizards, Lanthanotus, was found alive in recent years in Sarawak, Malaysia. Dr. Clifford Burdick has scientifically substantiated that life on this earth has existed in modern forms since earliest times through his research involving spores. Finally, no evolutionary scientist has yet gotten around the scientific truism that life comes from like life. It seems that many scientists who believe otherwise simply have allowed their beliefs to arise out of evolutionary prejudices. E. Kellenberger, writing in SCIENTIFIC AMERICAN, declared, *"Living things are enormously diverse in form, but form is remarkably constant within any given line of descent: pigs remain pigs and oak trees remain oak trees generation after generation." ("The Genetic Control of the Shape of the Virus,"* SCIENTIFIC AMERICAN, December, 1966).

The *"micro"* evolution argument is being challenged today. Micro-evolution says that development has taken place from a given state of complexity and order to an increased state of complexity and order.

Yet, we have seen from studies with DNA, mutations and thermodynamics that such net improvement is scientifically impossible. There is natural variation because there is variation in all living things. This is the result of genetic variation, which is a result of the genetic variation *"potential"* of the species, and mutation. Neither of these, however, produce any true *"evolution"* in any species. Genetic variation potential produces **horizontal** variation only. And, as previously discussed, scientists have found mutations to be degenerative and harmful, threatening the very existence of the species.

Evolutionary scientists also have not been able to conquer the Second Law of Thermodynamics, the tendency for things in the natural order to run down. Our natural system, our universe, is like a wound-up clock, which is winding down. The question becomes, *"Who wound it up in the first place? A Creator?"* According to the Second Law of Thermodynamics, systems, over time, move toward greater disorder. The universe is moving toward a state of maximum entropy. At some point, all space will be the same temperature. All energy will have been uniformly distributed in the cosmos. There will be no life, no light and no warmth, just perpetual and irrevocable stagnation. There is no way of avoiding this destiny, according to the Second Law of Thermodynamics, which is the exact opposite of evolution. Natural change moves irrefutably toward decay. The matter and energy of the universe are defusing. The sun is burning out. The stars are dying. Heat is turning to cold everywhere in the cosmos. Matter is dissolving into radiation. Energy is being dissipated into empty space. If, as under evolution, the universe and matter are eternal, then by now, according to the laws of thermodynamics, the universe should be already a weak, useless energy field. But, obviously it is not.

Scientists have attempted to venture into space to escape the limits of time, and the following implications of a Creator's judgment, as follows from the likes of the Second Law of Thermodynamics. There is one thing that evolution definitely requires, and that is lots and lots of time. An interesting evolutionary contradiction is that man, as an evolved *"animal,"* should not be able to think in terms of time, an abstract concept, unless he makes a *"leap of faith,"* which he has done under the religion of evolution.

The existence of linear time presupposes history, which further implies a judgment, and that man is responsible for how he uses his given time. Additionally, it is linear time plus Creator-given law that together produce patterns or cycles.

We are told how vast the universe is. And yet, at the University of Connecticut and MIT, scientists have shown, through Reimannian

Wealth for All

curved space astrophysics, that it takes only 15 years to reach the most distant stars, a far cry from what most of us have been taught in the evolutionary biased public (government) schools. Now, we have been taught, according to the physics of light, that as we accelerate to the speed of light, time stops, and matter becomes infinite and fills the universe. This is particularly interesting in light of the fact that Jesus said in John 8:12, *"I am the light of the world: . . . "* Also I John 1:5 declares, *"God is light, . . . "*

Studies of rapidly decaying radioactive elements and pleochroic halos suggest that creation was accomplished quite quickly and completely. If the earth had cooled down slowly over hundreds of millions of years, as evolutionists suggest, polonium halos could not have possibly formed because all the polonium would have decayed soon after it was synthesized, and would have been extinct when crustal rocks formed. The very fact that pleochroic halos exist are evidence of the simultaneous creation of radioactivity and rocks.

When Dr. Henry Morris, author of THE GENESIS FLOOD and a strong creationist, spoke to professional oil industry geologists in Houston, Texas several years ago, he received a standing ovation upon completion. Practicing oil industry geologists recognized that Dr. Morris' work on creation fit with the real world of geology. Reality science is far different than the evolutionary, academic variety.

Oil has been produced from garbage in a few hours, suggesting that the oil found in the earth could have been made rapidly and recently. C-14 dating of oil has confirmed this young life for oil. Most convincing is the fact that the excessive pressure found within oil beds, resulting in oil gushers, argues for trapped oil being less than 10,000 years old. Given the permeability of the rocks surrounding the oil beds, any pressure build up should have been dissipated and bled off into the surrounding rocks within a few thousand years. The fact that this has not occurred further supports the creation case for a young earth.

Robert Whitelaw, a nuclear consultant and Professor of Mechanical Engineering at Virginia Polytechnic Institute, has found that C-14 (Carbon-14) is not equal to disintegration. His conclusion is that the C-14 clock was turned on between 5,600 and 11,200 years ago, supporting evidence for a young earth, a far cry from the millions or billions of years that the evolutionists claim. Furthermore, C-14 dating has been found to be fairly reliable as a dating system until 4,500 years ago, the time of the global flood. This is also the time of the greatest fossilization. J. R. Jochmans has found evidence of the flood in 97 world cultures. If a water canopy existed above the earth before the global flood, which shielded out harmful radiation, and made it possible for men to live over 900 years, it possibly also prevented it from raining, which would have significantly altered the rate of C-14 production.

Niagara Falls is calculated to be between 5,000 and 10,000 years old based upon the rate at which its edge wears away. Evolutionists tell us that the great canyons of the world *"slowly"* cut through hard rock over millions of years, causing their tremendous depth. What we find, however, is that the lower rocks in the Grand Canyon, for example, provide clear evidence of great heat and pressure, suggesting that they were volcanic in origin. Furthermore, in the Grand Canyon, there is no evidence of *"wall polish"* which, if made *"slowly"* by the abrasive polishing agents in the waters of the Colorado River, would definitely be present. Effectively, *"wall polish"* is totally missing in the Grand Canyon. The probability is, in keeping with creationists' and catastrophic theory, that the Grand Canyon split open, for its elevation is higher than that of surrounding ground.

Evolutionists like to speak of uniformitarianism, that evolution took place slowly, smoothly and systematically over millions or billions of years. And yet, in addition to the above evidence, in March, 1982, bones of a land mammal were found in Antarctica, suggesting that this frozen region had once been lush with green plants and animals. A catastrophe obviously hit Antarctica. There have been sea shells found in the Himalayas of Tibet and huge boulders discovered on mountains in Vermont, weighing thousands of tons, that came from rock formations hundreds of miles away. All this suggests catastrophe, not uniformitarianism.

The age of the earth's magnetic field and its decay casts an important light on this evolution/creation controversy. The half-life of the earth's magnetic field has been computed to be 1,400 years. Calculating the rate of decay of the earth's magnetic field and extrapolating backwards just 20,000 years, we find that the earth has to be less than 10,000 years old. Going back just 20,000 years, scientists find that the Joule heat generated would liquify the earth. A NASA satellite's preliminary report showed a rapid decay of the earth's magnetic field. On a straight-line basis, the earth's magnetic field will be extinct in 3991 A.D. The decay is exponential. The earth's magnetic field is decaying faster than any other worldwide geophysical phenomenon.

The rotation of the earth is gradually slowing. If the earth had been slowing down uniformly for billions of years, its present spin would be zero. If we extrapolate backwards, we find that the earth's spin billions of years ago would have been so rapid that the centrifugal force would have pulled all the land masses toward the equator and extended them out to a height of over 40 miles. The oceans would have been displaced to the poles, and the shape of earth would have been transformed from a globe to a "fat pancake."

The earth is slowly cooling from inside to outside, in keeping with Stefan's Law of Radiation. Lord Kelvin calculated that the earth could not be billions of years old based upon the existing temperature gradient in the earth, its rate of cooling, and the assumption that the initial state of the earth was white hot.

Robert V. Gentry, Professor of Physics at Columbia Union College, found that Precambrian granites, the *"basement rocks"* of the earth, were formed very rapidly, which rules out all the evolutionary explanations for our planet.

Meteoritic craters are all dated at only a few thousand years old.

If there were no plants or vegetation on the earth, and no oxygen in the atmosphere, and vegetation was suddenly created by a Creator, which covered the earth, the number of years needed to generate the present level of oxygen found in the atmosphere is 5,000 years.

Bristlecone pines can, according to scientists, live for thousands of years or even tens of thousands of years. And yet, all of them date to less than 6,000 years old.

The radioactive elements, uranium and thorium, are continually decaying to form helium. Based upon the present rate of helium formation, the earth is approximately 10,000 years old.

The old Mississippi River supports the creationists' perspective also. It dumps 300 million cubic yards of sediment into the Gulf of Mexico each year. If the Mississippi River was millions of years old, the Gulf of Mexico would have been filled up by now. By measuring the rate of growth of the Mississippi Delta (about 250 feet per year), the age of the Mississippi River is calculated at approximately 4,000 years.

Ocean sediment is only several thousand feet thick. Given that there are 28 billion tons of sediment added to the oceans each year, if this erosion process had been taking place for billions of years, as the evolutionists say, the continents would have been totally eroded away hundreds of times over and the layers of sediment on the ocean bottoms would be 100 miles thick. Further study of the nitrates and uranium found in the oceans, which do not break down or recycle like salt, suggests that, due to their small concentration, that the oceans are only a few thousand years old. If the oceans were thousands of millions of years old, there would be far more uranium, sodium, nickel, magnesium, silicon, potassium, copper, gold, silver, mercury, lead, tin, aluminum, carbonate, sulfate, chlorine, calcium, lithium, titanium, chromium, manganese, iron, cobalt, zinc, rubidium, strontium, bismuth, thorium, antimony, tungsten, barium, molybdenum and bicarbonate concentrates than are found there presently.

Cosmic dust filters down to the earth from interplanetary space and enters the oceans at the rate of 14 million tons per year. The nickel content of this cosmic dust is much higher, more highly concentrated than that in earthly materials. If the earth was billions of years old, there should be 50 or more feet of this cosmic dust in the oceans' sediments. But, there is only enough cosmic dust on the earth, or the moon for that matter, to account for several thousand years of meteoritic dust influx.

It was long believed by space scientists that the moon was the same age as the earth. In fact, scientists were concerned that when men landed on the moon, they would sink into the moon dust. According to evolution theory, the moon is 5 to 10 billion years old. So, the astronauts should have had to contend with 20 to 60 miles of dust. But, the moon's surface, as many of us observed on television, was found to have only a few inches of dust at most, a real embarrassment for the evolutionists and a major victory for the creationists.

By this point, undoubtedly many of you are scratching your heads. Why wasn't all this scientific, creationist information presented on PBS, on Carl Sagan's COSMOS? Who controls PBS? The government. With whose funds? The taxpayers, yours and mine, just like with the public schools and universities. Is it farfetched to suggest that the continual bombardment of the general public with the theory of evolution in the government-financed schools, the government-subsidized universities, and the government-sponsored and subsidized media is anything less than government acting consistent with its own self-interest? Could government possibly be selling us the religion of evolutionary origin in order to justify its enormous existence and centralization of power? Could it be that an engineered worldwide economic collapse and the unreal threat of nuclear war might be enough to break down the United States of America, the last free nation on the face of this earth, in order to consolidate it into a one-world government, fulfilling the ultimate of evolutionary empire building dreams, going as far back as the Tower of Babel and the Egyptian Empire. We effectively gave the Soviets the atom bomb. Is the "Death Star" located in Washington, D. C.? Billions of dollars of loans and foreign aid given to the Soviet Union by the U.S. have helped create today's global economic mess, and have allowed the Soviets to build their military machine. Furthermore, Antony Sutton, in his 1982 book, TECHNOLOGICAL TREASON, listed over 150 U.S. multinational companies, which in the 1970s alone, have transferred important technology to the Soviet Union. Do you get the feeling that we so-called *"free"* Americans have been misled? Loyalty to country and loyalty to government are two different things entirely.

What about our scientists? Why do we hear from so few of them regarding these matters? First of all, most scientists are not rich men. Their livelihood and economic well-being depends, in most cases, on the generosity of their sponsors. The National Science Foundation is an agency of the federal government, supported by our tax dollars. How many college and university scientific research projects are federally funded in whole or in part? Most. How many private scientific research organizations are dependent upon multinational corporation and federal money, particularly where the military/industrial complex is concerned? Most. Ernest Borek in THE CODE OF LIFE (Columbia University Press, 1965) wrote: *"The overwhelming portion of scientific activity is financed by our federal government . . ."* As late as 1976, the Smithsonian Museum of Natural History allowed no exhibits which did not uphold evolution.

Scientists know which side their bread is buttered on. The real issue is money—economics! Money is the power that controls and manipulates everything in a fully-developed, evolutionary, economic empire, as ours is. Science is the most controlled area in our entire political/economic system.

The pyramid is the symbol of the international banking community, the money community. In ancient civilizations, such as the Mayan culture of central America, the kings were buried in pyramids and considered gods. One great Mayan king was called the *"lord of lords."* This is exactly what the BIBLE calls Jesus Christ, along with *"King of kings."* In Egypt, the pharaohs, considered sun gods incarnate, were buried in the pyramids. Shelley called Ramses, one of the great Egyptian pharaohs, *"king of kings"* in one of his sonnets. The pyramid is found on our Federal Reserve Note (U.S. dollar bill). We see the reality of evolutionary gods in the modern world even carried out through symbols from as long ago as the ancient Egyptian empire. Egypt made slaves of the Hebrews. Are God's children in the U.S., the New Israel, as our Founding Fathers called it, to be slaves also?

Science and technology cannot save us, as Colin Norman clearly argued in his book, THE GOD THAT LIMPS. The theory of evolution has about run out of rope and is gagging. Furthermore, science is running head-on into the same type of problems on the subatomic level that social scientists have run into with their disastrous collective dreams and schemes. While scientists are able to accurately predict activity in the physical universe at the level of, or larger than, the atom, by contrast, the subatomic world is not predictable. How the apparently random world of subatomic particles comes together and produces order that allows scientists to predict the movement and behavior of the atom and larger matter is still a mystery. This is much like the action of a random distribution of free individuals in the social realm, coming together to accurately form a predictable bell-shaped curve.

Scientists are learning the great lesson of humility, that they are not all powerful or all knowing. Scientists, too, it seems, walk by faith and not by sight. They depend upon a design they do not fully understand. They operate with faith in the uniformity of nature and the natural order. They are, like all other men, incapable of perfect truth. They do have a vested self-interest in promoting the God-like status of science, however, not only to support their egos, but also to ensure the continuation of government and multinational corporation grants and subsidies on which they economically depend. But, for this to occur, the public must be sold on the salvation of evolutionary science.

Ironically, the very base of science has been established, and still depends economically upon, the existence of a creationist Christian culture. Science depends upon excess capital, money, which allows scientific investigation to occur. Excess capital is only the product of a culture operating under the creation model, long-term.

Science means knowledge. Science is never complete. Scientists are continually learning and discovering new scientific applications. This is progress, not evolution. The tremendous scientific facts that science has given us precede from their underlying faith in a universe that is knowable (thanks to a Creator?). True progress does not come by way of the so-called circumstantial evidence of evolution which cannot be repeated. Rather, true progress (mistakenly called evolution) comes with the application of the scientific method, investigative doubt, and the discovery of laws which, in cause and effect manner, can then be utilized.

Down through the ages, men have always feared and worshipped what they did not understand. It is no different today. (Christian culture was/is the exception because it was/is uniquely reality-oriented.) Today, scientists are right up there at the top of the evolutionary spiral, held in awe, protected sacred cows, shielded from criticism and investigation by government, government-financed schools, universities and research centers, and multinational corporations. Reality and scientific truth, like freedom, must come from the grassroots up. Thus it has always been historically.

It has hopefully been clearly demonstrated by this point that man freely **chooses** which religious theory of origin he wants to live under, the creation model or the evolution model. We are living under the evolution model presently. It has brought us nothing but mass misery (good times are a debt illusion) with, of course, a few exceptions for those right up there at the top of the evolutionary order, in both the capitalistic and communistic systems. Isn't it time we at least consider reestablishing the creation model as basic? After all, it was the creation model which first built and sustained this great country. Human nature has not changed. So, we're not taking any real chances with the creation model, are we? The prosperous results in the future can already be predicted from successful past history. All we have to lose is our chains. But, before we willingly drop those chains, we'll have to overcome our pride and resistance to change, and in the process, deprogram ourselves from the Machiavellian evolutionary conditioning with which we have been bombarded all of our deceived lives.

We haven't come close to scratching the surface of all the fields and areas of scientific investigation, which can potentially be discovered and applied for the benefit of all mankind. We are still in the early stages of the scientific technological revolution. Science is reality-oriented. Christianity is reality-oriented. The two together are a natural, with *"Wealth for All,"* economic prosperity, the natural fallout. Our scientific dismay, just like our economic, political and social hopelessness, is a direct reflection of the bankrupt evolutionary theory which rules our scientific society today.

It is high time that free men again become responsible in all areas of their lives, first by getting their heads screwed on correctly religiously, with a workable creation theory of origin. Evil only can flourish when good men do nothing. A candle of light and truth drives out the darkness. We don't have to fight fire with fire. We can fight fire with water. Fighting fire with fire leads to revolution, which always results in a further centralization of power, the last thing we need. We need men and women to change their minds and approach life with a new optimistic and creative perspective. The future holds potentially tremendous scientific benefits. Within the upcoming trials and tribulations of the next 20 years lie the seeds for many glorious opportunities and breakthroughs, as our rigid institutions are forced to change and die. It is again time for men and women to draw comfort and strength from a living Creator, who is on their side, and can give them what they seek, including breakthroughs in the scientific realm. With this mental decision once made, victory on this earth and *"Wealth for All"* are just a breath away.

A Population Time Bomb?
5/21/82

Dr. David J. Rodabaugh, Associate Professor of Mathematics at the University of Missouri, has used several different mathematical models to show that evolutionary-based population figures for the earth are totally unreasonable. In fact, using the work of evolutionists Boyce, De Prima and May, Dr. Rodabaugh has concluded that **the world's population essentially grows exponentially until it reaches equilibrium.** As population nears equilibrium, growth slows.

Assuming that the earth's flood occurred 4,500 years ago, and the repopulation of the earth began with eight people, we are only half way to equilibrium.

Rodabaugh's work has been confirmed by studies with fish populations and various insects that naturally begin to level off at a certain density, even when there is plenty of food available. World population began slowing in 1977, even while life spans were increasing.

Holland is twice as densely populated as India. But, India is marked by economic poverty, squalor and human misery, while Holland, by contrast, is relatively prosperous, with twice as many people. India's population density is 400 people per square mile. Holland's population density is 1,000 people per square mile. India has more natural resources than Holland and a better growing climate, too. The logical conclusion is that the religion, philosophy, habits, motivational structure and attitudes of people are the primary determinants of human conditions, along with the economic and political structure.

Dr. Colin G. Clark, in June of 1980, speaking to a college audience in Santa Paula, California, said, *"Even at present levels of agricultural science, a properly cultivated world could support 10 times the present numbers on an American-style diet."*

We have the technology and creativeness, when harnessed with man's pursuit of his best self-interest long-term, to solve the world's problems. The solution begins with each individual being humble, giving, responsible, long-term oriented, and accordingly free. Man's choice, on both the spiritual and natural level, is to grow or die.

SCIENTIFIC DISCIPLINES ESTABLISHED
BY CREATIONIST SCIENTISTS

DISCIPLINE	SCIENTIST
ANTISEPTIC SURGERY	**JOSEPH LISTER** (1827-1912)
BACTERIOLOGY	**LOUIS PASTEUR** (1822-1895)
CALCULUS	**ISAAC NEWTON** (1642-1727)
CELESTIAL MECHANICS	**JOHANN KEPLER** (1571-1630)
CHEMISTRY	**ROBERT BOYLE** (1627-1691)
COMPARATIVE ANATOMY	**GEORGES CUVIER** (1769-1832)
COMPUTER SCIENCE	**CHARLES BABBAGE** (1792-1871)
DIMENSIONAL ANALYSIS	**LORD RAYLEIGH** (1842-1919)

DYNAMICS	**ISAAC NEWTON** (1642-1727)
ELECTRONICS	**JOHN AMBROSE FLEMING** (1849-1945)
ELECTRODYNAMICS	**JAMES CLERK MAXWELL** (1831-1879)
ELECTRO-MAGNETICS	**MICHAEL FARADAY** (1791-1867)
ENERGETICS	**LORD KELVIN** (1824-1907)
ENTOMOLOGY OF LIVING INSECTS	**HENRI FABRE** (1823-1915)
FIELD THEORY	**MICHAEL FARADAY** (1791-1867)
FLUID MECHANICS	**GEORGE STOKES** (1819-1903)
GALACTIC ASTRONOMY	**WILLIAM HERSCHEL** (1738-1822)
GAS DYNAMICS	**ROBERT BOYLE** (1627-1691)
GENETICS	**GREGOR MENDEL** (1822-1884)
GLACIAL GEOLOGY	**LOUIS AGASSIZ** (1807-1873)
GYNECOLOGY	**JAMES SIMPSON** (1811-1870)
HYDRAULICS	**LEONARDO DA VINCI** (1452-1519)
HYDROGRAPHY	**MATTHEW MAURY** (1806-1873)
HYDROSTATICS	**BLAISE PASCAL** (1623-1662)
ICHTHYOLOGY	**LOUIS AGASSIZ** (1807-1873)
ISOTOPIC CHEMISTRY	**WILLIAM RAMSAY** (1852-1916)
MODEL ANALYSIS	**LORD RAYLEIGH** (1842-1919)
NATURAL HISTORY	**JOHN RAY** (1627-1705)
NON-EUCLIDEAN GEOMETRY	**BERNHARD RIEMANN** (1826-1866)
OCEANOGRAPHY	**MATTHEW MAURY** (1806-1873)
OPTICAL MINERALOGY	**DAVID BREWSTER** (1781-1868)
PALEONTOLOGY	**JOHN WOODWARD** (1665-1728)
PATHOLOGY	**RUDOLPH VIRCHOW** (1821-1902)
PHYSICAL ASTRONOMY	**JOHANN KEPLER** (1571-1630)
REVERSIBLE THERMODYNAMICS	**JAMES JOULE** (1818-1889)
STATISTICAL THERMODYNAMICS	**JAMES CLERK MAXWELL** (1831-1879)
STRATIGRAPHY	**NICHOLAS STENO** (1631-1686)
SYSTEMATIC BIOLOGY	**CAROLUS LINNAEUS** (1707-1778)
THERMODYNAMICS	**LORD KELVIN** (1824-1907)
THERMOKINETICS	**HUMPHREY DAVY** (1778-1829)
VERTEBRATE PALEONTOLOGY	**GEORGES CUVIER** (1769-1832)

NOTABLE INVENTIONS, DISCOVERIES OR DEVELOPMENTS BY CREATIONIST SCIENTISTS

CONTRIBUTION	SCIENTIST
ABSOLUTE TEMPERATURE SCALE	**LORD KELVIN** (1824-1907)
ACTUARIAL TABLES	**CHARLES BABBAGE** (1792-1871)
BAROMETER	**BLAISE PASCAL** (1623-1662)
BIOGENESIS LAW	**LOUIS PASTEUR** (1822-1895)
CALCULATING MACHINE	**CHARLES BABBAGE** (1792-1871)
CHLOROFORM	**JAMES SIMPSON** (1811-1870)
CLASSIFICATION SYSTEM	**CAROLUS LINNAEUS** (1707-1788)

DOUBLE STARS	**WILLIAM HERSCHEL** (1738-1822)
ELECTRIC GENERATOR	**MICHAEL FARADAY** (1791-1867)
ELECTRIC MOTOR	**JOSEPH HENRY** (1797-1878)
EPHEMERIS TABLES	**JOHANN KEPLER** (1571-1630)
FERMENTATION CONTROL	**LOUIS PASTEUR** (1822-1895)
GALVANOMETER	**JOSEPH HENRY** (1797-1878)
GLOBAL STAR CATALOG	**JOHN HERSCHEL** (1792-1878)
INERT GASES	**WILLIAM RAMSAY** (1852-1916)
KALEIDOSCOPE	**DAVID BREWSTER** (1781-1868)
LAW OF GRAVITY	**ISAAC NEWTON** (1642-1727)
MINE SAFETY LAMP	**HUMPHREY DAVY** (1778-1829)
PASTEURIZATION	**LOUIS PASTEUR** (1822-1895)
REFLECTING TELESCOPE	**ISAAC NEWTON** (1642-1727)
SCIENTIFIC METHOD	**FRANCIS BACON** (1561-1626)
SELF-INDUCTION	**JOSEPH HENRY** (1797-1878)
TELEGRAPH	**SAMUEL F. B. MORSE** (1791-1872)
THERMIONIC VALVE	**AMBROSE FLEMING** (1849-1945)
TRANS ATLANTIC CABLE	**LORD KELVIN** (1824-1907)
VACCINATION & IMMUNIZATION	**LOUIS PASTEUR** (1822-1895)

*Source: **Institute for Creation Research**, 2100 Greenfield Drive, El Cajon, CA 92021*

CHURCH & STATE: SEPARATE OR NOT?

6/81

H. L. Mencken once remarked that there are two groups of people: those who work for a living, and those who *vote* for a living.

Let's say seven of us are standing around a dead tree which we desire to convert into firewood. We elect one man as supervisor (our government). He issues a decree (law) that the dead tree become firewood. Does the dead tree automatically become firewood because our elected government (supervisor) declared it to be so? Of course not. In the same way, laws legislated by Congress cannot produce goods and services.

Carrying our example a step further, let's say that three of us brought axes (capital) and chop all the wood so it can be used in fireplaces. The supervisor (government) arbitrarily gives approximately half of the firewood which the three of us cut to the other three fellows who sat around joking and laughing while we did the work.

What's the difference in the supervisor (government) taking the firewood from us without our permission and giving it to our three dead-beat friends, and our three dead-beat friends coming to our house in the middle of the night and stealing half of our firewood? There is no difference. The end result is the same.

Doesn't it stand to reason, therefore, that the three of us who cut the firewood will resent the fact that half of our work and production was taken from us? Doesn't it stand to reason that such legalized theft creates friction between the three of us who chopped the wood and the three who consumed the end product of our labors? Won't the three of us who worked have less incentive or desire to chop firewood next time? Won't the three of us who chopped wood resent the action taken by the supervisor (government)?

If this goes on for too long, at some point in time, won't the three of us who chopped the wood get into a fight (revolution) with those who consumed the wood we chopped? Isn't government transfer of wealth the essence of revolution? Isn't the supervisor (government) a parasite when he takes some of the wood for himself, as a result of his supervisory efforts? The supervisor (government) did not chop any wood.

Today, in the United States of America, 71 million people pay taxes (chop wood), while 81 million people depend upon government (supervisor) for their income (consume firewood). Don't producing Americans have a right to complain about the 50 percent tax bracket?

What happens when government gets too big, and becomes too much of a parasite? As time passed, our supervisor (government) took increasing amounts of our chopped firewood for himself, leaving less for those who did the work (chopped) in the first place, and less for those who received the firewood gratuitously. Won't both parties complain at some point in time, as the supervisor (government/ parasite) consumes increasing amounts of the firewood? Won't both the producers and the consumers of firewood turn on their supervisor (government) when it becomes too parasitic and consumes too much of the firewood? Of course. This is why all civilizations collapse when governments become fully developed. A parasite cannot long play the role of God. As a parasite and a false god, government can operate only erroneously, because it was conceived in spiritual error.

We need to realize that all of life is inescapably religious. Because man has a finite mind and limited time on this earth, he can never know everything about anything. Thus, he is forced to make some ultimate assumptions about the nature of reality. Assumptions about the ultimate nature of reality are, by definition, religious. Therefore, when you boil it all down, we come face to face with the fact that all of man's thinking is ultimately circular. The starting point becomes the religious presuppositions of the individual.

Man's mind also is limited. This is illustrated by the ongoing frustration of intellectuals who complain that the more they learn, the more they realize how little they know and how much more there is to learn.

In the scientific realm, the limits of man's mind run head-on into Heisenberg's indeterminacy principle and Godel's theorem.

Godel has shown that no description can be logically self-contained and total. The unknown always leaks in. For example, a mathematician must refer to things outside his system. All our natural systems ultimately are open, not closed, within our universe.

Heisenberg, in his indeterminacy principle, expressed that if an elementary particle's location is known, its momentum cannot be determined. If its momentum is known, the particle's location cannot be determined. Heisenberg's indeterminacy principle caused Einstein great consternation because it clearly revealed the fallibility of man. Thus, the humbling reality that man has had to face down through all the ages is that he is capable of only one thing perfectly: error.

There is a yawning chasm between a finite man with a limited mind, who is capable only of error, and a sovereign God who not only is absolute sovereignty and eternal, but who also is total perfection. It becomes logically ludicrous for a failing creature to believe he can work his way to perfection, or attain deity, because man's limits infinitely insure imperfection. Error plus effort still equals error.

For this reason, man needs a transitional bridge, a lifeline, between himself and God—something of a God/man whose deity will be revealed to man by revelation. It will be helpful if this God/man is both finite/infinite, physical/spiritual, human/divine, a second Adam who atones for the error of the first Adam. Thus, He restores a totally just God's fellowship with the elect members of the human race.

What we are coming down to, of course, is Christianity. In fact, the world can be divided into two basic religions. One is Christianity which historically is dependent upon a sovereign God providing salvation through Jesus Christ. The other is humanism which clusters all other world religions together. Instead of man operating from a base of humility, as in Christianity, he operates from one of pride, for humanism states that the creature (man), through an act of will, can obtain deity.

What we see in this earthly battle also is evident in the spiritual realm. Humanism is the religion of Satan. Satan, a creature, first desired to be like the Most High. Satan desired to be God. He was totally and completely humanistic.

One has to question the motives of political leaders and educators who give their blessing to literature, movies, magazines, and the like which emphasize sex and violence, but who tell us it is taboo to discuss politics and religion, when religion particularly is at the base of all human thought and resultant activity.

It also should be obvious that all education is religious. Education involves a search for truth which, as we have discussed, is based upon some ultimate religious assumptions about the nature of reality. Education also teaches a world view. All world views are religious, because the actions that result from a world view are based upon thoughts and preceding underlying assumptions—necessarily religious assumptions.

Humanism is the religion of the public school system. Shirley M. Hufstedler, who headed up the newly created Department of Education in the Carter administration, previously was a director of the Aspen Institute for Humanistic Studies.

In the early '60s, when John F. Kennedy was President and Robert Kennedy was Attorney General, a group of women in California asked Robert Kennedy to stop the public school system from teaching the religion of humanism. Attorney General Kennedy admitted that the public school system was religious, and that it was teaching the religion of humanism, but that he was not going to stop it.

The father of modern education, John Dewey, was thoroughly humanistic. He said, *"I cannot understand how any realization of the democratic ideal as a vital, moral and spiritual ideal in human affairs is possible, without a surrender of the conception of the basic division to which supernatural Christianity is committed."*

It now should be clear why local control of public schools is vital—to determine which religion the educational system will teach: humanism or Christianity. It will teach one or the other. One is of God, the other from the pit of hell.

On the political level, we have been taught there is such a thing as separation of church and state. We should treat such propaganda with skepticism. Government and religion historically have been combined time and time again. The Pharaohs of Egypt were sun gods incarnate. The Caesars of Rome were deified. Even the "divine right of Kings" is discussed in public school history books.

While church and state, politics and religion, can be separated *institutionally* in the real world, they are essentially the same in the abstract world, the world of ideas and the world of ethics. All governments are religious. The fundamental purpose of government is to rule, to issue laws. But laws are nothing more than enacted morality, ideas about right or wrong, ethics and values.

More than 50 percent of the Bible was written by politicians about government. Moses was the Prime Minister of his nation, Egypt. He also was the law-giver to Israel. The books that Moses wrote in the Bible dictate God's laws. These laws specify how He wants us to live. The books of Samuel, Kings and Chronicles relate the history of a theocratic nation. The very idea of the second coming of Christ is the second coming of a King, who establishes His dominion, His rulership. This event is inescapably political, as well as religious.

The philosopher George Santayana wrote, *"It should be observed that, if a systematic religion is true at all, intrusion on its part into politics is not only legitimate, but is the very work it comes into the world to do. Being by hypothesis, enlightened supernaturally, it is able to survey the conditions and consequences of any kind of action much better than the wisest legislature . . . so that spheres of systematic religion and politics—far from being independent—are in principle identical."*

So in terms of our *thought* processes, separation of church and state, separation of religion and politics, is impossible.

Why then do we separate the physical institutions of church and state? To prevent the concentration and subsequent abuse of power, in other words, for decentralization. Without the physical separation of church and state, tyranny results. The Crusades are an excellent historical example of this. When church and state are combined institutionally, freedom declines. Men cannot handle too much power. *"Power corrupts, and absolute power corrupts absolutely."* Men begin to think of themselves as God, which is humanistic to the core.

Freedom has been rare for the historical world because Christianity, as a pervasive national religion, has been equally rare. There were no free countries in the world, and virtually no personal freedoms in the 2,500 years between Jeremiah and the U.S. Declaration of Independence. Freedom, however, flourished in England following the completion of the King James Bible. At that time, the masses understood the relationship between Christianity, freedom and politics. England under Oliver Cromwell and the early history of the American colonies were both marked by pervasive Christianity *and* freedom.

Christianity makes freedom possible. *"If the Son therefore shall make you free, ye shall be free indeed"* (John 8:36). Why? Under Christianity, all men are equal because they are in equal need of the salvation provided by a sovereign God. As a result, each individual believer-priest is important, not only because he is under the domain and sponsorship of a sovereign God, but also because he is on equal status with all other men, regardless of his or her earthly political or economic status.

As the influence of Christianity diminishes in a political order, its vacuum is filled by government. Government always fills the vacuum of unbelief.

When men reject God's laws and drift away from the security of a sovereign, just and omnipotent protector, they look for security in numbers (synergism). This is exactly what government is, men acting collectively. The government then assumes responsibility for the needs of the people. Individuals no longer meet their own needs by following the instructions of an omniscient God. And because government assumes responsibility, it also usurps the peoples' freedom of action.

In the early history of this country, the health, education and welfare needs of the people were met by private and religious organizations. Today, approximately 60 percent of the federal budget goes for these needs. And the government has limited the freedom of the people as the people have become increasingly irresponsible.

What we see, in effect, is that government plays the role of God. Government is a substitute god. We must ask ourselves, "What kind of god is government?"

What is its ultimate source of power? We know it is not the provision of the Christian God. This leaves only one other option: government, playing the role of God, is an instrument of Satan.

But beyond the theological implications, government playing the role of God is the maximum distortion of reality. Why? Because government is inescapably a parasite. It produces nothing. It lives off its hosts. But, by the very fact that government issues laws, it plays the role of God. No wonder government always botches things up.

Government, or politics, is confiscatory economics. Taxes are legalized theft of economic goods—the transfer of wealth from a producing party to a consuming party. Inflation is a hidden tax. Government, the false god, the parasite, is creating something (money) out of nothing. But, because government is a false god and cannot really create something out of nothing, this ever-increasing amount of "play" money chases the same amount of goods and services which, in turn, drives up prices. This results in inflation.

Additionally, all gods demand tributes and sacrifices. Government, playing the role of God, demands tribute by way of increased taxes, and sacrifices by way of the shed blood of young men in wars. Death in war is the ultimate tax paid to government. The growth of government is always accompanied by increased taxation and increased wars.

Government is a curse. Government's legitimate responsibilities are limited to ensuring justice, enforcing contracts, and providing protection against enemies, both foreign and domestic. In I Samuel 8 of the Old Testament of the Bible, the elders of Israel demanded that Samuel, the prophet, give them a king. The Lord told Samuel that when the people asked for a king, they had rejected Him—God.

Samuel told the people that rejecting God in favor of a king would bring them misery: *"He (the king) will take your sons, and appoint them for himself, for his chariots, and to be his horsemen; and some shall run before his chariots. And he will appoint him captains over thousands, and captains over fifties; and will set them to ear his ground, and to reap his harvest, and to make his instruments of war, and instruments of his chariots. And he will take your daughters to be confectionaries, and to be cooks, and to be bakers. And he will take your fields, and your vineyards, and your oliveyards, even the best of them, and give them to his servants. And he will take the tenth of your seed, and of your vineyards, and give to his officers and to his servants. And he will take your menservants, and your maidservants, and your goodliest young men, and your asses, and put them to his work. He will take the tenth of your sheep: and ye shall be his servants"* (I Samuel 8:11-17).

Isn't this what we see today, with the 50 percent tax bracket, pervasive government regulation, inflation and wars? Isn't the situation in the U.S. today the realization of what Samuel said would be the case when government was asked to play the role of God? But, remember, government is a parasite. And when government is fully developed (the maximum distortion of reality), the collapse of the civilization comes. This was true in Egyptian, Babylonian, Chaldean, Greek and Roman empires. All of these collapsed when government power was maximized, the parasite playing the role of God.

All these empires were also, thus, thoroughly humanistic.

There are effectively two modern world empires—the Russian and the American. The Russian empire is the most apparent example of government playing the role of God. The U.S.S.R. is based upon the philosophical work of Karl Marx, a confirmed atheist. Marx's work, in turn, was based upon the ideas of the philosopher Hegel, who saw the state (government) as god walking on earth. So humanism is the religion of the Soviet Union. Humanism and atheism are identical. Both establish man, either individually or collectively, as God. Joseph Stalin once said, *"We have disposed the Czars of Earth. We shall now dethrone the Lord of Heaven."*

But, is the American empire any less humanistic?

Marxism is a religion. As Clarence B. Carson stated in WORLD IN THE GRIP OF AN IDEA, *"Marxism . . . is an anti-religious religion. It is an earthbound, materialistic, man-centered, cataclysmic, prophetic and dogmatic religion. Dialectical materialism is its revelation. History is its god. Marx is its prophet. Lenin is its incarnation. The revolution is its day of judgment. And Communism is its paradise. Its claim to being scientific even satisfies the intellectual's desire to have a rational religion."*

So, in the Soviet Union, government plays the role of God thoroughly. The U.S.S.R.'s government is a parasite.

How, then, has the Soviet Union survived? Because we, Western civilization, have supported the Soviet parasite. Over 95% of the technology in Soviet Russia has been provided by Western civilization capitalists. The U.S.S.R. owes Western bankers between $60 and $80 billion. The U.S.S.R. is now the world's largest importer of grain.

In Soviet Russia we see clear evidence of our theory that government, a parasite, results only in failure, personal and economic. We even see the lie of government, the parasite, as God in the Soviet Union. Poland demonstrated this point clearly, too.

According to the largest Soviet domestic propaganda agency, *Znaniye,* 37 million families in the U.S.S.R. have private garden plots of less than ½-acre per family. This represents less than 1.5 percent of all the farmed land in the Soviet Union. These private garden plots account for 61 percent of the potatoes, 34 percent of the vegetables, and 40 percent of the fruits raised in the U.S.S.R.

How important freedom is to economic production and the economic welfare of a society! Wood choppers take note.

In reality, communism creates human misery. It does *not* become a worker's paradise, leading to the withering away of the state. We see this clearly in the recent revolt in Poland. There, the workers (theoretically, the essence and beneficiaries of communism) are literally up in arms against the oppressive Soviet government. Obviously, the so-called government of the working class is revealed to all the world for exactly what it is—a sham.

It's interesting to observe that Karl Marx's most vicious attack was against the philosopher, Max Stirner. Stirner realized that government playing the role of God (humanism) would result in the collapse of the state (government). Marx saw socialism as the way out, that the sovereignty of man, collectively (government), would lead to the enslavement of man individually, in order to prevent the total breakdown of the established social order. Stirner saw that the logic of the humanistic state, government as God, was really nothing more than the collective sovereignty of man. But, because the sovereignty of man collectively (government—the parasite) has to break down, the end result would always be individual sovereignty or each man as his own god—anarchy.

We see this idea today captured by the phrase, *"Do your own thing."* Thus, revolution is the logical end result of a humanistic government as God because, when government fails, each man becomes his own god; each man becomes his own law. This is anarchy.

If each man is his own god, anyone who crosses his path or puts up barriers to his individual will, becomes his enemy. Therefore, each man stands alone in his lonely state, with every other man a competing god or enemy. This is the essence of revolution/anarchy. Power quickly fills the vacuum, usually in the form of a dictatorship.

Dictators, such as the Pharaohs or the Caesars are anti-Christs. Such tyrants are men playing the role of God, substituting themselves for the man/God, Jesus Christ. It was Friedrich Nietzsche's *"superman,"* the epitome of humanism, as God, that gave rise to Adolf Hitler. Adolf Hitler once commented, *"National Socialism is more than a religion; it is the will to create superman."*

One of the Founding Fathers of this country saw this man vs. God conflict clearly. He said, *"Men must be governed by God or they will be ruled by tyrants."* He also saw that the only way to keep government, the humanistic, parasitic monster, chained, was by individual religious faith. This faith, he knew, resulted in individual security, responsibility and freedom. It prevented government from filling the vacuum of unbelief and irresponsibility and, therefore, usurping freedom. He understood that the individual was more important than the state, because the individual is eternal, while the state is temporal.

In this discussion, we have observed that the battle in the heavens is between the forces of evil commanded by Satan, and the forces of good commanded by a sovereign God. So, too, is the earthly battle between Christianity and humanism, which dominates the governments and religions of this world.

Again, the definition of humanism is man, through an act of will, trying to achieve deity. Man can either attempt to do this individually, which is the motor of worldly religions, or collectively, through government playing the role of God. But, because man is capable only of error, and because government is a parasite, the humanism of world religions and governments is doomed to fail.

What we also are witnessing is a battle between humility and pride. Humanism, the essence of pride (man can become God), goeth before a fall. The source of humanism, Satan, the highest created being who desired to be like the Most High, failed and fell. Can man, a lesser creation, expect to do anything other?

In the U.S. today, we stand convicted as humanists. According to the HUMANIST MANIFESTOS I AND II, humanism denies the deity of God, denies the inspiration of the Bible, denies the divinity of Jesus Christ, denies salvation, denies heaven, denies damnation, and denies hell. Humanism believes in the removal of American patriotism and in the elimination of the free enterprise system. Humanism promotes disarmament and the creation of a one-world socialistic government. Humanism believes in the control of the environment, the control of energy, the limitation of energy, the equal distribution of America's wealth to reduce poverty and bring about equality, and the removal of the distinctive roles of men and women.

Humanism believes in the right to abortion, in mercy killing, in suicide and in sexual freedom between consenting adults. Humanism holds that there are no moral absolutes. Humanism endorses homosexuality, lesbianism and incest. Our culture embraces these humanistic goals. And humanism is the religion of Satan. Judgment can't be far away, unless there is revival. It doesn't even necessarily need to be divine judgment. We could simply reap what we have sowed.

We are headed for the collapse of our government, our economic and social order, and a bloody revolution. We are about to experience the blood sacrifice of the masses of our people as a result of our rejection of the only substitutionary blood sacrifice which God made available to us through Jesus Christ. Jesus said, *"I am the way, the truth, and the life: no man cometh unto the Father, but by me."* (John 14:6)

People have a choice—either mass revolution or individual

regeneration. When they accept regeneration by an act of faith, through the blood sacrifice of Jesus Christ, then through the indwelling of the Holy Spirit, they have the ability to grow and accept responsibility and enjoy commensurate freedom. When this occurs, there is no need for government. Government, the parasitic god, withers away.

This is in stark contrast with communism, which begins with a revolution (a blood sacrifice), which claims to create heaven on earth through a worker's paradise, which (theoretically) results eventually in a withering away of the state. But, we already have mentioned the hypocrisy, the lies, and the error of this theory, as evident in Poland today.

So government is a curse on the people, brought about initially by the falling away of religious faith, which ultimately results in the worship of government as God—the people looking to government to fill their needs.

The God of THE BIBLE states that the earth is cursed and that man must work by the sweat of his brow. THE BIBLE states that those who don't work, don't eat. This is basic economics.

Government, by contrast, the false god, tells us we don't have to work. The government will provide us with food stamps, welfare, and social security. So, we see that the spiritual conflict between a sovereign God of THE BIBLE and a parasitic, humanistic government as God extends to the economic realm. Now, we know government is a false, parasitic god. We also know who the false god of this world is—Satan.

Satan's religion is humanism. The religion of governments worldwide today, including the U.S., is humanism. Doesn't history reveal to us that humanistic government empires are historically satanic, and at their base, fueled by occult, mystery religions? Egypt was humanistic, with the man, Pharaoh, an incarnate sun god. Moses challenged Egypt's occult priests in Pharaoh's court.

The Babylonian mystery religions exist and are influential down to this day. It was in the Babylonian captivity that the people of Israel were led astray religiously. It's interesting to note that Egypt, Babylon, Assyria, Persia and Rome all oppressed the Israelites at one time or another. They were all humanistic empires.

We have discussed how modern Soviet Russia is a humanistic, satanic government. Hitler's Germany was a different manifestation of the same satanic, occult humanism. Rudolf Binding called National Socialism *"an authentically religious revolution."* Jean Michel Angebert in THE OCCULT AND THE THIRD REICH (McGraw-Hill) clearly documented how Hitler's Nazi movement was an occult religious movement. Hitler ended many of his speeches with, *"Amen."* He also was obsessed with mystery religions, the Holy Grail, and the legend of Parzival.

The swastika symbolized the mutation of superman. The swastika also is called the gamma cross. So we, too, have the contrast in symbols—the humanistic occultic gamma cross (swastika), or the cross at Calvary.

Occult religions ignore or minimize the work of Jesus Christ. Isn't it interesting that the slang use of *"Jesus Christ"* has become the ultimate in cursing in our country?

Rene Guenon writes about the use of the swastika in ancient China. It is intimately connected with Yin-Yang (the idea of good and evil being equal and opposite). If good and evil are equal and opposite, then Satan (evil) is equal to God (good). This is the essence of Luciferianism, the idea that Satan and Christ are equal and opposite sons of God, but that Satan is good and Christ is evil.

Good and evil are not equal opposites. Evil (sin) is separation from good, just as cold is an absence of heat.

The swastika, as discussed in THE OCCULT AND THE THIRD REICH, is linked to Masonry, the Rosicrucians, and in the form of the gamma cross, is a principle instrument of the Brahman (Hindu) religion.

Revolution—a satanic, blood-letting substitute for Christ's sacrifice on Calvary—is *intellectually occult.* However, the idea that revolution originates in occult, mysterious, secret, religious societies, has been traditionally rejected by the humanistic academic establishment. Only researchers such as Nesta H. Webster, in her works THE FRENCH REVOLUTION and WORLD REVOLUTION, previously documented the occult religious nature of revolution. Recently, however, the cover has been blown by James H. Billington who, since 1973, has been director of the Woodrow Wilson International Center for Scholars, located in the Smithsonian Institute Building, Washington, D. C. Billington received his doctorate as a Rhodes Scholar at Oxford and taught history for 17 years at Harvard and Princeton.

Billington takes *"seriously the notion that political revolution is the secular (humanistic) religion of our time."* In his recent book FIRE IN THE MINDS OF MEN: ORIGINS OF THE REVOLUTIONARY FAITH (Basic Books), Billington *"traces the course of revolutionary faith from its earliest origins in occult Freemasonry to the allegedly 'scientific' Marxism of today."* He, like Nesta Webster, also zeroes in on the French Revolution as occult in origin.

What about this occult influence through symbols such as the swastika? The earliest swastikas were tied to the solar system. Pharaoh was the Egyptian sun god incarnate. He used the swastika. This same symbolism is in evidence in India, Mexico, Palestine and Europe. The swastika was brought to Europe by the Druids who were Great Initiates, possessing occult knowledge from the Orient.

The gamma cross, known otherwise as the swastika, became a Buddhist sign. *"It symbolized the wheel of life to which man is chained, and from which he can succeed in freeing himself only through purification,"* says Jean Michel Angebert (THE OCCULT AND THE THIRD REICH). This purification idea, man through his own efforts becoming a god or acceptable to God, is totally humanistic.

Thor's hammer is of Egyptian origin. And Thor's hammer always has with it the swastika. Angebert writes, *"The solar cult transmitted to the Cathari by the Manichaeans, taken up by the Rosicrucians and the Illuminating Ones, was to crop up finally in the form of the swastika of the Third Reich."*

It's critically important to note that the American War for Independence was not a revolution. It was a fight by our Colonial forefathers to preserve what they already had. The philosophical base for the American War for Independence was found in the religious revival of the 1740s, led by such men as preacher/evangelist Jonathan Edwards. Colonial churches were the political town meeting halls. It was the threat of the British imposition of bishops on the American colonies that primarily stimulated American independence, along with their hatred of the Bank of England's money.

American colonies were issuing debt-free, non-interest earning money, commensurate with their economic production. The Colonies' economic power began to rival that of England. When Benjamin Franklin visited England, he was asked by members of Parliament why the Colonies were so prosperous. Franklin commented that the Colonies issued their own money, debt and interest free. There was no central bank, like the Federal Reserve. *"Wealth for All"* existed.

Immediately Parliament, at the behest of the Rothschild Bank, passed an act prohibiting the issuance of money by the Colonies. This act required the Colonies to use English money. It was the first time our money was based on debt. One year later, unemployment was rampant in the Colonies. Is it any different today? No. THE BIBLE condemns usury and debt for man's own good.

Let's focus on money for a moment. Governments create money. Yet, because money only *represents* goods and services, when excess money is created beyond production, inflation results. Inflation is a form of theft.

Money runs the world. Who is the temporary ruler of this world?

Satan. Satan runs the world with money. What does this tell us about banks and their occult symbol, the pyramid?

I Timothy 6:10 reads, *"The love of money is the root of all evil."* So, in the area of money, we have a spiritual conflict between God and Satan. Christ ran the money-changers (bankers) out of the Jerusalem Temple in great anger. So, here we see occult religion and banking combined in Christ's time.

How do we know the Jewish religion at the time of Jesus was occult? In the first place, it was a product of Babylonian occultism, assimilated during the Babylonian captivity. Secondly, in John 8, Jesus said to the Pharisees, *"Ye are of your father the devil, and the lust of your father ye will do."*

Let's become more contemporary. Who financed the Russian Revolution? International U.S. bankers. Paul Warburg, chief architect of the Federal Reserve Bank, and his brother, Felix, along with Jacob Schiff and others, gave $50 million to Lenin to overthrow a U.S. ally—Russia.

The influence of international money in establishing Adolf Hitler is well documented in Antony C. Sutton's work, WALL STREET AND THE RISE OF HITLER. W. Cleon Skousen's books THE NAKED COMMUNIST and THE NAKED CAPITALIST clearly reveal the connection between communism, international capitalism and international banking. It's important to observe that 50 percent of all the Trilateralists involved in the highest levels of the U.S. government today also are involved in banking.

From the "Church and State" perspective, let's look briefly at law in light of American history. Under our present evolutionary, humanistic system, we have less and less protection under law. Those in power (in the alphabet agencies, in the White House, in Congress and on the Supreme Court) have all but repudiated the U.S. Constitution, which was *the* law of the land and our source of freedom. The whole idea that *"ignorance of the law is no excuse,"* was based on the fact that the Constitution was the law of the land and grounded in Biblical law.

William Barclay's book THE TEN COMMANDMENTS FOR TODAY and R. J. Rushdoony's books LAW AND LIBERTY and THE INSTITUTES OF BIBLICAL LAW support this position. An article by John W. Whitehead and John Conlan, "The Establishment of the Religion of Secular Humanism and Its First Amendment Implications" (THE TEXAS TECH LAW REVIEW, Winter, 1978), is an extremely well-documented work, supporting the position that early American law was Biblical.

The greatest influence on American law and, in fact, the foundation of the American legal system, was William Blackstone's COMMEN-TARIES. Blackstone wrote, *"The doctrine thus delivered we call the revealed or divine law, and they are to be found only in the Holy Scriptures. Upon these two foundations, the law of nature and the law of revelation, depend all human laws. That is to say, no human laws should be suffered to contradict these."*

THE TEXAS TECH LAW REVIEW also comprehensively documents the destructive rise of secular humanism in the American system and its inseparable relationship with Darwinism and evolution.

In the Trinity case, the U.S. Supreme Court decided that Christianity was the common law basis of U.S. law. *Absolute* freedom of religion means no law exists since any ritual or activity can be justified religiously including polygamy, child sacrifice, bestiality, homosexuality, etc.

Perhaps now—finally—we will have the capacity to appreciate what our forefathers gave us. The First Amendment to the U.S. Constitution, *"Congress shall make no law respecting an establishment of religion,"* was meant to keep the federal government totally out of religion. Nine of the thirteen American colonies had a state-established Christian church. The U.S. Constitution puts chains on the federal government. It gives rights and privileges to the people first, to the state secondly, and last of all to the federal government. This is in keeping with the Christian principle we have discussed concerning the importance of the individual.

How thoroughly Christianity saturated the thinking of our American forefathers recently has been researched by Dr. M. E. Bradford of the University of Dallas. He discovered that of the 55 men who drew up the Constitution, only 5 were possible Deists, while 30 were militant Christians. And the remainder, while not vocal, were orthodox Christians.

The first act of the First Continental Congress was the passage of a resolution to open the Congress with prayer. On Saturday, July 15, 1775, the Congress resolved to attend, as a body, both morning and afternoon worship services on the following Thursday. In September, 1777, the Congress ordered the Committee of Commerce to import 20,000 Bibles for use by Americans. In September, 1781, the Congress recommended to all inhabitants of America an edition of the Bible, published by Robert Aitken.

Important books on our Christian roots include: THIS INDEPENDENT REPUBLIC and THE NATURE OF THE AMERICAN SYSTEM, by R. J. Rushdoony (Thoburn Press); THE ROOTS OF AMERICAN ORDER, by Russell Kirk (Open Court); THE LIGHT AND THE GLORY, by Peter Marshall and David Manuel (Revell);

and THE JOURNAL OF CHRISTIAN RECONSTRUCTION, by Dr. Gary North.

U.S. presidents were sworn into office with the Bible open to Deuteronomy 28.

During the American War for Independence, the British burned Bibles, churches, hymnals and church records. General George Washington, while commanding the Continental Army, required all soldiers to attend daily religious services. He called for repair and repentance during the harsh winter at Valley Forge.

At the signing of the Declaration of Independence, Samuel Adams commented, *"We have this day restored the Sovereign to Whom alone men ought to be obedient. He reigns in heaven. . . . "*

During the Constitutional Convention, Benjamin Franklin said, *"I have lived, Sir, a long time, and the longer I live, the more convincing proofs I see of this truth: 'that God governs in the affairs of man.'"*

After the Constitutional Convention, Alexander Hamilton stated, *"For my own part, I sincerely esteem it a system which without the finger of God, never could have been suggested and agreed upon by such a diversity of interest."*

George Washington wrote in 1778, *"The hand of Providence has been so conspicuous in all this, that he must be worse than an infidel that lacks faith."*

President George Washington in his inaugural address to Congress said, *"It would be peculiarly improper to omit, in this first official act, my fervent supplication to that Almighty Being, who rules over the universe, who presides in the councils of nations, and whose providential aids can supply every human defect. . . . "*

Our forefathers gave us a Christian Constitutional Republic. We have perverted it into a democracy. Our forefathers hated democracy. John Adams warned in 1815, *"Democracy has never been and never can be so desirable as aristocracy or monarchy, but while it lasts, is more bloody than either. Remember, democracy never lasts long. It soon wastes, exhausts, and murders itself. There never was a democracy that did not commit suicide."*

Alexander Hamilton said, *"We are a republic. Real liberty is never found in despotism or in the extremes of democracy."*

James Madison stated, *"Democracies have ever been spectacles of turbulence and contention; have ever been found incompatible with personal security, or the right to property; and have been as short in their lives as they have been violent in their deaths."*

John Marshall, a Chief Justice of the Supreme Court, declared, *"Between a balanced republic and a democracy, the difference is like that between order and chaos."*

Why did our Founding Fathers hate democracy? Because democracy is the rule of man—humanism—not the rule of God with man operating under God's laws.

We are on the brink of anarchy, to be followed by a dictatorship. The cycle of rule by governments over the 200-year national cycle is from the rule by one (a king), to the rule by few (a republic), to the rule by many (a democracy), to anarchy (revolution), and back to the rule by one (a king).

The average age of a country is 200 years. The United States celebrated its 200th birthday in 1976. The average age of a civilization is 510 years. The 510-year cycle of Western civilization fell due between 1975 and 1980.

Western civilization will collapse unless we have a Christian revival. The harsh climate which we are experiencing has, historically, led to the downfall of empires. Collapsing, godless, humanistic governments will do whatever they have to do, including destroying their own citizens, to survive. The pagan idea of a youthful phoenix, rising from the ashes of destruction, is the false hope of satanic, occult, godless, humanistic wars and revolutions.

Remember, it was Marx's idea of a revolution of the proletariat (the working class) against the bourgeoisie (middle-class capitalists and the property class) that was the essence of the Russian Revolution and the earlier French Revolution. Both the French and the Russian Revolutions ended with the occult phoenix (new order) attempting to rise from the ashes of revolution. Both failed miserably to achieve the objectives the masses expected.

We have seen where frightful humanism in our nation has set the stage for our own bloody revolution. The end of the 510-year cycle, which is where we are now, is noted for revolutions and nation-falling wars. Inflation has destroyed more lawfully constituted governments than any force except war itself. Inflation is still rampant today. Lenin said, *"The best way to destroy the capitalist system is to debauch the currency."* Crane Brinton's work, ANATOMY OF REVOLUTION, revealed that revolutions are preceded by the approaching bankruptcy of government. This is our present status.

We, as a country, are about to reap what we have sown. There is only one way to turn our nation around; that is through a massive Christian revival. II Chronicles 7:14 reads, *"If my people, which are called by my name, shall humble themselves, and pray, and seek my face, and turn from their wicked ways; then will I hear from heaven, and forgive their sin, and will heal their land."*

The foregoing evidence clearly documents that we were established as a Christian nation. God's promise in II Chronicles 7:14 applies to us. The salvation of our economic and political order begins with each of us, individually and responsibly, spending some serious time on our knees and in study. Then we need to get on our feet and begin changing things.

We are commanded to subdue the earth and exercise dominion. Faith without works is dead!

*   *   *

"Some consider it simply unfortunate that two of Archbishop Marcinkus' friends, Michele Sindona and Robert Calbi, turned out to be crooks, as well as members of a secret Freemasonic lodge and linked to the Mafia."

VISITOR
July 18, 1982
From Desmond O'Grady's
*"Italian Government
Presses Vatican on Bank
Scandal"*

OUR PUBLIC SCHOOLS: An "A" in Violence and Corruption; an "F" in Education

6/80

Humanism is such a pleasant-sounding word that it disarms most people. But unless this trend in education is rooted out of our public schools, the future of our nation is imperiled.

When Robert Kennedy was Attorney General, a group of women in California wrote him numerous letters, asking him to take action against government schools throughout the nation, since the schools were teaching the religion of humanism (man as god). Robert Kennedy responded that yes, the public schools were religious. They *were* teaching the religion of humanism, but he did not plan to do anything about it. Since then some Christians have attempted to do something about this.

All governments are religious. Laws are ideas about right or wrong, ethics, morality and values. These also are concerns of religion. Therefore since laws are *enacted* morality, and morality is a religious concern, the source of law in any society is the god of the society. Who is the law giver? A sovereign God or the federal government?

Public schools are religious institutions since they are extensions of the state (federal government). Schools which teach the doctrines of the federal government are an expression and reflection of the religious presuppositions of the government.

The German historian, Ethelbert Stauffer, in his study CHRIST AND THE CAESARS (1955), showed that the roots of the ancient conflict between church and state are religious. Where the state claims to be God walking on earth, the state will claim sovereignty and will seek to control every area of life and thought. A free society becomes impossible. The number of laws multiply endlessly.

The Christian claim, by contrast, is *not* that the church is sovereign over the world, for it is not; lordship or sovereignty is an attribute of God, not man. But the Christian insistence is on the freedom of the church, *"the realm of dominion in which the risen Lord continues to work,"* from the controls of the state or any other agency. It involves, moreover, a denial of the doctrine of state sovereignty.

The very word sovereignty is absent from the U.S. Constitution

99

because of the theological context of those times. The historian, A. F. Pollard, wrote, *"The colonies had been as anxious to get rid of James II in 1688 as they were to be free from Parliament in 1776. Their fundamental objection was to any sovereignty vested in any state whatsoever, even in their own. Americans may be defined as that part of the English-speaking world which have instinctively revolted against the doctrine of sovereignty of the state and have, not quite successfully, striven to maintain that attitude from the time of the Pilgrim Fathers to the present day."*

Since Pollard's time (1925), the state has steadily advanced its claims of sovereignty. The federal government has become increasingly humanistic in its view of the law. It has firmly established humanism as the religion of the public or state schools. The old historical question again becomes, *"Who is sovereign—God or the state?"*

The conflict between church and state, which is being fought today in the public schools, is the same as the war fought by the early church against the Romans, when Christians were martyred. It was then Christ versus Caesar. It is today Christ versus Caesar. The early church came into conflict with Rome. Rome sought to license, regulate, control, and tax all religions. The church refused to submit to controls. Its resistance was based on the lordship or sovereignty of Christ: Christ's domain cannot be under the dominion of Caesar. Caesar is under Christ, the creator and Lord, not Christ under Caesar.

The church thus engaged in several unlicensed activities. It held meetings which were instructional; worship meetings without permits. It collected abandoned babies, gave them to various church families, reared and instructed them; orphanages were maintained. Because of the Levitical nature of the church, i.e., a center of instruction, libraries and schools began to be built very early. Later, cathedral schools developed and universities.

The doctrine of academic freedom is a relic of the day when the academy was a part of the church and its functions, and hence entitled to the immunities thereof. How seriously this aspect was seen as basic to the church's life is apparent from the fact that, as soon as churches were built, libraries (and schools) were part of them.

George Washington, our first President, was an extremely religious man. In his Farewell Address, he warned against the notion that there could be morality without religion. He stated, *"We must above all else strengthen those institutions which further learning, promote them as an object of primary importance, institutions for the general diffusion of knowledge."* We must understand what Washington said in the context of his time and his beliefs. The only schools he knew were Christian schools. He was warning against atheism in action—The

French Revolution. He knew the only way the young nation could stand against the invasion of atheistic foreign ideas was by pervasive Christian education.

The historical concept of separation between church and state in this country came about as a result of separation of the federal government from the religious institutions. In fact, 9 of the 13 colonial states had an established state Christian church.

Early advocates of state controlled (federal) education were Unitarians who brought German ideas to this country. These included Horace Mann, James G. Carter, and Charles Sumner. Charles Sumner, the abolitionist Senator from Massachusetts, told Horace Mann that we must get rid of Biblical faith. Horace Mann saw public schools as the key religious institutions, *"all the children of the state,"* as he referred to them. John Dewey also declared supernatural Christianity to be the enemy or adversary. The idea of the saved and the lost, heaven and hell, good and evil, Dewey said, represented a *"spiritual aristocracy,"* and an alien creed.

Early American universities were church established. Between the ages of 5 through 7, children were learning Greek and Hebrew. They attended Harvard at ages 13 to 14. It was only after 1865 that the pagan doctrine of *"survival of the fittest"* became the educational doctrine of the schools.

After World War I, it was decided to hold children in school through the 8th grade to keep them from the job market. During the Great Depression, to keep children out of the labor market, the school age was raised to 16. This pragmatic approach developed into a belief in education as a panacea (salvation by education). After World War II, it was thought that there would be a depression if all the veterans returned to work. Therefore, the G. I. Bill of Rights was established to return the veterans to school.

But, public education has not been a panacea. In 1975, the preliminary report of the subcommittee to investigate juvenile delinquency was entitled, *Our Nation's Schools—A Report Card: "A" in School Violence and Vandalism.* This sub-committee, chaired by Senator Birch Bayh, revealed that from 1970 to 1973, in the public schools, homicides increased 18.5 percent, rapes and attempted rapes increased 41 percent, robberies increased by 36.7 percent, drug and alcohol offenses on school property increased by 37.5 percent.

These statistics were not confined to any single geographic region, but different regions had their *"specialties."* Robberies in the West increased by 98.3 percent. Assaults on other students increased in the South by 276.9 percent. In the North Central region, drug violations were up 97.4 percent, and rapes were up 60 percent.

Meanwhile, scores on the National College Entrance Examinations have fallen each year for 13 consecutive years.

The total spent by all levels of government on primary and secondary education in 1950 was $6.7 billion. Total expenditures by 1974 had risen to $61.6 billion. The cost per pupil, when adjusted for price inflation, rose 141 percent between 1950 and 1973. This means the public schools costs per capita rose 141 percent more than the general price level in these years.

The crisis in American public education is only beginning. The bad years lie ahead. The teachers who come into the school system now started the first grade in 1963-64—the year the academic decline became noticeable in the high school college entrance scores, the time of the beginning of curricula upheavals of the mid-1960s.

Just prior to World War II, Lawrence Dennis, anticipating the United States' involvement in the war, wrote a far-sighted book entitled, THE DYNAMICS OF WAR AND REVOLUTION. With regard to public education, he stated, *"The role of education in our present crisis is to make the masses susceptible as they never were before to propaganda and demogogic manipulation."*

Karl Marx' 10th Commandment called for free education for all children in the public schools.

Was there a master plan to control American public education? If so, when did it begin? In 1902, the General Education Board, a tax-exempt foundation, was created by John D. Rockefeller, Sr. Its *"Occassional Letter I"* laid down the plan for controlling American education in the following words:

> *"People yield themselves with perfect docility to our molding hands . . . We work our own good will upon a grateful and responsive rural folk. We shall not try to make these people, or any of their children, into philosophers, or men of learning, or of science. . . . of whom we have ample supply. The task we set before ourselves is very simple, to train these people as we find them to a perfectly ideal life just where they are. So we will organize our children into a community and teach them to do in a perfect way the things their fathers and others did in an imperfect way, in the homes, in the ship and on the farm."*

In 1929, the American Historical Society sponsored a Carnegie Corporation financed commission on social studies in the schools. Staff members and commissioners were drawn from various universities, from the Council on Foreign Relations, Rockefeller Foundation, etc. Prominent in the group were George S. Counts of Columbia University, Charles E. Merriam of Chicago University, Charles A. Beard, Isaiah Bowman representing the Council on Foreign Relations, Edmund E. Day of the Rockefeller Foundation, and others prominent in the promotion of social studies.

These educationalists conducted a 5-year study of the *"social science instruction"* and produced some 14 major and several supplementary volumes, one of them entitled, A CHARTER FOR THE SOCIAL STUDIES IN THE SCHOOLS. These volumes laid down the guidelines that were to be followed by the writers of textbooks, teachers and social administrators, and all others who had to do with the preparation of future generations for existence in the coming *"New Order."*

Here are some direct quotes from the *"Conclusions and Recommendations of the Commission":*

> *"Contemporary social thought and action in the realms of government, economy, and aesthetics . . . reflect more and more this growing integration and interdependence, and are increasingly concerned with increasing the functional efficiency of integrated and interdependent society . . . Under the molding influence of socialized processes of living . . . leaders in public affairs, supported by a growing mass of the population, are demanding the introduction of ever-wider measures of planning and control.*

> *"Cumulative evidence supports the conclusion that . . . the age of individualism and laissez faire in economy and government is closing and that a new age of collectivism is emerging. As to the specific form which this 'collectivism,' this integration and interdependence, is taking and will take in the future . . . it may involve the limiting or supplanting of private property by public property or it may entail the preservation of private property extended and distributed among the masses.*

> *"Whatever may be the exact character of life in the society now emerging, it will certainly be different in important respects from that of the past . . . and whether it will be better or worse will depend in large measure upon . . . the education of the rising generation . . . The implications for education are clear and imperative: . . . complete and frank recognition that the old order is passing . . . Organized public education in the United States, much more than ever before, is now compelled, if it is to fulfill its social obligations, to adjust its objectives, its curriculum, its methods of instruction, and its administrative procedures to the requirements of the emerging generation [and] the school . . . must recognize a new order and proceed to equip the rising generation to a co-operative effective in the increasing interdependent society . . ."*

How clearly is the school issue a religious issue! Madalyn Murray O'Hair, professional atheist, addressing an American Atheist Annual Convention in St. Francis, California in May, 1978, said, *"Let's face it. There is no way we could have held an atheist convention 10 years ago. Everything today is much better. Part of the reason is public education."*

The battle today between the church (private) schools and the public schools is a battle for the mind of the child. In fact, at a Notre Dame law conference recently, judges agreed that the issue that would predominate over the next 10 years would be this one: *"Who is Lord, Christ or Caesar? Will private schools be allowed to survive?"*

Let's look philosophically at this basic religious conflict between this religion of the state and state schools (humanism), and Christianity. Humanism is the worship of man. Man determines for himself what is right or wrong. Man is as God. In humanism, man is the measure of all things. Man is autonomous. Man is a rational being. Man is free under humanism to choose between good and evil. In other words, man is not tainted with sin. He has a neutral nature. This contradicts the Biblical perspective that none are righteous; that man is totally depraved.

Humanism assumes that if evil exists it is not the fault of man, but the fault of education, the churches, capitalism, social classes, etc. In other words, humanism promotes equality, and with equality evil will supposedly disappear. This has not been the case. Humanism assumes that whatever is normal (what the majority of the group accepts) is good. This is the same principle embraced by the Marquis De Sade. Christianity by contrast is abnormal. It is supernatural.

Humanism is a selfish perspective. And, as one would expect, selfishness has become clearly evident in our society. Such phrases as, *"If it feels good, do it,"* or, *"Do your own thing"* testify to it.

Let's look at some other contrasts. Under Christian education, God is God, and man lives by every word that proceedeth out of the mouth of God. Humanism states that man is God, and so situation ethics exist. However, if ethics are situational, who is to say what I can and can't do? No one! Therefore, the ultimate result of humanism in history has been: (1) a federal government with massive control, (2) anarchy and lawlessness as man recognizes his own independence as a god when the state fails, and (3) a dictatorship.

If man is God and ethics are *"what I establish for myself,"* then who is to say that it is wrong to commit incest with one's mother, sister or daughter? Why should I respect my teachers, parents, or anyone else? Aren't the lesbians logically correct in their thinking that the ultimate in sex, from a humanistic perspective, is masturbation?

Why not rampant abortion? After all, if it's what I want, why not?

Truth becomes pragmatic under humanism. If it works, it is supposedly helpful. The end justifies the means. As Friedrich Nietzsche effectively told us, a lie is more useful than the truth.

By contrast, in Christianity, God's word is the truth. As Jesus put it, *"I am the way, the truth, and the life."* The Christian perspective is that if God is sovereign, He is sovereign over all areas of life, including education. Either there *is* a single sovereign God, or there is no God at all.

Education, from a Christian perspective, requires discipline under God's laws. *"Thy law is truth."* Children are graded by God's standard. Under Christian education, formerly American education, the child's humanistic will is to be broken to the harness, to the truth of God's law and purpose. This is in blatant conflict with public education today, which promotes the so-called humanistic self-realization and self-development of the child. Self-development, under Christian education, is maximized once the Biblical foundation is established.

Public education denies the child's sin nature. It talks about truth being freedom from restraint; man doing his own thing. Today's schools meet the student's needs rather than teach and instruct. They promote ideas such as no punishment of the child, and letting the child unreservedly express himself. According to the humanistic perspective, mass human will, unrestrained by any outside teaching, is the road to truth. Man is his own truth. It is little wonder that in the '60s, it was the best and brightest students who demonstrated and rioted. In the '70s, it was the best and brightest who took the drug trips. This is the result of the *"best and brightest"* applying the humanistic perspective.

The Christian perspective and the humanistic perspective are in conflict in all subjects. In history, the question becomes: Who determines history, God or man? In science the question becomes: Are we living in an orderly universe created by God, where there is perfect cause and effect, or in one of chance? Is the universe winding down as the law of thermodynamics suggests, or is it evolving?

Today, God or Christ mentioned positively in school on the elementary, junior high, high school, or college level, or cited as authority, has become almost the ultimate in pornography.

Other conflicts in other instructional areas? You bet! In literature, who decides what is a classic? What are the presuppositions, the assumptions about the nature of reality of the writer? How about grammar? Will we have a Christian sense of time, with a past, present and future tense, or will we become an existentialistic society and culture, as we have already become, where the past and future are forgotten? After all, we are the *"now"* generation, and have become accordingly relativistic.

We see another manifestation of humanism in the economy where the savings rate among consumers is the lowest it has been in 14 years. *"Live for today,"* is the watchword. And the sexual revolution?

According to the humanistic perspective, these experimenters are the *"perfect pioneers,"* the natural result of the evolutionary faith. And in finance, in today's dog-eat-dog capitalism, we find the rape of the environment, the ruin of God's creation. Is this not the logical result of the pagan doctrine of the *"survival of the fittest"*?

And liberal arts? Liberal arts, the art of being a free man, is totally humanistic. By contrast, Christianity requires man to become free under the discipleship of Christ—freedom in bondage to Christ. Interestingly enough, it was Charles Norris Cochrane, a non-Christian, who, in his work CHRISTIANITY AND CLASSICAL CULTURE, noted that while on one hand the Roman Empire expounded a radical belief in individual freedom, on the other hand, it was the Christian church of that era that held to freedom under slavery to Christ. Cochrane's research revealed that the members of the early Christian church, in fact, enjoyed the greater freedom. There is freedom only under law, where boundaries are established.

Today's educational curriculum has become, for all practical purposes, irrelevant. Two of the most basic subjects—law and economics —seldom are taught in high schools, and are rarely required in college. Yet, we live in a world of physical economics and moral law.

The problems with which this nation is floundering are a result of its inaccurate educational premises. The destruction of centralized public education is, therefore, destined and necessary. Through its demise, humanism will be destroyed. Humanism, the doctrine of public schools today, is already in radical decline because it does not work. It is not the truth. The economic suffering and the political slavery which are about to descend upon Western civilization are the inevitable result of our educational folly.

What must be done? The federal government and the state must be kicked out of the education business. Local control of schools, textbooks, and teacher requirements must be reestablished. A return to education in the classical American sense, necessarily Christian, is required. All subject matter must be examined and the humanistic perspective eliminated.

School funds will have to be totally local in nature. A free market in education is desirable, where parents vote with their dollars to send their children to church, private, or locally controlled public schools.

Humanism

• Denies the deity of God, the inspiration of the Bible, and the divinity of Jesus Christ.

• Denies the existence of the soul, life after death, salvation and

heaven, damnation and hell.
- Denies the Biblical account of creation.
- Believes that there are no absolutes, no right, no wrong—that moral values are self-determined and situational. Do your own thing, *"as long as it does not harm anyone else."*
- Believes in removal of distinctive roles of male and female.
- Believes in sexual freedom between consenting individuals, regardless of age, including premarital sex, homosexuality, lesbianism, and incest.
- Believes in the right to abortion, euthanasia (mercy killing), and suicide.
- Believes in equal distribution of America's wealth to reduce poverty and bring about equality.
- Believes in control of the environment, control of energy and its limitation.
- Believes in removal of American patriotism and the free enterprise system, disarmament, and the creation of a one-world socialistic government.*

*   *   *

"The teaching profession attracts more than its share of the worst college students, and the least-qualified teachers stay in the profession the longest . . .

"Every year, incoming teachers are less academically able than their predecessors, . . ."

Associated Press
July 21, 1982
From a study conducted
by the University of
North Carolina at
Chapel Hill

* *Humanist Manifestos I and II, Prometheus Books.*

GOVERNMENT AND THE PEOPLE

6/11/81

The people of the United States are alienated from their government. The elected government doesn't run things. The bureaucracy does. While this phenomenon is most widely noted on a national level, it is also true at the state and local level. Senator Jackson said that the problem is that government doesn't work at any level.

We keep running presidents through the meat grinder—Kennedy, Johnson, Nixon, Ford and Carter (who aged 50 years during his 4 years). Remember that the 1978 Christmas special on ABC with Barbara Walters and Jimmy Carter in the White House ranked 63rd out of 64 special programs aired that week. The conclusions we can draw are obvious: The public couldn't have cared less about Jimmy Carter, or the public couldn't have cared less about Barbara Walters, or both of the foregoing.

Back in Spring of 1978, a Harris poll revealed that only 12 percent of the people in this country respected their congressman. So, basically, only 1 out of 10 people respect the office holders who rule this country. This is an extremely dangerous situation. It is a forerunner of revolution. People will put up with an obese, irrelevant government as long as economic times are good. But, when times turn bad, as they are doing now, the politicians are the ones whose necks are placed on the chopping block first, figuratively and literally, throughout history. The situation is aggravated by the underlying humanistic philosophical assumptions of the people.

The U.S. government was not always the monster that it is today. Some of us, who were educated in the public schools prior to the 1960's, may recall the all-important constitutional principle of limited government. But the liberals, who continued to cry for more government, have been successful. This is evidenced by the fact that the number of laws that have been put on the books during the past 5½ years are equal to the number of laws created from the beginning of this country up until the last 5½ years.

The conservatives decry this bureaucratic paper snowstorm. They call for a Constitutional Convention, an attempt to balance the budget, for the Liberty Amendment, a reduction of the number of government agencies and a reduction in taxes, if not the abolition of the IRS. But they (conservatives) are missing the boat, too. They rightfully complain that health, education and welfare payments, which are larger than the combined budget of all 50 states put together, are unreasonable. But, what they don't discern is that these health, education, and welfare needs must be met, and they will be met one way or the other!

In the early history of this country, a European named Alexis DeTocqueville wrote an insightful study entitled, DEMOCRACY IN AMERICA. He noted that the United States was marked by a conspicuous absence of what we call *"government."* But, the needs of the people, in a health, education and welfare sense, were still being met. Government was of the people, by the people and for the people. The people through their independent agencies on a **local** level, met the health, education and welfare needs of their neighbors and immigrants. DeTocqueville noticed, for example, that immigrants to the Eastern seaboard were **fed** by voluntary civic organizations, were **housed** by voluntary community organizations and were **taught** the English language and culture by schools established by the **churches.** Even though the Red Cross was established in Switzerland, in no place on this earth did it catch on like it did in the United States. Why? Because the people of this country were **self-governing** through their own independent agencies—agencies of all types. There was no need for what we today call *"government."*

When the **people** of a nation fail to take responsibility for meeting the needs of its citizens, then the government will fill the vacuum. And we can assume, from the foregoing statistics on how people feel about government, that the growth of government is a curse.

But, just what is this thing called government? The most important government we have is the government of ourselves—self-discipline, self-government. A man who minds his own business is not subject to group sanctions and the slavery of *"other's"* imposed norms and standards. A man who respects the rights and property of others is free to come and go as he pleases. He recognizes the principle that the law should not do for a group what an individual cannot legally do himself. The law should be limited to protecting the rights, privileges, and property of individuals who cannot protect themselves individually. Because an individual is responsible, he enjoys freedom of movement and action by contrast to the confinement and slavery of jail.

A man who takes the responsibility of starting a business has the freedom to make decisions and come and go as he pleases. By contrast, an employee does not enjoy that degree of freedom. The employee *"enjoys"* the *"security"* of the job in exchange for his loss of total freedom and decision making. The *"boss"* enjoys the fruits of his efforts. And, incidentally, there is no such thing as *"job security."* The ultimate in *"job security"* accrues to the boss who has assumed the risk and who makes the decisions. If his decisions and capital expenditures are incorrect, then the employee will be the first to lose his job. The boss gets fired last.

The point is, no matter how you look at it, there is no escaping the principle that freedom demands responsibility. A *"people,"* who individually do not accept responsibility for their own acts, will lose their collective and individual freedoms. If everyone obeyed the law, that is—respected the rights and properties of others—then there would be no need for laws and police forces, and therefore, there would be no taxes levied for these particular functions. In other words, individuals would enjoy personal freedom and financial freedom from these taxes. The basic element of government is, therefore self-government.

In our society today, we see a rapid movement away from self-government and commensurate responsibility. This is evidenced by the desire of the population, in mass, to enjoy unrestricted so-called freedom, which is really the maximization of selfishness—the concept of *"do your own thing."* The *"do your own thing"* vacuum is filled by the government. All we need to do is look at Cuba and the Soviet Union as two examples of this phenomenon. There, the people do **not** have freedom commensurate with responsibility. They have so-called *"unlimited"* freedom because they have no responsibility. The result is a constant bombardment of fiestas, festivals, carnivals and cultural activities, which keep the people constantly **entertained**. Isn't this what we see in our own country, as evidenced by the explosive growth of professional football to the status of America's most popular sport (witness the Superbowl). Isn't this what we see by the geometric growth of entertainment industries of all types? Was not the bull market in gambling stocks reflecting a frantic run by the people toward pleasure and away from real freedom commensurate with responsibility? Is not the obvious result of this mania slavery? For slavery is what comes with unlicensed liberty, as in the Soviet Union.

The second most basic form of government is family government. Make no mistake about it, the family, historically in this country, has clearly followed the order of: authority of father over mother, and the authority of mother and father over the children. Children have been governed by principles and by the rules for social conduct laid down in the home. Is it not obvious that a stable, loving, secure home which teaches respect for the rights and properties of others will result in reduced social costs, i.e., less need for the *"forces"* of law and order, and higher productivity than result from homes where the radical freedom of the child is encouraged?

The historical government of the family firmly directed the will of the child and disciplined him in the harness of principles of right and wrong. Isn't this a far cry from the doctrine of child development today, which calls for the unrestricted liberty of the child, the rights of the child, the International Year of the Child, with the underlying assumption being that the child's basic nature is neutral at worst, and good by implication. Make no mistake about it. This vacuum of irresponsibility **will be filled**. It will be filled by the government which sets up day-care centers and establishes public schools for the children. It is no accident that the day-care centers in this country are now patterned after those of the Soviet Union. At a Notre Dame law conference not too long ago the judges of this country stated that a primary legal issue in the next 20 years will be who owns the child, the parents or the state.

The next level of government is the government of the job. If you work it out, you'll find that we spend ⅔ of our waking hours either preparing for work, traveling to and from work, or on the job. (Man still earns his daily bread by the sweat of his brow.) The worker who becomes ego-identified with his job, who dives into it, works hard, and accepts responsibility enjoys not only promotions and pay increases, but sometimes also the freedom to establish work schedules, not to mention the easing of restrictions which apply to less responsible workers. (This assumes an honest economic system.)

The business, which understands and implements the principle that, *"Self-interest is best served by service to the community,"* will not have a policy of manufacturing defective products, of giving poor service in return for greedy, short-term profits. The business will, instead, look to the long-term, and recognize the *"responsibility of service"* as being in its best interest, and thereby, take corporate responsibility for the needs of its clients, workers and respect the environment. There can be no doubt that if businesses had assumed their responsibilities in keeping with the principle that self-interest is best served by service rather than by greedy, short-term accumulation, like the robber barons did, we would not be plagued with all the consumer protection agencies, with all the problems of unions and union legislation, and the environmental demons led by OSHA and the EPA. You see, in business, too, freedom is commensurate with responsibility.

The fourth level of government is social government. We are all, to some extent, ruled by the norms and standards of our peer group and the community-at-large. Where there are strong, interpersonal bonds, people are happier, less lonely and less alienated. They are also more sensitive to the rights and privileges of others. True meaning and happiness in life comes from relationships with people. When this sense of civic responsibility is widespread, when communities or people within a local community take responsibility for their actions, it follows that there is less crime and fewer government agencies to handle the maladjusted because there are fewer maladjusted. The local churches also help primarily to fill this vacuum.

How far are we from this principle? During the time of President Cleveland's administration, there was a severe flood in the South. Cleveland's response to the matter was that it would be a sad day in American history when the federal government had to provide flood relief instead of letting the people care for themselves. It used to be *"normal"* for the whole nation to pitch in and help a troubled area.

The buffer between local government and the federal government used to be the state government. But, with the destruction of state rights during the U.S. Civil War, the enactment of the 17th amendment, the growth of the federal bureaucracy and now federal revenue sharing, the state government has become impotent.

This brings us to the final level of government—what we call today the federal government. As mentioned earlier, when we do not have independent agencies, as we had previously in this country, to meet the health, education and welfare needs of the people, those needs will be met by the government. The vacuum will be filled; just like with the individual who refuses to take responsibility for his own actions and loses his freedom; just like with the misbehaving child who is increasingly subjected to restrictions imposed by his parents and society-at-large; just like with the worker who is negligent and uncaring and ends up with increased supervision and restriction; just like with the local community which fails to meet its responsibilities to its citizens and ends up with a monstrous central government over it. In all cases where a radical concept of freedom **without** responsibility is espoused —in all cases—liberty and freedom are lost. A form of slavery is the replacement. The result is human misery.

The buck stops at the federal government. All the lack of personal responsibility, family responsibility, work responsibility, and the lack of social and community responsibility is accrued by the federal government, with the result being increased restrictions, increased laws, increased taxation and enslavement of the people who have forfeited their freedom.

As misery becomes greater, the government (which is made up of miserable people) begins to fail. It can do nothing else. Government is a parasite. It thrives on what we feed it (taxes). The growth of government is suicidal. It kills the host eventually. The end result of government failure is anarchy, then totalitarianism which, of course, results in a total loss of freedom.

Is it clear now how the growth of government is a curse? This has always been true throughout history. The usual activity of government is to rule the people, to subject them, to make them miserable!

In the area of taxes, the *"tithe"* will always be paid. When local churches had meaning, the tithe was paid by its members to the local church. The church could then fulfill its community responsibilities of health, education and welfare in conjunction with local/self-government. There was no need for the high taxes which we have today. They are far above what is necessary to meet the needs of the people—in fact, four times above what is necessary. The bureaucracy chews up our wealth wastefully.

Look at all the corruption that comes from the **geographic** separation of the taxpayer from the tax collecting and distributing entity. Look at all the bureaucracy which is spawned at the state and federal level, which would be unnecessary if human needs were met at the local level.

There would be no need for Social Security if the extended family still took responsibility for the welfare of its older family members.

Citizens who give unselfishly to local agencies epitomize free-market charity. Citizens can withdraw their funds from a local welfare organization if it does not provide the services represented. This is a far cry from the situation we have in government today, where the power to tax is coercive. It is also an absolute monopoly which always results in less goods and services.

Every now and then someone brings to mind the old conservative adage, *"The government which governs best governs least."* The flip side of that statement is, *"Absolute power corrupts absolutely."* We have a government today which has, in reality, absolute power. Therefore, it should come as no surprise that it is almost absolutely corrupt and irrelevant. (There is not much difference.) Such a state is the spawning grounds of revolution, particularly when a radical concept of freedom is held by the population, the logical extension of which is anarchy. Ronald Reagan's election was the first hopeful sign we've seen of a potential change in trend. But, clearly, the Reagan Revolution has soured. It was without a true religious foundation.

The absolute corruption of government power is marked by the **combination** of economic and political power. This exists today. A mature civilization as ours is, furthermore, is evidenced by a pervasive central government, the majority of the population living within the cities, large corporate holdings of land, occupational specialization, sophisticated distribution and communication systems—all of which are characteristics of our civilization. Government accrues to itself the monopoly to create money and to tax. This economic power is the power of life and death. Its enforcement arm is political power.

When a person cannot provide for his own needs, money becomes the critical medium for survival; for it is only with money that persons within a mature civilization can purchase the basics. We are occupationally specialized. Therefore, today, the power to tax becomes the power to destroy. The IRS **is** the government's Gestapo.

Up until about the time of the U.S. Civil War, banks could create money; private mints could create money. There was a free market in money. And the marketplace worked just fine. In fact, in California where gold coins were minted, merchants often would not take U.S. government greenbacks. They preferred the money of the free market.

The result of this absolute power to create money is the corruption of inflation. Since inflation is the debauchery of a currency, the greater the inflation, the greater the corruption of government.

A bull market peaks and starts down when it looks strongest. Likewise, governments peak and fall when they have maximized their power—politically, economically, and legally. The economic corruption of inflation and the political corruption of Watergate, ABSCAM and the GSA are the clear evidences of corruption.

Government takes on the robe, puts on the crown, and seats itself in the throne room as a god. The maximum misery will be experienced by the people when they bow to the state, granting it sovereignty. Witness the Soviet Union.

All governments are religious. The key is to keep them from becoming a god as the U.S. government is becoming. Governments give us laws, but laws are ideas about right or wrong, ethics, values and morality. And these are the concerns of religion. Therefore, the source of law is the god of any society. Law **is** enacted morality. Today, the source of law and therefore the source of morality is, without question, the U.S. government.

Additionally, gods demand tribute and sacrifice. The government, as a god, exacts its tribute by way of taxes. It receives its sacrifices by way of the shed blood of its young men who fall on the fields of battle. This is why the concept of state sovereignty has everlastingly been accompanied by war after war. That is why the 20th Century has been so violent. State sovereignty, the government as God, has never been as widespread as it is today, globally.

For those who do not sacrifice their blood, there is the sacrifice of obedience and money. For, you see, government as God is the epitome of humanism, which is man as god. Believing, therefore, in the perfectability of man, laws enacted become all-encompassing and limit freedom, rather than few and punitive, whereby man enjoys freedom, and restitution is the penalty for crime.

It should now be obvious why the hope for our society lies in a massive reawakening, a change of mind, a new reformation, an assumption of responsibility, if you will. Individuals, families, businesses, and communities must reassume their responsibilities if they are to maintain their freedom. Passing the buck to the federal government which is less efficient, less effective, more corrupt and suicidal, can only result in greater taxes, misery, alienation, chaos and ruin both for the people and the government.

It all comes down to a spiritual issue. As Americans, we have historically held men individually responsible before God. Government had a minor role. There was great security as well as freedom and accomplishment. When men began to view themselves as glorified monkeys or as a meaningless combination of atoms, they became insecure and sought refuge in groups (governments). The placing of sovereignty in government is an unavoidable road to misery, loss of freedom, poverty, anarchy, and death. Massive individual reformation, and the resultant reestablishment of individual and community responsibility is, therefore, our only collective national hope for maintaining our freedom and wealth. The Reagan administration has tried somewhat to unshackle us and point us in the right direction, but each of us, individually, must be willing to assume the responsibility for our own load to achieve *"Wealth for All."*

ACTION: INACTION

6/25/82

One would assume that with the virtual explosion of information these days, coupled with speed-of-light communications, structural social changes would take place much more quickly than in the past. With the number of books and magazines published at record highs and a distribution system far more efficient than any in previously recorded history, we have, at almost a moment's notice, the data necessary to formulate or alter opinions and implement change. After all, people will change in a rational manner, won't they? A rational man, given satisfactory information, will form opinions and then **act,** based upon that information, consistent with his own long-term self-interests and/or value structure, won't he? So, all in all our society should be changing more rapidly and progressively than ever before. Right?

But what we see, in truth, is just the opposite—resistance to change and stagnation—economically, politically and socially, Marxist's activists to the contrary. This inaction and withdrawal is very well demonstrated by Howard Beale's monologue from the movie *"NETWORK"*:

> *"We sit watching our TVs while some local newscaster tells us that today we had 15 homicides and 63 violent crimes as if that's the way it's supposed to be. We know things are bad, worse than bad. They're crazy. It's like everything, everywhere, is going crazy, so we don't go out anymore. We sit in a house and slowly the world we're living in is getting smaller. And all we say is, 'Please, at least leave us alone in our living rooms. Let me have my toaster, and my TV, and my steel-belted radials, and I won't say anything. Just leave me alone!' "*[3]

Movies are reflections of social values.

We see this stagnation in other areas as well. Consistently, comprehensive surveys reveal that between 77 and 83 percent of the people in this country believe that most federal laws and regulations are irrelevant, unnecessary, and should be repealed. And yet, nothing is done. Increasing numbers of citizens withdraw from the political process.

116

With black youth unemployment approaching 50 percent, the seeds of social revolution are about to sprout. And yet, retreaded political rhetoric is the only response.

The tax rebellion grows, as Americans now pay more taxes than did a medieval serf. The underground economy approaches one third of our GNP. Yet, we find ourselves saddled with increasing taxes.

The primary responsibility of a government is to protect its citizens against all enemies foreign and domestic. The reality of our military vulnerability has been recognized for at least three years. Now, terrorists roam the streets of our cities and Russian Bear bombers and MIGs overfly the U.S. And yet to date, the political response has been all verbal.

The powerful trends which mark our escape from reality and movement toward illusion are evidenced by our increased interest in spectator sports rather than participating in sporting activity; the passive income system whereby millions depend upon food stamps, welfare and Social Security for their livelihood; and the fact that thirty million Americans depend upon drugs to get through each and every day.

We are witnessing the death of our culture. For what is not death, if it is not inactivity, the state of being inert? Resistance to change, our government's tendency to maintain the status quo, is an attempt to stop time, an indication of death. Our culture's infatuation with youth and staying young, as evidenced by such silliness as *"The Year of the Child"* are our attempts to turn back the clock and rebut the maturity and wisdom which comes with age. This is an insidious attempt to avoid the comtemplations of death. Thoughts concerning life's end in our civilization are taboo. They are taboo because we know we are dying!

In the economic arena, we see this preoccupation with today by way of the heavy use of debt (a sort of economic drug), which is borrowing from the future for consumption in the present. It is another way of trying to stop time. Deferred gratification is ejected in favor of present, conspicuous consumption. Also, in the economic arena, the continuing decline in savings and productivity in favor of consumption, and the constantly increasing mergers and acquisitions instead of creating new industries, are also evidences of a frozen, dying culture.

We are going through the process of decay similar to that of every other civilization which has preceded us. It was historian Arnold Toynbee who noted that when a civilization fails to meet a new challenge and cannot respond successfully, growth ceases and breakdown occurs. It was historian Oswald Spengler who noticed that the winter season of a culture, the time of civilization, is when the culture is frozen. It simply cannot (will not) respond to the challenges of its environment. It is as if, and perhaps we are, tired and ready to roll over and play dead. For, in reality, this is what we have done and are doing.

By contrast, look at the early days of America, when the seeds of our culture were sewn in strength by pioneer trail blazers and entrepreneurs who subdued the land and established new business enterprises. There existed a radical belief in freedom and the acceptance of the responsibilities which go hand-in-hand with freedom. Our ancestors understood all too well that freedom is never free. Have we reached the point when the responsibilities of freedom are just too great? It would seem so.

A culture cannot live long separated from its roots. The tradition of freedom in this country is both wide and deep. Because of this heritage, it is more likely that we will turn the responsibility for shepherding our freedoms over to Caesar, rather than slip totally into socialism. The tradition of the individual is still very strong in our culture's memory. The collectivist tendency is contrary to everything the vast majority of red-blooded Americans believe, even though that belief is no longer found extant in day-to-day reality. But, if it's true that 77 to 83 percent of Americans believe the federal government is basically an unproductive and useless parasite, why hasn't change come? We've already discussed the answer partially in terms of inaction. But increasingly what we have is a seething inaction, like a dormant volcano.

The sense of fair play which pervades Americans, that *"if you don't work, you don't eat,"* that *"you get what you earn and deserve,"* and that *"each receives according to his production,"* is ironically best seen in the rules which govern our spectator sports. A paradox exists here. On the one hand, spectators are marked by inaction and by a vicarious assumption of risk. On the other hand, the rules which govern the games played (football, baseball, etc.) are steeped in the deepest American tradition of *"you get just what you deserve,"* and *"nothing ventured, nothing gained."*

What has prevented this overwhelming cultural norm of, *"you get what you deserve,"* which is embedded in our games and culture, from being translated, in full force and effect, into our political system? It would seem quite logically that such an inconsistency would be widely recognized and worked out in time with the *"will of the people."*

Today, the liberals say, *"We're losing."* At the other end of the political spectrum, the conservatives cry out, *"We're losing the battle, too."* In the middle are the drones, the government bureaucrats, who just exist. They neither win nor lose because they are never the intellectual leaders nor the activists which trigger change. So, the questions become: *"Who wins?"* and *"Just what are the stumbling blocks to implementing widespread, publically desired, change?"* and *"Why the inaction?"*

"Who wins?" The only people who win are those who **control** the bureaucrats, a small elite group of power brokers. These are the folks who, historically, always win. The masses, throughout time, have seen far more slavery than freedom. We are talking about key politicians, leading multinational bankers, corporate executives and military personnel, who exert influence far beyond what is rightfully theirs. We are referring to the legislation writers at Brookings Institution and the policy formulators of the Aspen Institute for Humanistic Studies, who dream up the schemes that handcuff the masses.

Why are they able to keep a headlock on the citizens in our society? There is only one reason. We have sold ourselves cheap, for a pauper's wage. Our inaction has been bought for a mere pittance. The meager handouts from the federal government to each individual, catering to a particular special interest group, keeps the crowd in line and ensures the greatest good for the smallest number, the elite. It is our willingness, individually, to sell our souls for thirty pieces of silver, our Social Security check, our government-insured mortgage, our veteran benefits, our federal funding of education, our food stamps, our child support, ad nauseum—our willingness to sell our soul for an economic song is what keeps each of us in line and at each other's throats. Our greed and envy weave a web which wraps us into inaction. Such is the Machiavellian way of controlling the masses and ensuring power remains in the hands of a few, as it always does when civilization casts its long shadow, and the sun sets on a culture. At this bleak time, the civilization has lost the vision of responsible independence and following *"Wealth for All."* The people perish for lack of vision.

ME OR WE

9/26/80

Just what is it that causes talented, independent performers to be shunned by the *"establishment"* crowd? Mediocrity despises excellence. Envy is also part of it. We, as a society, no longer respect a man for his individual economic achievement. We, collectively, do not seek to emulate him as we improve ourselves. Rather, indoctrinated by the politics of guilt and pity, we wallow in the resulting envy which accompanies a democracy where mass levelling is the goal. Our society, thus, reinforces this attack on the individual achiever. It's the, *"If I can't be as good or better than he is, then I'll wreck him just for the sake of his destruction,"* attitude. It is a form of *"Misery loves company."* It is really envy run wild.

Are there any reasons for such a destructive attitude? Yes. One of the reasons is fear stemming from insecurity about one's self-worth and/or competence. Another is fear of loss of income due to, for example, subscribers gravitating to a better analyst. It has resulted, in economic practice, in the rejection of the free market. It is a resistance to risk and *"competition,"* wherein the *"cream"* is allowed to rise to the top. It is the desire for security where no one *"rocks the boat."*

The problem comes down to the ultimate political question: *"Whose rights are superior, those of the individual or those of the group?"* This question is, at its base, a theological one. In the United States, historically, men have looked to a sovereign God, who was both the individual and the group (the Christian Trinity—separate personalities, united), to direct the life of each individual. Thus, the individual was seen, in a classical American sense, as ultimately eternal and, therefore, more important than the state. The state, manifested by government at all levels, was seen as temporal and, therefore, secondary. Strength came, not from men huddling together in a pathetic attempt to mask their fears, insecurities, and inadequacies; rather, men joined hands, minds, or picked up weapons together on the basis of individual strength. They freely contracted because each had the ability to give and receive. They believed they had supernatural power. The state withered.

True strength in groups comes from men complementing each

120

other. It comes from each man contributing his part, voluntarily, not out of weakness, but from a base of strength.

Think of it this way: In our deteriorating democracy, what we effectively have are weak sisters coming together and collectively demanding tribute (blackmail) at the expense of other individuals/groups in society. Special interest groups today are collections of weaklings, each seeking to gratify themselves, in a parasitic way. The process is, of course, destructive long-term to both the group and the individual.

We also see these political confrontations, intrigues, and manipulations at the highest levels of business. Nearly everyone is scrambling to get *"his"*, in order to fulfill some personal need, to meet an inadequacy or satisfy a lust. This personal weakness results in the inability to give, and giving is a must in groups. Groups made up of such men are usually inefficient and ineffective, again particularly long-term.

The mind of a man is capable of only one thing perfectly—error. Man has limited time and a finite mind. He can never know everything about anything. So, the closest he can come to omniscience is by, in humility, cleaning up his own act, eliminating error in his own life, and then relying, in strength, on mature give and take, and upon the expertise of others in their particular areas of specialization. Good leaders, competent generalists, know this. They are not threatened by, nor do they threaten, experts in various fields of expertise. They welcome them readily. They grasp the insights of informed others in an attempt to solve the problem at hand. The result is mature leadership and progress in all areas of life—economic, political, or social.

This is a far cry from the group dynamics which are operative in our country today. We have taken a destructive course. Men who cannot, do not, and/or will not stand alone are, on a collective basis, hostile to everything for which this country stands. And they are poor group members as well. Contracts, mutual give and take, free enterprise, if you will, are the bases upon which independently strong men have worked together progressively and peacefully for the betterment of all. Those who seek security in numbers are slaves waiting for the collars. They value safety, not freedom. The only risks they are willing to assume are vicarious, which is exactly why the masses are infatuated with professional sports. This avoidance of risk is a rejection of reality. Men today love illusion more than truth.

American public education emphasizes the state (the group) rather than the individual. For the father of American education, John Dewey, true education meant not the development of the individual in terms of learning, but his socialization. Dewey was a closet communist. His influence has greatly contributed to our sad state of affairs.

Is there an answer to this conflict between the individual and the group? Yes. The secret lies in balance, what is referred to as the *"coexistence of apparent opposites."* In terms of buying power, both gold and cash can simultaneously be "king." This is an apparent contradiction. The same paradox exists for two skydivers freefalling out of an aircraft. Relative to the earth, they are in motion. Relative to each other, they are at rest. So it is also in the apparent conflict between the one and the many, the individual and the group. The balance comes when the individual man is responsible, seeks to eliminate error in his own life, develops his own talents, and progresses under his own strength. This type of man—a free, strong man—brings his individual strength to the group. He, therefore, not only has more to contribute voluntarily, but also lacks the weaknesses and lusts (security, power) which are destructive to the group's objectives. Under these conditions, groups can prosper because individuals maintain their freedom since they maintain their membership on the basis of their free will. The group benefits collectively due to the contractual arrangement. Socialistic and communistic group dynamics are, by contrast, cancerous. Weak individuals form weak groups. Misery loves company. Little is accomplished, which is exactly the reason why the U.S.S.R. has had to import foodstuffs and technology from Western Civilization to survive.

WHERE CONSERVATIVES GO WRONG

8/22/80

In today's confused world, marked by the failure to define one's terms, the same word can have many different meanings to many different people. This allows politicians to have a field day. Today, the political *"rabbit"* can call for some high sounding *program*, such as *"human rights,"* but never tell us what *"human rights"* are. *"Human rights"* mean different things to dissimilar groups with diversified frames of reference. Just what do we mean by *"human rights"*? No one really knows.

A stigma is attached to certain words. One such blemished word is *"conservative."* Ironically, individuals who consider themselves *"conservative"* today are often *"liberal"* in the classic sense of the word. Conservatives basically hold to the belief that each individual is personally responsible and accountable for his own actions. Conservatives believe each person should be given the freedom to work out his own destiny. Freedom is more important than security, in other words. This *"live and let live"* philosophy has been the cornerstone of classic *"liberal"* human rights. My, oh my, how fuzzy and distorted traditional word meanings have become. The result has been clouded thinking and resultant political manipulation.

Today, conservatives are held in low esteem by the liberal political establishment. Conservatives are viewed as selfish, self-seeking, cruel, rigid, old-fashioned, hard-headed, self-righteous, religious, regressive, warmongers—out-of-it! Since at least World War I, this view of conservatives has been the prevailing opinion of the *"do gooder"* establishment. But, the trend is changing. The Muskie, McGovern and Kennedy liberals are falling from grace. The conservatives have a chance to reinstate classic American values and principles, perhaps the best chance they have had this century. They are up to bat. Emerging events and time (cycles) are in harmony. Now, the conservatives can strike, if they just don't blow it, which they seem to be doing.

This writer has carefully monitored the conservative cause since the early 1960s. Goldwater had to lose. He was too far ahead of his time. But since Goldwater, conservatives time and time again have made three critical mistakes that have led to their demise. These mistakes are:

123

(1) Failure to define the *"time frame"* of issues discussed,

(2) Inconsistency in their view of big government, and

(3) Lack of recognition that the health, education and welfare needs of a society will always be met.

A society/civilization can only grow, prosper, and increase the spiritual, psychological and material well-being of its citizens when it takes, predominantly, a long-term view. A long-term view requires discipline, a characteristic more common to political conservatives than liberals. For example, an individual who expects to live a long, healthy life will discipline himself by watching his diet and exercising regularly. A truly successful businessman will build his business slowly, place his emphasis on customer satisfaction, in order to reap profits and be sustained long-term. An olympic athlete will discipline himself by training for years in order to reach world-class status. Parents will spend time with their children—weekly, monthly, yearly—in order to train them up to be solid, secure, adult citizens. In like manner, *"statesmen"* take a long-term view of what is good for the country, rather than cop-out for the short-term expediency which is espoused by *"politicians."* Politicians always react to **urgent** matters. States-men, with a broader view of time, discount the urgent and act on prin-ciple, on what is **important.** That is why most statesmen have been conservatives. They hold to a longer view of time, to what is impor-tant. Statesmen resist the tyranny of the urgent. The urgent, the short term, is usually related to selfishness as well. (*"What can I get for me, now?"*) Tragically today, in our welfare democracy, statesmen are referred to as *"dead politicians."*

Where conservatives go wrong in debates (discussions) with liberals is in their failure to recognize the time perspective of each party in the debate. Liberals almost always argue the short-term view, while con-servatives take the long-term perspective. The short-term need is **urgent** and always captures the interest of the politicians, lobbyists and welfare masses. The conservative, though he recognizes the urgent need, sees that long-term, urgency is not important. Stated differently, the liberal always wants to eat up the seed corn now. The conservative sees that long-term survivability is only guaranteed by holding the seed corn in reserve for spring planting.

Is there an equitable solution to this conflict? Surely. A transitional bridge is needed whereby the **urgent** is satisfied near term, with only minimal damage to the **important** long-term. Put simply, some of the seed corn is eaten, but not nearly all of it. By and large, the unending programs, the programs of income distribution (aid to dependent chil-dren, unemployment benefits, foreign aid, veteran benefits), the actions of government agencies (OSHA, EPA, the Department of Education, the Department of Energy) are reactions to a sense of urgency. To ensure the preservation of the important, at the time these programs are enacted, there needs to be a date set for their termination. In this way, the long-term perspective, which in all areas of life is the most healthy and progressive, maintains priority in our society. Otherwise, the tyranny of the urgent destroys the important.

The second problem with conservatives is that they do not consistently argue against big government. To be uniform, conservatives must ground themselves in the Constitution of the United States. The Constitution vested power in the people primarily, the states secondarily, and the federal government last of all. The federal government, to put it another way, is at the bottom of the governing totem pole. The Constitution is basically a negative document regarding the federal government. It limits what the federal government can do. It reserves rights and freedoms for the individual. It provides checks and balances in government. Unique in history, the Constitution of the United States established government as a servant of the people, rather than a sovereign over the people.

Conservatives correctly rail against all the income redistribution programs which are fomented at the federal level. All the social programs, all the alphabet agencies, all the departments of the federal government that lead to bigger, bureaucratic government, conservatives rightfully condemn. But, in contradiction, conservatives turn around and argue for big government when it comes to the areas of national defense and nuclear energy. Let's look at these two subjects separately.

Conservatives can rightfully state that the three legitimate purposes of government, as established by the Constitution, are protection against foreign enemies (invasion), maintenance of law and order domestically (putting down insurrection and riots), and ensuring justice (enforcing contracts). Conservatives, thus seeking defense against enemies, foreign and domestic, demand a big military budget. A military budget is fine, to the extent it does not spend tax money to send American munitions and troops overseas. This is imperialism. Imperialism is the course upon which the U.S. embarked at the turn of this century. It has resulted in an increasing number of wars, which in turn further concentrate power in the hands of the federal government. We have lost the constitutional concept of a militia, with local control of the military.

Until World War I, it was clearly understood, constitutionally, that all foreign military escapades were to be fought with volunteer troops. Volunteer troops were used for our military ventures into Cuba, the

Philippines and Mexico. Nearly 20,000 lawsuits were filed prior to World War I. Why? It was understood by the American people of that time that it was unconstitutional for American youth to be forced to fight on foreign soil. Conservatives should recognize this limited government principle as they insist upon a strong military. Tax receipts should be spent solely for the protection of American territory. All foreign ventures must be fought exclusively with volunteer troops. As Eisenhower warned, the incestuous military/industrial complex, with its corruption, waste, and evil (Permindex) must be reformed. It is an unholy sacred cow. It has led to the power of the American flag-waving gun, supporting the investment of the multinational *"buck"* abroad.

It goes without saying that goverment welfare payments to domestic businesses (Chrysler) is fascism. So-called *"conservatives,"* who call for this type of redistribution, are wolves in sheeps' clothing.

The call for federally-controlled nuclear energy is just as egregious a mistake. Just as the control of money and the control of land has historically been the primary means of controlling people, so today, in our sophisticated, technological society, is control of energy a key way to control people. As nuclear energy, (perhaps, in the future, solar energy) may be the key to the harmonious continuation of our civilization, do we really want to assign control of such critical technology to the federal government? Control of energy today is the control of people. (The budget of the Department of Energy is greater than all oil company profits.) Decentralized electrical generating plants and decentralized locally controlled nuclear power facilities prevent power from accruing at the federal level (if nuclear power is desirable).

Along this same line, let's chase a rabbit, momentarily. It was mentioned above that the control of land has historically been a primary means of controlling people. The states, through their legislatures, should declare that the federal government, which was formed by the states, no longer has the right to, or ownership of, any land within the boundaries of that particular state. With such actions, all federal lands would be returned to state ownership immediately. The states would then have the means of raising their own funds. Federal land planning should be stopped cold. (The federal government presently owns one-third of the land in the United States. This is equivalent to all of the land east of the Mississippi, plus Louisiana and Texas.) This land action must be taken through the state legislatures because the courts in this country, by law now, must hold the United Nations Charter to be supreme, not the Constitution. In 1964, the Senate of the United States declared that the Charter of the United Nations was the supreme law of the land, over and above our Constitution. That is why state legislative action is so critical. The courts must be isolated, left out in the cold, particularly until juries again make the law.

Another rabbit. With the power to tax being the power to destroy, the progressive income tax must be repealed. In its place, a *"head"* or *"flat"* or *"national sales"* tax should be established. Why? First of all, such taxes restore the power to collect taxes at the local level where true power should lie. Secondly, with such taxes people will painfully realize just exactly how much they are being taxed. In the case of a national sales tax, they will pay through the nose when they buy any finished goods or services. This will result in immediate public interest in the level of taxation. Government's size will be reduced. People will demand it. Thirdly, such taxes discourage consumption and encourage long-term savings. This makes available capital for the construction of plants and production of machinery. This, in turn, increases the number of jobs and ultimately the goods and services available to the people for consumption. The fourth positive point is that such taxes are fair. People are taxed equally, or for just what they consume, nothing more. Finally, such taxes abolish the IRS Gestapo and turn all the *"make-work"* accountants and attorneys, who are specialists in non-productive tax law, out to pasture. They will once again be afforded the opportunity to seek gainful employment.

The final mistake conservatives make is in their failure to recognize that the health, education and welfare needs of a society will always be met. The only question is, *"Where and how will they be met?"* Governments always fill the vacuum of irresponsibility. When conservatives are selfish, when conservatives hoard their money and fail to meet their social and civic responsibilities commensurate with their economic standing in the community, government will come in and fill that vacuum. Freedom is commensurate with responsibility. Conservatives, on the local and state level, must work to establish substitute programs that meet the health, education and welfare needs of their community. Once this is done, expensive, over-staffed, and inefficient federal "HEW" programs can and will be abolished.

It is well established that the real beneficiaries of all federal government wealth transfer programs are the bureaucrats and those **who control the bureaucrats.** The poor don't get the goods. The bureaucracy chews up the gingerbread man.

The conservatives must return the HEW issue to where the issue belongs—the local and state level. Until conservatives take the initiative, become less selfish and greedy, in terms of both time and money, and assume their responsibilities commensurate with their elevated economic and resultant political status, our society will continue to suffer a loss of freedom. Freedom is only commensurate with responsibility.

Conservatives talk a lot. The love to complain about big government. They criticize the silent majority with the phrase, *"Silence is not golden; it is yellow."* But, words are cheap. Actions always speak louder than words. Conservatives must assume leadership responsibilities in all areas of life. Faith without works is dead!

WHY DEMOCRACY DOES NOT WORK

8/18/78

The more this writer reads concerning early American history, the more he holds the wisdom of our Founding Fathers in reverent respect. Our early leaders had a disdain, if not contempt, for democracy —the rule of the mob.

John Adams warned in 1815, *"Democracy has never been and never can be so desirable as aristocracy or monarchy, but while it lasts, is more bloody than either. Remember, democracy never lasts long. It soon wastes, exhausts, and murders itself. There was never a democracy that did not commit suicide."* Alexander Hamilton stated, *"We are a Republic. Real liberty is never found in despotism or in the extremes of democracy."* James Madison declared, *"Democracies have ever been spectacles of turbulence and contention; have ever been found incompatible with personal security, or the rights of property; and have been as short in their lives as they have been violent in their deaths."* John Marshall, a chief justice of the Supreme Court commented, *"Between a balanced Republic and a democracy, the difference is like that between order and chaos."*

Why is democracy never as desirable as aristocracy or monarchy? Why is real liberty never found in the extremes of democracy? Why are democracies spectacles of turbulence and contention, incompatible with personal security or the rights of property, and have had short lives and violent deaths? Why are democracies chaotic? Why are the answers to all these questions important? . . . . **Because we live in a democracy.** And, if history repeats, as it should given human nature as a constant, then understanding the *"whys"* will give us clues as to how far down this treacherous road we have traveled as a nation.

Democracies are dumb. That's right, plain dumb. The world's evolutionary economic and political arena is an arena of competition where the nations vie for limited resources in an effort to produce the most efficient goods and services. As in any competitive sphere, probabilities favor the victory going to those who are quick to recognize opportunity, smart enough to grasp the problem and develop a solution, and possessed of the energy and drive necessary to translate their insight into reality. This type of talent is not widely distributed, which is obvious from observations of science, of sporting contests, or of business ventures, e.g., Albert Einstein, Bill Walton, and Henry Ford. Also, it is obvious from observation of governments. Democracies necessarily encompass those who fall within the first standard deviation under the bell-shaped curve (if the curve is not in fact skewed to the left). Therefore, by law, the **most** intelligent thinking will be, at bare minimum, watered down by the *"masses."* Additionally, the nature of the democractic process is a slow one. So, it is likely that the slow, average thinking that results from the democractic process will not be the early bird, and will not get the worm. Probabilities for success favor instead, the talent monarch, enlightened aristocracy, or the republic.

Next, consider the nature of the democractic politician, the choice of the masses. People tend to choose one of their own (again, mediocrity), and tend to vote for their own self-interests. Therefore, the dominance of the politician instead of the statesman is the norm. (Statesmen appeal to standards, not short-term self-interest.) The politician, insecure, with a craving for power and approval from the masses, can never lead, but instead must follow. Why? The politician reacts to the *"will of the people."* This is just dandy, except for the fact that the masses are slow, emotional, and mediocre, and never recognize the problem until it is upon them, and often not until it has engulfed them. Then, they cry out. Then, the politician scrambles to put out the latest fire. Thus, the politician is in a continual state of *"crisis management."* He never **anticipates** the problem. He just **reacts** to the masses. He follows. He does not anticipate or plan. He only **reacts** to the leaky faucet after it has flooded his house. After all, it took weeks for the democratic process to agree that the problem was a leaky faucet, and another three weeks to decide how to solve the problem (cut off the water, or pull out the plumbing, or hire a plumber), and yet an additional three weeks of squabbling to determine who would get the plumbing contract. Yes, the plumber who put the *"john"* in the politician's house for free got the contract. Who else? After all, the *"majority,"* emotional in nature, can be easily manipulated.

Can one imagine such a process running a business, or attempting to buy or sell pork bellies, or for that matter, working efficiently and making a profit in any market? No way! Then, why should the process succeed in the political marketplace? Democracy is a turtle, at best. But unlike the children's tale, the turtle doesn't win any races because the rabbit doesn't take any naps. He leaves the dreaming for the turtle.

In short, democracies do not respond quickly or accurately to their environmental challenges. This is why they have short lives, are chaotic and are turbulent. Their susceptibility to political patronage makes contention inevitable.

The most dangerous aspect of all in democracy is the inevitable loss of liberty, and the loss of personal security and property rights, which leads eventually to its bloody and violent death. Democracy focuses upon the equality of man. After all, are not all men created equal? Doesn't one man have one vote? Aren't men and women equal?

Since the focus of democracy, then, is on equality, why not carry it to its logical extension? Equality of property rights. Redistribute property through the common, standard measure of property, which is money. Use a graduated income tax. Utilize inflation. Go the Robin Hood route. Take from the rich and give to the poor, by insidious and direct coercion. It's the will of the majority (democracy). Personal security and property rights thus die, not only because the unstable democractic process has the power to take them away, but also because it is logically an application the doctrine of equality, which is the doctrine of democracy. (Equality was formerly seen as legal, not economic.)

The next step? Who receives the proceeds of the redistribution of wealth? Listen to the hens cackle. Envy and greed take hold. Everyone wants his piece of the pie. Look at all the contention. Who is to say what is fair. We are all equal. We are all gods, as it were. We all have equal claim to the plunder. . . . Power and clout will ultimately decide. But, hold it! Power and clout are not supposed to be part of a democracy. Error, error, error. . . .

As the talented withdraw (ATLAS SHRUGGED), due to their inability to reap the fruits of their efforts, as they resign due to the frustration of over regulation, of being forced to deal with the mediocre, the redistributed pieces of pie become smaller. The doctrine of envy, which resulted from the doctrine of equality, now gives way to violence, as the *"I want my share"* attitude takes hold in a demonic circus of warped competition. The process of bloody suicide is under way. How sad! How tragic! But, oh how real. . . . And we, participants in the U.S. democracy, are in the center ring.

Our Founding Fathers understood there is no free lunch, which democracy not only tries to create, but also redistribute. Our leaders gave us the benefit of their wisdom in the Declaration of Independence and the Constitution. How clearly they saw the nature of man. How pitifully we have squandered our priceless heritage, our Republic, and our opportunity for *"Wealth for All."*

GOOD TO EVIL. . . . TO GOOD?

11/16/79

One of the great wits, thinkers, and cartoonists in this country is Jules Feiffer. His *"words and picture frames,"* in typical cartoon manner, say more than many books.

Back in 1975, Feiffer did a *"piece"* which progressively revealed how good men are corrupted. (Power corrupts. Absolute power corrupts absolutely!) Below is the copy, exactly as written by Jules Feiffer, on October 19, 1975. It was distributed by the Field Newspaper Syndicate:

> *"I awoke one morning knowing the truth. Knowing the truth led to inner peace. Inner peace lead to self-assurance. Self-assurance led to authority. Authority led to power. Power led to the thirst for more power. The thirst for more power led to compromise. Compromise led to selling out. Selling out led to riches beyond my wildest dreams. Riches beyond my wildest dreams led to enemies around every corner. Enemies around every corner led to sleepless nights. Sleepless nights led to not waking up any more knowing the truth."* [4]

In the last four years, this writer has read Feiffer's words innumerable times. In the above case, the thirst for power was the Achilles' heel which led to the downfall. It was the fatal character flaw. **It seems to be THE fatal character flaw among politicians in this country.**

The United States is a desert when it comes to leadership. There are no signs of hope on the horizon either. Self-interest no longer means service as a means to reaching one's goals. Self-interest has come to mean almost total selfishness. With the crises approaching—economic, military, political—the leadership void will be filled! The capability of those who now reside in positions of power is akin to that of a butcher in a garment factory. Their clumsy techniques make a consistent mess of things. Ineptitude is unfortunately coupled with lack of credibility.

Whomever *"he"* is who finally ends up with the reins of power will probably have them handed to him. He will be the lesser of many evils (politicians). It will be widely admitted that crisis decisions must be made immediately. Such preempts a democratic process.

It is unfortunate that there are so few men today who are willing to make tough decisions. This lack of character accelerates the day of judgment when these decisions will be made, by default, and result in a Caesar.

Where are our statesmen? Where are our true leaders? After we flounder through a few more incompetent ones, after the population-at-large has greatly suffered, we will be ready for a true Caesar. Remember, Caesar will be **loved** by the people.

What must Caesar be like in order to be loved? He will probably come out of the masses. He will therefore **not** be identified with the political bungling on this side of the next great war and depression. He will be untainted.

He will probably be uplifted by the masses and placed in the position of power against his will. After the massive amount of power abuse that the people have endured during the first 80 years of the 20th Century, they will only trust someone who has no power lust. Also, he will not be motivated by money. He will not be for sale.

He will undoubtedly be an intellectual leader, an avant-garde thinker, who will inspire the masses. At the same time, he will lead by example. He will, therefore, provide a blanket for the people. He will be out front intellectually and inspirationally; he will lead from behind in the sense that he will be a servant of the people. He will be like a river which naturally assimilates all the streams which flow into it.

He will probably be a religious leader. The masses will have learned the hard way that there can never be ethical separation of church and state.

In summary, Caesar will most probably be a common man, who is able to identify with the masses. His strength, power, and public support will come from the fact that he does not desire power, prestige or money. He will not need *"people"* to support his ego. He will be able to give, to truly serve. He will, at the same time, be a loner. He will be able to make tough decisions based on principles. No other individual will be able to sustain the credibility of the then-enlightened masses.

He will not be proud. He will know that wisdom comes from the counsel of many. He will not let his ego interfere with the evidence that supports the national interest.

He will know the truth. The truth will lead to inner peace. Inner peace will lead to self-assurance. Self-assurance will lead to authority. Authority will lead to power. But, the Caesar who rules this country, who is loved by the people, will be able to handle power, for he will recognize his own weaknesses, his own humanity. He will be a good man, for all it takes is one good man to stop the march of evil.

Power and Authority
11/16/79

(Source: LIBERTY Magazine, Sept./Oct., 1979. Article by Haven B. Gow, pg. 23.)

POWER

"In his book POWER, Adolph Berle discussed what he believed are five laws of power: (1) Power invariably fills any vacuum in human organization; (2) power is invariably personal; (3) power is invariably based on a system of ideas or philosophy; (4) power is exercised through and depends on institutions; (5) power is invariably confronted with, and acts in the presence of, a field of responsibility.

"Power, in other words, is the capability of accomplishing something; it means control over others; it can mean, but does not necessarily imply, the legal ability to do or accomplish something."

AUTHORITY

"Authority, on the other hand, involves the moral right (and sometimes, too, the legal right) to settle issues or disputes; it means the right to control, command, or determine. Authority . . . is natural: that is, it emanates from the demand of man's nature. Human beings require and desire authority, even as they desire and demand friendship, love, family. Any human group, organization, or institution demands authority. . . .

". . . any tolerable social order demands a delicate balance between freedom and authority, for authority helps to teach man self-control and keeps human beings from committing mayhem against their neighbors.

"A harmful breakdown of authority in one area of life almost inevitably leads to erosion of authority in other areas, as well."

Statesmen
11/16/79

"The great difference between the real statesman and the pretender is that the one sees into the future, while the other regards only the present; the one lives by the day, and acts on expediency; the other acts on enduring principles and for immortality." Edmund Burke

Caesar: on Schedule
1/23/78

This writer recalls the ridicule he received while instructing at the U.S. Air Force Academy (early 1970s), when he proposed that the timing for a U.S. Caesar would be in the 1980s. This projection has not changed one bit. Dr. Hans Sennholz, Professor of Economics at Grove City College, Pennsylvania, confirms my analysis. Dr. Sennholz was a German fighter pilot in Hitler's Air Force in World War II.

There are three reasons why Caesar is a likelihood:

1. Times of great change do not allow for democratic processes. We are on the threshold of cataclysmic changes. Caesar will be a necessity. Witness how the President and the Congress are accomplishing absolutely nothing. In a crisis, one man must make fast decisions. Plato recognized this principle of government, and longshoreman philosopher, Eric Hoffer, has reiterated it as one of his greatest concerns.

2. The state (government) is failing badly in its role as God. Men will take it upon themselves to play God as things unravel (anarchy). But, anarchy never lasts long and will be replaced by a Caesar.

3. Our nation has become a nation of cowards who seek security under the leaky umbrella of government. We refuse to say *"no"* to special interest groups who trample our rights. We refuse to rebuke an aggressive individual who breaks in line and who exhibits his courage vicariously through such events as football games. Cowards fall in line behind the protective skirts of a Caesar.

The Reflection in the Mirror
9/21/78

The early 1980s are predicted to be troublesome times for this country on a social, political, economic and climatological basis. Which one of our leaders will then make the following remarks which will, in turn, draw the public to him:

> *"The streets of our country are in turmoil . . . Communists are seeking to destroy our country. Russia is threatening us with her might and the Republic is in danger.*

> *"Yes, danger from within and from without. We need law and order. Without law and order our Nation cannot survive.*

> *"Elect us and we shall restore law and order. Without law and order our Republic will fail."*

Who shall utter these words? A charismatic George Wallace? Well, all we know to give us a clue is the identity of the person who spoke them in the first place. That individual is . . . Adolph Hitler, 1932.

STRAWS IN THE WIND

4/25/80

This writer is increasingly coming to the unpleasant conclusion that the U.S. government is about to clamp down hard on its citizens' freedom. Those in power, who have controlled for so long, have undoubtedly seen the handwriting on the wall. The days of expanding government power, with behind the scenes multinational manipulation, is coming to a close. Stated differently, the jig is up. But power is never relinquished easily. If there is to be a power play, a move for total control by the federal government over U.S. citizens, it must come soon. The threat of an increasingly independent citizenry is contrary to the self-interest of the power brokers.

The signs of the build-up for a coming power play are:

1. Preparation of the country for war. War always concentrates power in the hands of the federal government. No administration has ever been voted out of office in time of war. A small limited war with Iran, for example, would benefit the administration nicely.

2. A severe recession/depression. In such an event, the outcry from government workers and the unenlightened, unemployed masses will be for government to *"do something."* The U.S. government will naturally respond with more controls and regulations, with a resultant loss of individual freedom. We are seeing this now in the housing industry.

3. The created energy shortage (thesis) resulted in the call for the government to *"do something"* (antithesis). The solution was the creation of the Department of Energy (synthesis). The control of energy today is control of people.

4. Public schools are/have been producing illiterates who, due to their illiteracy, cannot question or think through government statements or policy. The illiterates are a problem (thesis). The public has therefore demanded better education (antithesis). The solution is the Department of Education (synthesis). Therefore, further indoctrination in the humanistic philosophy of the federal government is bound to accelerate with the establishment of the Department of Education. Christian and free schools will be under greater attack.

5. Judges appointed at the federal level are increasingly alien to

136

those over whom they preside. Appointed judges remove the ultimate control of the judicial system from the people. These appointed judges can effectively *"wash out"* decisions made by juries at a lower judicial level. Without jury decisions being final, the people no longer make the law or have the final say.

6. Congress only legislates approximately 400 laws per year. The Federal Register includes 66,000 pages of law. These laws, if not challenged within 30 days, become the law of the land. The bureaucrats, who establish them, are accountable to no one. The agency-created laws circumvent historic constitutional checks and balances.

7. Federal revenue sharing puts state and local governments at the mercy (under the thumb) of federal government proclamations.

8. Regionalism (ten federal districts), which administers federal agency law, results in the ability to exercise total control over the population during a national emergency.

9. Executive Orders are on the books which effectively establish a dictatorship. It is not difficult to imagine a threatening situation in today's unstable world that is perceived as a national emergency. A declaration of national emergency would be all the excuse needed to implement all the in-place federal measures for total control.

10. The recently passed banking act (Monetary Control Act) brings all banks under control of the Federal Reserve. Thus, legislation is in place to control all financial and economic freedom at the federal level. The new banking bill allows the Comptroller of the Currency to impose selective banking holidays, city by city, state by state, without the prior approval of Congress.

11. HR-5961 seeks to limit the amount of money an individual can take out of the United States. It restricts freedom of movement, because it restricts the movement of assets which are necessary for free travel.

12. Debt has weakened the economic strength of the people. What debt service doesn't sop up, inflation and taxes do. People are vulnerable economically to federal control. Taxes are up 63 percent since 1974. Payments to individuals now account for 50 percent of the total federal budget. The rise in payments to individuals since the mid-1960s accounts for 93 percent of the total rise in federal spending that has occurred. Is such theft wrong?

13. The government has increasingly regulated major industries: steel, automobile, and now oil. Meanwhile, small businesses are being bankrupted and taken over by multinationals. The small business failures are due to heavy debt and sharply declining economic activity triggered by high interest rates.

14. The federal government owns the equivalent of all the land east

of the Mississippi, plus Texas and Louisiana. And, the great federal land grab continues. Interior Secretary, Cecil Andrus, seized 40 million acres of Alaskan land when the Senate did not approve a land bill. The Central Idaho Wilderness Act has passed the Senate and is now in the House. It places 2.3 million acres in a government-protected wilderness area which happens to be the richest known source area for cobalt in the United States. Cobalt is in short supply.

15. The progression of human action in a civilization is from bondage, to spiritual faith, to great courage, to liberty, to abundance, to complacency, to apathy, to dependence, to decadence, and then back to bondage. We are somewhere in the dependence/decadence category. It is during these times when government seizes power and dictatorships are established.

16. Our civilization is 200 years old. The average age of a civilization is 200 years.

17. The average household views 7 hours and 22 minutes of TV daily. The general public is thus well-conditioned and susceptible to the *"logic"* of a political power play that is sold over the boob tube. Media organizations are in place to parrot the establishment line. The *"in house"* media organizations that are represented on the Council on Foreign Relations are: NBC, CBS, TIME, FORTUNE, NEWS-WEEK, NEW YORK TIMES, WASHINGTON POST, LOS ANGELES TIMES, NEW YORK POST, DENVER POST, LOUISVILLE COURIER JOURNAL, MINNEAPOLIS TRIBUNE, THE KNIGHT NEWSPAPERS, MCGRAW-HILL, SIMON AND SHUSTER, HARPER BROTHERS, RANDOM HOUSE, LITTLE BROWN AND CO., VIKING PRESS, COWLES PUBLISHING and THE SATURDAY REVIEW. . . .

One of the recurring things I've noticed as I get older is that while the players, the environment, and the level of sophistication changes, the games remain the same. There were the little *"social cliques"* in elementary school. The *"social set"* existed in junior high school. An *"elite"* (football players and their girl friends) ran the high school. The fraternity/sorority power bloc ruled at the university level. Different folks in different situations, all playing the same games. It seems there is always a money/power/social status club that runs things. The more things change, the more they remain the same. Just take a look at a local neighborhood club, church, or business organization. Why should things be any different in big business/politics? Is it too far-fetched to believe in a national *"Super Club"*?

Beyond a doubt, one of the most damning pieces of evidence to support the idea of collusion between multinational corporations, banks, and the U.S. government (the Super Club) is published by the Fund to Restore an Educated Electorate (F.R.E.E.), Box 8616, Waco, Texas 76710, John Stewart, Director. The organizational charts which are reproduced here are approximately 25 percent of the work accomplished by F.R.E.E.

Study these organizational charts carefully. What is the probability of all these men and women coming to power **coincidentally**—all members of the Council on Foreign Relations and the Trilateral Commission? . . . ZERO! Clearly, the mechanism is in place to accomplish what governments have always done best historically—**rule absolutely!** Perhaps I am just grasping at straws in the wind. But these straws seem to indicate that unless the American public stands up to defend its constitutional freedoms, the days of liberty will be numbered, and *"Wealth for All"* will be a dead dream.

IRREFUTABLE EVIDENCE OF C.F.R./TRILATERA

Influence or Control of Money, Mail, Media, Military, IRS/Tax Courts, Commerce, Energy, Unions, Domestic and Foreign Policy, etc. Provides an Apparent Opportunity for Massive Fraud, Robbery, and Control of the American People!

10% (190) of 1,948 CFR members are journalists, correspondents and communications execuitves.

DAVID RO
CHAIRM

COUNCIL ON FO
58 E. 68th St.,
Phone (2

MEDIA
Past & Present CFR/TC Members (partial listing)
(Brought up to date — 1982)

CBS
William Paley	CFR
William Burden	CFR
Roswell Gilpatric	CFR
James Houghton	CFR
Henry Schacht	CFR TC
Marietta Tree	CFR
C.C. Collingwood	CFR
Lawrence LeSueur	CFR
Dan Rather	CFR
Harry Reasoner	CFR
Richard Hottelet	CFR
Frank Stanton	CFR
Bill Moyer	CFR

NBC/RCA
Jane Pfeiffer	CFR
Lester Crystal	CFR
R.W. Sonnenfeldt	CFR
T.F. Bradshaw	CFR
John Petty	CFR
David Brinkley	CFR
John Chancellor	CFR
Marvin Kalb	CFR
Irvine Levine	CFR
H. Schlosser	CFR
P.G. Peterson	CFR TC
John Sawhill	CFR TC

ABC
Ray Adam	CFR
Frank Cary	CFR
John Connor	CFR
T.M. Macioce	CFR
Ted Koppel	CFR
John Scali	CFR
Barbara Walters	CFR

CABLE NEWS NETWORK
Daniel Schorr	CFR

PUBLIC BROADCAST SERVICE
Hartford Gunn	CFR
Robert McNeil	CFR
Jim Lehrer	CFR
C. Hunter-Gault	CFR
Hodding Carter	CFR

ASSOCIATED PRESS
Keith Fuller	CFR
Stanley Swinton	CFR
Louis Boccardi	CFR
Harold Anderson	CFR
Katharine Graham	CFR

U.P.I.
H.L. Stevenson	CFR

REUTERS
Michael Posner	CFR

BOSTON GLOBE
David Rogers	CFR

L.A. TIMES SYNDICATE
Joseph Kraft	CFR TC

BALTIMORE SUN
Henry Trewhitt	CFR

NEW YORK TIMES CO.
Richard Gelb	CFR
James Reston	CFR
William Scranton	CFR TC
A.M. Rosenthal	CFR
Seymour Topping	CFR
James Greenfield	CFR
Max Frankel	CFR
Jack Rosenthal	CFR
Harding Bancroft	CFR
Amory Bradford	CFR
Orvil Dryfoos	CFR
David Halberstram	CFR
Walter Lippmann	CFR
L.E. Markel	CFR
H.L. Matthews	CFR
John Oakes	CFR
Adolph Ochs	CFR
Harrison Salisbury	CFR
A. Hays Sulzberger	CFR
A. Ochs Sulzberger	CFR
C.L. Sulzberger	CFR
H.L. Smith	CFR
Steven Rattner	CFR
Richard Burt	CFR

TIME INC.
Ralph Davidson	CFR
Donald M. Wilson	CFR
Louis Banks	CFR
Henry Grunwald	CFR
Alexander Heard	CFR
Sol Linowitz	CFR TC
Rawleigh Warner, Jr.	CFR
Thomas Watson, Jr.	CFR

NEWSWEEK/WASH. POST
Katharine Graham	CFR
Philip Graham	CFR
Arjay Miller	TC
N. deB. Katzenbach	CFR
Frederick Beebe	CFR
Robert Christopher	CFR
A. De Borchgrave	CFR
Osborne Elliot	CFR
Phillip Geyelin	CFR
Kermit Lausner	CFR
Murry Marder	CFR
Eugene Meyer	CFR
Malcolm Muir	CFR
Maynard Parker	CFR
George Will	CFR
Robert Kaiser	CFR
Meg Greenfield	CFR
Walter Pincus	CFR
Murray Gart	CFR
Peter Osnos	CFR
Don Oberdorfer	CFR

DOW JONES & CO.
(Wall Street Journal)
William Agee	CFR
J. Paul Austin	TC
Charles Meyer	CFR
Robert Potter	CFR
Richard Wood	CFR
Robert Bartley	CFR
Karen House	CFR

NATIONAL REVIEW
Wm. F. Buckley, Jr.	CFR
Richard Brookhiser	CFR

ROBERT McNAMARA
CFR
Hollis Chenery — CFR
Edward Fried — CFR
Ernest Stern — CFR
INTERNATIONAL BANK FOR RECONSTRUCTION & DEVELOPMENT

ROBERT McNAMARA
CFR
Richard Richardson — CFR
INTERNATIONAL FINANCE CORPORATION

ABBOTT WASHBURN
CFR
FEDERAL COMMUNICATIONS COMMISSION

ROBERT McNAMARA
CFR
WORLD BANK

ANNE WEXLER
CFR
ASSISTANT TO THE PRESIDENT

HENRY KISSINGER
CFR **TC**
ADVISOR

FEDERAL RESERVE
G. William Miller	CFR
Paul Volcker	CFR TC
Anthony Solomon	CFR TC
Henry Wallich	CFR
Emmet Rice	CFR
Henry Woodbridge, Jr.	CFR
Donald Platten	CFR
Robert Knight, Esq.	CFR
Steven Muller	CFR
Gerald Hines	CFR
Geo. H. Weyerhaeuser	CFR TC
Harold Anderson	CFR
Mark H. Willes	CFR

NORTH AMERIC

TRILATERAL
345 E. 46th St.,
Phone (2

James Earl
(Charter member,
Selecte
The TRILATERAL
Trained for the Pre

INTERNATIONAL BROADCASTING AND COMMUNICATIONS
Olin Robison	CFR
John Reinhardt	CFR
Charles Bray	CFR
R. Peter Straus	CFR
Rita Hauser	CFR
Glen Ferguson	CFR
Alice Ilchman	CFR

NATIONAL SEC

BRZEZINSKI	MONDALE	VANCE
CFR **TC**	**CFR** **TC**	**CFR** **TC**
NATIONAL SECURITY ADVISOR	VICE PRESIDENT	SECRETARY OF STATE Replaced by Edmund Muskie CFR

T.TANNENWALD, Jr.	JOHN SAWHILL	J. C/
CFR	**CFR** **TC**	**CFR**
U.S. TAX COURT	DEPT. OF ENERGY John Deutch CFR	Rep Patricia Albert HE\

EMERGENCY COURT OF APPEALS
Dudley Bonsal — CFR

INTERNATIONAL COURT OF JUSTICE
Richard R. Baxter — CFR

OFFICE OF MANAGEMENT AND BUDGET
Peter Szanton — CFR

OFFICE O
Ernest Boye
Peter D. Bel
Joseph Cali
Joel Cohen

PLEASE NOTE

The "NEW WORLD ORDER" views of Rockefelle are not shared by all members. Some join for pre dow dressing". All Americans should closely exa mulated and implemented by the CFR through

	CFR MEMBERSHIP BREAKDOWN (1978-1979)	
Scholars & Educators	370	(19%)
Business	555	(28%)
Lawyers	190	(10%)
Government	292	(15%)
Non-Profit Organizations	272	(14%)

CONGRESSIONAL RESEARCH LIBRARY
Ann L. Hollick	CFR

CONGRESSIONAL COMMITTEES
William B. Bader	CFR
William J. Barnds	CFR
Pauline R. Baker	CFR
William G. Miller	CFR

1980 PRESIDENTIAL CANDIDATES
(It is standard practice for members to resign before running for public office.)
John Anderson	CFR TC
Howard Baker	CFR
George Bush	CFR TC
Jimmy Carter	TC
Ted Kennedy (Boston Affiliate)	CFR

DEPARTMENT O

Cyrus Vance (Sec.)	CFR TC
Edmund Muskie (Sec.)	CFR
Warren Christopher	CFR TC
Harry G. Barnes, Jr.	CFR
(Director, Foreign Service)	
Douglas J. Bennet	CFR
(Congressional Relations)	
Lucy Wilson Benson	CFR TC
Priscilla A. Clapp	CFR
Stephen F. Cohen	CFR
(Human Rights)	
Richard N. Cooper	CFR TC
(Economic Affairs)	
Mark B. Feldman (Legal)	CFR
Leslie H. Gelb	CFR
(Politico-Military)	
David Gompert	CFR
Robert D. Hormats	CFR
(Economic-Business)	
Jerome H. Kahn	CFR
(Deputy Director)	
Paul H. Kreisberg	CFR
(Policy Planning)	
W. Anthony Lake	CFR
(Policy Planning)	
Karin Lissakers	CFR
(Policy Planning)	
David E. Mark	CFR
(Intelligence-Research)	
Edward Morse	CFR
David D. Newsom	CFR
(Board of Foreign Service)	
Matthew Nimetz (Legal)	CFR
Robert H. Nooter	CFR
(International development)	
Stephen A. Oxman	CFR
E. Raymond Platig	CFR
(Intelligence-Research)	
Ben H. Read (Management)	CFR
Stephen M. Schwebel (Legal)	CFR
Marshall D. shulman	CFR
(Soviet Affairs)	
Paul Warnke (Salt)	CFR
R.E. Earl, II (Salt)	CFR

AMBASSADORS
Andrew Young (UN)	CFR
Donald F. McHenry (UN)	CFR
James F. Leonard (UN)	CFR
Richard R. Baxter (UN)	CFR
Roger J. Cochetti (UN)	CFR
W. Tapley Bennett, Jr. (NATO)	CFR
Morton I. Abramowitz	CFR
(Thailand)	
Richard Bloomfield (Portugal)	CFR
Kingman Brewster, Jr.	CFR
(Britain/Northern Ireland)	
Walter L. Cutler (Zaire)	CFR
Arthur R. Day (Jerusalem)	CFR
Lawrence Eagleburger	CFR
(Yugoslavia)	
Donald B. Easum (Nigeria)	CFR
Hermann F. Eilts (Egypt)	CFR
Thomas O. Enders (Canada)	CFR
Richard N. Gardner (Italy)	CFR
Raymond L. Garthoff	CFR
(Bulgaria)	
Robert F. Goheen (India)	CFR
Arthur A. Hartman (France)	CFR
Ulric St. Clair Haynes, Jr.	CFR
(Algeria)	
Philip M. Kaiser (Hungary)	CFR
Samuel W. Lewis (Israel)	CFR
Stephen Low (Zambia)	CFR
James G. Lowenstein	CFR
(Luxembourg)	
William H. Luers (Venezuela)	CFR
Warren D. Manshel (Denmark)	CFR
Rozanne L. Ridgway (Finland)	CFR
William E. Schaufele, Jr.	CFR
(Poland)	
James W. Spain (Tanzania)	CFR
Ronald I. Spiers (Turkey)	CFR
Walter J. Stoessel, Jr.	CFR
(Germany)	
William H. Sullivan (Iran)	CFR
Terence A. Todman (Spain)	CFR
Milton A. Wolf (Austria)	CFR
W. Howard Wriggins	CFR
(Maldives and Sri Lanka)	

HOUSE & SENATE CFR/TC MEMBERS
(Past & Present)

SENATE
● Howard Baker	(Tenn.)	CFR
● Birch Bayh	(Ind.)	CFR
● Lloyd Bentsen	(Tex.)	CFR
● William Brock	(Tenn.)	CFR TC*
● Edward Brooke	(Mass.)	CFR
● Clifford Case	(N.J.)	CFR
● Frank Church	(Idaho)	CFR
● Dick Clark	(Iowa)	CFR
William S. Cohen	(Maine)	CFR TC
● Alan Cranston	(Calif.)	TC
John Cooper	(Ken.)	CFR
● John Culver	(Iowa)	CFR TC
● John Danforth	(Mo.)	TC
● John Glenn	(Ohio)	TC
H.H. Humphrey	(Minn.)	CFR
● Jacob Javits	(N.Y.)	CFR
● Ted Kennedy	(Mass.)	CFR
(Belongs to Boston Affiliate)		
Gale McGee	(Wyo.)	CFR
● George McGovern	(S.D.)	CFR
● Charles Mathias	(Md.)	CFR

● Walter Mondale	(Minn.)	CFR
● Daniel Moynihan	(N.Y.)	CFR
● Edmund Muskie	(Ma.)	CFR
● Claiborne Pell	(R.I.)	CFR
● Abraham Ribicoff	(Conn.)	CFR
William Roth	(Del.)	CFR TC
● Paul Sarbanes	(Md.)	CFR
● Adlai Stevenson	(Ill.)	CFR
Stuart Symington	(Mo.)	CFR
Robert Taft, Jr.	(Ohio)	TC

HOUSE
● John Anderson	(Ill.)	CFR TC
● Les Aspin	(Wisc.)	CFR
● J.B. Bingham	(N.Y.)	CFR
● John Brademas	(Ind.)	CFR TC
● Barber Conable, Jr.	(N.Y.)	TC
● William R. Cotter	(Conn.)	CFR
● Dante Fascell	(Fla.)	CFR
● Thomas Foley	(Wash.)	TC
● Donald Fraser		CFR TC
● Stephen Solarz	(N.Y.)	CFR

*William Brock, Chrmn., Republican National Committee CFR TC
● Voted to transfer ownership of the American canal in Panama to a Marxist dictatorship.

COMMISSION CONTROL OF THE UNITED STATES

KEFELLER
OF THE
EIGN RELATIONS
York, NY 10021
734-0400

CHAIRMAN OF

OMMISSION
York, NY 10017
661-1180

nmy) Carter
teral Commission)
973 by
MISSION & CFR
ency by Brzezinski

RITY COUNCIL

TREASURY	
William Simon	CFR
Michael Blumenthal	CFR TC
C. Fred Bergsten	CFR TC
Anthony Solomon	CFR TC
Arnold Nachmanoff	CFR
Helen B. Junz	CFR
Richard Fisher	CFR
Roger Altman	CFR
John Heimann	CFR

Since 1920, fourteen (14) CFR members have served as Secretary of the Treasury.

CFR: Indicates past or present membership in the Council on Foreign Relations.

TC: Indicates past or present membership in the Trilateral Commission.

W.B. DALE	R.A. DUNGAN
CFR	**CFR**
INTERNATIONAL MONETARY FUND	INTER-AMERICAN DEVELOPMENT BANK

HEDLEY DONOVAN	LLOYD CUTLER	HENRY OWEN
CFR TC	**CFR TC**	**CFR TC**
SENIOR ADVISER TO THE PRESIDENT	COUNCIL TO THE PRESIDENT	SPECIAL REPRESENTATIVE OF THE PRESIDENT

H. BROWN	GEN. DAVID JONES	S. TURNER
CFR TC	**CFR**	**CFR**
SECRETARY OF DEFENSE	CHAIRMAN, JOINT CHIEFS OF STAFF	CENTRAL INTELLIGENCE AGENCY

ARMS CONTROL AND DISARMAMENT AGENCY	
S.M. Keeny, Jr.	CFR
A.S. Fisher	CFR
Adam Yarmolinsky	CFR
John Newhouse	CFR
Barry M. Blechman	CFR
Thomas Halsted	CFR
Thomas Watson, Jr.	CFR
Harold Agnew	CFR
McGeorge Bundy	CFR
Paul M. Doty, Jr.	CFR
Lane Kirkland	CFR TC
Wolfgang Panofsky	CFR
Jane Pfeiffer	CFR
Brent Schwcroft	CFR
William E. Jackson	CFR

ANO

R. TRAIN	FRANK CARLUCCI
TC	**CFR**
CFR TC	

by
is CFR
r CFR
HUD

Replaced by
Douglas Costle CFR
W. Drayton CFR

ENVIRONMENTAL PROTECTION AGENCY

CENTRAL INTELLIGENCE AGENCY

UCATION
CFR
CFR
CFR TC

JUSTICE DEPARTMENT	
Eric Richard	CFR
Ruth Glushien	CFR

LICENCES · PERMITS	
D. Michael Deutch	CFR

A.C.I.R.	
Bruce Babbitt	CFR TC
Governor of Arizona	

singer, Brzezinski and others in the CFR/TC "inner circle" e and to further their careers. Some are invited in for "win- the disastrous results of foreign and domestic policy for- ears without public knowledge.

STATE

Deane R. Hinton (Extraordinary/Plenipotentiary)	CFR
Alfred L. Atherton, Jr. (At Large)	CFR
Henry D. Owen (At Large)	CFR TC
Elliot L. Richardson (At Large)	CFR TC
Gerard C. Smith (At Large)	CFR TC
Herbert Salzman (USOECD)	CFR
Ellsworth Bunker (Panama Canal)	CFR
Sol Linowitz (Panama Canal)	CFR TC

*PLEASE NOTE: These CFR/TC members head State Department bureaus where dramatic shifts in American foreign policy appear to work against allies of the United States and in favor of revolutionary forces.

BUREAUS
INTER-AMERICAN AFFAIRS
(Cuba, Nicaragua, Panama, El Salvador)

*Viron P. Vasky, Bureau Head	CFR
*Luigi Einaudi, Policy Planning	CFR

AFRICAN AFFAIRS
(Rhodesia, South Africa, Angola)

*Richard M. Moose, Bureau Head	CFR
*Goler T. Butcher, Asst. Administrator	CFR

NEAR EASTERN/SOUTH ASIAN AFFAIRS
(Iran, Afghanistan)

*Harold H. Saunders, Bureau Head	CFR

EAST ASIAN & PACIFIC AFFAIRS
(Taiwan, Korea, Vietnam, Cambodia, Laos, Thailand)

*Richard Holbrooke, Bureau Head	CFR TC

EUROPEAN AFFAIRS

James E. Goodby, Deputy Assistant Secretary	CFR
Sandra L. Vogelgesang, Policy Planning	CFR

INTERNATIONAL ORGANIZATION AFFAIRS

C. William Maynes, Bureau Head	CFR
George Dalley, Deputy Assistant Secretary	CFR

OCEANS, INTERNATIONAL ENVIRONMENTAL & SCIENTIFIC AFFAIRS

Thomas R. Pickering, Bureau Head	CFR
John D. Negroponte, Deputy Asst. Secretary	CFR
William Sullivan	CFR

PUBLIC AFFAIRS

Hodding Carter, Bureau Head	CFR

PRESIDENTS COMMISSION ON THE COAL INDUSTRY	
John D. Rockefeller IV	CFR TC

COUNCIL ON WAGE AND PRICE STABILITY	
Michael Blumenthal	CFR TC
Juanita Kreps	CFR
Patricia Harris	CFR TC

EMPLOYMENT POLICY	
Harold Brown	CFR
Juanita Kreps	CFR
Joseph Califano	CFR TC

GENERAL MOTORS	
Reuben R. Jensen	CFR
Roger B. Smith	CFR
Marina v. N.Whitman	CFR TC

SMALL BUSINESS ADMINISTRATION	
Arthur P. Cyr	CFR

INTER AMERICAN FOUNDATION	
Peter Jones (Levi Strauss & Co.)	CFR
Charles Meyer (Sears Roebuck & Co.)	CFR

TRADE NEGOTIATIONS	
Richard Rivers	CFR
Robert Strauss	CFR
Alonzo McDonald	CFR

DEPT. OF COMMERCE	
Juanita Kreps	CFR

FOREIGN TRADE ZONES BOARD	
Juanita Kreps	CFR

PENSION BENEFIT GUARANTY CORP.	
Michael Blumenthal	CFR TC
Juanita Kreps	CFR

FORD MOTOR CO.	
Donald E. Petersen	CFR
Carter L. Burgess	CFR
Clifton Wharton, Jr.	TC
Philip Caldwell	TC
Arjay Miller	TC

UNION BOSSES

I.W. Abel (Former President, United Steelworkers of America)	TC
Sol Chick Chaikin (President. Int Ladies' Garment Workers)	CFR TC
Thomas R. Donahue (Secretary/Treasurer. AFL-CIO)	CFR TC
Murray H. Finley (President. Amalgamated Clothing & Textile Workers)	CFR
Victor Gotbaum (American Fed of State. County and Municipal Employees)	CFR
Lane Kirkland (Pres AFL-CIO)	CFR TC
Howard D. Samuel (President. Industrial Union Dept AFL-CIO)	CFR
Martin J. Ward (President. United Assn of Journeymen and Apprentices of the Plumbing and Pipe Fitting Industry, U.S.A & Canada)	CFR TC
Glenn E. Watts (President. Communications Workers of America)	CFR TC
Leonard Woodcock (Former President U A W.)	CFR TC
Jerry Wurf (President. American Federation of State. County and Municipal Employees)	CFR

Have Workers Been Sold Out to International Socialism, or Worse?

THE CARTER ADMINISTRATION

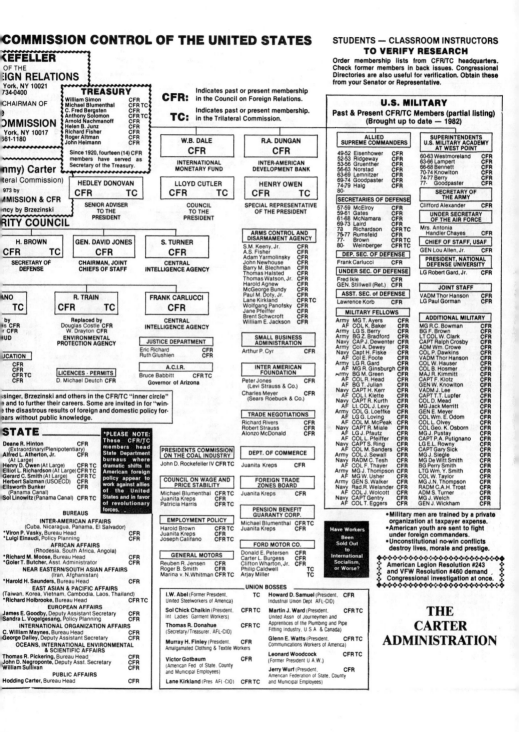

Who Is Responsible For:

Good Times — Bad Times

Influence or Control of Money, Mail, Media, Military, IRS/Tax Courts, Commerce, Energy, Unions, Domestic and Foreign Policy, etc. Provides an Apparent Opportunity for Massive Fraud, Robbery, and Control of the American People!

10% (216) of 2,164 CFR members are journalists, correspondents and communications executives.

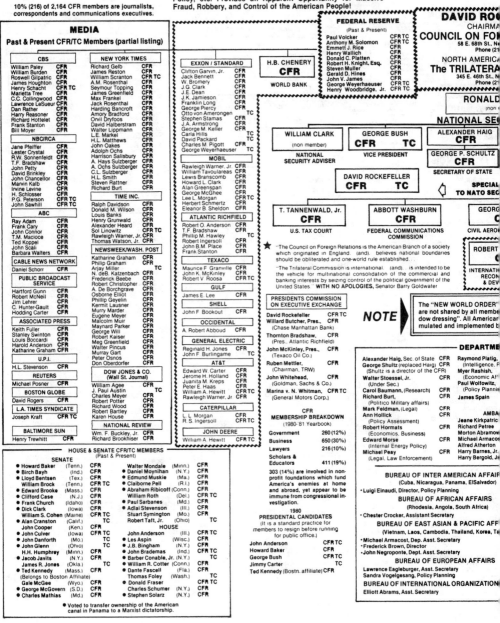

MEDIA

Past & Present CFR/TC Members (partial listing)

CBS
William Paley	CFR
William Burden	CFR
Roswell Gilpatric	CFR
James Houghton	CFR
Henry Schacht	CFR TC
Marietta Tree	CFR
C.C. Collingwood	CFR
Lawrence LeSueur	CFR
Dan Rather	CFR
Harry Reasoner	CFR
Richard Hottelet	CFR
Frank Stanton	CFR
Bill Moyer	CFR

NBC/RCA
Jane Pfeiffer	CFR
Lester Crystal	CFR
R.W. Sonnenfeldt	CFR
T.F. Bradshaw	CFR
John Petty	CFR
David Brinkley	CFR
John Chancellor	CFR
Marvin Kalb	CFR
Irvine Levine	CFR
H. Schlosser	CFR
P.G. Peterson	CFR
John Sawhill	CFR TC

ABC
Ray Adam	CFR
Frank Cary	CFR
John Connor	CFR
T.M. Macioce	CFR
Ted Koppel	CFR
John Scali	CFR
Barbara Walters	CFR

CABLE NEWS NETWORK
Daniel Schorr	CFR

PUBLIC BROADCAST SERVICE
Hartford Gunn	CFR
Robert McNeil	CFR
Jim Lehrer	CFR
C. Hunter-Gault	CFR
Hodding Carter	CFR

ASSOCIATED PRESS
Keith Fuller	CFR
Stanley Swinton	CFR
Louis Boccardi	CFR
Harold Anderson	CFR
Katharine Graham	CFR

U.P.I.
H.L. Stevenson	CFR

REUTERS
Michael Posner	CFR

BOSTON GLOBE
David Rogers	CFR

L.A. TIMES SYNDICATE
Joseph Kraft	CFR TC

BALTIMORE SUN
Henry Trewhitt	CFR

NEW YORK TIMES
Richard Gelb	CFR
James Reston	CFR
William Scranton	CFR TC
A.M. Rosenthal	CFR
Seymour Topping	CFR
James Greenfield	CFR
Max Frankel	CFR
Jack Rosenthal	CFR
Harding Bancroft	CFR
Amory Bradford	CFR
Orvil Dryfoos	CFR
David Halberstam	CFR
Walter Lippmann	CFR
L.E. Markel	CFR
H.L. Matthews	CFR
John Oakes	CFR
Adolph Ochs	CFR
Harrison Salisbury	CFR
A. Hays Sulzberger	CFR
A. Ochs Sulzberger	CFR
C.L. Sulzberger	CFR
H.L. Smith	CFR
Steven Rattner	CFR
Richard Burt	CFR

TIME INC.
Ralph Davidson	CFR
Donald M. Wilson	CFR
Louis Banks	CFR
Henry Grunwald	CFR
Alexander Heard	CFR
Sol Linowitz	CFR TC
Rawleigh Warner, Jr.	CFR
Thomas Watson, Jr.	CFR

NEWSWEEK/WASH. POST
Katharine Graham	CFR
Philip Graham	CFR
Arjay Miller	TC
N. deB. Katzenbach	CFR
Frederick Beebe	CFR
Robert Christopher	CFR
A. De Borchgrave	CFR
Osborne Elliot	CFR
Phillip Geyelin	CFR
Kermit Lausner	CFR
Murry Marder	CFR
Eugene Meyer	CFR
Malcolm Muir	CFR
Maynard Parker	CFR
George Will	CFR
Robert Kaiser	CFR
Meg Greenfield	CFR
Walter Pincus	CFR
Murray Gart	CFR
Peter Osnos	CFR
Don Oberdorfer	CFR

DOW JONES & CO.
(Wall St. Journal)
William Agee	CFR
J. Paul Austin	TC
Charles Meyer	CFR
Robert Potter	CFR
Richard Wood	CFR
Robert Bartley	CFR
Karen House	CFR

NATIONAL REVIEW
Wm. F. Buckley, Jr.	CFR
Richard Brookhiser	CFR

EXXON / STANDARD
Clifton Garvin, Jr.	CFR
Jack Bennett	CFR
J.G. Clark	CFR
J.E. Dean	CFR
J.K. Jamieson	CFR
Franklin Long	CFR
George Piercy	CFR
Otto von Amerongen	TC
Stephen Stamas	CFR
J.A. Armstrong	CFR
George M. Keller	CFR
Carla Hills	TC
David Packard	CFR
Charles M. Pigott	CFR
George Weyerhaeuser	TC

MOBIL
Rawleigh Warner, Jr.	CFR
William Tavoulareas	CFR
Lewis Branscomb	CFR
Howard L. Clark	CFR
Alan Greenspan	CFR
George McGhee	CFR
Lee L. Morgan	CFR
Herbert Schmertz	CFR
Eleanor B. Sheldon	CFR

ATLANTIC RICHFIELD
Robert O. Anderson	CFR
T.F. Bradshaw	CFR
Phillip M. Hawley	TC
Robert Ingersoll	CFR
John B.M. Place	CFR
Frank Stanton	CFR

TEXACO
Maurice F. Granville	CFR
John K. McKinley	CFR
Robert V. Roosa	CFR TC

GULF
James E. Lee	CFR

SHELL
John F. Bookout	CFR

OCCIDENTAL
A. Robert Abboud	CFR

GENERAL ELECTRIC
Reginald H. Jones	CFR
John F. Burlingame	TC

AT&T
Edward W. Carter	CFR
Jerome H. Holland	CFR
Juanita M. Kreps	CFR
Peter E. Haas	CFR
William A. Hewitt	CFR
Rawleigh Warner, Jr.	CFR

CATERPILLAR
L.L. Morgan	CFR
R.S. Ingersoll	CFR TC

JOHN DEERE
William A. Hewitt	CFR TC

H.B. CHENERY
CFR
WORLD BANK

FEDERAL RESERVE
(Past & Present)
Paul Volcker	CFR TC
Anthony M. Solomon	CFR TC
Emmett J. Rice	CFR
Henry Wallich	CFR
Donald C. Platten	CFR
Robert H. Knight, Esq.	CFR
Steven Muller	CFR
Gerald D. Hines	CFR
John V. James	CFR
George Weyerhaeuser	CFR TC
Henry Woodbridge, Jr.	CFR TC

DAVID RO[CKEFELLER]
CHAIRMA[N]
COUNCIL ON FO[REIGN]
58 E. 68th St., Ne[w]
Phone (21[)]

NORTH AMERIC[A]
The TRILATERA[L]
345 E. 46th St., N[ew]
Phone (2[)]

RONALD [REAGAN]
(non [member])

NATIONAL SEC[URITY]

WILLIAM CLARK	GEORGE BUSH	ALEXANDER HAIG
(non member)	**CFR TC**	**CFR**
NATIONAL SECURITY ADVISER	VICE PRESIDENT	GEORGE P. SCHULTZ **CFR**
		SECRETARY OF STATE

DAVID ROCKEFELLER
CFR   TC

SPECIAL [NEGOTIATOR]
TO NATO SEC[RETARY]

T. TANNENWALD, Jr.	ABBOTT WASHBURN	GEORG[E]
CFR	**CFR**	C[ ]
U.S. TAX COURT	FEDERAL COMMUNICATIONS COMMISSION	CIVIL AERO[NAUTICS]

ROBERT [ ]
C[ ]
INTERNATIO[NAL]
RECON[STRUCTION]
& DEV[ELOPMENT]

★ "The Council on Foreign Relations is the American Branch of a society which originated in England. (and). believes national boundaries should be obliterated and one-world rule established.."

"The Trilateral Commission is international. (and). is intended to be the vehicle for multinational consolidation of the commercial and banking interests by seizing control of the political government of the United States." **WITH NO APOLOGIES, Senator Barry Goldwater**

PRESIDENTS COMMISSION ON EXECUTIVE EXCHANGE
David Rockefeller	CFR TC
Willard Butcher, Pres., (Chase Manhattan Bank)	CFR
Thornton Bradshaw, (Pres.: Atlantic Richfield)	CFR
John McKinley, Pres., (Texaco Oil Co.)	CFR
Ruben Mettler, (Chairman, TRW)	CFR
John Whitehead, (Goldman, Sachs & Co.)	CFR
Marina v. N. Whitman, (General Motors Corp.)	CFR TC

NOTE ▶ The "NEW WORLD ORDER" [goals] are not shared by all membe[rs as a win-]dow dressing". All American [policy is for-] mulated and implemented b[y ...]

CFR MEMBERSHIP BREAKDOWN
(1980-81 Yearbook)
Government	260	(12%)
Business	650	(30%)
Lawyers	216	(10%)
Scholars & Educators	411	(19%)

303 (14%) are involved in non-profit foundations which fund America's enemies at home and abroad, yet appear to be immune from congressional investigation.

1980 PRESIDENTIAL CANDIDATES
(It is a standard practice for members to resign before running for public office.)
John Anderson	CFR TC
Howard Baker	CFR
George Bush	CFR TC
Jimmy Carter	TC
Ted Kennedy (Bostn. affiliate)	CFR

DEPARTME[NT]
Alexander Haig, Sec. of State	CFR	Raymond Platig,	
George Shultz (replaced Haig)	CFR	(Intelligence, R[ ])	
(Shultz is a director of the CFR)		Myer Rashish,	
Walter Stoessel, Jr.	CFR	(Economic Af[ ])	
(Under Sec.)		Paul Wolfowitz,	
Carol Baumann, (Research)	CFR	(Policy Plannin[g])	
Richard Burt,	CFR	James Spain	
(Politico Military affairs)			
Mark Feldman, (Legal)	CFR		
Ann Hollick	CFR	AMBA[SSADORS]	
(Policy Assessment)		Jeane Kirkpatric[k]	
Robert Hormats	CFR	Richard Petree	
(Economics, Business)		Morton Abramow[itz]	
Edward Morse	CFR	Michael Armacos[t]	
(Internal Energy Policy)		Alfred Atherton	
Michael Peay	CFR	Harry Barnes, Jr.[ ]	
(Legal, Law Enforcement)		Harry Bergold, J[r.]	

BUREAU OF INTER AMERICAN AFFAIR[S]
(Cuba, Nicaragua, Panama, ElSalvador)
• Luigi Einaudi, Director, Policy Planning

BUREAU OF AFRICAN AFFAIRS
(Rhodesia, Angola, South Africa)
• Chester Crocker, Assistant Secretary

BUREAU OF EAST ASIAN & PACIFIC AFF[AIRS]
(Vietnam, Laos, Cambodia, Thailand, Korea, Ta[iwan])
• Michael Armacost, Dep. Asst. Secretary
• Frederick Brown, Director
• John Negroponte, Dept. Asst. Secretary

BUREAU OF EUROPEAN AFFAIRS
Lawrence Eagleburger, Asst. Secretary
Sandra Vogelgesang, Policy Planning

BUREAU OF INTERNATIONAL ORGANIZATION[S]
Elliott Abrams, Asst. Secretary

HOUSE & SENATE CFR/TC MEMBERS
(Past & Present)

SENATE
● Howard Baker	(Tenn.)	CFR
● Birch Bayh	(Ind.)	CFR
● Lloyd Bentsen	(Tex.)	CFR
William Brock	(Tenn.)	CFR TC
● Edward Brooke	(Mass.)	CFR
● Clifford Case	(N.J.)	CFR
● Frank Church	(Idaho)	CFR
● Dick Clark	(Iowa)	CFR
William S. Cohen	(Maine)	CFR TC
● Alan Cranston	(Calif.)	TC
John Cooper	(Ken.)	CFR
● John Culver	(Iowa)	CFR TC
● John Danforth	(Mo.)	TC
● John Glenn	(Ohio)	TC
H.H. Humphrey	(Minn.)	CFR
● Jacob Javits	(N.Y.)	
James R. Jones	(Okla.)	TC
● Ted Kennedy	(Mass.)	CFR
(Belongs to Boston Affiliate)		
Gale McGee	(Wyo.)	CFR
● George McGovern	(S.D.)	CFR
● Charles Mathias	(Md.)	CFR

● Walter Mondale	(Minn.)	CFR
● Daniel Moynihan	(N.Y.)	CFR
● Edmund Muskie	(Ma.)	CFR
● Claiborne Pell	(R.I.)	CFR
● Abraham Ribicoff	(Conn.)	CFR
William Roth	(Del.)	CFR TC
● Paul Sarbanes	(Md.)	CFR
● Adlai Stevenson	(Ill.)	CFR
Stuart Symington	(Mo.)	CFR
Robert Taft, Jr.	(Ohio)	TC

HOUSE
John Anderson	(Ill.)	CFR TC
● Les Aspin	(Wisc.)	CFR
● J.B. Bingham	(N.Y.)	CFR
● John Brademas	(Ind.)	CFR TC
● William R. Cotter	(Conn.)	TC
● Dante Fascell	(Fla.)	CFR
Thomas Foley	(Wash.)	TC
● Donald Fraser		CFR TC
Charles Schumer	(N.Y.)	CFR
● Stephen Solarz	(N.Y.)	CFR

● Voted to transfer ownership of the American canal in Panama to a Marxist dictatorship.

To Whom Do Americans Owe Allegiance?

EFELLER
F THE
GN RELATIONS
rk, NY 10021
-0400

CHAIRMAN OF
COMMISSION
rk, NY 10017
-1180

EAGAN
er)

ITY COUNCIL

TREASURY
(Past & Present)

Donald Regan	CFR
John Heimann	CFR
C.D. Lord	CFR
William Simon	CFR
Michael Blumenthal	CFR TC
C. Fred Bergsten	CFR TC
Anthony M. Solomon	CFR TC
Arnold Nachmanoff	CFR
Helen B. Junz	CFR
Richard Fisher	CFR
Roger Altman	CFR

W.B. DALE
CFR
INTERNATIONAL
MONETARY FUND

CHASE MANHATTAN CORP.

David Rockefeller	CFR TC
Willard C. Butcher	CFR
William S. Ogden	CFR
Robert R. Douglass	CFR
John C. Haley	CFR
Charles F. Barber	CFR
J. R. Dilworth	CFR
Richard M. Furlaud	CFR
Theodore Hesburgh	CFR
Ralph Lazarus	CFR
Edmund T. Pratt, Jr.	CFR
S. Bruce Smart, Jr.	CFR
Wm. T. Coleman, Jr.	CFR TC
James I. Ferguson	CFR
Alexander Haig, Jr.	CFR
John D. Macomber	CFR
Leo Martinuzzi, Jr.	CFR
Franklin Williams	CFR
John D. Wilson	CFR

U.S. MILITARY
Past & Present CFR/TC Members (partial listing)

ALLIED
SUPREME COMMANDERS

49-52	Eisenhower	CFR
52-53	Ridgeway	CFR
53-56	Gruenther	CFR
56-63	Norstad	CFR
63-69	Lemnitzer	CFR
69-74	Goodpaster	CFR
74-79	Haig	CFR
80-		

SUPERINTENDENTS
U.S. MILITARY ACADEMY
AT WEST POINT

60-63	Westmoreland	CFR
63-66	Lampert	CFR
66-68	Bennett	CFR
70-74	Knowlton	CFR
74-77	Berry	CFR
77-	Goodpaster	CFR

SECRETARIES OF DEFENSE

57-59	McElroy	CFR
59-61	Gates	CFR
61-68	McNamara	CFR
69-73	Laird	CFR
73	Richardson	CFR TC
75-77	Rumsfeld	CFR
77-	Brown	CFR
80-	Weinberger	CFR TC

PRESIDENT, NATIONAL
DEFENSE UNIVERSITY

LG Robert Gard, Jr.	CFR

C. WEINBERGER
CFR TC
SECRETARY
OF DEFENSE

GEN. DAVID JONES
CFR
CHAIRMAN,
JOINT CHIEFS OF STAFF

WILLIAM CASEY
CFR
CENTRAL
INTELLIGENCE AGENCY

BANKERS TRUST CO.

Alfred Brittain, III	CFR
David O. Beim	CFR
Carlos Canal, Jr.	CFR
Richard L. Gelb	CFR
Calvin H. Plimpton	CFR
Patricia Stewart	CFR
John W. Brooks	CFR
Vernon Jordon, Jr.	CFR
Wm. Tavoulareas	CFR

DEP. SEC. OF DEFENSE

Frank Carlucci	CFR

UNDER SEC. OF DEFENSE

Fred Ikle	CFR
GEN. Stillwell (Ret.)	CFR

CHIEF OF STAFF, USAF

GEN Lou Allen, Jr.	CFR

SECRETARY OF THE NAVY

John Lehman, Jr.	CFR

VISERS
Y COUNCIL ▷

HENRY KISSINGER
CFR **TC**

ASST. SEC. OF DEFENSE

Lawrence Korb	CFR

JOINT STAFF

VADM Thor Hanson	CFR
LG Paul Gorman	CFR

ALLEY
k

JAMES DUFFY
CFR
POSTAL RATE COMM.

ADM. BOBBY INMAN
CFR
DEPUTY DIRECTOR
C.I.A.

MORGAN GUARANTY

Lewis T. Preston	CFR
Alex. Vagliano	CFR
Rimmer deVries	CFR
Jackson B. Gilbert	CFR
Ray C. Adam	CFR
Carter L. Burgess	CFR
Frank T. Cary	CFR
Emilio G. Collado	CFR
Alan Greenspan	CFR
Howard Johnson	CFR
James I. Ketelsen	CFR
Walter H. Page	CFR
Ellmore Patterson	CFR
J. Paul Austin	TC

MILITARY FELLOWS

Army	MG T. Ayers	CFR
AF	COL K. Baker	CFR
Army	LG S. Berry	CFR
Army	BG Z. Bradford	CFR
Navy	CAP J. Dewenter	CFR
Navy	Capt H. Fiske	CFR
AF	Col E. Foote	CFR
Army	LG R. Gard	CFR
AF	MG R. Ginsburgh	CFR
Army	BG M. Green	CFR
AF	COL R. Head	CFR
AF	BG T. Julian	CFR
Navy	CAPT H. Kerr	CFR
AF	COL I. Klette	CFR
Navy	CAPT R. Kurth	CFR
AF	Lt. COL J. Levy	CFR
Army	COL G. Loeffke	CFR
AF	LG G. Loving	CFR
AF	COL M. McPeak	CFR
Navy	CAPT R. Miale	CFR
AF	LG J. Pfautz	CFR
AF	COL L. Pfeiffer	CFR
Navy	CAPT S. Ring	CFR
AF	COL M. Sanders	CFR
Army	COL J. Sewall	CFR
Navy	RADM C. Tesh	CFR
AF	COL F. Thayer	CFR
Army	MG J. Thompson	CFR
AF	MG W. Usher	CFR
Army	GEN S. Walker	CFR
Navy	Rad.R. Welander	CFR
AF	COL J. Wolcott	CFR
Navy	CAPT Gentry	CFR
AF	COL T. Eggers	CFR

ADDITIONAL MILITARY

	MG R.C. Bowman	CFR
	BG F. Brown	CFR
	LT COL W. Clark	CFR
	CAPT Ralph Crosby	CFR
	ADM Wm. Crowe	CFR
	COL P. Dawkins	CFR
	VADM Thor Hanson	CFR
	COL W. Hauser	CFR
	COL B. Hosmer	CFR
	MAJ R. Kimmitt	CFR
	CAPT F. Klotz	CFR
	GEN W. Knowlton	CFR
	VADM J. Lee	CFR
	CAPT T.T. Lupfer	CFR
	COL D. Mead	CFR
	CAPT Gary Sick	CFR
	MG J. Siegle	CFR
	MG De Witt Smith	CFR
	BG Perry Smith	CFR
	LTG Wm. Y. Smith	CFR
	COL W. Taylor	CFR
	MG J.N. Thompson	CFR
	RADM C.A.H. Trost	CFR
	ADM S. Turner	CFR
	MG J. Welch	CFR
	GEN J. Wickham	CFR

Additional from the "ADDITIONAL MILITARY" column continued:
	GEN E. Meyer	CFR
	COL Wm. E. Odom	CFR
	COL L. Olvey	CFR
	COL Geo. K. Osborn	CFR
	MG J. Pustay	CFR
	CAPT P.A. Putignano	CFR
	LG E. L. Rowny	CFR
	MG Jack Merritt	CFR

AMARA

BRUCE BABBITT
CFR
ADV. COMMISSION ON
INTERGOVERNMENTAL RELATIONS
(GOVERNOR OF ARIZONA)

J.R. WEST
CFR
ASST. TO
SECRETARY OF
THE INTERIOR

BANK FOR
CTION
MENT

CHEMICAL BANK

Donald C. Platten	CFR
Charles Carson, Jr.	CFR
Richard LeBlond, II	CFR
Walter V. Shipley	CFR
Robert J. Callander	CFR
Frederick L. Deming	CFR

s of Rockefeller, Kissinger, Brzezinski and others in the CFR/TC "inner circle" ome join for prestige and to further their careers. Some are invited in for "win-uld closely examine the disastrous results of foreign and domestic policy for-CFR through the years without public knowledge.

OF STATE

	CFR	Richard Blomfield	(Portugal) CFR
ch)		Charles Bray, III	(Senegal) CFR
		Arthur Burns	(W. Germany) CFR
		Horace Dawson	(Botswana) CFR
	CFR	Angier Duke	(Morocco) CFR
		James E. Goodby	(Finland) CFR
	CFR	Arthur Hartman	(U.S.S.R.) CFR
		Deane Hinton	(El Salvador) CFR
		Samuel Lewis	(Israeli) CFR
		James Lowenstein	(Luxmbg.) CFR
ORS			
(U.N.)	CFR	William Luers	(Venezuela) CFR
(U.N.)	CFR	Ronald Palmer	(Malaysia) CFR
hailand)	CFR	Thomas Pickering	(Nigeria) CFR
illipines)	CFR	Maxwell Rabb	(Italy) CFR
(Egypt)	CFR	Ronald Spiers	(Pakistan) CFR
(India)	CFR	R. Strausz-Hupe	(Turkey) CFR
lungary)	CFR	Terence Todman	(Spain) CFR

TEXAS INSTRUMENTS

Mark Shepherd, Jr.	CFR TC
J. Fred Bucy, Jr.	CFR

CITIBANK

Walter B. Wriston	CFR
G.A. Costanzo	CFR
Hans Angermueller	CFR
George J. Vojta	CFR
Lief H. Olsen	CFR
Thomas Theobald	CFR

1st NATL. OF CHICAGO

Wm. McDonough	CFR
Robert S. Ingersoll	CFR TC
Brooks McCormick	CFR
Lee L. Morgan	CFR

MANUFACTURERS
HANOVER

Charles J. Pilliod, Jr.	CFR

ROBERT ANDERSON
CFR
DEPT. OF LABOR

William Brock, Jr. CFR TC
(Special Trade Rep.)
Eleanor Norton CFR
'Nat'l Comm. for
Employment Policy)

MALCOLM BALDRIGE
CFR
SEC. OF COMMERCE

CFR

• Military men are trained by a private organization at taxpayer expense.
• American youth are sent to fight under foreign commanders.
• Unconstitutional no-win conflicts destroy lives, morale and prestige.

American Legion Resolution #243 and VFW Resolution #460 demand Congressional investigation at once.

CHRYSLER

Jerome Holland	CFR
Najeeb Halaby	CFR
Tom Killefer	CFR
J. R. Dilworth	CFR
Gabriel Hauge	CFR

GENERAL MOTORS

Reuben R. Jensen	CFR
Roger B. Smith	CFR
Marina N. Whitman	CFR TC

Have Workers Been Sold Out to International Socialism, or Worse?

INTERNATIONAL

Andrew Brimmer	CFR TC
Brooks McCormick	CFR

FORD MOTOR CO.

Donald E. Petersen	CFR
Carter E. Burgess	CFR
Clifton Wharton, Jr.	CFR
Philip Caldwell	TC
Arjay Miller	TC

CFR

CFR

CFR
CFR
CFR

CFR
CFR
AIRS

UNION BOSSES

I.W. Abel (Former President. United Steelworkers of America)	TC
Sol Chick Chaikin (President. Int Ladies Garment Workers)	CFR TC
Thomas R. Donahue (Secretary/Treasurer, AFL-CIO)	CFR TC
Murray H. Finley (President, Amalgamated Clothing & Textile Workers)	CFR
Victor Gotbaum (American Fed. of State, County and Municipal Employees)	CFR
Lane Kirkland (Pres AFL-CIO)	CFR TC
Howard D. Samuel (President. Industrial Union Dept. AFL-CIO)	CFR
Martin J. Ward (President. United Assn of Journeymen and Apprentices of the Plumbing and Pipe Fitting Industry. U S A. & Canada)	CFR TC
Glenn E. Watts (President, Communications Workers of America)	CFR TC
Leonard Woodcock (Former President of U A W)	CFR TC
Jerry Wurf (President. American Federation of State. County and Municipal Employees)	CFR

*PLEASE NOTE: These CFR/TC members head State Department bureaus where dramatic shifts in American foreign policy appear to work against allies of the United States and in favor of revolutionary forces.

THE
REAGAN
ADMINISTRATION

A Quote and a Table are Worth a Thousand Words
1/9/81

'The Trilateral Commission doesn't secretly run the world. The CFR does that.'' Winston Lord, President of the CFR and a Trilateral Commission member.

PRESIDENT

1929-33	Herbert Hoover*	CFR
1953-61	Dwight Eisenhower	CFR
1961-63	John Kennedy	CFR
1969-74	Richard Nixon*	CFR
1977-80	Jimmy Carter	T

VICE PRESIDENT

1925-29	Charles G. Dawes	CFR
1953-61	Richard Nixon*	CFR
1965-69	Hubert Humphrey	CFR
1974-77	Nelson Rockefeller	CFR
1977-80	Walter Mondale	CFR, T

SECRETARY OF STATE

1920	Frank Polk	CFR
1921-25	Charles Hughes	CFR
1925-29	Frank Kellog	CFR
1929-33	Henry Stimson*	CFR
1944-45	Edward Stettinius	CFR
1949-53	Dean Acheson	CFR
1953-59	John Foster Dulles	CFR
1959-61	Christian Herter	CFR
1961-69	Dean Rusk	CFR
1969-73	William Rogers*	CFR
1973-77	Henry Kissinger	CFR, T
1977-80	Cyrus Vance	CFR, T
1980	Edmund Muskie	CFR

SECRETARY OF TREASURY

1920-21	David Houston	CFR
1921-32	Andrew Mellon	CFR
1932-33	Ogden Mills	CFR
1933-34	William Woodin	CFR
1934-45	H. Morgenthau, Jr.	CFR
1957-61	Robert Anderson	CFR

1961-65	Douglas Dillon	CFR
1965-69	Henry Fowler	CFR
1969-71	David Kennedy	CFR
1972-74	George Shultz*	CFR
1974-77	William Simon	CFR
1977-79	Michael Blumenthal	CFR

SECRETARY OF WAR/DEFENSE

1916-21	Newton Baker	CFR
1940-45	Henry Stimson*	CFR
1945-47	Robert Patterson	CFR
1947-49	James Forrestal	CFR
1951-53	Robert Lovett	CFR
1957-59	Neil McElroy	CFR
1959-61	Thomas Gates, Jr.	CFR
1961-68	Robert McNamara	CFR
1969-73	Melvin Laird	CFR
1973	Elliott Richardson*	CFR, T
1975-77	Donald Rumsfeld	CFR
1977-80	Harold Brown	CFR, T

ATTORNEY GENERAL

1941-45	Francis Biddle	CFR
1958-61	William Rogers	CFR
1973	Elliot Richardson*	CFR, T

SECRETARY OF H.E.W.

1956-68	John Gardner	CFR
1970-73	Elliot Richardson*	CFR, T
1977-79	Joseph Califano, Jr.	CFR, T
1980	Patricia Harris*	CFR

SECRETARY OF COMMERCE

1921-29	Herbert Hoover*	CFR
1946-48	Averill Harriman	CFR
1958-59	Lewis Strauss	CFR
1967-68	Alexander Trowbridge	CFR
1972-73	Peter Peterson	CFR
1975-77	Elliott Richardson*	CFR, T
1977-80	Juanita Kreps	CFR

SECRETARY OF H.U.D.

1973-75	James Lynn	CFR
1977-79	Patricia Harris*	CFR

SECRETARY OF LABOR

1953-61	James Mitchell	CFR
1961-62	Arthur Goldberg	CFR
1969-70	George Shultz*	CFR

(*more than one office)

THE DEMANCIPATION PROCLAMATION

7/11/80

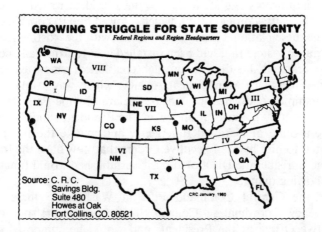

GROWING STRUGGLE FOR STATE SOVEREIGNTY
Federal Regions and Region Headquarters

Source: C. R. C.
Savings Bldg.
Suite 480
Howes at Oak
Fort Collins, CO. 80521

CRC January 1980

In the chapter *"Straws In the Wind,"* it was asserted that the federal government might move to seize total control of the country. A *"laundry list"* of recent Federal actions was presented to support this thesis. DON BELL REPORTS (P. O. Box 2223, Palm Beach, Florida 33480) lays out the *"in place"* federal machinery to annihilate our freedoms. . . .

"It should be understood that whenever the President of the United States desires to declare a state of National Emergency, he can seize absolute dictatorial power over every individual, and the property and assets of every individual in the United States. The President merely issues an Executive Order declaring that a National Emergency exists; then the federal government can do as much or as little in the way of exercising dictatorial power as may seem expedient to the Bureaucracy. . . . FDR was the first president who used an Executive Order to declare a State of National Emergency. That was on March 9, 1933, when he declared that 'bank holiday.' Later he used Executive Orders for other purposes. But the U.S. Supreme Court stepped in and ruled against many of FDR's EOs. Speaking for the Court in 1934, Chief Justice Hughes wrote: 'Emergency does not create power. Emergency

145

does not increase granted power or remove or diminish restrictions imposed upon power granted or reserved. The Constitution was adopted
in a period of grave emergency. Its grants of power to the Federal government and its limitations of the power of the States were determined
in the light of emergency and they are not altered by emergency.
(Home Building & Loan Assoc. v. Blaisdell, 290 U.S. 426-
1934)'. . . .

"On July 24, 1979, President Carter issued E.O. 12148, which gave
him more dictatorial powers than any President had ever had under
the original orders and statutes. . . . the President issued an accompanying executive order, 12149, which allowed him to coordinate and
combine these National Emergency Powers with the existing Regional
Governance system that had been installed as a fourth branch of federal government. He did this through creation of a new agency, the
Federal Emergency Management Agency, which was to manage the
dictatorship, if and when it might be declared by the President.

"As presently planned, if and when the President should decide to
declare a State of National Emergency and invoke the full powers
delegated to him by the Executive Orders that now have the force of
law, the Bureaucratic Dictatorship thus established would function in
the following manner:

"At the Central Command Post in Washington there is the
Interagency Coordinating Council. This would work out of the
Executive Office of the President, and would be composed of the
heads of the following departments and agencies: Department of the
Interior, Department of Agriculture, Department of Commerce,
Department of Labor, Department of Health and Human Services,
Department of Education, Department of Housing and Urban
Development, Department of Transportation, Department of Energy,
Environmental Protection Agency, Community Services Administra-
tion, General Services Administration, ACTION, Small Business
Administration, U.S. Army Corps of Engineers, Regional Action
Planning Commissions, Office of Management and Budget, and the
Federal Emergency Management Council. This Interagency Co-
ordinating Council might be compared to the Supreme Soviet which
operates out of the Kremlin in Moscow.

"To further coordinate and consolidate, manage and direct the activities of the Interagency Coordinating Council, there is a special,
top-level bureaucratic council, known as the Emergency Management
Council. According to Section 3 of Executive Order 12148 of July 20,
1979: 'There is hereby established the Emergency Management Council. The Council shall be composed of the Director of the Federal
Emergency Management Agency who shall be the Chairman, the

Director of the Office of Management and Budget, and such others as
the President may designate. The Council shall advise and assist the
President in the oversight and direction of Federal emergency programs and policies. . . . The heads of Executive agencies shall
cooperate in the performance of functions vested in him.'

"Under this Federal Emergency Management Council and the
Interagency Coordinating Council in Washington, there are the Ten
Federal Regional Councils that govern the Ten Federal Regions from
their Ten Regional Capitols. Each of these Ten Regional Councils is
composed of a representative from each of the before-named executive departments and agencies which make up the Interagency
Coordinating Council. The Chairman (Commissar?) of each of the
Ten Regional Councils is named by the President. Then, from each of
the Ten Regional Capitols there is a network of sub-regional councils
and commissions which will supervise, oversee, and/or replace State,
County, local and community governments and services.

"This network of bureaucratic agencies, operating under orders
issued by the Executive Office of the President by the Federal
Emergency Management Council, could:
—Take over all communications;
—Seize all sources of power (electric, nuclear, petroleum, gas, etc.);
—Control all food resources;
—Seize all forms of transportation;
—Control all highways and seaports;
—Seize railroads, inland waterways and storage facilities;
—Commandeer all civilians to work under federal supervision;
—Control all activities relating to health and human services;
—Control all activities relating to education;
—Register every man, woman and child in the United States;
—Shift any segment of the population from one locality to another;
—Control all devices capable of emitting electro-magnetic radiation;
—Take over farms, ranches and timberland;
—Freeze all wages and prices;
—Demand emergency welfare services (food, clothing, lodging) in
private homes for those said to be in need;
—Regulate the amount of your own money you can withdraw from
your bank or savings and loan institution;
—Close all banks, stock exchanges, etc., and freeze stock and bond
prices;
—Institute extraordinary measures with respect to any facility, sys-
tem, or service said to be essential to national survival.

"Communism within the form of a Representative Republic is an
apt description. Under almost any pretext, a President can declare a

State of National Emergency and this will become a Bureaucratic Dictatorship. Such a potential dictatorship depends upon that fourth and unconstitutional branch of federal government called Regional Governance. It can be eliminated only through action by State Governments. That is why coming elections are important: not at the federal but at the state and local level. The fight to reclaim the Republic and restore national righteousness begins at the doorpost, not the Capitol dome."

POLITICS AND PRINCIPLE

9/5/80

I sat down for lunch last week with a gentleman who is running for a seat in the U.S. House of Representatives. The lunch turned into a fascinating conversation lasting some two hours. What I learned about what it takes to get elected in this country made me ill.

Here's what I discovered:

1. It is expected that less than half of the potential voters will vote in this fall's critical elections.

2. Of those who do vote, only 6 percent will vote based upon the issues.

3. Of these 6 percent who decide to vote on the basis of the issues, most of them will vote based upon the candidate's stand on **local** issues, not those of regional, national or international importance.

4. It is quite simple to get voters to vote **against** their self-interest. In fact, it has been proven in campaigns that the most effective way of obtaining votes is shaking hands, going door-to-door. It seems that if the American voter feels he can talk to you or touch you, then you are an OK guy. It doesn't matter if you endorse Fidel Castro for president, just so long as the voter feels he has access to you.

5. A politician must be all things to all people, in an age when everything is acceptable, nothing is barred, and all lifestyles and attitudes are permitted; principled statesmen have no chance to get elected. Put bluntly, a statesman is a dead politician.

The chances of getting elected by running against government benefits are next to nil. The majority of Americans now depend upon government for their income. The only lucky exceptions, who are elected, are extremely well-known and rich individuals who have high placed sponsors.

6. Polls are a sure-fire campaign aid. But polls can be manipulated, like statistics. If you want a press release, just take a poll. The press latches on to polls like hound dogs do rabbits. By choosing the sampling group carefully, and by conducting the poll in an advantageous way, politicians can make polls show almost anything they desire.

7. The media play games with the candidates. Candidates who refuse to advertise in certain newspapers, on particular radio stations,

or on selected TV stations will find their press releases are *"black-balled."* The candidate either puts up the bucks to advertise in a weekly newspaper, for example, or he receives no press coverage by that paper. It's hardball economics. It's cut-throat and dirty.

8. There are schools that teach candidates how to run successful political campaigns, just like there are schools that teach investors how to make money in leveraged real estate. There are computer programs for sale that spell out how to run a successful campaign (manipulate the voters).

Is anyone interested in running for political office?

Race and Reality/Privilege and Opportunity
9/5/80

A letter to the editor in the August 4, 1980, issue of the U.S. NEWS AND WORLD REPORT stated concisely the relationship between special interest groups and government, and the problems that have resulted as a by-product of the federal government's intrusion into all areas of American life, particularly economics.

> *"The fire is dying under the melting pot, and the mix is congealing into separate tribes. The fire that once made 'American' more than a suffix was an eager belief in opportunity and the harsh realization that the state would grant no favors: As Americans, we were on our own. But this ethic of individual enterprise has given way to one of tribal privilege. An ethnoaristocracy has emerged that extorts guarantees in the name of opportunity and waves the word 'prejudice' as a mugger waves a knife. A society once united against privilege has split into multiple tribes that arrogantly demand it. With every heated cry against 'prejudice,' the melting pot gets colder."*

Alan Siddons
Boston

CONGRESS: GUILTY AS CHARGED

9/5/80

In 1959, a commission was created by Congress to study how well government is doing its job. This Advisory Commission on Intergovernmental Relations has just concluded that the federal government is out of control. A surprise? No way! Furthermore, it has laid at the feet of Congress the blame for wasteful and unmanageable domestic aid programs. The Commission's study, "A Crisis of Confidence and Competence," found that Congress is so preoccupied with trivial issues that it does not have time to deal with the economy or foreign affairs either. Congress itself was found primarily responsible for *"the crisis of confidence."*

There is also such a hodgepodge of programs which are unnecessary, wasteful and mismanaged that overlap at the federal, state and local level, that the result is an unwieldy, out-of-control bureaucracy.

This Advisory Commission on Intergovernmental Relations was manned by twenty-six citizens, including representatives of the executive branch, governors, mayors, congressmen, county officials, state legislators, and private citizens. This study, publicized by the NEW YORK TIMES, places the *"official"* stamp of incompetence on government, something we already knew, practically, was the case. Question: If we do not reform the system peacefully in the next four years, who believes we can then avoid violent change?

151

CORRUPTION?

6/22/78

The setting is Mill Valley, California, the 7th grade government class of one Mr. George Muldoon. The year is 1978. George decides to let his 7th graders experiment in self-government. The students set up a capitalist democracy. (Interesting. This is the type of government the United States has. Well, imprinting is still *"taking,"* we assume.)

The students printed money. (Great! The U.S. Treasury should beam with pride. Another all-American activity is underway.) Students had to pay to use the pencil sharpener, books, wastebasket, or door. Bids were taken for concessions. (Oh, how ideally capitalistic!) Even the police force was active, issuing citations for sitting on desks and messing up the room. (Law and order prevailed. George Wallace, where are you?)

But, unfortunately, the story does not end here. Human nature enters the picture, and its painting is much less than a sight for sore eyes.

Some members of the class got arrested. But they simply bought off the police. People with money had more power than the president. (Oh, Mr. Rockefeller?) The police eventually fingerprinted the whole class and kept dossiers on them. (Do you hear the cheers from the KGB, the IRS, and the SEC?) And the banking system? It was up to its ears in scandal. (John Law, alive and well in the boardrooms of NYC banks.)

The bank president paid off other students for favors rendered and work done. (Shah of Iran, don't you smile so widely!) Some banking employees stole from the coffers. (Is all the gold in Ft. Knox?) But still the system persisted. (Hang tough!)

What led to its downfall? COUNTERFEITING! (The whole world now nods. Inflation is a form of counterfeiting, for it creates something like paper called money, out of nothing. See, over there is the U.S., with the biggest grin of all.)

What happened when the system collapsed? George Muldoon assumed dictatorial power. (He must have had Executive Orders.)

We should all give thanks such children's games never happen in real life! Yes, this is a source of great comfort to us all.

152

MULTINATIONALS

7/7/78

Chapter 14 and 16 in CYCLES OF WAR heavily hit the multinationals and their unhealthy impact on Western society. The ECONOMICS section in the Appendix expanded upon this subject and took it to its logical conclusion. Without question, Jimmy Carter was made president by the multinationals. And, as I pointed out in the book, one of the reasons we have a weaker dollar is due to the benefits of a weaker dollar for the multinationals. Now, the June 19, 1978, WALL STREET JOURNAL, front page *"Outlook"* confirms that research.

> *"To the more skeptical Europeans, America's seeming indifference over the years has merely masked a cynical strategy. During their eagerness to buy up European industries in the 1960s, American companies doubtless benefitted by the dollar being held artificially high under the old gold-pegged, fixed-rate monetary system. Now that the American emphasis is on exporting more and bringing home profits from past investments, it is advantageous to the U.S. for the dollar to be lower."*[5]

Profits and greed is one sorry motive for the destruction of the ties to old allies. Make no mistake about it. The Europeans are rightfully disgusted with the U.S. of A., thanks to Carter and Co.'s dollar imperialism.

A special congressional study initiated by the late Sen. Lee Metcalf (D. Mont.) recently revealed, *"An extraordinary pattern of directorate concentration"* and, in effect, stated that an elite group of interlocking directors control all the major financial institutions, utilities, transportation companies, industrials, retailers, and broadcasting companies. In the thick of things are the big multinational banks—Chase Manhattan, J. P. Morgan, Citicorp, Manufacturers Hanover, Bankers Trust, First Chicago, Chemical New York, and that's just for a starter. (Hear John Law cheer from his grave.)

This big happy family of multinational financial power, according to the subcommittee, *"have at least the appearance of providing ready channels for communication and information which could lead to coordinated, rather than competitive, financial policies among the nation's largest banking institutions."*

CYCLES OF WAR chapters entitled *"The Powerful Elite"* and

"Civilization Cycles and War" discussed these points at length.

The report also stated, *"These patterns of director interrelationships imply an overwhelming potential for antitrust abuse and possible conflicts of interest which could affect prices, supply and competition, and impact on the shape and direction of the American economy."*

Small wonder that Vice President Mondale, in an address, praised the multinationals. He is a charter member of the elite club, The Trilateral Commission. Someone had to come to the multinationals' defense. And lo and behold, the elitists' think tank, The Brookings Institution, released a 535-page treatise on the "multis." Nice things were said. Brookings knows which side its bread is buttered on.

Abraham Lincoln warned us. He stated in his second inaugural address, *"I see in the future a crisis arising that unnerves me and causes me to tremble for the safety of my country. As a result of the war, corporations have been enthroned and an air of corruption in high places will follow. The money power of this country will endeavor to prolong its reign by working upon the prejudices of the people until all the wealth is aggregated in the few hands and the Republic is destroyed. I feel at this time more anxious for my country than even in the midst of war."*

Literature predicts coming reality. The following is taken from the movie, NETWORK. Mr. Jensen, Chairman of the Board of CCA (Combined Communication Assoc.) is lecturing Mr. Howard Beale, network news anchorman for UBS (Union Broadcasting System). Heed carefully Mr. Jensen's remarks.

> *"We no longer live in a world of nations and ideologies, Mr. Beale. The world is a college of corporations, inexorably determined by the immutable bylaws of business. The world is a business, Mr. Beale! It has been that way since man crawled out of the slime, and our children, Mr. Beale, will live to see that perfect world without war and famine, oppression and brutality— one vast ecumenical holding company for whom all men will work to serve a common profit, in which all men will hold a share of stock, all necessities provided, all anxieties tranquillized, all boredom amused. And I have chosen you to preach this evangel, Mr. Beale."*
>
> *"Why me?"* Howard whispered humbly.
>
> *"Because you're on television, dummy. Sixty million people watch you every night of the week, Monday through Friday. . . ."*
>
> *"I have seen the face of God!"* Howard said. . . .
>
> *"You just might be right, Mr. Beale."*[6]

A Den of Thieves
11/20/81

The only difference between the Republican Party and Democratic Party is that they are different gangs of bandits. The Republicans steal for the rich from the poor in the following ways:

1. Republicans formulate complicated tax packages which allow the rich, who can afford high-priced accountants and attorneys, to escape the tax hook. Republicans also support the corrupt military/industrial complex, padding the *"gun"* companies' pockets.

2. Republicans do not attack the fractional reserve banking system which is the primary engine of inflation. The rich, having assets that they can collateralize, are able to borrow money from the banks and thrift institutions (where the poor have made deposits) to purchase more assets which increase in value during inflationary times. Effectively using other people's money (OPM) by borrowing, the rich get richer while the poor get poorer. The poor lose during inflationary times because they do not have the moxie or money to invest wisely. Their meager monetary deposits in establishment financial institutions are chewed up by accelerating inflation.

While the Republicans appeal to the special interests of the rich, the Democrats, on the other hand, appeal to the special interests of the poor. Every dog has his own day, but the Democrats have a bigger *"dog."* There are more poor.

The Democrats steal, too. They legislate social welfare programs, the *"butter"* side of the *"guns and butter"* equation, which transfers real wealth from the rich through taxes to the poor. The Democrats steal for the poor from the rich.

Question: How can there ever be any social or political harmony in this country when both political parties are a den of thieves? How can there by any confidence or peace of mind in our economic system when everyone is always politically attempting to pick everyone else's pocket? Pragmatic politics is eating us alive. We need to return to the principle that *"theft is wrong,"* at all levels, individual and collective.

We need to reestablish a sense of fair play. It is a tremendous paradox, but no accident, that the general public is increasingly flocking to the one area of life in our society where fair play and competition is manifested to the maximum—professional sports!

Who wins long-term if we continue down this sad road? Elitists, bureaucratic elitists. Why? The next stage in our social cycle is anarchy. Anarchy is followed by dictatorship, the extreme form of elitism. A dictatorship requires an elite bureaucracy in order to function. Remember the Nazi S.S.? Well, both the Republicans and Democrats support the IMF and World Bank for the good of the elitists' New World Order.

THE AMERICAN PRESIDENCY

3/28/80

It might have been interesting to have lived in England under Cromwell, or in the United States in the 1830s-1850s. In any case, there is great difficulty identifying with 1980, 20th Century America. There is great interest in the character and vision of scientists and statesmen who are part of our past. Equally engaging is the prospect for our future.

This writer's American *"cultural black box"* was shattered when I was in college. I was fed propaganda by a communist revolutionary who was sentenced to 35 years in the penitentiary at Huntsville, Texas. In our Business Values class, she used American literature to criticize the American system, to destroy the cultural values and perspectives of her young students, including yours truly. She stated, at that time, that the communist plan was for an American revolution in the 1980s.

Looking back now at her arguments and criticisms, I find them to be almost entirely correct. Her solutions, however, were in error. The point is this: As a result of that experience, this writer became permanently alienated from the run-of-the-mill thinking, values and perspectives of 20th Century Americans. Living 2,000 miles away from my family and my roots has further enabled me to become increasingly aloof and more objective about our American system.

Along this line, I found Joel Garreau's article in a WASHINGTON POST, discussing dividing the United States into eight different nations, quite creative, illuminating and instructive. Garreau has seen America as it really is. If one understands his viewpoint, one sees the political nature of the American system. Briefly, the 8 *"nations"* within the United States are broken down as follows: 1) Ecotopia—Made up of Western Washington, Western Oregon, and Northern California. Members of this nation are rugged individualists who are ecologically concerned. 2) The Foundry—This nation is composed of Newark, Trenton, Camden, Schenectady, Buffalo, Wilkes-Barre, Pittsburgh, Wheeling, Detroit, Akron, Toledo, South Bend, Gary and Cleveland. These cities are in decline, are "gritty." They are noted for hard work with heavy machinery, utilizing coal and iron to manufacture goods. 3) The Empty Quarter—Composed of Montana,

156

Eastern Washington, Utah, Idaho, Nevada, parts of Northern Arizona and New Mexico, Western Colorado and Wyoming. This is the last great colony of all the other *"nations."* It is the land of *"wide open spaces,"* the majority of which is owned by the federal government and big corporations who are bleeding the area of its raw materials. 4) The Islands—Composed of Miami, Puerto Rico and the Caribbean Islands. This is a Latin nation. Miami is the capital. Its specialty is arms and drugs. 5) MexAmerica—Composed of Texas, New Mexico, Arizona, and Southern California. It is influenced by the growth of the Mexican population which is exceeding that of Bangladesh. Major cities include Phoenix, El Paso, Houston and Los Angeles. Its primary population are Hispanics. 6) New England—This is the poorest nation in America. It is composed of Maine, Vermont, Rhode Island, and New Hampshire. It is the center of the nation's so-called higher education, which has supported such extreme ecological positions that the citizens of this country live near the subsistence level. 7) Dixie—The capital of this nation is Atlanta. It is composed of Louisiana, Mississippi, Alabama, Georgia, Florida, Tennessee, Virginia, the Carolinas and other southern states. It is the center of America's popular music—Nashville, Memphis and New Orleans. Its unifying history, language, food, dress, xenophobia and charm are well understood. It is in the process of becoming another Foundry. 8) The Breadbasket—Commonly known as the Plains, it includes Nebraska, Iowa, Kansas, the Dakotas, Minnesota, and parts of Colorado, Illinois, Wisconsin, Missouri, Oklahoma and Texas. The entire United States eventually comes around to the way the Breadbasket thinks. As Garreau put it, *"It's the breadbasket where social change meets its most important test. If new ideas or style prevail here, they become fully American.*

"These folks take their regionalism seriously, yet they are internationalists. They understand the world's interdependence because of their proximity to the missile silos, and to the machinery of food export. They are sobered by their links to the land.

"Very straightforward. No time-and-a-half. No arbitration. No strikes, even as the farmers discovered last year.

"People are affected by the land around them, all of us. Nothing else in all America is as straightforward as the land of the Breadbasket.

"The Nixon people had the right question: Will it play in Peoria?"

Barry Goldwater was a man out of touch with the political realities of his time. So was Richard Nixon, but Nixon tried to change his stripes. In the end, however, he was recognized for what he was and was effectively booted out of office. The political, economic and actual climate is again changing. Ford and Carter were/are the transitional bridge. A Ted Kennedy or a Jimmy Carter elected President in 1980 would be precisely the wrong man at the wrong time. The era of the Kennedys, Muskies and McGoverns is dead. The colder, harsher climate will demand a leader who is in touch with the new primary trends, those being: 1) a return to fundamental religion; 2) a bootstrap, individualistic economic perspective; 3) limited government; 4) a strong military; and 5) a revised judicial system. Such have been the requirements at every major turning point in history marked by a colder, drier, and more harsh climate. A revolution will occur if a *"liberal"* is elected in 1984.

*   *   *

"Business cycles have been integrated with weather trends throughout history. They still are."

". . . the current evidence shows that we are heading now into the cold-dry phase of the 100-year cycle which means a rapid sequence of depressions in the near future."

"The conclusion that business trends have followed the weather trends down through history, and that the wet periods have been prosperous and the dry periods 'unprosperous' is borne out by the relationship of the Rogers price curve for British wheat, that goes back to 1260 A.D., to the weather trends."

"Dark Ages seem always to have their peaks during the cold-dry periods of history. When the Dark Ages have been at their worst, climatic desiccation has occurred and along with it economic destitution."

"Cold-dry periods have always been the times in history when piracy, both on sea and land, has reached its highest peaks, and when most of the famous migrations of history have occurred."

"Cold-dry periods have generally been periods of anarchy, chaos, piracy, depression, and poor government."

"Cold-dry periods are periods of class struggle, civil war, palace wars, palace murders and mutilations and the collapse of dynasties."

Dr. Raymond H. Wheeler

Source: Foundation for the Study of Cycles
124 South Highland Ave., Pittsburgh, PA 15206

THE MEAT GRINDER

10/17/80

Over the past twenty years, we have put five presidents through the meat grinder—Kennedy, Johnson, Nixon, Ford, and now the Pepsodent Peanut, Jimmy Carter. On the surface, there are many reasons why this has occurred. First of all, this country is going through the throes of change, making major readjustments. Presidents get caught up in his maelstrom.

The climate has become more harsh and variable. As all true economic prosperity stems ultimately from the combination of land and labor. When the land becomes more niggardly, as it has now, economic distress becomes more widespread. Tough times make folks more conservative and ornery.

The family unit, the basis of authority, training, psychological stability and, thus, the foundation of national strength, has become fragmented. The divorce rate has doubled in the past ten yers. We are adrift.

How many Americans today can name their great grandparents? Few. So, we have lost our family roots, too.

Militarily, we now think we have become second rate. We, thus, feel naked, vulnerable to the Soviets.

Inflation plagues us all and increases the level of social tension.

Our institutions, due to government over-regulation and their inherent resistance to change, have become frozen and unresponsive to the needs of the people.

The above are just a few of the unsavory situations which contribute to our national unrest, which ultimately settles out at the president's desk.

The problem with the presidency goes much deeper than the foregoing analysis. We have just celebrated our 200th anniversary, the average termination point for a society. Also, we have just completed the 510-year cycle of Western civilization. The president is climbing up the down staircase. At this time, all of our complex problems demand an assumption of *individual* responsibility and *de*centralization. But, we collectively refuse to respond to the danger signals. Natural trends (climate) reinforce this decentralization direction, which is

159

necessary if we are to cope effectively and meet our challenges. Needless to say, our presidents have led us in the opposite direction—toward greater centralization, with further assumption of responsibility by the executive branch. It's as if everything is backwards, which it is.

One of the reasons that we are chasing our own tail, so to speak, is that the men who run for president seek the office because they *need* to be president. They seek the office out of weakness. Stated somewhat differently, all of the past five presidents have been marked by deep-seated insecurity, with the resulting need for public approval. They needed the presidential power in order to demonstrate to the public that they were worthy of our love. It was/is their way of saying, *"Look folks, I'm O.K. I deserve your love and approbation."* Men, particularly presidents, who are under extreme stress, who have to rely upon fickle public opinion for their sense of self-worth, are, at the very least, unstable. They could be dangerous. Nixon was dangerous during Watergate. He was rejected. He could have struck back at the nation. He considered it.

The rejection by the American public today of an American president is deeply threatening to the holder of the highest office in this land. Jimmy Carter tried to get Mama Lillian to love him as much or more than she loves Billy. And he struck out. How can a president deal with the needs of a nation, or even analyze them rationally and objectively, when his own needs are not being met? He does not have the ability to give, or more dangerously in some cases, even listen to, or face reality. Only a secure individual can give and perceive reality accurately.

The media has *"pumped up"* presidential candidates in the minds of the emotional public to the point where the candidates are expected to be *"supermen."* The word *"superman,"* just like in the movie and the earlier comic book, should not be taken lightly. A *"superman"* is exactly what we expect our American president to be. It does not matter that this expectation is truly insane, and illogical. Why? Because *"superman"* is the epitome of the social humanistic evolutionary spiral. And we all believe in social evolution, don't we? And, *"superman"* is the logical end result of our humanistic faith—man as God. Isn't he?

The American president today attempts to fill the bill, meet the demands of our humanistic culture. The fact that he consistently fails miserably is a primary threat to our whole social order! It rattles our very foundation. And, the fact that our humanistic perspective is egregiously erroneous, as is painfully obvious by the bumbling performance by our elected *"supermen"* (presidents), is beside the point. As a culture, we are unwilling to face the reality that our theology of humanistic, evolutionary rationalism and materialism is breaking down. Talk about culture shock! This is far more than we can handle. We'll even risk nuclear war to avoid facing this issue. We might even invite it.

It should be apparent, that like all other decaying civilizations, we are weak and sick. But, the blame for the sickness does not just lie in the power lusts and unfulfilled needs of the presidential candidates, nor in simply the unrealistic expectations created by the media, nor in just the outworkings of our evolutionary humanistic faith. The blame ultimately rests on the backs of the American public.

Concomitant with the breakdown of the classic American family, there has been, in an action and reaction manner, the overwhelming, deep-seated, psychological desire by the masses for a loving, omniscient and omnipotent father—the father that the public, individually, and therefore collectively, never had. Black youths have few fathers. The illegitimacy rate among blacks is now over 50% in many parts of the country. The Mexican population is not much better off. What a sad beginning and insecure foundation from which to face a prejudiced, demanding world.

Divorce is rampant among whites, too. The working out of the humanistic objective, that man can do what he well pleases, *"Do his own thing,"* has resulted, quite logically, in easier and more numerous divorces. And, as if this was not enough, with both parents working in an attempt to stay ahead of inflation and enjoy the good life, children are put on the back burner. Adding insult to injury is our social norm that success and self-worth are directly related to material abundance. It is no small wonder that fathers give their children low priority. The *"cat's in the cradle."* When our society tells a man, *"Look, you're only worth what you own,"* why shouldn't he view his children as a burden and spend as little time with them as possible?

Since World War II, the children of the depression-conscious parents, grown-ups now ages 25 through 35 (the egg through the snake group), have deep seated insecurities. They long for the father, the example, they never had. The media promises they will find him in the American president. The media is wrong, as president after president's failure bears testimony. We, *"the children,"* feel betrayed. And, the anger which accompanies this betrayal is akin to that of a woman scorned. It follows no logic. It just manifests itself in hatred and the desire to destroy the betrayer.

So, as in the Greek tragedies, the American public, longing for a father figure, sets up a man on a pedestal, only to jerk him down and roll him in the dust once our unreasonable expectations go unfulfilled. And the poor president, who allows himself to be put up on that pedestal, is part and parcel of the whole tragic scene. He lets himself be placed in the mouth of the meat grinder in an effort to fulfill his deep-seated need to feel important, to be loved, which is something he can never get from the ever changeable and whimsical public.

The public does not have the ability to give. The president does not have the ability to give. Giving requires a full vessel, which begins with the fulfillment of the basic psychological needs in the first six years of life. These needs must be met by the family. But, our families are disintegrating. No wonder we are headed to hell in a handbasket.

Our last, best chance may be to grab hold of a loving Heavenly Father. If not, this self-destructive scene will continue until our society collapses or a man arises from the masses, a Caesar, if you will, who truly has the ability to give. He will be both loved and hated. But, he will be respected. He will fulfill the *"Great White Father"* needs of the insecure public. And, he will be able to handle the power of the presidency, because, unlike at least our past five presidents, he will not need the approval of the masses in order to feel important.

"MARES EAT OATS, AND DOES EAT OATS, AND LITTLE LAMBS HOST THE GONG SHOW"

3/10/78

Like a bolt out of the blue I was awakened last night. I sat right up in the middle of my bed when a voice said to me, *"Dummy, you have it all wrong. The U.S. has no problems. War is not a threat to mankind. The Middle East is a chess game. The Russian Bear belongs to Grizzly Adams." "But, wait,"* I said. *"No, you wait,"* said the voice. *"Our world isn't real. It can't be taken seriously. It is all a gigantic Gong Show. How stupid of you to have never have seen it."*

"But," I protested, *"Jimmy Carter is not a perfect clone of Chuck Barris." "Ah,"* said the voice, *"but he is. . . . You, all wrapped up in your commodity markets, just never could see the obvious. You thought Jimmy Carter was a lamb in the presidency. And you thought little Jimmy got himself all confused with the Lamb of God. How terribly religious of you."*

"Listen to me," said the voice. *"The American public is right. They are always right. Eat, drink and be merry. The audience of the Gong Show does. The audience of the Gong Show is the American public, along with Congress."*

"Why is Congress part of the audience?" I asked. *"Because, dummy, somebody has to play the part of errand boy and explain to the American public exactly what is not going on. And, besides, who can serve cold pop and popcorn as well." "I see,"* I said. *"No, you don't,"* said the voice. *"You thought there was something to Oswald Spengler's words that, 'world peace involves the private renunciation of war on the part of the immense majority, but along with this, it involves an unavowed readiness to submit to being the booty of others who do not renounce it.'. . . Don't you know we have fought the war to end all wars?" "But." "No buts,"* said the voice, *"Those are reserved for Congress and besides BUT is hardly the appropriate word. It's much too mild. But, I digress.*

"You also thought there was something to John Adams' words, 'Democracy has never been and never can be so desirable as aristocracy or monarchy, but while it lasts, is more bloody than either. Remember, democracy never lasts long. It soon wastes, exhausts, and

163

murders itself. There never was a democracy that did not commit suicide.' No wonder Adams was gonged. Bring on Barbara Walters.

　"Now, look at all the other fluff you have fed your readers. You tell them to keep a close eye on how the coal miners react to Chuck Barris', opps, Jimmy Carter's Taft-Hartley directive. You said it is critical because it is a crucial test of America's willingness to obey the law at a time in world history when the relativism of Hegel's dialectic reigns supreme and the world sits on the brink of anarchy-massive lawlesness. My sakes, man, it is just another act on the Gong Show! Don't you remember when Jimmy introduced his energy bill? And the human rights issue? And how about the 'I will never lie to you charade?' They were all acts, and they were all gonged! . . . So what if we renamed the Ship of State, the Hesperus. Another one on the rocks is fine by me. And the panel you ask? That TRIUNE of judges? Uh, it is about time for this commercial to end. The next act coming up is Sadat. He is to do a clever version of 'Froggy Went a Courting.' He'll get gonged too. Jimmy does a great job of picking acts that will get gonged. The audience loves it.

　"No, no time for any more questions. Yes, yes I am on my way to a costume party. Glad you like my red tights. No, no, there must be a malfunction in your air conditioning system. Why else would it be so hot in here. Now, lie back down," the voice said, *"and don't worry your red head. You have every reason in the world to rejoice. Houston beat Arkansas and Texas back to back and is going to the NCAA basketball playoffs. What else could you ask for? No one else asks for more. And the Gong Show? Relax! Everything is in total control. Didn't you know? I direct that show,"* said the voice, *"and Chuck Barris, opps, scratch that, Jimmy Carter, works for me."*

THE MAKING OF A PRESIDENT: 1980

1/31/80

If the Republican and Democratic primaries continue in the same vein as the Iowa caucuses, the American people will once again **not** have a choice for president of this country. The smiles must be broad and the champagne glasses uplifted in Eastern academic, political, and multinational circles. London, which influences U.S. foreign policy, should also be pleased. After all, their boys, both Republican and Democrat, lead the pack. Jimmy Carter is a *"former"* member of the Trilateral Commission. George Bush is also a *"former"* member of the Trilateral Commission. They, of course, resigned when investigators began digging too deeply into their connections with the Trilateral elitists.

Haven't we seen an interesting turn around by the press as this campaign has developed? First, Teddy Kennedy was the *"darling"*. . . until he announced. Next, lo and behold, Iran exploded, and Jimmy Carter was brought back from journalistic rags to riches. His revival is nothing short of remarkable, a true tribute to media power. And, then there's George Bush, straight from Eastern establishment wealth and academic training (Yale). Bush, a part-time Texan, spent some time in the barrel. But, then again, you don't become a U.N. ambassador, an envoy to China and Director of the CIA unless you are really well connected with the powerful elite.

Wasn't it interesting to watch the press build-up of George Bush? How cleverly they ignored John Connally and clipped old Ronald Reagan. A Trilateral victory for sure.

You remember the Trilateralists? Those are the boys who just happen to hold the most powerful positions in this country. Of course, they mean no harm. There is never any such thing as an abuse of political power, is there?

Let's refresh our memory. Who are some of the Trilateralists whose names keep popping up: Paul Volcker, George Weyerhaeuser, Harold Brown, Michael Blumenthal, Zbigniew Brzezinski, Jimmy Carter, Walter Mondale, Elliot Richardson, Cyrus Vance, Paul Warnke, Andrew Young, Anthony Solomon, Henry Kissinger, Sol Linowitz, Alan Cranston, John Culver, Robert Ingersoll, John H. Glenn, Jr.

Hedley Donovan, Robert Taft, Jr., William Scranton, Robert Roosa, John D. Rockefeller, IV, David Rockefeller, David Packard, Paul McCracken, J. Paul Austin, and Arthur Burns. My, oh my! These names have appeared time after time on the TV evening news (pick your network). Oh, they deserve the air time all right. They pull the strings, run the government, and are all members of the **same** organization, the Trilateral Commission. It has to be a coincidence, right?

There are some other similarities between Bush and Carter. Neither of the men are inspiring. The American people are ready for a leader, a masculine, somewhat macho type, who may be a little rough around the edges, but who speaks his mind and hangs tough. Neither Bush nor Carter fit this mold. This allows the powerful elite more control. They willingly fill the power vacuum left by an apathetic public. Can you imagine either Jimmy Carter or George Bush getting mad, rolling up his sleeves and by so doing inspiring some hero worship? Not on your life. Nevertheless, if the press ever needed an excuse to railroad either Jimmy Carter or George Bush into the White House, they have it now. And, the American public will bite—hook, line and sinker, maybe. Let's hope not.

Let's just go back and review the rise to power by Jimmy Carter. It was in London, in the fall of 1973, that Jimmy Carter was introduced to David Rockefeller. The setting was a private dinner. The Trilateral Commission had just been formed by David. Jimmy Carter, ambitious sort that he is, signed on as a founding member. The Trilateral Commission, of course, was the work of an obscure Columbia University Professor named Zbigniew Brzezinski. Now, Brzezinski had experience in the State Department and was sympathetic to communism. He felt that what we needed was a one world government. He didn't put it quite that bluntly. He wanted, more euphemistically stated, a *"community of nations."* The original group was made up of Japan, the United States and Western Europe.

Brzezinski's bright dream has darkened. Things haven't worked out so well for the Trilateralists. Protectionism is on the rise.

Mr. Carter had the necessary backgound support in '76. Coming from Georgia, as an unheralded governor of the state, he was tied into J. Paul Austin (Coca Cola). Doesn't his name appear up there in our list of Trilateralists? Why, yes it does. And, wasn't it TIME magazine that gave Jimmy Carter the support and publicity that helped propel him successfully through the campaign? And, wasn't Hedley Donovan, Editor-in-chief of TIME, a Trilateralist? Sure enough. You remember TIME magazine. It's the periodical that named both Adolph Hitler and Ayatollah Khomeini as the *"Man of the Year."*

Just maybe there is some connection to the give away of the Panama Canal and the loans that Panama owed to big Eastern establishment multinational banks. There are now some 31 Trilateralists who sit on the boards of banks in Panama, the *new* international banking center. Perhaps there is also some relationship to the United States' 300 million dollar emergency loan to Portugal and Coca Cola being able to enter that country for the first time in 50 years. Since Carter has been in The White House, Coca Cola has entered China for the first time in 30 years. Also, former Coca Cola executive, Charles Duncan, was appointed Secretary of Energy. My, oh my, things do go better with Coke.

But, lest we think ourselves too clever, we must go back in history. None of this is new. There is nothing new under the sun. We don't even have to go back as far as Rome to find strange bedfellows. We can just explore the election of Franklin D. Roosevelt, whose son-in-law wrote a thought-provoking book, F.D.R., MY EXPLOITED FATHER-IN-LAW. In that volume, FDR's son-in-law discusses a meeting he had with Bernard Baruch. (It was in 1932 that Bernard Baruch financed FDR's campaign.)

FDR's son-in-law, being a struggling broker, went to the king of investors, Mr. Bernard Baruch, for advice. He asked Mr. Baruch what he ought to invest in. Baruch commented that he had just purchased 5/16 of the world's silver on 10% margin. Mr. Baruch suggested that he invest in silver, too. Now, what was one of the first things FDR did as President? He doubled the price of silver! His excuse? He said he had to help the poor Western miners. How kind-hearted of F.D.R. How nice for Baruch.

Baruch had earlier financed Woodrow Wilson's presidential campaign. And Woodrow Wilson, naturally, recognizing that Bernard Baruch was the best man for the job, put him in charge of war production. It was purely coincidence, of course, that $11 billion worth of U.S. government contracts were funneled through Bernard Baruch's own company. Patriotic Baruch made a paltry $4 billion on the deal.

The faces and the names change, but the game goes on and on, at least until the civilization cycle ends. And, perhaps, this is where we are now. Wheeler's Drought and Civil Warfare Clock indicates this to be the case. So, perhaps we do have a basis for hope long-term. Radical change may be the only way to break the back of the power brokers and restore the fundamentals of our once great country, to allow the common folk a shot at *"Wealth for All."*

WASHINGTON: WONDER OF WONDERS

1/30/81

Washington, D.C., particularly during inauguration time, carries one to undreamed of heights of personal interaction (positive). Such lofty levels, however, also remove one to the kingdom of fantasy where reality exists only somewhere in the foggy distance or the remote past (negative). Being both by upbringing and by inclination a small-town country boy, this writer has lived in and sampled the world's cities long enough to confirm and correct intellectual and cultural impressions. Knowing where we stand in the 510-year cycle of Western civilization (at the end of it), a time of world cities, it stood to reason to this thinker that living close to reality, avoiding illusion, and finding real meaning in life would be more easily accomplished in the hinterlands. It is all too easy in the environment of the city, particularly the likes of Washington, D.C., where pomp and circumstance, pride and power, ego and one-upmanship are the continual activity of the many, to lose touch with what is really important to one's self, one's family, one's country, and one's God.

I am convinced that one of the reasons that the United States was able to conceptually formulate the miracle which became our Constitution was the fact that nine out of ten of the early colonists tilled the soil. They were in touch with reality. The spiritual and material planes were related and integrated. Such a concept is difficult and usually foreign to those born, bred, and/or captured by the city.

So, the reason I have continued to maintain my isolation in Montana, is not only for the purity and clarity of thought that comes without environmental static, but also so I can maintain touch with the land, the soil, with all the humility that relationship brings. When you work daily with chickens, llamas, horses and goats as I do, fulfilling the basic needs of dependent animals who return affection in kind, one has a hard time developing a sense of self-importance.

Self-importance, sensation, show and style are the modus operandi of the Washington Establishment. And, it is difficult to believe that in the midst of such a surrealistic environment, trying in the sense that it militates against hard work and character, that the changes needed by

168

this country will come with accuracy or alacrity. Perhaps, most insidious of all, is the influence, the incredible overwhelming intimidating influence of money and power exerted on those who partake of the Potomac offering day in and day out. How can they think clearly?

It is all too easy to be distracted, to be swayed, and to be carried away by wave after wave of parties, receptions, luncheons and limousines, minks and money, which are part and parcel of Washington's daily life. When men play God, it is difficult not to act like one. And so, the poison of pomp and circumstance takes its toll on both humility and thus clarity of thought. Such vulnerability does not exist so readily in the rural country.

There are two ruling elites in this country: The Democratic ruling elite, and the Republican ruling elite. At the inauguration of Ronald Reagan, we saw the transfer of power from one ruling elite to another. Partisan politics aside, the Republican ruling elite is more deserving of its political position. It is made up, and primarily financed by, what Jefferson called the *"natural aristocracy."* The *"new rich"* have, for the most part, earned and deserve their positions of power and prestige, OPM debt capitalism aside. They have made it all on their own. By contrast, the Democratic ruling elite primarily consists of old Eastern Establishment wealth, third generation and later wealth, wealth which is marked by guilt and/or a lack of understanding of how wealth is created. Other members of the Democratic ruling elite have acquired wealth and power at the expense of *"the people."* That is to say, some Democrats have attained their lofty positions by promising to deliver the moon, and by robbing Clyde Citizen to pay Walter Welfare. In the process, these leeches skim enough off the top to satisfy their lusts to exercise influence and power, and perhaps even become financially well-heeled. We are speaking in generalities here. What applies to the Democratic goose also is somewhat applicable to the Republican gander, and vice versa.

I think I now understand why our Founding Fathers hated political parties. Political parties quickly become elite groups in which decisions are made, based upon their benefit to the in-crowd. **Who** you know is far more important than **what** you know, **or** doing the right thing, heaven forbid. Principle is sacrificed to compromise, the price continually paid for favors owed. Change comes slowly, if at all, and usually only when the threat of being expelled from public office becomes so great that it cannot be dismissed through rhetoric or forgotten in time. Nine out of ten U.S. citizens distrust politicians. Folks have a keen sense of things.

Compromise, often a polite word for hypocrisy, is not only demonstrated by the political process, but also by the very institutions which carry on the charade. Strolling down Constitution Avenue, I was struck by the irony of how all the *"Alphabet Agencies"* have lined up their stone monuments, like dinosaurs in a row, in haughty defiance of the street named after the document which was intended to prevent their very existence. The *"Alphabet Agencies"* fill ten pages of the Washington, D.C. phone book (small print). Constitution Avenue is pocked by the headquarters of the Department of Commerce, the Internal Revenue Service, the Interstate Commerce Commission, the Department of Justice, the Department of Labor, and other goodies created by the federal government which have compounded the misery of the common man. God help us. These gray, dull, cold, structures, which house the equally cold and creatively dead bureaucrats, seem eternal, and at minimum, intimidating to the common man. But, then again, so did the Shah of Iran. It is no wonder that CFR members dominate administration after administration. No one else knows their way through the bureaucratic maze.

What about Ronald Reagan? Did he **sell** out? No, he just **sat** back in California. And when he did, the power vacuum he left was filled by the old, Republican, Washington Establishment. In the process, the *"Old Guard"* also captured RR's ear. Absence makes the heart grow fonder for someone else. And absent after election time were the Moral Majority, Conservative Caucus, the Republican platform, and others. These groups weren't absent willingly. They were blocked out. Thus, came the *"Old Guard"* appointments.

The *"political operatives"* I spoke with declared that Nancy Reagan was the driving force and ambition behind RR's march to the presidency. This being the case, then we have an old, tired actor running things, who desperately wants to do right by the American people, who dearly desires to be liked and to please all. One has to wonder if the night of the election, the gala and the inauguration may be the highlights of the presidency for this decent man. One also has to wonder if when battered by the frustration, long hours and daily strain of the presidency, this elder politician will long for the quiet, peaceful days of California. He was hesitant to leave California in the first place. The insufferably hot and humid Washington summers and the cold, gray, damp winters will not be to RR's liking. A noted general does not believe RR will last four years. We recall reluctantly the old Indian curse which has condemned every president elected on a zero-numbered year since 1840 to die in office. Come 1983, if Ronald Reagan's administration is failing, if the economy is falling apart, if he is rejected by the people after three tiring years of effort to make things right,—one has to wonder if RR's subconscious will give it all up and trigger the mental and physical reaction. This country needs more than an Eisenhower or Coolidge, Reagan's role models. We need a Jefferson or a Jackson. Reagan has chosen the wrong presidents to emulate.

The *"new rich"* of the Republican ruling elite, our country's *"natural aristocracy,"* has a very apparent Achilles' heel. They are still so engaged by the trappings of their new-found financial, economic, political and personal power, that they get all too easily wrapped up in status symbols and one-upmanship games, activities common to those new to the arena of the super rich. In these distractions, we find an understandable unwillingness to climb a few wrungs back down the ladder, to first listen, and then to come to the aid of the common man. Private sector programs, which give hope, are vital to make believers out of the mass of Americans who are becoming increasingly impoverished by high food and fuel prices, taxes, and the demon of inflation. The American dream is dying. The Reagan election is disbelieving America giving its dream a final chance.

The danger is that the Republicans will appear to be uncaring, that they will become too much engaged with the fact that they now rule, and, in the process, lose this limited opportunity given them by the already skeptical public. Republican thinking is in the minority. With only 72 million people paying taxes and 81 million dependent upon government income for a living, the Democrats have the deck stacked in their favor. And, so, with each passing day, the dark clouds of 1982 and 1984 loom more ominously, when inaction keeps time with the clock. Robert Prechter (P. O. Box 262, Chappaqua, NY 10514) who analyzes the stock market from an Elliott Wave perspective, brought this political graph to my attention. (See graph next page.) The bell may toll for the Republicans in 1984, unless they move quickly. The Republicans had best discard their limousines, their $10,000 dresses, and their minks which were as numerous at inauguration as popcorn at a Saturday afternoon movie, if they are to capture the trust of an impatient American public. Republican clout won't count for long with the masses. The Republican elite is already victimized by the doctrine of envy which has been preached persuasively in this century at least since the times of FDR. A Democratic landslide in 1984 and a concomitant Republican burial will not be met by surprise, but by cynicism and the phrase, *"Oh well, I knew conservative politics was obsolete."*

A real hot spot was all the grassroot PACS (Political Action Committees) which are springing up like mushrooms in the nation's capital. Also, an elite group of Republican businessmen are finally putting their money where their mouths are, and supporting candidates and causes which promote individual advancement and preserve freedom. There seems to be a growing recognition among rich Repubicans that government, particularly the Democratic party form, will always fill the vacuum of rich Republican irresponsibility.

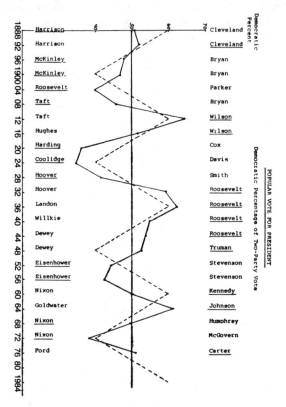

Remember how all true wealth comes ultimately from resources taken from the good earth. The best contemporary example of this truth on the international level is OPEC with its oil. It is a point still lost on Washington. . . . And where did the majority of the Republican *"Megabucks"* earn their wealth? In the South and the West. And in what areas? Oil and gas and real estate—from the EARTH! It's a paradox. Washington, which only understands paperwork, bureaucracy, connections and high society, is now subjected to the influence of EARTHmen.

PACS exert **enormous** political influence. *"Megabucks"* (the Republican financial superstars) and PACS are the one-two punch which create or kill many of the politicians and much of the legislation which is ground through the hopper in Washington, D.C. Politicians are men of action. Their tremendous workload, heavy constituency and correspondence requirements and party functions—all eat up their time and their estates. This makes them (politicians) vulnerable as well as in need of good input. Having had the opportunity to personally visit with over half a dozen senators, one on one, I am convinced that they will listen to and heed good counsel, if enough pressure is applied. I found this to be unquestionably the case, for their questions reflected a political desire for information which would help them make better decisions. The politicians are worried, which is probably why they escape (party) so much. They know the mood of the public is restless. We count, now as never before. Letters to our congressmen and senators marked *"personal,"* with concise, factual bits of information, documenting why a particular stand is justified, may be carefully evaluated. Politicians are only moved by influence. It's far better for you to move them than for the decadent Washington establishment to have its merry way. Money to Washington *"lifers"* is like water from a faucet—to be wasted. One well-known conservative senator has no clout with his colleagues because he has too much integrity. He won't compromise. No joke. We must exert our rightful influence. Otherwise, we risk revolution, long-term.

Now, as never before, do I realize how little truth and facts are understood by the financial powers that influence legislation, and even more tragically, how little is known by those who enact it. Money is power, and politics is power. But wisdom, knowledge and understanding is necessary for the survival of either financial or political power. The conversations I had this past week with those who govern the greatest country on earth have convinced me to go to the mat if necessary on this point.

On a personal level, Linda and I thoroughly enjoyed the four days of glitter and sparkle, pomp and circumstance, ceremony and celebration afforded us at this both festive and solemn time in our political life. *"Tux and tails"* were the order of the day for meetings, luncheons, receptions and parties with congressmen, senators, department heads, dignitaries, *"megabuck"* financiers and movie stars. Performers met included Donnie and Marie Osmond, Debbie Reynolds, Wayne Newton, Elizabeth Taylor (That's right, I even got to embrace Elizabeth and her two Oscars.), Mel Tillis and a host of other superstars which gittered in the night both above and below Washington. By the time Wednesday rolled around, Linda and I had had enough, so that even an offer to attend another reception at the White House was refused in lieu of a plane home.

On the flight back, I had the opportunity to reflect upon the suggestions that I seriously consider running for the U.S. Senate from Montana. It was a very flattering offer, and certainly one with appeal. But what kept coming back to me were Waylon's words in *"Luckenbach, Texas."* You remember them, *"I don't need my name in the marquee lights. . . . So baby let's sell your diamond ring, buy some boots and faded jeans, and go away. . . . This coat and tie is choking me, and in your high society, you cry all day. We've been so busy keeping up with the Jones', four car garage and we're still building on. Maybe it's time we got back to the basics of love."*

Waylon's wisdom is lost on the D.C. establishment.

One of the greatest blessings for a man in this life is to be able to live with a woman he loves and witness the miracle of the family which blossoms as a result of that relationship. Another is to be able to live modestly and comfortably beneath his financial means and also limit the demands on his time. A third is to know what is really important. I am blessed with all of these jewels.

I hail from a long line of teachers and entrepreneurs. My roots are blended and energized in THE REAPER. I have turned down countless opportunities to manage multimillion dollar commodity funds, simply because there is no joy for me in just making money. I have to feel I am making a contribution in order to be fulfilled.

The whole concept of self-interest being best-served by service is not only financially rewarding, but tremendously self-fulfilling. What I wouldn't give to have this concept thoroughly understood and embraced not only intellectually, but also emotionally, by the entire business and political community which rules over our country. When I no longer feel this way, I will find something else to do. But, until then, there is something very special about writing for *"the salt of the earth."*

REAGAN'S TREADMILL

3/13/81

The Reagan administration is running on an ever-steepening treadmill, which is threatening to frustrate its efforts to curb federal spending. The culprits are high interest rates with concomitant compound interest, and federal social spending programs which are indexed to inflation. Stated differently, the Reagan administration has to run faster just to stay even. It has to cut the budget more, just to keep the deficit from increasing.

According to some monetary theorists, the tremendous monetary growth allowed by the Federal Reserve during the last months of the Carter administration is an inflationary black cloud closing in on this country. If these theorists are correct, even in the face of present high interest rates and U.S. Treasury borrowing *"crowding out,"* the Federal Reserve cannot let the money supply increase now. This would be like throwing gasoline on a fire. While it is my analysis that interest rates could be about to soften some, it should be only a short-term event. If the economy softens, borrowing to stave off bankruptcy will again push rates higher, as will federal borrowing to finance the social programs triggered by unemployment in a declining economy. It is my analysis that the economy is now turning down again into recession.

It is no secret that rates have stayed high, due to the recent rededication of the Fed to keep money expensive (interest rates above the rate of inflation), tremendous U.S. Treasury borrowing, tax-time borrowing, and oil industry procurement of loans for expansion following decontrol. Interest rates, at their present high levels, have already resulted in corporate losses and have washed some companies up on the shores of bankruptcy. Even high interest rates later on this year will, of course, aggravate this unfavorable economic situation.

It has been estimated that a 1% increase in unemployment results in as high as a $25-billion increase in federal spending. In other words, as a result of a reduction of both personal and business tax intake due to poor economic conditions, plus the requirement for increased government spending (borrowing) for transfer payments triggered by soft economic conditions, a $25-billion deficit is assured for every 1% increase in unemployment.

175

The Reagan administration and the Fed try to fight inflation by maintaining high interest rates. However, high interest rates frustrate the Reagan administration's program to reduce federal spending, since high interest rates pressure the economy, cause companies to go bankrupt, which results in worker layoffs, which triggers more federal spending. It's a vicious cycle. And, of course, higher interest rates mean it costs the government more to borrow. For these reasons, the Reagan administration must reduce social spending now—immediately! But, yet, the Reagan cuts in the **increase** in the federal budget are only a drop in the bucket. And, already, special interest groups and the Congress are becoming recalcitrant. It's a *"damned if you do, damned if you don't"* situation. The Reagan administration is between the *"devil and the deep blue"* in an effort to reduce the federal deficit. Perhaps Jimmy Carter, the ultimate pragmatist, saw that the tidal wave of federal deficits must self-destruct the country in order for the problem to be finally solved. Carter knew all too well that no one man is going to stop a tidal wave of federal transfer payments brought on by a generation of economic ignorance and debt.

The only hope for the Reagan administration is to be triumphant quickly, and then to accelerate the budget cuts once an initial victory is under their belts. The clock is ticking. Already, high interest rates have forced cancellation of business expansion plans. Federal borrowing could zoom from an estimated $80-billion to $130-billion. The federal deficit is zooming out-of-sight!

Let's review the cycle again: High interest rates maintained in an effort to fight inflation results in declining business activity. This leads to employee layoffs, which trigger federal social spending. This social spending, or transfer payments, must be financed by Treasury borrowing in the capital markets, which is expensive, which results in more crowding out and the driving up of interest rates along with an increased federal deficit. This leads to further business stagnation, and so the vicious cycle goes. The only way out is to painfully cut social spending, federal loans and loan guarantees now, given a debt capitalistic system.

The Federal Reserve has to sit this one out on the sidelines. Investors, both domestically and internationally, are so attuned to inflation and watching the Fed, that the Fed can no longer increase the money supply without triggering a further bond market collapse, which results in yet higher interest rates. Also, with so many dollars being held by OPEC countries and in Europe and Asia, any hint of the Fed relaxing their monetary restraint will result in accelerated inflationary expectations with all that implies by way of higher gold prices and a dollar crisis. The Reagan administration has a tiger by the tail.

Actually, it is going round and round with a skunk in a blender. The smell of a financial debacle is in the air.

The pressure of higher interest rates could begin easing now and fall off more in April. However, we should not expect a decline in interest rates to last too long, or fall off too far. There is tremendous demand for money bubbling not too far below present interest rate levels. Consumers are waiting in the wings for mortgages. Businesses have billions of dollars of bonds to float. The federal government pig is increasing its take at the borrowing trough. And, there are no savings due to illiquidity throughout the economy.

Due to the volatility, uncertainty, and emotional nature of today's economic and financial environment, as investors, speculators, and business people, we want to get out of debt and stay liquid. It is prudent to avoid making long-term business or personal financial decisions at this time. Cash and T-Bills are king, in addition to survival precious metals. We will play the swings in commodities, because we can move quickly in these markets, and *"go with the flow."* If the Fed caves in, if the Reagan administration throws in the towel, or if Congress capitulates to special interest groups, we will expect the first hint of this inflationary activity to be best manifested in the commodity markets. While we should do everything we can to encourage our elected representatives to pass Reagan's program for budget cuts, economic and political realism suggests that the Republicans will fail.

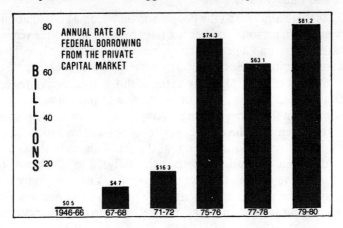

Source: Economic Meteorology, RR 13, Kansas City North, Missouri 64161

WASHINGTON HOT SEAT

7/31/81

For the purpose of listening to, and visiting with, Budget Director, Dave Stockman, Secretary of the Treasury, Donald Regan, and Defense Secretary, Caspar Weinberger, I prepared the following questions. It has occurred to me that your personal and financial planning will benefit from reviewing these questions since there is so much hard data in the questions themselves. I was unsuccessful in pulling answers to these inquiries from these government officials. Perhaps your congressman or senator can help you out with the answers.

Economic and Financial Questions

1. Isn't it accurate to state that even with the Reagan administration's recent success with Congress in spending and tax cuts, in truth all that has been accomplished is a cut in the increase in government spending and a cut in the increase in taxes? When and how can we expect real budget cuts?

2. Is there any reason the people should become excited about a 25 percent cut in personal income tax rates over the next three years when it barely offsets a 22 percent tax increase that individuals will have to endure from higher Social Security taxes and bracket creep?

3. Aren't present high tax rates a thorn that could fester into outright rebellion given that there are now 2 million active tax protestors; given that more and more Americans are in the 50 percent tax bracket; given that the average serf only worked two to three days a week for his feudal lord; given that the Black slaves in the Old South provided their plantation masters with only 10 to 12 percent of the production; and given the fact that even the Viet Cong only took 30 percent tribute from the Vietnamese? Are you concerned enough about tax protests to move aggressively to further cut spending and taxes?

4. Doesn't the American public's infatuation with professional sports reflect not only an escapism from the harsh and unfair political and economic system perpetuated by the federal government today, but also provide the one arena where fair play is observed consistently? What ever happened to the perspective that people are equal at

178

the starting line, not at the finish line? Is there a chance that we will have a consumption-based tax system initiated, consistent with 17th century English social philosopher Thomas Hobbes' perspective that people should be taxed on what they take out of society rather than on what they contribute to society? If not, why?

5. Why haven't we eliminated the Department of Education and the Department of Energy which cost $26 billion to operate, particularly when we observe that the Department of Energy's budget is greater than the combined profits of at least the ten largest major oil companies, and that the public's vote of *"no confidence"* for the Department of Education is evidenced by private schools springing up in this country at the rate of better than one a day?

6. What makes this administration believe that with a tax cut the consuming public will save the money and business will make capital expenditures, given the fact that consumers are loaded up with debt and illiquid, and that the liquidity of corporations presently is at dangerously low levels? Isn't the probability of consumer saving and business spending decreased with the almost certainty of an upcoming recession, and the fact that such investment activity seldom occurs at the peak of the 54-year Kondratieff Wave cycle as confirmed by studies at MIT, and as discussed as far back as 1932 by economist James M. Funk at the Department of Commerce?

7. In an age of coming decentralization and emerging conservative trends worldwide, by what thinking does the administration consider allowing the bankrupt S & Ls to be absorbed by the big multinational banks who have already made uncollectible loans in excess of twice their equity to Third World countries?

8. How can the Reagan administration count on 15 percent of GNP business fixed investment when such has never exceeded 11.6 percent and rose only to 11 percent in 1966, when the U.S. economy peaked on a non-inflationary basis?

9. What are the government discussions about, or probabilities of, using The Monetary Control Act which allows the Federal Reserve not only to monetize the debt of the U.S. government, but also to buy up the bonds of private corporations and foreign countries?

Military Questions

1. Given the United States' reliance on imported strategic metals, such as chromium, platinum, manganese, bauxite, cobalt and tin for the continued successful operation of our industrial plants, and given the Soviet's strategy to secure and control the 14 choke points in the world's oceans, namely the five inland seas—South China, Mediter-

ranean, North Sea, Norwegian and Caribbean; the seven critical passage points—Malacca Straits, Ceylon, Horn of Africa, Mozambique Channel, Cape of Good Hope, Gibraltar and Cape Horn; along with the two interoceanic canals—Suez and Panama; what naval counter-measures has the U.S. taken to protect these 14 choke points through which our critical strategic metals and the world's seaborne commerce pass?

2. Is the reason the Department of Energy has not been abolished because 50 percent of the Energy Department's budget goes for the making of nuclear warheads and the management of the strategic oil stockpile?

3. Dr. Antony Sutton, in his book, NATIONAL SUICIDE, has documented that 95 percent of the technology provided the Soviet Union has come from the West. According to Dr. Sutton, the Watkins-Johnson Company sold the Soviets their missile guidance system. General Al Knight declares that the Bryant Chucking and Grinding Company of Springfield, Vermont has been selling equipment to the Soviet Union since 1931, including the precision grinding tools needed to make the ball bearings required by the inertial guidance system for the MIRV missiles. The Kama River Factory in the Soviet Union was financed to the tune of $2 billion by Chase Manhattan and the U.S. taxpayer supported Export-Import Bank. This factory manufactures a substantial portion of trucks, tanks and rocket launchers for the Soviet Union. The White House has approved the sale of V-12 engines to the Soviet Union, which are used in tanks. By what logic or insanity do we sell the Soviet Union the rope to hang us, the technology necessary to build up their military machine? Isn't this totally hypocritical if we take the Soviet Union at their word, that they are sworn to our destruction, and given the fact that the military spending budget for the United States is scheduled to increase $1.5 trillion over the next five years? If we are going to sell the Soviet Union technology and equipment so they can manufacture weapon systems to destroy us, then why do we need a national defense? Or, switching the question around, if we are going to have a national defense and a huge military budget, why do we sell such critical technology to the Soviets? Who benefits from such sales? Who finances them?

4. Isn't it true that half of the U.S. defense budget goes for defending other nations? Given the illiquidity and heavy debt throughout all levels of government, and the dangerous debt level of businesses and consumers, by what logic can these huge military expenditures be defended, particularly in light of the fact that the United States is a constitutional republic and not a world empire? What is being done to cut the waste of the military budget? Do we really need four air forces and

three military academies?

5. Given the debate over fighter bombers and particularly the B-1, what, if anything, has been done to investigate the feasibility of using the Burnelli aircraft design?

6. Given the increasing number of media hints and intelligence reports suggesting a move militarily by the United States against Cuba, what are the probabilities of such aggression occurring? In considering military action against Cuba, does the fact that Cuba's airfields are being expanded to accommodate Soviet strategic Backfire bombers influence your decision? Is one of the reasons the Cubans are constructing this airfield on Grenada due to the fact that Grenada commands the water channel through which 52 percent of all U.S. imported oil passes?

7. How do you respond to Major General John Singlaub's statement, *"The Soviets could bomb us with cargo planes?"* What are the implications of his remarks, given the holes in NORAD's radar system, our limited number of interceptor aircraft and Russian aircraft sightings along the East Coast?

8. Is it true that the MX system is basically useless and vulnerable without an ABM system to protect it?

9. Is it accurate that the U.S. has one missile submarine in the Pacific and all the rest in the Atlantic Ocean? If so, what's being done about it?

10. To what extent will the space shuttle be used to carry x-ray lasers or light lasers into space for use against Soviet missile attacks, given the successful tests of the x-ray laser at the Lawrence Livermore Laboratory and the light laser at Kirkland Air Force Base in Albuquerque, New Mexico?

11. Is it true that we have no ICBM production lines in operation while the Soviets have five assembly lines? Is it also true that we have no ABM defense? If so, what's being done about it?

12. Is it correct that the U.S. missile warning system is so delicate that it produced 147 false indications of a Soviet missile attack on the U.S. during the last 18 months? If so, what's being done about this?

13. What has been done to protect the electronic equipment of this country against the EMP (Electro Magnetic Pulse)? How accurate is the data that projects that the EMP resulting from a nuclear weapon exploded 200 miles above this country would destroy every piece of unprotected electronic equipment in the country, including bank accounts on computers?

14. What do you make of the Supreme Allied Commander of Europe's comment regarding the U.S.' ability to sustain its forces in combat: *"The U.S. is flat on its ass."*?

15. What are we going to do about the fact that 70 percent of the United States' defense budget goes for salaries and pensions and that the Reagan Administration is planning to spend $1.5 trillion on defense in the next five years while defense costs are escalating at twice the national inflation rate?

16. Why are we continuing with the M1 battle tank which costs $2.5 million each when a 1980 GAO study says these tanks have never had a successful cold weather start and a blue ribbon committee of technical experts discovered that the engines' durability and reliability levels are so low that the levels could be doubled and the engines would still fall short of their durability and reliability requirements?

17. Why aren't we going ahead with the neutron bomb when it's only a $50 million program, and it would put us back in a position of superiority over the Soviet Union?

18. Given chemical warfare usage as a major part of the tactics planned for invading Europe by the Soviet Union, why are our soldiers presently not equipped to fight against this type of warfare? Is it true that our soldiers have no gas masks or chemical weapons for their own protection? How many rounds (days) of ammunition do our troops have in Europe?

19. Is it true that only ten of the United States Army's 16 combat divisions are ready to fight and that the remaining 6 would need several weeks to deploy in an emergency? Is it also correct that the Soviet Union has 46 divisions under arms with 15 along the Turkish border alone and nearly 16 divisions in full readiness against our ten? If so, what's being done about this?

20. Is it correct that the amount of money spent on military hardware from 1959 through 1979 could have recapitalized U.S. industry six times?

21. How is the Pentagon's $100 million, 4,000-person, full-time program against drug and alcohol abuse in the military progressing? Are one out of three U.S. soldiers still involved in drugs?

22. Is it true that Soviet bombers could penetrate undetected through NORAD radar gaps until 1985? If so, what's being done about it?

23. Given British intelligence confirming Russian planned terrorism for Saudi Arabia, the probable overthrow of the Saudi Arabian government and the fall of the Saudi royal family by 1986, what contingency plans has the U.S. made militarily to ensure the continuation of the oil flow from the Middle East, particularly from Saudi Arabia?

24. What is the probability of the reinstatement of the draft, given the drug-related problems and the low level of morale in our military,

plus the fact that 50 percent of the Army's enlistees cannot read above the sixth grade level, and the fact that young blacks make up 12 percent of the country's population but 30 percent of the Army and 33 percent of the enlisted grades?

25. What has been done to upgrade the technical competence of our military, given that in 1979, 86 percent of all artillery crewmen failed the Army's skill qualification tests for their assigned specialty, that the failure rates were 89 percent for track vehicle mechanics, 90 percent for nuclear weapons maintenance specialists, and 98 percent for artillery repairmen?

26. Is it true that while allotting only $98 million per year to provide for the nuclear defense of the entire United States, the U.S. Congress has spent more than ten times that amount, approximately $1 billion, to build massive blast shelters in a 300-mile arc around Washington, D.C., designed to protect the members of Congress and government bureaucrats? What is being done in national civil defense for the people?

A SHOT IN THE DARK

9/11/81

The August 21st REAPER discussed the possibility of suitcases rigged with bombs being placed aboard jetliners, the bombs engineered to explode in midair. A few days after that REAPER was written, a Taiwanese jetliner exploded in flight, killing all 110 people on board. That same August 21st REAPER discussed how Libya's madman, Muammar Qadhafi, was livid and embarrassed beyond words when U.S. F14s shot down his *"rootin'-tootin'"* SU22s. Qadhafi's terrorist network, allied with the PLO, let the world know in no uncertain terms what it thought about the U.S.A. the next week as bombs exploded all over the globe, from Peru to Germany. It seems it would clearly be a mistake for the Secret Service not to take seriously Qadhafi's threat to *"liquidate"* President Reagan. On September 2nd, Qadhafi declared a *"holy war"* against the U.S. Our Phoenix office has informed the White House regarding this matter. (Federal government intelligence is often as bad as federal Postal Service.)

Let's gather a perspective on this distasteful subject. Your editor first brought to contemporary light (CYCLES OF WAR, 1977) that every president elected on a zero number year since 1840 had died in office. Mr. Reagan was elected on a zero number year—1980. The April 3rd REAPER's lead article, *"An Inch is as Good as a Mile,"* was written a day after John Hinckley's alleged assassination attempt on the President. That REAPER stated:

> *"On Monday, March 30, 1981, we came within an inch and a heartbeat from having George Bush as President of the United States of America. In this case, an inch was as good as a mile. . . ."*

It was two to three weeks after President Reagan took that bullet that it was first made known that the bullet had indeed lodged a mere inch from the President's heart. This writer received more than a few comments and phone calls about the fact that *"An Inch is as Good as a Mile,"* written the day following the assassination attempt, was confirmed by actual evidence some two weeks later. You may recall from squaring of price and time analysis of late March, that we were expecting important events to occur at that time.

It is additionally ironic that your editor's photograph appeared on

184

the June cover of CHRISTIAN LIFE; that President Reagan's photograph graced the July cover of CHRISTIAN LIFE; that this writer's *"Church and State"* piece was in both issues; and that I had the opportunity to present both issues to the President in July.

Carrying this intrigue further, the July 24th REAPER's *"Washington: Might and Right?"* article reviewed this writer's latest visit with the President and members of his cabinet. In that REAPER I reported on a disturbing conversation I had with a gentleman who was attending the White House reception also. I wrote,

> *"It is still mighty easy to get close to the President, real close. One gentleman, who attended the White House reception with me, commented that his rented limousine and driver were ushered right through the White House gates with no identification check of the license plates, driver or himself. Furthermore, this man declared, with considerable concern, that he strolled right up into the White House, unushered, unquestioned and unchecked. He was early for the reception, he stated, and so he strolled around for awhile on two levels of the White House unencumbered. He commented, rightfully, that it really worried him that he was able to roam so freely. It bothered me, too. I would have thought White House security would have been far more professional."*

Given just this evidence so far, one has to be concerned about the safety and well-being of our president. Terrorist organizations now have *"processed"* far more sophisticated *"Manchurian candidates"* than ever before. And, as professional security agencies and body guards will testify, it's almost impossible to prevent an assassination if the assassin is willing to die in the process. I have visited at length with a professional body guard who advises the Secret Service. I have talked for long hours with an FBI agent who was at Wounded Knee. This writer has listened to men who were part of the clandestine intelligence network in Vietnam. And, a man even traveled to Montana to speak to me, after reading CYCLES OF WAR, to tell me how grim things really were in the real world of espionage. This particular gentleman claimed he was the only survivor of an ambush perpetrated by our U.S. government, after his network had fulfilled their U.S. government assignment, knocking off a drug warehouse in Mexico. He related how it's no fun to take a shower and sleep with a 45 automatic all the time.

Robert Moss, co-author of THE SPIKE, recently commented on terrorism:

> *"I have been struck in recent months by the complacency in many quarters about the supposed invulnerability of the U.S. to terrorist attacks. If I were an international terrorist, there is almost no other country in the world where I would prefer to operate. That is because crucial installations and targets are wide open in this country. . . .*
>
> *"Finally, we have to anticipate and prepare for an increase in the*

number of attempted assassinations of prominent figures."
(Source: Daily News Digest)

We read the works of history, which are punctuated with assassinations and assassination attempts, and find it all very plausible. But yet, because it is too grim a subject to contemplate, our minds automatically reject such possibilities in this day and age. One of the *"leftovers"* of our formerly Christian culture is the idea that *"life is dear."* In fact, in many places in the world today—Russia, China, India, Iran, Africa—*"life is cheap."* *"Maggots in a flour sack"* is the contemptuous description of mankind expressed by one Eastern Establishment elitist. Throughout history, as in our world today, *"life is cheap."* This is the majority view. And there can be some interesting parallels drawn between the high level of abortions in the United States empire today, and the readiness with which the midwives of liberated Roman women threw their newborn babies into canals to drown. One-third of all U.S. pregnancies are being aborted today.

Please recall that our civilization is very similar to Rome. Chapter 13 of CYCLES OF WAR is entitled, *"Cycles of War and Caesar."* Therein the parallels between the two civilizations were abundantly presented. The United States is a world empire, as was Rome. We have U.S. multinational corporations, overt and covert political operatives globally, and military units stationed worldwide. These are all evidences of an empire! We have a president, who in a time of crisis, can exercise Executive Orders which give him the power of a Caesar. The likelihood of a president becoming dictatorial, in Caesar-like fashion, was a consistent thread running throughout CYCLES OF WAR. French historian, Amaury De Riencourt, projected this historically in his 1957 work, THE COMING CAESARS. Riencourt reached the same conclusion that Oswald Spengler did in his THE DECLINE OF THE WEST, published over 50 years ago.

Caesar had his Praetorian Guard. This imperial bodyguard had a great deal to say about who became Caesar. The U.S. military/industrial/banking complex has a great deal to say about who becomes Caesar, oops, president in this country, too.

The greatest enemy, the most dangerous enemy, is always the enemy within. Why? Because the enemy within is never recognized. Whether it's God and Satan, Adam and Eve, Joseph and his jealous brothers, Pharaoh and Moses, Moses and the Israelites, Saul and David, David and his sons, Jesus and Judas, Caesar and Brutus, the Catholic Church and Luther, Lincoln and Stanton, or Hitler and his generals—in each case, the greatest enemy was the enemy within. Have you noticed the increasing number of cartoons recently which depict Ronald Reagan as a Hitler-type? It's scary.

At first blush, it would appear that the most dangerous enemies from within are U.S. citizens. The John Hinckley experience supports this perspective. And just the other week, Isom Joseph Dean, Jr. was taken into custody by Secret Service agents after being stopped on a routine traffic complaint. Dean, as it turns out, armed with a 22-caliber pistol, three rifles and a shotgun, was on his way, allegedly, to kill President Reagan.

Even a grandmother, Mary Hardman of Belmar, New Jersey, is being forced to appear in court on the charges that she threatened to kill the President. Such a backlash by beneficiaries of the U.S. welfare system, who are politically and economically naive, should not be surprising. The violent reaction is deeply ingrained and conditioned by the *"survival of the fittest"* philosophy and the use of violence as an acceptable solution to problems presented on TV. Reagan being portrayed as a Hitler-type doesn't help matters any, given the aggressive reaction that Americans have to any and everything that has to do with Hitler and the Nazi era. But perhaps the greatest enemy from within is not the ordinary, disenchanted, cynical U.S. citizen. Perhaps the enemy within is far more sophisticated and insidious. Perhaps it is the banking system, particularly if Reagan moves toward a classic gold standard. Perhaps it is the military/industrial complex.

It was Dwight David Eisenhower, military hero of World War II, *"the best and the brightest"* that the U.S. military/industrial complex produced, who, as President, warned us in no uncertain terms about the dangers of the military/industrial complex. It was Gary Powers' U-2 incident which led to an acceleration of tension between the two superpowers, the U.S.S.R. and the U.S.A., at that time. Who profited from the U-2 scandal? The military/industrial complex, of course. And what did Gary Powers claim? He stated that the bomb had been **planted** on board his aircraft. Question: Who put it there? Whatever happened to Gary Powers?

Now, let's get to the guts of this unpalatable issue. *"The Great Right Turn"* in American politics, the *"Reagan Revolution"* as it is being called, has hinged upon the popularity, political skills, conviction and dedication of primarily one man—President Ronald Reagan. Gary North, who served on Capitol Hill, and who is still well-connected with political in-fighting, has written that following Reagan's election, from the time of the transition team forward, the ideological constitutional conservatives lost out to the Eastern Republican Establishment.

Reagan, in his effort to cut back big government, has been aided handily, primarily by one man, OMB Director, Dave Stockman (a political zealot if there ever was one). And recall, that Dave Stockman's appointment was a fluke. He was Reagan's personal choice because the President was so impressed with how Stockman consistently beat him in preparatory debates during the presidential campaign. And Stockman, who now has a comprehensive grasp of the myriad budgetary problems, has zeroed in on the only two areas where meaningful budget cuts can be made to salvage the budget—Social Security and **defense spending**. The Social Security trial balloon was quickly shot down by volleys streaming from all over the American landscape. Major Social Security cuts are politically impossible. Social Security will be, at most, subjected to cosmetic surgery.

That leaves us with the **real** sacred cow—military spending, **the** *"untouchable,"* if you will. Stockman has locked in on the military/industrial/banking complex's *"pet."* And Stockman has President Reagan's ear. The projected defense budget cuts—$30 billion.

Remember what happened to Representative Ron Paul of Houston when he fought the battle for taxpayers against subsidizing the Export-Import Bank and all the other *"development"* banks?

> *"On May 12, 1981, the House of Representatives voted to remove $876 million from the 1981 budget of the Export-Import Bank. The big banks' and corporations' executives went to work that very night. The next day, May 13th, 71 votes were switched and $876 million was reinstated. That's real power in action! The U.S. taxpayers have subsidized the Export-Import Bank to the tune of $13 billion already, historically."*

And what's happened to Representative Ron Paul as a result of his efforts to bring all these banking/industrial boondoggles to light? For this, along with his exposure of the devilish Monetary Control Act of 1980, Representative Paul has become the victim of *"redistricting."* He has been shuffled over into a district where he has a real tough go at getting reelected. *"Big bucks"* have lined up against Congressman Ron Paul.

Will the military/industrial/banking complex have any less sympathy for Ronald Reagan or Dave Stockman if they take a sharp knife to the defense sacred cows? It's a disturbing question.

Now, let's turn to the man who would become the next U.S. president if the unthinkable happened to President Reagan. While some more suspicious writers have pointed out the connection between the Hinckley and Bush families, and while the Hard Right Wing has observed that George Bush as President would be the *"darling"* of the Eastern military/industrial/banking complex, there is no reason, absolutely none at all, to even suspect that George Bush would be in any way involved with a nefarious plot to become this nation's chief executive officer. One, though, has to be bothered by the recent observations of long-time, rational, astute political observers, who have now become alarmed at the base that Bush and the BUSHmen have established in the Executive Branch. Again, these are not the observations of the far out, off-the-wall, lunatic fringe, that sees conspiracy under every rock.

It has been pointed out that George Bush for vice-president was a reluctant Reagan selection, one, in fact, Reagan was pushed into. And yes, it has been observed that Bush's people have dominated communications and political appointments in this administration. Yes, it is also true that Bush has established a *"cabinet-in-waiting."* All these occurrences are disturbing a number of patriotic Americans, political thinkers and analysts.

Beyond question, George Bush, educated at Yale, with only a 27% conservative rating as a congressman from Texas, as the former Ambassador to the U.N., as the former U.S. Envoy to Red China, as the former Director of the CIA, as a former member of the Trilateral Commission, is overwhelmingly the preferred president of the Eastern military/industrial/banking complex. And, with President Reagan strongly considering taking a sharp knife to the jugular of some of the military/industrial/banking complexes' pet projects, the powers that be, will, at minimum, grumble. Let's hope that's all they do.

The greatest enemy always comes from within because he is never suspected. If one honestly and openly just surveys the vast number of publicized books written on clandestine U.S. military/industrial/banking activity over the last 20 years, one cannot help but come away with the clear impression that the *"end"* has been seen to justify whatever *"means"* were necessary in far too many cases. Books written by former insiders expose all the dirty laundry. These works appear only in the underground press. They are blackballed by the establishment press for the most part.

What we must unfortunately consider is the possibility that George Bush could find himself installed as President, in spite of himself. History, both ancient and modern, about terrorist and military/industrial/banking activities, forces us to consider this possibility. The rampant violence extant in the 20th Century, coupled with our nation's tendency to put all of its past five presidents through *"The Meat Grinder,"* makes the picture even darker. And, I write this piece with a letter here on my desk inviting me to a reception and dinner at George Bush's home in Washington, D.C. on the evening of September 21st.

It is important to consider this unpleasant subject for two reasons:

1. It's critical that we have a grasp, an all encompassing grasp, of a series of distasteful events, which, if they come to pass, will most probably lead to an economic crisis and financial panic of mammoth proportions. There is little question that if George Bush is elevated to President of the United States suddenly, gold will soar, bonds will crater, and we could be faced with an instant depression. Such a political surprise **should** lead to a panic. Panics are the result of surprise.

One astute political writer observed that if it's Mondale vs. Bush in 1984, the American people have a *"lose-lose"* situation. If this turns out to be the case, gold should be squirrelled away domestically and internationally. Also, a residence should be established in a small town as a back-up to an urban domicile.

2. For personal planning, as well as contemporary political perspective, which vitally affects **financial** and **economic** activity in our **political democracy,** I felt it imperative that we have a handle on how these *"straws in the wind"* were coming together. The *"squaring of price and time in history"* takes place in much the same manner as the *"squaring of price and time in markets."* Indicators come together in markets and trigger a trade. Activities come together in history and trigger an event. It's disconcerting the way activities are coming together with Qadhafi, the international terrorist's bombings, the early assassination attempt on President Reagan, the threats of other would be assassins, the news releases which state that Reagan is only working two-three hours a day, leaving the impression he is expendable, the Hitler-type cartoons, the military/industrial/banking complexes' concerns, and the power which George Bush is gathering behind the scenes, intentionally or unintentionally.

Power always fills a vacuum. The presidency of the United States is the *"power plum"* of the world. When Ronald Reagan delegates authority, he also delegates responsibility and **power!** It is simply natural for George Bush to assimilate his fair share of it, in a perfectly innocent and ethical way. It's those out there in the shadows, terrorists and the military/industrial/banking types, who put the bomb on board Gary Powers' U-2 spy plane, that are worrisome, along, of course, with deranged U.S. citizens. The evidence is clearly that *"they"* would prefer George Bush as President!

This country doesn't need any more replays of, *"The Manchurian Candidate,"* or *"Seven Days in May,"* or *"Three Days of the Condor."* For the first time, in a long, long time a president has decided to try to light the constitutional candle of freedom, which our forefathers established for the American people. Being human, and thus only capable of one thing perfectly—error—President Reagan has made his share of mistakes. Most of his mistakes, I am convinced, are errors of ignorance, stemming from poor advice or inadequate information. Any politician who stays more than a fortnight in Washington, D.C. contracts the infectious *"power"* disease which distorts judgment. Nevertheless, President Reagan has struck a match and lit freedom's candle. President Reagan has slim odds, slim to none, of succeeding. But he deserves his chance to try. The global winds of violence are blowing, and causing that candle's flame to flicker.

D.C. BLUES

6/12/81

A good friend just returned from Washington, D.C., where he was involved in some high-level political meetings. I was told without equivocation, that the political conservatives have lost, that the battle is over for control of the Reagan administration. As you will recall, this was my concern, that Reagan would wilt or be outgunned by the Bush-led establishment. The latter is the case. Reagan has been BUSHwhacked.

These controlling Republicans, like the Democrats which preceded them, believe in the centralization of power at the federal level, only they accomplish it more surreptitiously. The Democrats subsidize the poor. This is easily visible. The Republicans subsidize the rich. This is not so visible. Both subsidies lead to the concentration of power at the federal level.

Corporate welfare via subsidies granted to the Export-Import Bank, the World Bank and other international banking agencies far overshadow what we normally consider to be *"welfare."* Support of the military-industrial complex with all the waste, graft and corruption involved with that bureaucracy, coupled with an interventionist foreign policy, makes the international bankers squeal with glee. After all, it is the international bankers and corporations who benefit most from this Republican welfare and war preparations.

The buzzard which is flying away with our freedoms has two wings —a left wing and a right wing. The Democrats control the left wing— with wasteful social spending. The Republicans man the right wing— with inefficient military spending and international financial boondoggles. Guns and butter, right and left, when concentrated at the federal level, result in the loss of personal freedoms. Remember, freedom only comes to anyone long-term with the assumption of responsibility. If, as individuals, we neglect to assume responsibility in any area of life, that vacuum will be filled by the government, the price being our commensurate loss of freedom.

We will not restore true principles of freedom to this country until the federal government is again established primarily as a limited institution intended to protect the **freedoms** of the individual, rather

192

than as an agency whose purpose is to provide for the **needs** of the people. The first embraces risk, the second security. As long as our people want their needs met and their security provided for by the government, the federal government will accommodate them, at the expense of freedom. But, in the process, we all commit suicide. Government is a parasite, which eventually devours its host (us).

Bush's key governmental appointments so dominate the Reagan administration, that if something tragic should happen to President Reagan, the transition to the Bush administration would come off without a hitch.

"Honeymoon Sours"
6/12/81

When political commentators start writing that the wrong monkey was placed in the White House, we know the Reagan honeymoon is about over. It is just waiting for a significant crisis or bungling to herald its conclusion. Most significant is the fact that President Reagan, at the height of his popularity, backed off quickly from his hard stance favoring significant, painful cuts in Social Security benefits. With R.R. backing down now, while his popularity is still soaring, is there any question that he will back off when the economic going gets really tough?

Also extremely significant is the confirmation that the American public has no concept of the desperate straits this country is in regarding debt economics, Social Security chaos, and the runaway federal budget. Approximately 90 percent of the mail received by the White House was against President Reagan's proposed Social Security reductions.

REAGAN ON THE RUN

10/30/81

It's important that we again review our personality sketch of President Reagan. President Reagan is by career choice, an actor. He enjoys people. He thrives on pleasing people. But, he also believes in doing the right thing. His personal desire to please the masses is, therefore, in conflict with his presidential actions. One wonders how long the President can maintain this tension.

The depth of this internal conflict was demonstrated by the fact that after the unions snubbed the President at the Labor Day Parade in New York City, he stated his desire to walk **with** the workers in next year's parade. The October 16th WALL STREET JOURNAL reported, *"Union workers all across the country generally agree that Mr. Reagan favors the rich, . . ."*

The President has yet to recognize that we have an ideological split in this country. We have the classic, Judeo-Christian, free enterprise, constitutional Americans, who believe that the federal government's only purpose is to provide for the protection of its citizens and maintain justice. In other words, the government's only function is to protect **freedom.** Then, we have the evolutionary, socialistic, humanistic Americans, who believe it's the federal government's purpose to provide for the **security** of the American people. There is no resolution to this ideological conflict. It is an either/or situation. **Freedom and security are antagonistic in this sense.**

When a nation is not ethnocentric or geographically condensed, as ours is **not**, it must have shared values and like-minded ideologies in order to survive. This ideological conflict is at the crux of what is ripping our social fabric apart. Our Christian ethic is gone.

Unfortunately, President Reagan is being increasingly surrounded by insensitive bureaucrats who thwart his natural instincts to do the right thing. Expect riots and terrorist acts in the cities. Have a *"country retreat"* established in a small, sleepy, rural town.

The reasons why the masses will be in revolt are high unemployment (particularly among the volatile minority groups), high taxes (taxes have not really been cut), and the fact that the public, with media prodding, is increasingly perceiving the Reagan administration as *"living*

194

high on the hog," while only the masses are forced to sacrifice. Recent political cartoons clearly portray Reagan as living an easy lifestyle. Mrs. Reagan's untimely purchase of $1,000 a place setting White House china didn't help this growing, negative, public perception either ($209,508 tax deductible for contributors). Fifty-two percent of Americans now believe that Reagan cares most about the rich, up from a mere 23% just last February.

It is a disastrous political mistake for the Republicans to underestimate how deeply entrenched is the liberal doctrine of *"envy,"* which has been hammered into the minds of the masses over the past 50 years. Again, the Republicans' perception of government is basically one of protecting the liberties of the people and ensuring justice. However, over the past 50 years, the masses have been taught, in the public schools, that the primary purpose of the federal government is to provide economic security for the people. **This means wealth transfer!** By flaunting wealth *("millionaires on parade"),* the Republicans are literally adding fuel to the fire of revolt which cyclically is projected to lead to a Democratic landslide in 1984.

As we are entering a recession or depression now, which will result in tough times for the masses (middle class included) between now and 1984, we can expect the Republicans to be driven out of office with a buggy whip when the election rolls around. The *"envy"* backlash will be horrible to behold.

Reagan's Right Wing coalition, which was instrumental in getting him elected, is totally disillusioned. Reagan's appointments, including Armand Hammer, a multinational industrialist with strong Soviet ties, as chairman of the President's cancer panel, came as a real shock. Reagan's approval of the subsidized low interest loans to Romania and China aggravated matters. His signing of Executive Order #12314, *"Federal Regional Councils,"* was a low blow, too.

That we are going to have an economic contraction, whether a deflationary recession/depression or an inflationary recession/depression is a foregone conclusion. Our whole economic system is based upon the viability of our long-term money markets. The destruction of these long-term money markets has been a logical, cause and effect consequence of our pervasive humanistic short-term social, political and financial perspectives. We have been committing *"elegant suicide,"* living for the present, the here and now, with no sense of *"deferred gratification."* It is the height of folly to think that the long-term money markets in bonds and mortgages can survive when all the short-term pressures throughout our entire social system militate against it. This newsclipping from the WALL STREET JOURNAL speaks clearly of this financial crisis.

Some Traders See State of Near-Paralysis As Investors Hesitate to Commit Funds

By Tom Herman and Edward P. Foldessy
Staff Reporters of The Wall Street Journal

NEW YORK—Reeling from last week's steep declines in bond prices, financial executives fear even more trouble ahead.

Bond traders say the credit markets are in danger of slumping into a state of near-paralysis' because of the growing reluctance of pension funds, insurance companies and other institutional investors to commit funds to long-term debt issues. Trading volume has slowed to a trickle lately as prices have plunged, and many analysts say it's unlikely this situation will change soon.

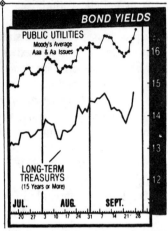

If you have assets, it's time for you to move. A portion of your portfolio should be located outside of the country. Next, become involved in politics on the local level. Become of service to your local community. Become someone who is trusted and respected by being active in local civic or charitable organizations and affairs. This backlash of *"envy"* from the impoverished masses could hit head-on by 1985 at the latest. Goodwill had best be established by then.

Hell hath no fury like a woman scorned, and the emotional, effeminate mentality of the masses will react violently against the *"silver spoon"* Republicans who promised economic Minerva, but delivered only Dante's Hell. The vindictive backlash of the common man, in his short-term state of economic ignorance, will target the Republicans for crushing his last grasp at the American dream. He will effectively throw economic acid into the face of the rich and powerful, who, correctly or incorrectly, are associated with the Republican Party.

When the public elected Ronald Reagan, they expected to see John Wayne in the White House. Instead, they got a drugstore cowboy, a Chase Manhattan, Standard Oil, General Electric, Merrill Lynch, Goldman Sachs' type, with a pinstripe suit **under** the cowboy's outfit. It's a facade the public doesn't buy, and one they will shoot full of holes with their own six-gun, figuratively and perhaps literally, no later than 1985.

THE GOLDEN HOPE

12/18/81

Since this is the season of hope and good cheer, a time when temporarily all is well with the world, it seems appropriate to share with you what may be becoming an increasingly realistic hope: **a return to the gold standard!** I've talked to Senator Steve Symms and Congressman Ron Paul about it. Congressman Paul puts the odds of a gold standard being adopted at only 1 in 10. It could be closer to 2 out of 3. A member of the White House staff recently *"slipped"* when he told me that President Reagan was seriously considering re-establishing the gold standard. The way events are coming together feels like the way a good trade comes together, too.

The Gold Commission releases its final report on March 31st. If there are several options the President can take listed in that report, and one of them includes a gold standard, then the President will have the justification he needs to do what he instinctively feels is correct— re-establish the gold standard.

In addition to our gut instinct regarding a gold standard, and the White House source information, other powerful Capitol Hill sources, who are very sensitive to the gold standard issue and well connected with the White House, too, confirmed this strong Reagan bias toward gold. They are accordingly optimistic.

It's important that we take note of the President's mental, psychological and physical condition in light of these golden considerations. President Reagan is becoming increasingly isolated. Since the first assassination attempt on his life, he has been more willing to take strong stands and trust his instincts. The latest Libyan threat has only reinforced that intuitive stance. President Reagan is trending more toward reflection, with a strong attraction for nostalgia. He is increasingly finding that his desire to be loved by the American general public, as well as his dream to re-establish the idealistic American free enterprise republic, are both crumbling. His recent concessions to labor and his near pleading remarks to the old folks are reflections of his actor's desire for applause and approval. President Reagan is feeling the stress and strain of the Oval Office. The inability to control internal bickering, news leaks and in-fighting within his

Executive Department are worrisome. He is also irritated with the pettiness which is part and parcel of Washington's way of life. All this is taking its toll on this 70-year-old man. He is not as stable as he once was.

The recent spending confrontation with Congress was terribly difficult and left the taste of a bittersweet win. The recent attacks by the establishment press, particularly the devastating Stockman article in THE ATLANTIC MONTHLY went down hard. The silly Richard Allen and William Casey affairs have been time consuming and painful. Attacks recently by THE HOUSTON POST, THE WASHINGTON POST, THE NEW YORK TIMES, James Reston and THE SAN FRANCISCO CHRONICLE have all been hard blows to our nation's Chief Executive Officer. As the pressure builds, he is more likely to do the one thing monetarily that his instincts tell him to do—re-establish the gold standard.

Recall the Barbara Walters' Thanksgiving Special with President Reagan. One of the old presidential campaign posters, which graced the President's California ranch house walls, placed emphasis on sound money.

The monetarists are discredited. The Keynesians are long gone. The supply-siders are out of favor. The economy has fallen like a stone. Gold may be the last anchor of credibility and economic salvation. And, the President, who has a way of snatching victory from the jaws of defeat, may very well sense this and act.

Let's track some more recent occurrences which may force the President, perhaps even at the urging of the more typical politicians, to grab hold of gold. Without a golden anchor, the economy cannot withstand the potential panic stemming from the bankruptcy of Chrysler, International Harvester, Ford, the S & Ls and/or the savings banks. Small business is being crucified by these high interest rates. A gold standard, particularly one linked to U.S. government bonds, could bring the still high long-term interest rates down more sharply.

The labor unions are hostile because their members are out of work. Unemployment is soaring. The gold standard might be the only confidence builder available to prevent yet more layoffs.

Congress is considering additional military spending cuts and social spending budget cuts in the face of my long projected $100 billion deficit. This is something President Reagan definitely does not want to see happen. In order to keep the federal deficit from increasing even more, to prevent increasing taxes and cutting military spending, the President just may have to go to gold.

Autos and housing definitely need the relief that a gold standard will bring to these interest rate sensitive industries. The typical

American's dream of owning his own home, with two cars in the garage, has been crushed.

The cities are in financial trouble. Some 60 percent of the cities are furloughing workers. The mayors are beating down the White House door.

The President needs to solve the economic crisis now. A gold standard might restore enough confidence to give the President a temporary reprieve. Foreign affairs are heating up. The Middle East, Poland, Europe, arms in Cuba, the military build-up in Nicaragua, the fracturing of NATO—all need the President's total attention now. He can't fight the lions of foreign affairs and the domestic economy at the same time without being eaten alive.

In the first nine months of 1981, the Soviet Union has shipped more military equipment to Cuba since the Cuban missile crisis of 1962. Arms are flowing from Vietnam to Nicaragua. Central America and the Caribbean require immediate attention.

The federal government is looking at increasing its debt 40 percent over the next three years. How can we refinance or obtain new sources of funds without gold? Monetize it all? Inflationary!

It's just possible that a gold standard could lead to a rush to purchase bonds and boost the stock market as confidence is restored. The liquidity could come from a mass exit from the money market mutual funds. This could possibly provide us two financial aspirins, which would temporarily relieve this nation's migraine economic headache.

In the WALL STREET JOURNAL's widely-read article *"Heard on the Street,"* Khaled Abu Su'ud, the investment and financial advisor of the Emir of Kuwait said he *"hopes the Reagan administration will take steps to strengthen the dollar as the international trading currency, perhaps by restoring the gold standard."*

What would gold do to the Third World countries? It would probably dramatically increase their commodity prices instantly, as we should expect would be the case in this country. A return to a gold standard should lead to an immediate adjustment, or a *"parity"* between gold and other commodities. For example, gold re-established at $400 an ounce could trigger 1973 or 1976 parity with corn at $8.00 a bushel. Can you imagine $8.00 a bushel corn? Other commodities should be similarly bullishly affected.

Real new wealth commodity prices multiply themselves seven times as they work through the economy. Thus, a return to the gold standard, leading to sharply higher commodity prices, could very well give us a two-year boom as stocks, bonds, business, and confidence rise, along with commodities. Such a dramatic increase in commodity prices, while they appear to be dramatically inflationary on the surface, should not be that much of an economic problem, given all the other built-in costs of finished goods these days. The cost of raw materials (commodities) is only a fraction of the price of a finished good today. There might be a temporary spurt of inflation in the price of goods and services, then stability for awhile.

Remember Senator Laxalt's comment way back on September 27th on NBC's MEET THE PRESS. He said, *"Gold is an option."*

Do you get the feeling that we are slowly but surely being drawn toward gold, that we have no other good option left?

The Third World countries could even pay back their debts to the international bankers with higher commodity prices. The farmers would return to solvency. They might even buy some automobiles and homes, along with all the other dream-hungry Americans. Interest rates would undoubtedly come down, particularly if the debt instruments were attached to gold. Small business could revive. Real estate and construction would perk up. Confidence would definitely be restored and the flow of funds out of money market funds might very well provide enough cash in the economy for the time necessary for the economy-at-large to get geared back up into a recovery. Gold just might work, for a time.

Now we turn to the one big, obvious stumbling block—the central bank, the Federal Reserve. But now, even the Fed is scared. The economic decline has turned into an avalanche. A flaming liberal Democrat, Congressman Henry B. Gonzales of San Antonio, Texas, has sponsored HR4358 that will eliminate the Federal Reserve. That's a real threat. If interest rates continue up, it could very well be enough to tip the Fed's hand toward gold and, as a result, give the President all the support he needs to do what he wants to do anyway—put the U.S. back on a gold standard.

All President Reagan has to do to establish the gold standard is to call up U.S. Secretary of Treasury, Donald Regan, and tell him to initiate the Mundell-Zijlstra proposal.

Jude Wanniski in a December 7th BUSINESS WEEK article entitled, *"A supply-side case for a gold standard,"* may have told us why the Fed will now support a gold standard.

> *"Without gold, the Federal Reserve is helpless. With the dollar floating, it is not possible for Paul Volcker to know the supply of money in the economy or the demand for it. The idea that he can somehow control that which he cannot know is the basis of the monetarist experiment that has undermined the people's faith in our currency. . . .*
>
> *"The bank [Federal Reserve] is guided in its purchase or sales of securities in the open market by the marginal changes in the public's demand for currency as observed at the gold window. The Fed now has no such guidance. . . ."* [8]

Get the drift of Wanniski's statements? **A gold standard will benefit the Federal Reserve as well as the U.S. government and the American people!** Notice that the gold standard will not do away with the Federal Reserve (the central bank), or the fractional reserve banking system. **What we face, in effect, is a prostituted gold standard!** But, the general public won't know it; most financial analysts won't know it; the press will trumpet this compromised gold standard as a return to stability and good times; and the instant psychological *"fix"* will be on.

Confidence rules our economy. A golden whore, dressed up as a virgin, could very well do the trick to turn the confidence factor positive and thus turn the economy around in an instant. **And this euphoria could carry us for a couple of years!** And, why not? What have we got to lose? At least, this will be the view of all who pragmatically survey the situation.

Are we really going on a gold standard? Do we really have a choice? Besides, 60 percent of the world's central bank's reserves are in gold. And less than 6 million Americans own gold. Few Americans are likely to demand gold when the dollar becomes convertible. It's a confidence game.

Wanniski has given the central bank (the Fed), the one big stumbling block, a graceful out. Actually, he has done more than that. He has given the Federal Reserve a golden sacrifice.

If we can't have real freedom, with a free market in money, or real new wealth commodities monetized on the local level, then the next best thing is a gold standard. Gold is monetary reality and disciplines governments, restoring power to the people.

THE CHINA CAT ATE THE CANARY

1/21/82

Richard Allen resigned as National Security Advisor. He was replaced by William Clark, a man far more cooperative with the Eastern Establishment. Did you catch Henry Kissinger on national TV talking about what a great replacement Clark was? The cat was talking about how great it was to eat the canary.

The projections in the December 11th and December 18th, 1981 REAPERs, concerning the resignation of Richard Allen, brought about behind the scenes by Henry Kissinger and Armand Hammer, should boost your confidence in the credibility of our international sources. It should also alarm you to the reality that the Eastern Establishment is again firmly in control.

The centralization of power and control by the major world governments, the United States and the Soviet Union, and its economic counterparts, the multinational banks and corporations, at an ever increasing pace, reminds me of a bull market that is approaching the vertical, blowing its top. It goes limit day after day and seems invulnerable. And yet, as wise traders know, bull markets that go limit and approach the vertical are experiencing their last gasp of power prior to a panic and collapse, the onset of a new bear market. So it is with the centralization process of the world's political systems.

In terms of reality, the truth that *"good"* for individual man and collective man long-term is based upon self-discipline, assumption of personal responsibility and personal productivity, thus, decentralization, means the present escalating centralization tendency is doomed to failure. It has always failed in the past because human nature is a constant. It is already sowing the seeds of its own major bear market, that of emerging decentralization and the renewal of independence and freedom as people again reclaim responsibility for their own lives. The theology that the government, the parasite, can play the role of God, and thus centralize everything unto itself, along with its parasitic offshoots, the multinational banks and corporations, is now bankrupt. It's impressive show of power today is akin to that of a bull elk raging through the woods with a bullet lodged in its heart. It's only a matter of time until it drops and dies. Outward power masks internal

202

deterioration. The trick is not to get trampled during the death throes.

Riskless Loans
2/5/82

$71 million of our tax money has just gone to bail out the multinational banks. The Reagan administration has now committed to honor its guarantees to bail out $71 million of loans that Poland owes to hotshot American banks. Which banks are involved? The *"Old Faithfuls"* of multinational debt capitalism: Citibank, Chase Manhattan Bank, Morgan Guaranty Bank, Chemical Bank, Marine Midland Bank, Bank of America, First National Bank of Chicago and two lesser known entities, First Wisconsin National Bank and Girard Bank of Philadelphia.

The question becomes, *"Would you have loaned your money to Poland?"* Answer: Of course not. Then why did these banks loan **our** money to Poland?

Adding insult to injury is the fact that these multinational banks are going to be bailed out from their bad investment decisions (loans) by our tax money, to the tune of $71 million! The federal government is going to use our tax money to reimburse these multinational banks for their stupid loans to Poland!

The solution to this problem? Don't deposit our funds in these banks in the first place. By so doing, we finance boondoggles. These multinational banks loan our money foolishly and then we have to pay taxes to get our own money back, which we put in the banks in the first place for safekeeping. Crazy, isn't it?

Notice (rubbing salt in the wound) that these *"world saving"* banks did not assume any risk. They had our government **guarantee** their lousy loans, meaning our tax money guarantees (insures) that they can make loans to communists that no prudent individual would ever consider. And now the Reagan administration has established the precedent to bail out these banks to the tune of $396.5 million, which is owed by Poland this year!

What department of the federal government guaranteed these loans? The U.S.D.A. For what purpose? U.S. grain exports to Poland. The bottom line? The communists get a free lunch courtesy of you and me! And Reagan is cutting free lunches in the U.S.?

POLITICS, THE PRESS AND INTEREST RATES

8/28/81

Here in Montana, we are saddled with three of the *"leading"* Democratic *"Big Spenders"* in Congress—Senator John Melcher, Senator Max Baucus and Representative Pat Williams. Their ratings by the Conservative Index and by The National Taxpayers' Union are consistently low on the taxpayer's totem pole.

During the recent Congressional recess, Senator John Melcher put his traveling political circus on the road, went from town to town, and asked people to *"come on in"* and express their opinion about high interest rates. Not surprisingly, Melcher's series of economic *"tent"* meetings were a tremendous draw. It was a beautiful political ploy. The Montana masses were given an opportunity to vent their pent-up hostility to their *"understanding"* U.S. senator. Given the economic ignorance of the general public, including unfortunately the general public in Montana, and further given the total lack of understanding about money and interest rates, the common folk urged Senator Melcher to do what he wanted to do in the first place—pass a Congressional Resolution that calls for President Reagan to ask the Federal Reserve to lower interest rates in the next 90 days.

How are these *"miracle"* lower interest rates to be achieved? By flooding the banking system with credit, of course.

Pause a moment. Can you imagine the immediate impact upon the gold, silver, bond, stock, international currency and commodity markets if the Fed opened the gates to the money supply? Commodities would soar. The bond market would crash. We'd have financial chaos worldwide, overnight.

At the urging of some prominent and informed Montana citizens, I submitted a statement to the *"press,"* explaining what was wrong with Senator Melcher's program. My criticisms and corrective suggestions appear just below. Following my remarks is a newspaper article published in THE INDEPENDENT RECORD, one of this state's leading newspapers. This news clipping was the *"summary"* of my remarks. Is there ever a difference.

Even more disturbing is the media release which was broadcast on statewide radio stations. The radio broadcasts were even farther

204

removed from my original remarks. And the *"press"* was **friendly** to my statement. . . . My Comments:

"It's both obvious and unfortunate that Montana Senator John Melcher has no understanding of either economics or the root causes of high interest rates. Senator Melcher's current statewide meetings to discuss the Federal Reserve Board's policy of artificially pushing up interest rates is clearly a political ploy intended to distract voters from the real issues and his own dismal voting record. Inflation is the direct result of: 1) the federal government issuing printing press dollars; 2) deficit spending by the federal government which is monetized, for which Senator Melcher is directly responsible, and 3) the creation of credit by our fractional reserve banking system.

"High interest rates now are a symptom of the inflationary disease. Interest rates are high primarily due to the illiquidity of the economy. With the defacto deregulation of interest rates, the free market forces of supply and demand have come into play. Throughout the late 1970s, consumers and businessmen have been on a borrowing binge, buying goods and services on credit in an effort to beat inflation. As inflation soared, credit was cheap and, in some cases, interest rates were at a zero or negative cost when adjusted for inflation and taxes. Thus, consumers and businessmen did the natural thing. They borrowed to buy goods and services today which cost more tomorrow. This reckless inflationary and credit atmosphere was created in the first place by the economic naivete of the Carter administration and the reckless and frivolous spending by the Democrats which controlled Congress at that time. We are reaping now what our liberal spending politicians such as Senator Melcher, Baucus and Pat Williams, via federal deficits, have sowed.

"While our fractional reserve banking system as used by consumers and businessmen, is the engine of inflation, the creator of inflation is the federal government. Inflation is simply an increase in the supply of money. The supply of money is determined at the federal level. It has been politicians' (such as Senator Melcher) unwillingness to balance the budget and cut back on federal spending programs, which makes inefficient use of resources, which led us to the brink of runaway inflation in 1980. Inflation is a drug. Once an economic system has caught the habit, it only gets worse unless the economy is willing to go cold turkey, which is what our economy is attempting to do now via the Reagan administration's programs. High interest rates are a by-product of the inflationary fever in our economy as it fights the inflationary disease.

"With pervasive illiquidity and the increased demand for money, interest rates can only go higher or stay high. Interest rates have remained high because federal government borrowing to finance extravagant programs voted for by Senator Melcher, is competing with private sector demand. But, businessmen can't afford to bor-

row at these high interest rates for long, and consumers can't af-
ford mortgages for home loans because the federal government is
the pig at the lending trough, borrowing what little money is
available, to finance federal programs, both social and military.

"*In Senator Melcher's ten years as a member of Congress or in*
the United States Senate, he has voted once and only once against
expanding the federal budget deficit. If Senator Melcher was
really interested in investigating and curing the cause of these high
interest rates, he would denouce his own liberal, high-spending
voting record. He would make aggressive steps to see that the fed-
eral budget was balanced, so that deficit spending and monetizing
of the deficit would not result in the inefficient use of resources
and/or the creation of inflation. Senator Melcher would act to see
that monetary growth was consistent with real production of
goods and services. He would work toward the abolition of the
fractional reserve banking system, recognizing that, historically,
debt long-term has never been beneficial for any society. In any
case, he would work to provide an incentive for productive, job
creating debt and disincentives for consumer debt. Next, Senator
Melcher, consistent with 17th Century English social philosopher
Thomas Hobbes' perspective that people should be taxed on what
they take out of society rather than on what they contribute to so-
ciety, will work for tax reform. He should work for the abolition
of the progressive income tax. He should work for the establish-
ment of something along the lines of a national sales tax. And
Senator Melcher should work to see that the Federal Reserve Act
and the Federal Reserve System are abolished. This could be done
in accordance with Section 30 of the Federal Reserve Act, which
provides that the government can buy back the stock from the
Federal Reserve Banks at any time, thereby saving the taxpayers
the interest cost on money which has been created by the Federal
Reserve out of thin air.

"*Such bold moves by Senator Melcher would truly be in the*
best interests of the people of Montana and this country. It would
mark him as a statesman rather than a politician. Unfortunately,
the National Taxpayers Union has long labeled Senator Melcher
to be one of the truly big spenders in the United States Senate."

Here's the Radio version of the above:

MORNING-MONTANA-MORE-MORNING-MONTANA IN BRIEF

-8-

(HELENA) -- INVESTMENT COUNSELOR R-E MCMASTER JUNIOR CHARGES THAT SENATOR JOHN MELCHER OF MONTANA IS MORE OF A THREAT TO THE NATION'S ECONOMIC HEALTH THAN INFLATION. MCMASTER MADE THE COMMENT THIS WEEK AFTER SENATOR MELCHER HELD HEARINGS IN GREAT FALLS AND MISSOULA ON THE EFFECTS OF HIGH INTEREST RATES. MELCHER SAYS HE WILL USE THE TESTIMONY TO SUPPORT HIS PUSH FOR A DROP IN THE RATES WITHIN 90 DAYS. MCMASTER... WHO AUTHORS A NATIONALLY CIRCULATED INVESTMENT LETTER... SAYS LOWERING INTEREST RATES OR PRINTING MORE MONEY WOULD CREATE WHAT HE CALLS HYPER-INFLATION. MCMASTER SAYS THE ONLY WAY TO "WRING (INFLATION) OUT OF THE SYSTEM" IS TO USE HIGH INTEREST RATES. MCMASTER SAYS THE CAUSE OF THE INFLATION IS DEFICIT SPENDING BY THE FEDERAL GOVERNMENT... AND HE BLAMES THAT ON BIG SPENDERS IN CONGRESS. MCMASTER SAYS MONTANA SENATORS MELCHER AND MAX BAUCUS, AND MONTANA CONGRESSMAN PAT WILLIAMS ARE AMONG THOSE BIG SPENDERS.

I he Independent Record, Helena, Mont., Sunday, August 9, 1981—5A

Melcher hears defense of high interest

BY JAMES DeWOLF
IR State Bureau

Sen. John Melcher is more of a threat to the nation's economic health than inflation according to Kalispell-based investment counselor R.E. McMaster Jr.

"If Sen. Melcher was really interested in investigating and curing the cause of these high interest rates, he would denounce his own liberal, high-spending, voting record," McMaster said.

Melcher is using the congressional recess to hold hearings in Montana on the impact of record high inflation rates. Most of those who have testified so far have said inflation is threatening to destroy them.

And the senator says he will use that testimony when he returns to Washington to argue for passage of a resolution he has already introduced. The resolution calls on the president to ask the federal reserve board to lower interest rates in the next 90 days.

McMaster is the author of a nationally circulated investment letter called the Reaper.

He says clients for his advice in the past have included the Shah of Iran and currently include nationally known investment author Howard Ruff.

According to McMaster lowering interest rates or printing more money would have the effect of creating hyper-inflation.

He said government, businessmen and individuals in the recent past have taken advantage of interest rates that were lower than inflation. The result has been spiraling debts in both the public and private sectors.

"We have reached the point where there are no good choices," McMaster said. "We are going to have to suffer (with high interest rates) to wring this out of the system."

Federal debt is so large and the government is willing to pay so much to borrow that the nation's money supply is shrinking McMaster said.

"We are reaping now what our liberal spending politicians such as Sen. Melcher, Sen. (Max) Baucus, and Rep. (Pat) Williams, via federal deficits, have sowed," McMaster said.

McMaster accused Melcher of practicing "snake oil" economics by telling the public that interest rates can be artificially lowered. He said the senator should be working for an end of the fractional reserve banking system (that can multiply the effect of deposits to create more money), trying to see that monetary growth matched the growth of production, promoting the end of the progressive income tax, and pushing for creation of a national sales tax. He said Melcher should also be trying to abolish the Federal Reserve System instead of manipulating it.

McMaster said he sent the senator a letter outlining what should be done but the letter was never answered.

"Such bold moves (as those suggested by McMaster) would truly be in the interests of the people of Montana and this country," McMaster said. "It would make him as a statesman rather than a politician. Unfortunately, the National Taxpayers' Union has long labeled Sen. Melcher to be one of the truly big spenders in the United States Senate."

What's the point? Each of us, and the markets, are influenced daily by the press. Newspapers, news magazines and radio and TV news programs provide the overwhelming majority of Americans with all of their news input. From these limited sources, the American general public formulates its opinion about economics, politics, society and the *"real world."* But, every word spoken on a radio or television newscast, just as every word written in a newspaper or news magazine, is, in and of itself, an editorial opinion. The above sequence of *"news"* information, from my original news release, to the radio broadcast, shows how much is lost or altered for effect in our communication's system. We must be skeptical about what we hear and read, particularly when it comes from the established media. We must remain on guard and distrust the apparent *"truth"* of a news item, just because it is logical. The bias among the establishment press is liberal. The inclination among the establishment press is to do whatever is necessary to entertain or to *"sell"* its perspective, and to maintain its advertising corps. The established networks—ABC, NBC, and CBS, along with PBS, are monopolies. Monopolies, by definition, restrict competition. We all know that an uncompetitive environment, a monopoly situation, such as exists with the TV networks, is never in the best interest of the common man.

Post poll reports people think major media cover up news

WASHINGTON (AP) — More than half the people polled nationwide by The Washington Post believe the major news media often cover up stories and frequently violate individual privacy, a survey reported.

A majority believes the media when government officials issue denials.

Fifty-three percent of 1,507 people interviewed by telephone agreed with the statement, "the major news media often cover up stories that ought to be reported," the newspaper said. Thirty-five percent disagreed.

Sixty-three percent felt "the major news media frequently violate the privacy of individual citizens." Twenty-eight percent disagreed.

Questioners defined "major" media for respondents as the news organizations of the ABC, CBS and NBC television

networks; The New York Times, The Washington Post and the Los Angeles Times; Time and Newsweek magazines, and "a few other" unspecified publications.

Some other findings:

● Fifty-seven percent of respondents said that when a high government official denies a news story, they believe the media. The officials are believed by 17 percent.

● Forty percent said the major news media are not critical enough of the federal government. Twenty-five percent said the media are too critical.

● Fifty-nine percent disagreed with the proposition that the media, in covering anti-government protests, always support the demonstrators and criticize the government.

● On complex or controversial subjects, 46 percent trust national television for their understanding. National news magazines were second with 25 percent, major newspapers had 17 percent and radio 5 percent. Seven percent had no opinion.

WAR, IN PERSPECTIVE

5/30/80

As the storm clouds build for the upcoming war, it is important that we make the appropriate observations about this, the ultimate in human folly. It is all too easy, once we have quickly considered the prospect of war, to dismiss it until it is really upon us. Such seems to be the consistent operation of the human mind. We forget the unpleasant. We remember the positive. Hopefully, by reviewing the background which projects an approaching war, we can focus on the unsavory reality, be more rational, and therefore, better prepared.

We must remember, first and foremost, that war is a political act. As Karl Von Clausewitz stated in his classic ON WAR, *"It is . . . a continuation of policy by other means; the political intentions are the objects, and the war is the means. The nature of war is therefore determined by political objects. . . . It is, therefore, a political act."* But, we need not look to such ancient observers as Von Clausewitz for enlightenment. Rear Admiral Robert A. Theobald, in his 1954 book, THE FINAL SECRET OF PEARL HARBOR, stated, *"Our main deduction is that President Roosevelt forced Japan to war by unrelenting diplomatic-economic pressure, and enticed that country to initiate hostilities with a surprise attack by holding the Pacific Fleet in Hawaiian waters as an invitation to that attack."* He further commented, *"The President and his military and naval advisers well knew on October 9, from the Tokyo dispatch to Honolulu of September 24, that Japan intended to plan a surprise air attack on the American Fleet in Pearl Harbor, and had daily evidence from the late decodes of certain Tokyo-Honolulu dispatches during the period, December 3-6 inclusive, that the planned attack was soon to occur."* [9]

This side of history we never read in public school accounts. But, as Whittaker Chambers, former TIME editor stated, *"No one who has, even once, lived close to the making of history can ever again suppose that it is made the way history books tell it."*

Antony Sutton, in his two-volume work, WESTERN TECHNOLOGY AND SOVIET ECONOMIC DEVELOPMENT, documented how Western technology has been supplied to the Soviets for the past 53 years. Sutton has impeccable credentials. He was a research fellow at the Hoover Institute on War, Revolution and Peace at Stanford University. Sutton stated, with regard to Soviet technology, *"Almost all—perhaps 90-95 percent—came directly or indirectly from the United States and its allies. In effect, the United States and the NATO countries have built the Soviet Union—its industrial and its military capabilities. This massive construction job has taken 50 years since the revolution in 1917. It has been carried out through trade and the sale of plants, equipment, and technical assistance."*

Why would the West supply the Soviet Union with the technology necessary to make her the greatest military threat in the history of the world? There are only two motivations—greed/profit, and/or the desire for a one-world government brought on by a worldwide communist revolution. Carroll Quigley, a history professor at Princeton, Harvard and Georgetown University, wrote in TRAGEDY AND HOPE, *"There does exist, and has existed for a generation, an international Anglophile network which operates, to some extent, in the way the radical Right believes the Communists act. In fact, this network . . . has no aversion to cooperating with the Communists . . . The American branch of this organization (sometimes called the Eastern Establishment) has played a very significant role in the history of the United States in the last generation. . . . In New York it was known as the Council on Foreign Relations . . ."*

But the U.S.S.R. is not the only octopus financed by the West. It is well-documented that the West financed the rise of Hitler. Antony Sutton, in another book, WALL STREET AND THE RISE OF HITLER, concluded:

> *"First: that Wall Street financed the German cartels in the mid-1920s, which in turn proceeded to bring Hitler to power.*
>
> *"Second: that the financing for Hitler and his S.S. street thugs came in part from affiliates or subsidiaries of U.S. firms, including Henry Ford in 1922, payments by I.G. Farben and General Electric in 1933, followed by the Standard Oil of New Jersey and I.T.T. subsidiary payments to Heinrich Himmler up to 1944.*
>
> *"Third: that U.S. multinationals under the control of Wall Street profited handsomely from Hitler's military construction program in the 1930s and at least until 1942.*
>
> *"Fourth: that the same international bankers used political influence in the U.S. to cover up their wartime collaboration and to do this infiltrated the U.S. Control Commission for Germany."*

Whenever we want to determine the real issue in a confusing situation, we should ask ourselves, *"Where does the financial interest lie?"* Remember, the love of money is the root of all evil. Money is power. Politics is power. The synthesis of the two (money and politics) in the

Hegelian dialectic is collusion between multinational corporations/ banking interests, and governments. This synthesis is the evolutionary pinnacle. The *"fittest"* are at the top, possessing near absolute power which corrupts absolutely.

As responsible citizens, we are forced to choose between the two theories of history. The two theories are: 1) Things just happen, or 2) Somebody wanted something to happen.

It has always bothered this writer that we dropped the atomic bombs on Japan. Why? Would not Japan have surrendered if we had exploded an atomic bomb off her coastline? Why was it necessary to devastate Japan? Is it true that in March, 1945, the Japanese government notified the American Embassy in Moscow, the Russian Embassy in Tokyo, and the U.S. government directly that Japan was ready to negotiate conditions of surrender on any terms the U.S. would dictate? In other words, is it true that Japan offered to unconditionally surrender? Is it true that the U.S. stated it had trouble deciphering the message?

On May 9-10, 1941, American bombers destroyed 90 percent of Tokyo with incendiary bombs. The atomic bombs followed, but brought about less than 3 percent of the destruction of Japan. Eighty-five percent of the Japanese railroads and all of the industrial capacity were destroyed.

We know that industrial production is always built out of the surplus of a society, that which is not consumed. Question: Who financed the rebuilding of the Japanese railroads and industry? Whoever built them, owns them. There is a tremendous rate of return for internationalists involved in post-war reconstruction. And remember, too, Eisenhower warned us that the most dangerous threat to this country was the military/industrial complex. Even wily old Henry Ford once wrote, *"War is an orgy of money, just as it is an orgy of blood."*

In 1933, Major-General Smedley Butler, who fought wars on three continents, gave a speech at an Armistice Day celebration in Philadelphia. He confessed, *"War is just a racket. A racket is best described, I believe, as something that is not what it seems to the majority of the people. Only a small inside group knows what it is about. It is conducted for the benefit of the very few at the expense of the masses."*

Butler elaborated, . . . *"The trouble with America is that when the dollar only earns 6 percent over here, then it gets restless and goes overseas to get 100 percent. Then, the flag follows the dollar and the soldiers follow the flag. This is done to defend some lousy investment of the bankers. . . .*

"There isn't a trick in the racketeering bag that the military gang is blind to. It has its 'finger men' to point out enemies, its 'muscle men' to destroy enemies, its 'brain guys' to plan war preparations, and a 'Big Boss'—supernationalistic capitalism.

". . . I spent most of my time being a high muscle man for big business, for Wall Street and for the bankers. In short, I was a racketeer, a gangster for capitalism.

"I helped make Mexico—and especially Tampico—safe for American oil interests in 1914. I helped make Haiti and Cuba a decent place for the National City Bank boys to collect revenues in. I helped in the raping of half a dozen Central American republics for the benefit of Wall Street.

"The record of racketeering is long. I helped purify Nicaragua for the international banking house of Brown Brothers in 1909-1912. I brought light to the Dominican Republic for American sugar interests in 1916. In China, in 1927, I helped to see to it that Standard Oil went its way unmolested. . . ."

Perhaps we should ask some questions about our Korean involvement also? After U.S. troops marched up and down that country, blowing it to bits, all to no avail, the conflict was called to a halt. Today, S. Korea is a modern, 20th Century industrial power. S. Korean goods and services compete with those manufactured stateside. Question: Who financed the rebuilding of Korea? Who owns Korea?

In three modern-day cases—Germany, Japan, and Korea—countries which were devastated and then rebuilt, we should ask, *"Who financed the reconstruction?"* The profits in these reconstruction endeavors were huge.

The countries were well chosen. Germany, Japan, and Korea are known for their industrious, hard-working people. And hard-working, productive people help investors' profits soar.

In Vietnam, why wasn't that oil refinery in Hanoi bombed? Why were all those petroleum tank farms in communist hands left untouched? The U.S.A. sure burned up a lot of fuel and wasted tons of munitions there. Is it true that a major multinational oil company is now building one of the most modern oil refineries in the world on the western side of Vietnam?

Back to our two theories of history. Franklin D. Roosevelt told us which theory is correct. He effectively said, *"Things do not just happen; they are planned that way. . . ."* We must never discount the financial interests which operate behind the scenes before and during a time of war. Wars are tremendously profitable for the munition suppliers and bankers who finance them. They are also profitable for the debt capitalists involved in the post-war rebuilding effort.

We should ask, *"Why has Representative Hansen of Idaho received a press blackout since he traveled to Iran? Did President Carter, or more specifically, Brezinski and Jordan, know that if the Shah was brought to this country, the U.S. Embassy in Iran would be seized? Was this done, in part, to enable Chase Manhattan to freeze Iranian deposits?"* This is a question being asked by many journalists. It never receives any media exposure.

Previously, we have noted how the relativism of the Hegelian dialectic (thesis, antithesis, synthesis), coupled with social humanistic evolution, has resulted in government sovereignty. Money is power. Politics is power, etc. Government sits at the summit of the evolutionary spiral, the survival of the fittest, at the top of the heap. Government has a right to rule because, under relativistic, Hegelian, Social Darwinistic ethics, *"Might makes right."* Both liberals and conservatives philosophically support this theology. State sovereignty is obviously supported by liberals. Liberals look to government to play God, to solve all problems. Conservative support of state sovereignty is somewhat more insidious. Conservatives, through their call for federal construction of an international military machine, lend support to the concentration of power at the federal level. It is important to remember, that prior to World War I, all military escapades on foreign soil were fought with volunteer troops. It was clearly understood that it was unconstitutional to use draftees to fight abroad.

The economic policy of a government sovereign is that of protectionism. Free markets are increasingly abolished because free markets are not sovereign. Government is sovereign. The raising of trade barriers between various national entities increases tension. When goods are unable to freely cross borders, armies will pave the way for them.

With national government sovereignty today, economics is elevated beyond its proper level. Nations maintain their power by appealing to the envy of the economically less fortunate. Votes are bought. In return, goods and services are redistributed. Today, under both Marxist communism and Western capitalism, resulting envy is rampant. The result: Power is maintained by redistributing economic wealth. Thus, salvation for all nations worldwide today is **materialism**, a hedonistic distortion of free market economics. Salvation by materialism, with its underlying envy, increases tension. Government sovereigns then opt for protectionism, a certain prelude to war. Behind the scenes are the rich and powerful vultures, the product of a relativistic, humanistic, evolutionary culture. How can it be that the victors in the vestige of our constitutional Republic feast upon the carrion of free men? It is one thing to be loyal to a country and its people. It is entirely another consideration to be supportive of its government.

* * *

"American petroleum corporations, steel and aluminum industries, electronic companies, chemical industries, food production agencies, etc., did openly and willfully, for personal gain, trade and give comfort to our enemies and their allies throughout the many years of the Vietnam War, with full knowledge and consent of the Congress and Executive Branch of government. . . .

"Whereas such unscrupulous trade with the enemy in time of war is clearly definable as treason in the Constitution of the United States of America, Article III, Section 3."

District I of the Veterans
of Foreign Wars in Philadelphia,
May 12, 1982, from *"Moratorium
on the Registration for the Draft"*

AS WAR THREATENS: WE NEED A
"THINKING REVOLUTION"

11/1/78

History never repeats itself. Man always does. The geography, climate, language, culture, government and level of technology may change, but man's nature is the common thread. This is why we have cycles in human action. Man has not yet escaped the chains of his animal nature, which locks him into slavery in the natural realm and cycles. The anchor provided by a sovereign God is the only escape. Man builds up. Man destroys. Businesses prosper. Businesses fail. Civilizations rise and civilizations fall. Wars recur.

This most ghastly of all man's activities, war, is linked in the same harness with death, a taboo subject in our culture. So, despite its devastating consequences, its on-rushing approach is blindly ignored.

Our present situation is very similar to that of Great Britain prior to World War II, when that country ignored the Nazi build-up and dismissed the warnings of Winston Churchill who later called World War II, *"the unnecessary war."* England, after World War I, just as this country after Vietnam, had an intense revulsion against war. It felt it had slaughtered its youth senselessly. Britain condemned itself, as America does today. The will to fight and defend its allies disappeared. Jogging was the fad in Britain prior to WWII.

Five years ago, one third of the countries on this earth were free. Today, the number has shrunk to less than 20 percent. Over 50 years ago, Oswald Spengler warned us that this would be the case. In his frightening THE DECLINE OF THE WEST, he stated, *"World peace involves the private renunciation of war on the part of the immense majority, but along with this, it involves an unavowed readiness to submit to being the booty of others who do not renounce it. It begins with the state-destroying wish for universal reconciliation, and it ends in nobody moving a finger so long as misfortune touches only his neighbor."*

Are we the mirrored image of the Romans who sat in their stadium, watching the games, while the barbarians invaded and burned the city? We, too, have our games and our stadiums. Professional football is America's number one sport. For many in the cities who are disenchanted with life, the game has become reality. For them, like the

214

Romans, life has become an illusion.

It does no good to attempt to turn a straw house into bricks when the wolf is at the door. And, even now, we hear his howls off in the distance. The Foreign Affairs Research Institute of London has revealed that there is no parallel to the present Soviet build-up, since that of Nazi Germany in the 1930s. Shall we have to endure our own trial by fire, as Britain did?

We have provided the Soviets with 90 to 95 percent of their technology, the bulk of which has been used in a war-making capacity. We are naive to believe that the USSR's economic dependence on us will prevent military aggression. Former Deputy Secretary of Defense, Robert Ellsworth, has documented the fact that throughout history, economic health has never been particularly effective in the international struggle for power. It has not prevented war! For example, Germany traded very heavily with England immediately prior to World War I. Germany also traded extensively with Russia until entering World War II. In fact, throughout history, barbarians have overrun more advanced, economically superior civilizations.

Military power is the Soviets' only strong suit. Their economy is collapsing. They will have to import Middle East oil in the 1980s. They face internal social unrest, maybe revolution. But, they have seen the utilization of their military might as their best means of expanding influence abroad. Witness Africa!

More disturbing, Harvard's Russian Research Center has concluded that the Soviets believe they can fight, win and survive a nuclear war. The House Armed Services Committee has reported that the U.S. strategic position has deteriorated so greatly that we now are unable to deter a first strike by the USSR. The Stockholm International Peace Research Institute has warned that the probability of nuclear war is *"steadily increasing, is virtually inescapable."* The INTELLIGENCE DIGEST of England has concluded that the most probable time for the Russians to be militarily agressive is within the next five years.

The Russian fleet is now more than triple the size of our fleet, which is the smallest it has been since Pearl Harbor. Nearly 50 percent of our oil is imported along with practically all of our rubber, chromium, cobalt and manganese ore—all of which are vital to our industrial system. Ninety-nine percent of these resources are brought to our shores by ship. Isn't it obvious why the shipping waters of the Persian Gulf, the Red Sea, the Horn of Africa, and the Cape of Good Hope are so strategically important?

We have the threat of chemical and biological warfare, an area in which the Soviets have conducted extensive research and have achieved terrifying results. And, what about weather warfare and particle beam weapons, where the Soviets enjoy considerable expertise, thanks to our giving them the work of probably the greatest scientist of this century, Nikola Tesla. Arnet and Hoffman have additionally reported on America's inability to fight even a conventional land war.

Dare we look to the U.S. government for help? Hasn't the government already failed in its primary legitimate purpose—to provide for the national defense? The Soviets have enough food stored underground to feed their population for a year. They have a massive civil defense effort. It is estimated that in a nuclear exchange, the U.S. would lose 160 million of its over 220 million population, while the Soviets would lose only 5 to 10 million. Even the Chinese believe that our lack of civil defense preparation is insane, suicidal. Their Vice-Premier has stated that World War III is *"unavoidable."* These questions must be asked by any thinking individual, *"Is our government naive or stupid?" "Are we being sold out?" "Is the U.S.S.R. really as strong militarily as we have been led to believe?"*

We should know better than to look to our government for help. Our government, for the most part, is made up of inferior, uncreative bureaucrats and politicians, the natural consequence of a majority of the citizenry who have become disinterested in their Republic. Politicians rarely anticipate or lead. They only follow. Politicians wait for the *"will of the people."* But, the *"people"* rarely anticipate. They only react. Thus, a continual state of crisis management is insured.

We seem to have forgotten that the usual activity of government is to rule, to subject its people. Only in fleeting moments of history, such as in the time of the Eastern Roman Empire, England under Cromwell, and the early history of this country has government been a servant of the people, instead of a god. Gods demand tribute and sacrifice! Federal expenditures are up 4,000 percent since 1940. Today the government spends 40 percent of the national income. It has its tribute. Are we about to become its sacrifice? Already it has embarked upon the destructive road of protectionism—tariffs, trade restrictions, import quotas and the like. The sagacious Ludwig Von Mises, in his treatise, HUMAN ACTION, stated, *"The philosophy of protectionism is a philosophy of war."*

Our economy is desperately ill. War is the magic elixir. Victory in war prevents economic chaos and preserves the government. If defeated, the opportunity to begin anew exists for the government. In either case, the people lose.

The Hudson Institute study, entitled REPORT FROM IRON MOUNTAIN, stated, *"War has provided both ancient and modern societies with a dependable system for stabilizing and controlling national economies . . . the permanent possibility of war is a foundation for stable government; it supplies the basis for general acceptance of political authority."*

What this country needs is a massive change of mind, a thinking revolution, for thoughts always precede action. Is there hope for our society in the immediate future, or in the long run, without massive reawakening, a new reformation? Should we return to the absolutes and stability of the Hebrew-Christian law, which provided the foundation on which this country has enjoyed freedom and achieved greatness?

More important to our discussion is the fact that our traditional Hebrew-Christian ethics are militant ethics. Our forefathers took seriously their manifest destiny, the commandment to subdue the earth, to exercise dominion. These sound ethics have provided the basis for a strong well-equipped military and a secure national defense.

A few years ago, our country imported a management consultant, as it were, who brought with him all his historical and philosophical tools and insights. He observed our *"eat, drink and be merry"* attitude. He noted the reckless debt assumption on the part of the consumer, the spending for things as if there were no tomorrow. He watched a decadent legalistic society, operating on the cold letter of the law, which had lost its sense of justice and mercy. He told us the next war may well bury Western civilization forever. He concluded that we had lost our concept of a Supreme Complete Entity, a God, which used to restrain our passions and irresponsibility. His name, Aleksandr Solzhenitsyn.

Another great thinker, the elder statesman of Western civilization's 20th Century historians, was Arnold Toynbee. He is best known for his massive work, A STUDY OF HISTORY, the writing of which took 40 years, including 3 million words, with more than 19,000 footnotes. Toynbee, just before his death, produced his last major work entitled, MANKIND AND MOTHER EARTH: A NARRATIVE HISTORY OF THE WORLD. In it, he reached the same conclusion of Solzhenitsyn, that religion is the most important of human experiences. Toynbee also wrote that war has been following war in an ascending order of intensity. And, if the series continues, this process of intensifying the horrors of war will result in the self-annihilation of the war-making society.

W. D. Gann was the best analyst, and stock and commodity trader this country has ever seen. His genius was confirmed by the fact that, for over 50 years, he was correct in better than 85 percent of his predictions. He was called *"The Authority on Predictions of Securities," "The Guru of Wall Street,"* and *"The Master Economic Forecaster."* Gann pulled over $50 million in uninflated dollars from the stock and commodity markets. On April 5, 1954, two years before his death, Gann wrote his most significant letter, *Why Time Cycles Predict Trend of Commodities, Stocks and Business.*

"After 52 years of experience and research, going back hundreds of years, I have proved to my entire satisfaction that history repeats, and that when we know the past we can determine the future," he said.

"I am a firm believer in the Bible. It makes it plain that the future is but a repetition of the past. The Bible teaches us that men and nations reap what the sow. Time cycles repeat because human nature does not change. That is why wars occur at regular cycles. Old men do not want wars. Neither do they want to go into war after they have been through one. Young men fight the wars because they read history and want to be heroes. Leaders of nations appeal to the young men who have no experience, and induce them to fight."

Do we dare ignore the conclusions of these caring and honest men who have dedicated their lives to the pursuit of truth? Truth does kill those who hide from it. The Hebrew-Christian truths are the historical roots of all of our social institutions. The authorities I have cited give clear testimony to the fact that we are a civilization floundering in error and headed for war. Error is the result of faulty assumptions about the nature of reality, false religious assumptions.

We reap what we sow. We must sow seeds of righteousness. The resulting fallout in the military sphere will be immediate emphasis upon civil defense and local militias for decentralized, grassroots defense. This basic defense, once established, will provide us with enough security so we can more clearly ascertain the Soviet threat. We must act now. The United States is the last *"battlestar"* of freedom, and our children are on board.

HAS THE RUSSIAN BEAR STOPPED DANCING?

6/16/78

It has been widely established that New York bankers helped finance the Russian Revolution of 1917. And certainly, even a casual observer should have noticed how easily David Rockefeller and entourage visit the Russian capital with considerable regularity. Now, this writer is not going to get off on a right wing conspiracy kick. It is just an acknowledgment of history, that at the point in a civilization's history when it is mature, when it has a pervasive government, sophisticated communication and distribution systems, corporate agriculture, and a concentration of population in the cities, that there is inevitably the concentration of power in the hands of a few.

Much establishment press coverage has been given recently to the sad state of affairs of the Western military machine (It's rusted), and the shiny new war-making galleons (with condiments) owned by the Soviets. The *"network evening news"* and such newspaper headlines as *"Russians Perfect New, Better Missile"* and *"Carter: NATO Must Meet Red Buildup"* echo the now recognized danger. Do we believe the press?

The Collins Report, which has been recently revealed by the establishment press as an alarming discovery of our military weakness, was available September, 1977. Do the Soviets have NATO and the U.S. over a military barrel, both in conventional and nuclear war-making? The U.S. position is similar to that of Great Britain between WWI and WWII. The Nazi buildup was ignored. And Great Britain paid the piper. Will the U.S. pay the Russian piper? Was it planned that way? Is it all a sham?

Some conservative American journalists believe that Soviet and U.S. cooperation exists internationally, as evidenced by the truth of what is happening in Africa, particularly South Africa where the Soviet and U.S. aims seem to be identical. (The mouth of Andrew Young could well be hooked up to a Kremlin tape recorder.) American journalists point to how the White House is now controlled by the Trilateralists (NY banks and multinationals), whose tentacles permeate the Soviet Union. Therefore, even though these journalists readily concede, that if the Russian military machine is awesome, and

219

the Western effort by comparison is puny, they still believe all the noise about the Soviets presently is just a ploy to generate support for Mr. Carter's sagging public support. After all, what else but a *"Get tough on the Soviets"* attitude could better bolster Mr. Carter's image and unite the country.

There is another perspective. The Soviets have been under the thumb of the U.S. for better than 5 decades. The New York banks helped finance the Russian Revolution. The Soviet society would have collapsed long ago if it were not for Western loans ($60-80 billion), Western technology, and Western wheat. We have literally provided the Russians with all the rope necessary to hang us.

Now, there is a basic psychological principle that states that an ego cannot be indebted with no means of repaying and not retaliate in some manner. We have evidence of this in U.S. foreign aid programs and welfare to minorities, where such *"gifts"* are met with hatred and violence in time. Could such be the growing Soviet attitude toward the U.S.? Possibly so. Just like a student likes to better his teacher, wipe him out if you will, so too could this be the Soviet psychological position.

Such an attitude is consistent with the Soviet culture. The Russian climate is cold and harsh, and this harshness is reflected in Russian literature and music. Power is the basis of respect from the Soviet frame of reference. And, we have become weak. It just could be that the Soviets now find us disgustingly puny, with concomitant lack of respect. Statements made to U.S. leaders recently certainly reflect such an attitude. And, Richard Pipes' studies at Harvard's Russian Research Center confirm the fact that the Soviets believe that they could fight, win, and survive a nuclear war. What else could the Russian massive civil defense efforts, huge grain storage undertakings, and aggressive military build-up be for? We must think from their frame of reference, not our own. (Is this information on the Soviets correct? Do we dare trust Harvard?)

Additionally, if, in fact, the Kremlin is having trouble with internal restlessness and satellite country unrest, such an aggressive military posture might be justified under a *"now or never"* attitude. The apparent Soviet need to import oil from the Middle East could figure into their strategy. And, with the technological lead time for war now for Western *"catch up"* standing at a frightening 6 years, undoubtedly the Soviets recognize that the most advantageous time to move aggressively is during the next six years.

But underlying it all, one has to suspect that the Soviets are just sick of the West, and hold us up to ridicule and general disdain. The Russians are simply tired of being NUMBER TWO; they have been patient, and *"Try Harder."*

On Sunday, May 28, 1978, Zbigniew Brzezinski, Special Assistant to the President for National Security Affairs, went before the country on *Meet the Press* and issued a general alarm about the aggressiveness of Soviet military action throughout the world. Coming from the most important mind behind the Carter administration (*"If there is one book in Carter's gospel, it is Zbigniew Brzezinski's BETWEEN TWO AGES . . ."*, said Jeremiah Novak in "The Trilateral Connection," ATLANTIC MONTHLY, July 1977), what Brzezinski said left one in a state of shock. The clear impression was that the Soviets are OUT OF OUR CONTROL. Add that to Mondale's speech on the Soviet nuclear threat, and the almost frantic trips to China, and a case can be made that the Soviets now feel comfortable that they can tell the U.S. to *"Stick It!"*

The entire thrust of the Carter and Trilateralists' administration has been based upon the work of Zbigniew Brzezinski in his book, BETWEEN TWO AGES, AMERICA'S ROLE IN THE TECHNETRONIC ERA. In BETWEEN TWO AGES, Brzenzinski wrote (in October 1969), *"The world is ceasing to be an arena in which relatively self-contained, 'sovereign,' and homogeneous nations interact, collaborate, CLASH, OR MAKE WAR."* (Emphasis added)

Brzezinski further stated, *"Nuclear weapons—never used in conflict between nuclear powers—pose the possibility of such mutual annihilation that they tend to freeze their possessors into passive restraint, with sporadic outbreaks of violence occurring on the pheripheries of the confrontation."*

Ideas precede action. The thoughts of Brzezinski have provided the basis of policy for the Carter administration. On Sunday, May 28th, on *Meet the Press,* Brzezinski, in effect, admitted that he had been WRONG in his book, BETWEEN TWO AGES. The Soviets **ARE** CLASHING AND MAKING WAR. THE KREMLIN LEADERS THINK MUTUAL ANNIHILATION IS NO LONGER A POSSIBILITY. THE UNITED STATES TOOK A GIGANTIC GAMBLE, BASED ON THE WORK OF BRZEZINSKI, AND LOST! DO WE DARE BELEIVE BRZEZINSKI?

So, in a nutshell, it is entirely possible that the Russian bear has stopped dancing to the tune of the Western Pied Piper. If so, the jig is up, . . . really UP! And what comes to mind are the words of famed historian Arnold Toynbee, who stated,

"If the analogy between our Western Civilization's modern history and other Civilization's 'Time of Trouble' does extend to points of chronology, then a Western 'Time of Trouble' which appears to have begun sometime in the sixteenth century may be expected to find its end sometime in the twentieth century; and this prospect may well make us tremble."

We are approaching the final 20 years of the 20th Century.

RUSSIAN ROULETTE

1/9/81

The Soviet Union may be a military threat to the survival of the United States of America. The U.S.S.R. apparently is a far greater danger to our nation than she has ever been before for three reasons:

1. The Soviet empire is collapsing.
2. The U.S.S.R.'s only strength lies in her military power.
3. The Soviets presently enjoy a military window of advantage over the United States through 1983. After that time, it will begin to close with Reagan in the White House, calling for increased defense spending.

Let's assume the press has told us the truth about the Soviet's military strength (a dangerous assumption). A wounded bear is far more dangerous than a fat and full one. The Russian Bear is wounded, lean and hungry. It may be tempted to react, rather than think things through and follow its historical chess-like pattern. There have been unpublicized food strikes within the Soviet Union. The Soviet Union's Russian population is very restless, too, due to the continued failure by the Soviet political leadership to provide consumer goods and services.

The Soviets face an increasingly antagonistic Moslem population along the southern border, which is identifying with the Moslem Middle East. In Southern Russia, few of the Muslims can even speak the Russian language. And, their population numbers are exploding.

Drifting to the east, Russia is paranoid about China. Not only does China's rapidly expanding population concern the Soviet Union, but the fact that Japan and the United States are forming alliances with China, which will significantly advance her technologically and militarily, makes the Soviet Union even more wary. Soviet tacticians know their military history. They realize all too well the historical basis of the conflict between the Russians and the Chinese.

All is far from quiet on the Western front. The Poles were given an inch, and now they intend to take a mile. There is no satisfying Poland's new labor revolutionaries. The shock waves of the Polish experience are being felt in Czechoslovakia, Hungary and East Germany, too.

To pour salt in the wound, the Russian economy, along with the economies of their Eastern European satellite states, is collapsing.

How could it be otherwise? In the Soviet Union, the government plays God. Yet, government is always a parasite. The parasite, government, has destroyed and is destroying, the country and the Russian people. Only the insanity of billions of dollars of Western loans ($60-$80 billion), plus the fact that the West has provided the Soviet Union with 95% of its technology, have kept the crippled Bear on its feet. The Russian Bear is bleeding badly, and it doesn't have much time.

There are only three reasons why the West would provide the Soviet Bear with the necessary transfusions now: (1) The West is greedy/ stupid (2) It's in the best interest of international bankers, who have made loans to the Soviet Union, to keep the Russian Bear alive. These bankers have the political clout to ensure a continuation of the financial transfusions. (3) It is necessary for the transition to a one world empire.

Let's look at some of the recent activities and statistics concerning the Soviet Union to help us expand our perspective:

1. Russia has now been forced to take Afghanistan's fertilizer, cement and natural gas without paying for it.

2. West German banks loaned Poland $674 million. Better than 65% of this amount has to go to pay off existing loans.

3. Yugoslavia owes the West $20 billion and has no way of repaying the loan.

4. Czechoslovakia is considered one of Eastern Europe's best credit risks. Nevertheless, only $30 million of a $150 million loan to Czechoslovakia's central bank could be placed.

5. A four-year $300 million loan to Hungary's central bank ran into resistance.

6. Poland almost defaulted on an $18.5 billion loan to the West. The debt service was $4.5 billion. Poland couldn't even come up with that amount. The Soviet Union covered $1 billion of that amount with gold sales.

7. The Soviet Union is having to sell gold to buy grain.

8. The U.S.S.R. is having great financial difficulty supporting its empire expansion plans in the Middle East, Africa, Central America, the Caribbean and South America. These *"tentacles"* are literally draining the Russian Octopus dry. Russia is having to Bear down.

Lenin said, *"War is a continuation of politics, war is political, it serves political aims, and is undertaken to achieve definite purposes."* The Soviet Union will go to war in order to achieve its grand design for a worldwide communistic state, to preserve its influence over its unwilling satellites, and to stay alive as a national power. The smell of war is in the Russian air. But, at this point in time, the Russian Bear is a wounded, military King Kong. The Soviets are having trouble in the army. Drafted men from over 130 nationalities, who speak 50 different languages, are hard to coordinate. Russian troops bumbled and fumbled in Afghanistan. Meanwhile, we are told that due to ideological differences, cultural dissimilarities, and language barriers, that there is no way we can communicate with this monster.

HOLD IT! . . .

While the Soviet conventional, naval, biological and chemical, and nuclear military might could devastate the West, the unleashing of such destruction by the U.S.S.R. will be the initiation of Soviet suicide. The Soviet Union knows that if it destroys the West, it self-destructs. The West is its lifeline. And this writer believes this reality is known and understood by the Kremlin leaders. Not only should mutual self-interest, but mutual survival, be the middle ground upon which the two superpowers come to a peaceful agreement. For, we **can** communicate with the Soviet Union. International bankers do. Chase Manhattan has a branch bank in Moscow! But, beyond that, Vasily Kuznetsov could become President of the Soviet Union. And dear old Mr. Kuznetsov RECEIVED HIS MASTER'S DEGREE FROM CARNEGIE-MELLON UNIVERSITY IN PITTSBURGH, PENN-SYLVANIA, IN THE UNITED STATES OF AMERICA!

It takes two years, minimum, to earn a master's degree in this country. It is U.S. military *"Red scare"* propaganda to believe that we cannot communicate with the leaders of the U.S.S.R., particularly when one of their top leaders has been educated in the U.S.

The Soviet Union's trade with the West is expanding faster than with either the Third World countries or with other socialist countries. The U.S.S.R. desperately needs Western machinery and equipment, and is willing to export oil in exchange for them, plus sell gold. At one time, Russia was a major exporter of grain. In 1981, the U.S.S.R. will be the world's largest importer of grain for the second consecutive year. If Russia does not get the grain, the Soviet people will revolt!

Sixty percent of the grains and 50 percent of the oilseeds which are shipped in world trade each and every year come from the United States. The U.S. exports 65 percent of its wheat. Seventy-five percent of the world's soybeans are grown in the United States, 40 percent of which are sold overseas. Half of the world's exported corn is grown here in the United States of America. Without the U.S. agricultural production, the Soviets will starve.

The United States has incredible leverage over the U.S.S.R. The Soviet Union needs us. In reality, the U.S. is the Soviet Union's lifeline to survival—financially, biologically and technologically. Only a fool or a traitor would be unable to negotiate a favorable deal with such fine bargaining chips, unless the Soviets are already so strong that we are presently being blackmailed. During the next four years, the U.S.

government's response to, and relationship established with, the Soviet Union will clearly reveal whether we are governed by fools/traitors/cowards, or by statesmen who really have the best interest of the American people at heart.

Assuming all is on the up and up, economic warfare might not work, and might not buy us time anyway. Such economic protectionism is a catalyst for war. But, what choice do we have? The Soviets, if they are in fact as strong as we are led to believe (a real question, given our lack of confidence in the honesty of the established propaganda mills), they may well decide to risk military aggression in the Middle East and or Western Europe, calculating that the Western Allies are too weak to respond effectively. Such action might be seen as necessary by the Soviets to hold together their own economy short-term (without relying on the West for support), as necessary to prevent internal civil unrest, as necessary in terms of the Soviet military window of opportunity, or as necessary as part of a plan to install a worldwide communist empire. In any case, if the West gives in readily to the Soviets by way of granting the U.S.S.R. more loans, more technology and/or more grain at this critical time in history, then we are ruled by fools or traitors, or cowards being blackmailed. Given our lack of civil defense preparation, and the conditioning the American public has received on the horrors of nuclear war (much of which is totally false), will we knuckle under to nuclear blackmail by the Soviets, when it may be a hoax? In any case, we desperately need civil defense and local militias.

THE IRON MAIDEN

5/25/79

A hundred years from now, when historians write about Western civilization's fight for survival, they may conclude that the election of Mrs. Thatcher and the Conservative Party in Britain was the turning point—the point where Western civilization tried to end its 60-80 year drift toward destructive socialism.

The well-worn phrase, *"As goes Britain, so goes the United States"* still rings true and cannot be ignored. It will behoove Americans to keep a close watch upon the *"Battle of Britain"* during the next year. It will be not only an ideological fight, but a fight for national survival, the outcome of which could determine the future of Western civilization. Let us pray that Thatcher's election has not come too late, and is all it has been trumped up to be.

Economics will be in the forefront of the news as Thatcher's Conservative Party crosses swords with Britain's powerful labor unions. The battle for open shops, cutting income taxes and restoring free enterprise will not be a quick or easy one. The fact that 76 percent of the voters turned out is indicative of the tremendous human interest and the energy which will be expended in the coming months.

As I discussed two years ago in CYCLES OF WAR, when climates become cooler and more harsh, obese, bureaucratic governments are overthrown. People become more conservative. We saw that in this country with Proposition 13, the drive against the ERA, and the call for a Constitutional Convention to balance the budget. Britain's establishment of those similar ideological principles in a majority government, represents a fulfillment of my predictions, and is in keeping with Wheeler's Drought and Civil War Clock, which calls for a major turn in Western civilization around 1980.

But, there is more at stake here than politics and economics, much more. Western Europe is increasingly vulnerable to Soviet attack, or so we have been told. Mrs. Thatcher's nickname, *"The Iron Maiden,"* was given her by the Soviet Union, due to her strong stand for national defense. Under her leadership, Great Britain will become increasingly concerned with the Soviet arms build-up.

226

This hard line stand against Communist Russia has spread across Europe. On April 14, 1979, in Boston, a Social Democratic member of the West German Parliament, Conrad Ahlers, who formerly served as Press Secretary to Willy Brandt, called detente *"useless."*

In our own country we have seen a resurgence of interest in establishing military superiority. ABC's "World News Tonight" had a 2-week military feature, "Second to None." The vicious battle over SALT II, which is taking place in the Senate, the outcry by retired generals and admirals against America's military weakness, the consistently hawkish editorials and feature articles in the WALL STREET JOURNAL, coupled with booming book sales that deal with *"war"* further support this observation. The ABC movie *"Ike,"* wherein Eisenhower is portrayed much like Patton, takes the cake!

This writer has been asked if I would be interested in sailing with the Pacific fleet when it leaves San Diego in June for military maneuvers enroute to Pearl Harbor. Naval preparation is under way. Later on this year, the Strategic Air Command (SAC) will hold its largest simulated nuclear war maneuvers ever. The exercise is entitled, Global Shield—'79. Over 120,000 SAC personnel will be involved in this exercise. Interestingly enough, the Soviet Union will **not** be notified of the time of this exercise, and there will be SAC bombers flying toward Mother Russia. (Is this wise?) Additionally, no foreign observers will be permitted to watch the war games.

On the surface, all this *"awakening"* is encouraging. It is high time that Western civilization took a stand. But, it also increases the probability of war. Don't expect the Soviet Union to roll over and play dead. That is not the nature of a *"Bear."* The new idol for the young Soviets is the brutal hardliner, Joseph Stalin. The young *"Turks"* have found a butcher to emulate. In the recent May Day celebration in Moscow's Red Square, military marching units were included **for the first time** since 1969. This is a blatant statement by the Soviets that detente is dead. (It has long been absent from their in-house literature.) Increasing the probability of confrontation is the fact that the top Soviet leadership is old. The Politburo's average age is 69 years. Brezhnev is 72. His probable successor, Andrei Kirilenko, is 72 also. The young aggressive Marxists, who are having increasing clout in the Party, are waiting in the wings to cut their teeth during military confrontation.

As if all this was not enough to convince us of an upcoming war, we must realize that the Soviet Union faces other problems which will increase the probability that it will utilize its only *"ace in the hole"*— its military superiority.

The Wednesday, April 25, 1979, WALL STREET JOURNAL summarized what I have been saying for years. In an article entitled, *"The State of the Soviet Union,"* by Karen Elliott House, we read, *"At home its leadership is decrepit, its economy is sliding and severe labor shortages loom. Abroad, China's determined drive to modernize with Western help poses a growing challenge on the Soviet's longest border. Around the world, Moscow's effort to win allies has produced more dependents than partners. And, anti-Soviet sentiment is rising in the U.S., perhaps portending new American resolve to thwart Soviet adventures."* [10]

In other words, the Soviets don't have anything going for them, except military power! The U.S.S.R. may have to invent a war to survive. Governments have done this historically. Given their present predicament, coupled with their harsh climate, language, culture and **respect for only brutal power,** one should expect the Soviets to continue their financing (with the support of Western banks) of insurrections world-wide, to move aggressively to obtain control of the Persian Gulf, the Indian Ocean, the Mediterranean Sea and the African shipping routes. By cutting off the West's mineral resources imported from Africa, coupled with blocking the oil tankers' shipping lanes, the Soviets can shut down Western civilization. The threat of a Soviet 48-hour blitz into Western Europe, a nuclear *"first strike"* against the United States, or a nuclear *"first strike"* against the East Coast of the United States, followed by a land invasion via Siberia, Alaska and Canada—none of the possibilities can be ruled out. What about nuclear blackmail?

The Soviets need to move, and move soon. They cannot allow the cruise missile or MX missile to come *"on stream."* The cruise missile would force a complete re-organization of the Soviet defense system. They cannot allow a rebuilding of NATO, and/or an aggressive re-armament program by the United States. They cannot permit the Mexican oil to become a potential wartime reserve for the United States. The U.S.S.R. must move by 1984. They are stockpiling strategic metals now. (gold, lead, titanium, aluminum, cobalt, copper, molybdenum)

Time is running out in other areas as well. As the WALL STREET JOURNAL noted, *"The rate of economic growth has dropped sharply in recent years to 3.2 percent,"* in 1978. This economic decline is accelerating. Therefore, increased defense spending will be difficult in the future for the Kremlin, particularly after 1984. Soviet Russia will have to import oil by the mid-1980s, so energy is a problem, too. Labor, also, is scarce as *"Russians are becoming a minority of the various Soviet peoples."* The labor problem is compounded by an exploding Muslim population which is anti-Soviet.

Can Soviet Russia allow China to become a military and economic power which threatens its longest border, particularly if China remains antagonistic, which seems to be the case? How long can Russia stand the economic drain by all the little countries which are in the Soviet camp—Afghanistan, Cuba, Vietnam, South Yemen, Angola, Mozambique, Ethiopia, etc? All of these *"satellites"* are pressures on an economically declining Russian Bear.

In short, the Soviet Union sees itself as being backed into a corner from which it has no alternative except to strike out in the way it knows best—militarily, particularly if it feels threatened by the West, which is now the case.

In a recent speech, I upped the probability of war occurring within the next 6 years from 60 percent to 80 percent. Let's up it another 3 percent now, to 83 percent.

What does this mean to you by way of your personal and investment planning? It means you must look seriously at having some assets abroad. It means a personal *"battle plan"* (no pun intended) to face the threat of war, including a nuclear war and/or a war for national survival.

I know all this is grim. But, we are unwise if we fail to act on the evidence at hand. Failure to act now, when time and resources are available, can only result in a painful crisis down the road. The truth of a difficult matter, not faced and dealt with today, becomes a far greater problem tomorrow. Truth kills those who hide from it.

On Tuesday, May 22, 1979, in the Arabian Sea, the U.S. Naval Aircraft Carrier Midway was *"buzzed"* by Russian aircraft. This harassment almost resulted in crash landings by American naval aircraft. This is the third such incident perpetrated by the Soviets (who also have an aircraft carrier in the area) in the last 10 days. . . . The Soviets are becoming more aggressive.

From an impeccable confidential, high-level source comes the following: *"The SS-20s, which the Soviets are installing on the Eastern European frontier, are offensive weapons. The Soviets believe they have to move before the Trident II comes on stream in the 1980s. At present, the Trident submarines cannot take out the Russian missile silos. In fact, of the 16 missiles aboard the Trident, only 4 could be launched before the sub would be hit by a counter strike. The Trident missiles are not too accurate, either.*

"Soviet-launched ICBMs could take out all of our land-based ICBMs in a first strike in less than 30 minutes. Upon such an occurrence, the U.S. would have no means of taking out Russian missile silos. Russia could then issue an ultimatum to the United States, 'Either disarm, or we will use our second wave of missiles to destroy

your cities and 160 million of your people. If you retaliate, you could only annihilate 5 to 10 million of 'protected' Soviet citizens. No President in his right mind would push the button. The Soviets could then take over Europe and the Middle East."

Dress for War
6/8/79

Styles that show off the body have come back in fashion for 1979. When did this style last become fashionable? In the 1930s and 1940s, the time of the Great Depression and the WWII. Does history repeat?

CARTER SPELLED CHAMBERLAIN

1/19/79

The evidence continues to mount that we are headed for a major military conflict in the 1980s. The latest building block toward destruction comes from a column by Smith Hempstone, writing in the January 6, 1979, SALT LAKE CITY TRIBUNE. Hempstone stated, *"To find a year as disastrous for Western diplomacy as that which has just ended with a whimper rather than a bang, one must go back 40 years to 1938, the last act of the pre-World War II era . . . In fact, the capitulations of 1938 sowed the seeds of World War II, beggared the West and cost the lives of tens of millions of human beings.*

"And if this is the year the Carter administration fails to recapture that sense of purpose and high resolve necessary to defend freedom, historians of the future may well look back on 1978 as the year in which the tide of events, by default, turned irreversibly against the West."[11]

Area by area, let's look at Carter's retreat:

1. **The Western Hemisphere**—a) The Carter administration is becoming friendly with Cuba and Fidel Castro. Cuba has shown nothing but hostility toward the West as evidenced by troops in Africa and MIG-23s in Cuba, which have the potential of hitting Washington, D.C. with nuclear weapons. b) The control of the Panama Canal was surrendered to an unfriendly government. c) The serious conflicts in Nicaragua were ignored. d) In El Salvador, the terrorist activity seldom received State Department comment. e) The U.S. has lost the respect of Argentina and Chile. It took Pope John Paul II to try to arbitrate the dispute between these two countries.

2. **Africa**—a) Ethiopia has now entered the Soviet's sphere of influence. b) Somalia cannot be considered a friendly nation, particularly since it was allowed to be beaten by Cuban mercenaries. c) Rhodesia, an old ally, has been abandoned. The communist guerrillas there have not become friendly to the U.S. d) In Namibia, South Africa and SWAPO rejected the peace plan of the West. e) Old ally, South Africa, has been betrayed by Washington.

3. **The Far East**—a) Taiwan, a long-time Western ally, was sold down the river in order to accommodate Red China, who will **borrow**

231

billions from the U.S. to rearm their army and build up their industry. b) South Korea's defenses have been weakened.

4. **The Middle East**—a) We alienated the Israelis and the Arabs (with the exception of Egypt) in attempting to arrange a peace settlement. b) Lebanon is in a continuous crisis state. c) Afghanistan is now clearly in the Soviet's sphere of influence as a result of the bloody coup. d) Pakistan withdrew its pro-Western ambassador. e) The Shah of Iran lost his regime while Carter waffled and backed down to Soviet threats.

5. **Europe and the Eastern Mediterranean**—a) Greece and Turkey are still at odds due to the Cyprus problem. As a result, the influence of the U.S. there has been weakened. b) The October monetary crisis revealed the disdain that Europeans have for the U.S. dollar.

6. **Russia**—The SALT talks are the *"give-away"* of the West.

Retreat, retreat, retreat! Feed your neighbor to the hungry alligator and hope that he won't come back tomorrow and eat you. This is the foreign policy of the Carter administration. It's hard to sleep well at night when there is a hungry alligator on the loose (communism), particularly since the Carter administration has already fed nearly all the neighbors to the alligator in the false hope that it will go away. Shouldn't we shore up domestic U.S. defenses?

SOLDIERS? . . . NONE

9/28/79

The week of September 17th, 1979, Senator Sam Nunn of Georgia requested a closed session of the U.S. Senate. He sought to convince his colleagues that the draft registration of 18-year olds needed to be reinstated. Perhaps the following were some of his considerations:

General Bernard W. Rodgers, former Army Chief of Staff, recently called for the drafting of 75,000 men a year. Rodgers is a knowledgeable military veteran. He studied philosophy, economics and politics at Oxford. He has served in combat in three wars. At the end of June, 1979, he became Supreme Allied Commander in Europe. He knows the score. Ernest Conine, in a LOS ANGELES TIMES article noted, *"Unless large numbers of reserve and national guardsmen could be mobilized and made ready for combat within 30 to 90 days, the only choice would be surrender or* **nuclear** *war."* When a columnist starts to write in these terms, we should begin to shudder.

The Navy, Marines, and Air Force expect the reserves to fill 15 to 20 percent of their manpower requirements. The Army's reserve requirements—45 percent. Presently the Army's *"individual ready reserve short fall"* is 500,000. It is expected to become worse in the 1980s, a time when the danger of war will be greatest. To add to the problem, there are less young men and women reaching military age. The *"baby boom"* following World War II has passed the military draft age. To further make matters worse, most of today's Army is made up of the poor and minority groups who do not have the background training necessary for military discipline. Thirty percent, or 234,000 of the 780,000 members of the All-Volunteer Army use marijuana. Approximately 6.7 percent are on hard drugs. A recent Congressional Task Force found that 90 percent of U.S. troops stationed in Germany were using hashish, and that approximately 30 percent were using heroin. Obviously, these troops couldn't fight their way out of a bad trip, much less defend themselves in a military confrontation. A hundred American soldiers stationed in the Hanau-Frankfurt area of West Germany were recently arrested for pushing drugs. What a way to earn a living! Join the Army and see the world—a world of increasing drug-instilled illusion.

233

As author of CYCLES OF WAR, I have had hundreds of Vietnam veterans and draft age young men ask me, *"When will the next war be?"* I ask them, *"Will you fight it?"* To date, the response has been 100 percent— *"No!"* They are not willing to fight on foreign soil for a government that sponsored Korea and Vietnam. We may be about to see the reality of, *"What if they gave a war and nobody came?"*

The Next War

In 1977, when I wrote CYCLES OF WAR, THE NEXT SIX YEARS, in Chapter 10, *"Cycles of War and the Military,"* I stated, *"Finally, the question must be asked, 'What if they gave a war and no one came?'"* At least, the question should be asked on the U.S.' side of the conflict. The active duty forces are at minimal manpower requirements and are plagued by illiteracy, poor discipline, and drug problems, just for a start. The reserves are acknowledged as an 'Achilles' Heel.' The men who fought in Korea and Vietnam aren't likely to be *"suckered in"* the third time around. Those who avoided the draft and were let *"off the hook"* have no reason to show up should the draft be reinstituted. Certainly they would be let *"off the hook"* again. And, what about volunteers and new draftees? Considering the no-win policy, the low credibility of the government, thanks to Mr. Nixon (among others), not to mention the deep suspicion of the military itself, it is a question that deserves some thought. What if the U.S. was involved in a war, a serious one, not a Vietnam chess game? Could the nation pull together? . . .

It is abundantly clear that it is highly doubtful that we could generate the manpower necessary for a *"conventional"* war. To complicate the problem, we have incompetent, corrupt leadership, as Anthony B. Herbert, Lt. Col. Ret., so clearly revealed in his best-seller, SOLDIER, a startling expose of the sorry military leadership which dominated Vietnam. Rag-tag troops and immoral, incompetent leadership increases the probability of **nuclear war**! Why? As William Irwin Thompson wrote in DARKNESS AND SCATTERED LIGHT, *"With moral decay encouraging the growth of incompetent leadership and short-sightedness, the likelihood of nuclear war increases. To fight a conventional war you need good generals and patriotic troops dedicated to the ideals of self-sacrifice. If you cannot trust your generals. . . . and if the soldiers are simply a pack of undisciplined, pot-smoking civilians, then you know that you cannot maintain a conflict over any length of time in a conventional war. And so in war all dictatorships [wars/crises all end up being run by pseudo-dictators] will be tempted to use nuclear weapons in the hands of small and* *trusted battalions. If the dictator can hope to achieve a lightning-swift strike over the enemy, then he can dream of increasing his power with the people in a stunning victory."*[12]

During the next **major** economic crisis, the government, probably a dictatorship via Executive Orders, will **seek** to increase its power with the people. Even now, the federal government is ineffectual and considered to be incompetent. Better than 80 percent of the people in this country believe that federal government regulations are useless. Only approximately 1 out of 10 respect their congressman. Approximately ¾ of the population think the energy crisis is a hoax. In short, the federal government is losing power.

Dr. Raymond H. Wheeler of Kansas, who created the Drought and Civil Warfare Clock, stated, *"The present 500-year cycle is due to end around 1980."* Wheeler felt that where we are presently in the cycle is where governments break down and nations collapse! Along with this breakdown there occurs a wave of international wars—nation-falling wars—wars that give way to civil strife and revolution.

Fundamentals are confirming Wheeler's cyclic research. Expect the next **major** economic downturn in the 1980s to result in civil unrest and resulting decline in government power. The inevitable result will be war. As Rousas John Rushdoony wrote in THE ESCHATOLOGY OF DEATH, *"War is a sign of impotence. A system or philosophy of life which has no power to convert becomes imperialistic."* The U.S. has been imperialistic since the late 1880s. Wars have increased accordingly. Rushdoony further commented, *"A failing faith resorts to war because it lacks the contagion of faith and conviction and can only force men into its own system. War is the resort of those who lack true power and are declining."*

What's true for us is also true for the Russians. The U.S.S.R.'s deteriorating situation is becoming widely known.

During the past seven economic booms, a *"peace"* boom has been followed by a war. Since we are presently in the latter stage of a *"peace"* boom, we should expect a war after the economy turns down **sharply**. Evidence favors that war being of the nuclear variety due to the demise of government power, the lack of military readiness, and incompetence among the troops-at-large.

THE U.S. AND IRAN: TWO PEAS IN A POD

12/14/79

Feelings run deep on both sides of the U.S./Iranian conflict. Some of Iran's resentment against the U.S. stems from longstanding U.S. meddling in Iranian affairs.

From a U.S. perspective, nothing could be more insulting than for a third rate power to hold hostage U.S. citizens. Perhaps one of the best indications of the depth of the anger and resentment which pervades this country is the fact that there was an anti-Iranian demonstration held by high school students in a small town in Montana. A large gathering of students outside of the school carried signs which read, *"Nuc the Ayatollah," "No freedom, No food," "Nuc Iran," "Down with Iran," and "Boycott Iran."* When students in sleepy Montana become incensed, you can bet your cowboy boots that the whole country is enraged! But, we should really expect as much. These events are occurring exactly **when** they should. Occurrences are confirming cycles. We are seeing a *"squaring of events with time."* How so? Dr. McClelland's literature cycle progression is:

1. A high need for affiliation **and** power.
2. A low need for affiliation.
3. Social reform (the Civil Rights movement of the 1960s) followed fifteen years later by,
4. **War.** (1980)!

It was Dr. McClelland's projection (in 1975) that psychologically our country would be more prepared for war in 1980 than at any time since 1825. Stated differently, we are leaning more heavily toward organized violence **now** than we were at the time of the U.S. Civil War, World War I or World War II.

The Iranian crisis fulfills the requirement that military action by the U.S. **must** be self-righteous in nature. We have an idealistic leader who is **perfect** to lead us into self-righteous conflict. Good old Jimmy Carter may at last fulfill his ambition to be *"The man on a white horse."*

The war feeling is so intense, particularly among the younger *"war-fighting-age"* generation, that it does no good to try to communicate to them the horrors of war. I've tried and failed. They don't really

236

understand or care that war is hell. They have seen the TIME/LIFE programs on TV which glorify war. They have visions of Patton and Ike, and are pumped full of all the other movies which depict the grandeur of war. The youth who will be fighting this next war have already forgotten Vietnam. Some of them don't know the first thing about Vietnam. Even *"Apocalypse Now"* has had little impact on them.

I remember Vietnam. I was hospitalized for nearly a month in Wilford Hall Hospital, San Antonio, Texas. The Air Force's Vietnam War veterans returned there for treatment and rehabilitation. I will never forget the mangled bodies, the burned arms, legs and faces, which were scarred for life; the young men who were missing a hand, an arm, one or both legs; those whose faces had been blown away; the free-flowing tears of fathers and mothers who witnessed what was left of their sons—this tragic scene is indelibly in my memory.

Why is it that we have such difficulty recalling the pain and suffering of war? Do our minds blot out pain that effectively? Why is it that we are unable to communicate now the previous personal tragedy of thousands of young men and families as a result of the vicious act of war? How can short-term economic self-interest justify the personal calamity of war? How can we condone a war economically when it only leads to greater inflation and multinational profits? It seems that when the nation becomes obsessed with aggressive, self-righteous violence that no logic can alter the course of that vehemence until it has worked its way through the system. The socialized violence of pro-football is just not enough anymore, or so it seems.

Iran is equally self-righteous in its desire for violent vindication. For, it was Iran that was pulled kicking and struggling into the 20th Century and saddled with Western technology and lifestyle far too rapidly. Iran is now reacting, indignantly and belligerently, to that U.S.-imposed cultural abuse. Iranians believe they have been violated culturally, economically, socially and religiously. They have nothing but contempt for the United States. It is the type of resentment which has no basis in reason. It is self-destructive. The emotional desire to *"get even"* with the United States is so great that many Iranians simply do not care if they suffer or die as long as the United States *"gets theirs."*

I write with personal insight in this area. As a former U.S. Air Force instructor pilot, I flew with Iranian students. And, it was this time last year that I expected to be in Iran, visiting with the Shah. It was the Iranians, after all, who first became interested in CYCLES OF WAR. In early 1978, Dr. Assad Homayoun, Minister Counselor for Political Affairs for the Shah, requested autographed copies of CYCLES OF

WAR for himself, the Iranian Ambassador to the United States, and the Shah. They feared, at that time, upheaval in their country. In March, 1978, I was concerned about riots and possible revolution in Iran. How could Jimmy Carter, some eight months later, go on national TV and straight-faced tell the nation that he had no knowledge of potential trouble in Iran? Bunk! What I wouldn't give for one good statesman to lead this country!

Lloyd Demause has done us a service in his psychological research on group dynamics as they relate to violence/war. Demause's work is important in understanding the meaning and depth of the U.S./Iranian crisis.

In THE JOURNAL OF PSYCHOHISTORY, Demause authored *"Historical Group Fantasies."* Demause's thoughts about group fantasies apply to Iran. *"The most dramatic examples . . . are those found in anthropologists' accounts of groups who are suddenly 'deculturated,' who lose their rituals and beliefs through traumatic contact with Western or other cultures. This dramatic loss of traditional group-fantasies generally leads to such severe outbreaks of personal anxieties that new group-fantasies with apocalyptic and millenarian contempt are usually quickly formed to replace them."* [13] Certainly the words *"apocalyptic"* and *"millenarian"* apply to Iran. The Ayatollah is the personal embodiment of such concepts. And, Iran had its rituals and beliefs *"ripped off"* by the West.

Demause's research also predicts the ultimate fall of the Ayatollah. *"Since group-fantasies require that the fantasy-leader be under continuous attack for his possession of the group, and since the leader's attempts to counter these attacks through magical and heroic efforts to prop up his image are doomed to fail, every group-fantasy eventually reaches a 'collapse' stage where the leader is experienced as being extremely weak, unable to nurture the country, and increasingly powerless to contain the growing rage and anxiety within the group."* [14] Ironically, this was the fate of the Shah, too. It should also befall the Ayatollah before the Iranians settle down (under Soviet influence?).

How can the Ayatollah and a small group of fanatics control Iran? Demause's work gives us a clue: *"Minority millennial groups, often overtly bizarre in membership and purpose, are delegated the task of acting out the anxieties of this collapse period—groups which previously the larger society paid little attention to, but which now capture widespread interest and even awe as delegates of the majority's emotional state."* [15]

The Ayatollah provides ideal transitional leadership. *"It is only when a group's emotional values seem to have fallen apart that it looks for fantasy-leaders who are activists in foreign policy, who will provoke other nations in order to set up as many crisis areas as possible out of which new group-delusions may be formed in order to restore the group's psychological stability.*

"The country is now seen as infinitely precious and superior, but endangered from the outside, not from one's own hostility."[16] How clearly Demause's work expresses Iran's hostile projections on the United States.

"If the group delusion is millennial, the group can unite under a 'tough' messianic figure who will effectively split the world into those to be saved and those to be killed in the coming apocalypse."[17] This explains what appears to Americans as irrationality—the holding of American hostages.

Perhaps the height of irony is that Americans are involved in a similar group dynamic struggle. The internal tension and conflict that Americans are feeling stems from having violated their long-standing value structure. We have assumed too much debt, wallowed in the undeserved easy life via inflation at the cost of ruined families and an insecure future. We have been kicked around as a nation (Vietnam, Panama). We now must work our way through a national program of penance, a national *"soul cleansing,"* if you will. We are ready for WAR!

Jimmy Carter could be a perfect leader in such an environment. Demause comments, *"If the group-delusion focuses on an enemy external to the group and the group goes to war, the once weak fantasy-leader is now seen as 'tough,' 'fighting.'*

"The 'personalized' reactions of the group-trance state all assume that the world outside the group is suddenly full of others who, for some strange reason, are out to humiliate the nation, and especially its leader."[18]

How powerful is the fantasy of war? *"So powerful is the derealization process of a group-trance, that I have never been able to find any nation anywhere in history going to war which bothered to estimate the number of dead and injured expected to result from their actions.*

"One of the most bizarre results of group-trance thinking is that no war, revolution, or other group-delusion is ever begun with a goal of what is expected to be accomplished by the actions. One's logical assumption that any world leader actually has a plan for what to do when the war is over is quite mistaken. . . . The action itself is, in fact, the goal, not the consequences of the action."[19]

Now, we understand why the danger of war is so great between Iran and the U.S. For both countries, **action** is what is important, a national cleansing, not the consequences of the action. The demonstrations in Iran, as well as in this country, could not express this *"group"* tragedy more clearly.

WAR, 1984: CONTRARY OPINION?

1/15/82

The September, 1981, issue of PSYCHOLOGY TODAY, in a nation-wide survey, found that fear of communist aggression in the United States has dropped to 8 percent. Hold it! When better than 90 percent of the American general public no longer fear communism or Soviet military aggression against them, a contrary opinion stance of the first order is generated!

Ironic, and perhaps somewhat schizophrenic, is the fact that - PSYCHOLOGY TODAY reported, in the same survey, that Americans' greatest fear for this nation is the fear of war! Some 41 percent fear war. Interesting, isn't it? Next to no one in this country fears communist aggression, and yet 41 percent fear war. Question: Who is the war going to be with if it's not with the communists? Even if such a war is a ruse, who else is there around to fight? The federal government? A recent AP/NBC poll revealed that three-fourths of all Americans believe the U.S. will go to war in the next few years. By 1984? Will we fight Iran? Libya?

The Soviet Union, who is considered by most Americans to be our greatest enemy, is caught in somewhat of a paradox. The leaders of the Soviet Politburo are old men who have no desire for war. And yet, Soviet military muscle is the U.S.S.R.'s only real strength. The Soviet economy and empire are collapsing.

Soviet military personnel have been caught and killed this past year by South African troops in Angola. Africa, particularly South Africa, is the resource and shipping jugular vein of the African continent for Western civilization, not to mention the free world's primary producer of gold.

It was during this past year that a 4-ship Soviet naval force was seen operating only 230 miles off the coast of Oregon for the first time in ten years. Three of those four Russian ships were equipped with guided-missiles.

The U.S.S.R. is hastily building up Cuba militarily, as well as installing missiles and military arsenals in Central America. Russia has been (is?) flying fighter aircraft and bombers off the United States' east coast.

The Soviet Union has been drawing huge amounts of money out of Western banks during the past year. Russia has been (is?) stockpiling strategic metals and foodstuffs. The U.S.S.R. is on the move militarily. Perhaps this is what General Robert Schweitzer was referring to when he declared that the Soviet Union is on the move. *"The U.S. is facing the greatest danger the Republic has ever encountered since its founding days."* (Just why was he fired?)

General Schweitzer confirmed the thoughts of many other competent military analysts. For example, Hans Ulrich Rudel, a respected German WW II pilot, recently declared, *"I fear there will be war within 2 or 3 years."* That brings us right up close and personal to 1984, doesn't it?

Mr. Digby Dodd, a knowledgeable Englishman and a researcher of Raymond H. Wheeler's climatic work, projected that if 1982 and 1983 are warm, dry years in the cold/dry cycle, as he projects will be the case, then these years are very likely dates for international conflict.

Anita Kemp, writing in the March, 1981, issue of CYCLES, in an article entitled *"Cycles Foresee the Future of International Violence,"* used a set of six cycles linked with international violence, arms races, United Nations' voting behavior and business shocks to project a peak period for international violence between 1980 and 1990.

Other respected military leaders have also confirmed General Schweitzer's remarks. General Bernard W. Rogers, NATO Supreme Allied Commander for Europe, stated not too long ago, *"By 1982, we'll reach the most vulnerable point of our ICBM fleet. The first half of the '80s may well be the most critical period that the West will face for many decades to come. It will be a time of testing and perhaps of crisis."* Up close and personal to 1984 also, wouldn't you say?

Not only are military commanders, climatic specialists and cycles analysts in harmony by predicting war possibly by 1984, but we also find that the economic environment is ripe for the distraction of war. In 1980, Soviet trade with the United States fell 47 percent from 1979. Free trade, economic interdependence, is the primary salve for the itch of war. When men exchange goods and services, economic exchange, they have a vested interest in not fighting. War becomes contrary to a nation's self-interest. Fighting hurts the respective economies. In 1980, trade with the Soviet Union fell to $2.17 billion, down from $4.1 billion in 1979.

(Whether the United States should have unrestricted trade with an acknowledged enemy like the U.S.S.R. is certainly open to question. But that question aside, it is established that lack of economic exchange heightens tensions which lead to war.)

The political climate, where both superpowers are concerned, is conducive to military conflict, too. Arthur Schlesinger, Jr., writing in the November 18, 1981, WALL STREET JOURNAL, stated, *"The Reagan crowd, for better or worse, is well on the way to persuading the world that it regards military power as its primary instrument in the conduct of foreign relations."* INTELLIGENCE DIGEST (Intelligence International, Ltd., 17 Rodney Road, Cheltenham, Flos. GL50 1HX, United Kingdom) headlined an article, *"1984 a Soviet 'target year.'"* INTELLIGENCE DIGEST went on to write:

"In a projected Kremlin scenario it is calculated that Soviet military potential will reach its peak in 1983-85, but "NATO's *rearmament is unlikely to become effective, even under President Reagan's more aggressive policy, until the 1990s . . . It is therefore suggested that the target year should be 1984 when the American people will be busy with the election of their President to the exclusion of all international interests.*

"The Soviets' plan is to isolate Europe as much as possible, diplomatically and politically, and then exert pressure to bring about revolution through subversion, but using military force where necessary; the objective being:

"To secure the objectives, the surrender of Western Europe without running the risk of war, let alone nuclear war. The USA can then be dealt with whenever this is expedient."

The final nail in our war coffin is recognition of the reality that the social environment is also ripe for war. As Ernest Hemingway stated, *"The first panacea for a mismanaged nation is inflation of the currency; the second is war. Both bring a temporary prosperity; both bring a permanent ruin. Both are the refuse of political and economic opportunists."*

Certainly a war would prove to be a viable distraction from the economic problems (recession) which exist presently in the Soviet Union, Europe and the United States.

Young men are the cannon fodder for war. There is plenty of cannon fodder available now. Recently, the U.S. unemployment rate for black teenagers hit 45.7 percent; for other young men of prime military age, 20-24, 12.7 percent. Some 40 percent of the unemployed Europeans are under 25 years of age. The E.E.C. unemployment level is the highest in 23 years. West Germany has its highest unemployment since 1952. Over 700,000 British youth are graduating from high school with no hope for jobs.

The economically sick global economy has already seen extremely damaging riots in Great Britain, West Germany, Denmark, the Netherlands, France, Italy and Spain, instigated by the restless young. Riots are projected to hit the United States, particularly among minorities in the cities. What is a politically expedient way, a pragmatic answer to reducing unemployment and eliminating riots fomented by energetic young men, as well as redirecting dissident public opinion away from the political and economic malaise? Send the youth to war! It is a tried and true, historically workable, politically acceptable solution. And we are closing in on 1984, when *"events and cycles"* are square.

The Dance of the Kali
1/15/82

The six years during which the CYCLES OF WAR were projected to occur end with calendar year 1984. Will *"price and time"* be *"square"* in 1984 for war? Will *"cycles and historical events"* be in harmony?

When CYCLES OF WAR came off the press in 1978 and public interest in the book began to mushroom, this writer formed an organization to promote and distribute CYCLES OF WAR. War Cycles Institute had sole responsibility for distributing and marketing CYCLES OF WAR.

By all logic, War Cycles Institute should have been located in Columbia Falls, Montana, where we lived and worked at the time. Columbia Falls has both UPS and U.S. Postal Service.

So, there was no logical reason for not locating WCI in Columbia Falls. And yet, for some strange reason which escapes me to this day, this writer established War Cycles Institute in **KALI**spell, Montana, which is situated 18 miles from Columbia Falls, Montana.

What sense did it make for the staff of War Cycles Institute to drive 36 miles round trip to pick up our mail, when we had a post office located 50 yards from our office and a mile from my home? None! And yet, we all drove that 36-mile round trip twice a week. So, effectively, to the world-at-large, War Cycles Institute operated out of **KALI**spell, Montana.

Notice the first four letters of **KALI**spell—K A L I. The meaning of the word spelled out by the first four letters of **KALI**spell is very significant.

Late in 1978, an American, who is also a Hindu priest, and who actually practiced his religion in India, wrote to tell us that the **KALI, the Hindu goddess of death and destruction,** was about to begin her dance. We'll never forget the day we received that letter. A cold chill ran down our spines. You see, **KALI**, the Hindu god of death and destruction, is spelled the same way as the first four letters of **KALI**spell. And War Cycles Institute is located in **KALI**spell, Montana!

Remember, there was no logic for WCI being located in **KALI**spell. And, the sole purpose of War Cycles Institute, located in **KALI**spell, Montana, is to distribute CYCLES OF WAR: THE NEXT SIX YEARS. Coincidence? Destiny? Fate? A squaring of price and time (events and cycles) in history? Whatever, the first book on the subject of the potential upcoming war to occur by 1984 (CYCLES OF WAR) was publicized and distributed out of the city in Montana whose first four letters spell out the name of the Hindu goddess of death and destruction. THE ENCYCLOPAEDIA BRITANNICA, Vol. 13, 1961, describes the **KALI**:

> *"Usually regarded as a goddess of death and destruction, she is depicted as black, four-armed, with red palms and eyes, her tongue, face and breasts blood-stained, matted hair, and fang-like teeth. She wears a necklace of skulls, corpses as earrings, and a girdle of snakes."*

There you have it, just why that cold chill went down our spines when we received the letter from that Hindu priest. The **KALI** is not exactly the girl of our dreams.

The War Kettle: A Potpourri
1/15/82

To this point, in focusing on the unsavory subject of war, we have discussed the probability of war from the standpoints of contrary opinion, general public consensus, Soviet economic desperation and Russian military buildup, military experts' opinions, climatic factors, cycles, economic protectionism, political hawks in the Reagan administration, U.S. military weakness at a time of maximum Soviet strength, global economic difficulties, particularly unemployment among military-ripe young men, and a touch of the mystical (KALI).

Now, there are a few other ingredients we would like to drop into our war pot to round out the flavor which rises, building the clouds of war.

The GNP of all the world's developed countries is equal to the entire world's spending on military hardware—approximately $500 billion. Are these arms to be a waste of money?

Given worldwide educational indoctrination in socialism, including in the U.S. public schools, the probability of war increases. The philosophy of socialism is a philosophy of envy and a philosophy of war. When people are educated into the socialistic doctrine, that the government transfer of wealth from one party to another is justified, that legalized theft is okay, then it's a short step into public support for powerful governments to attack the governments and peoples of other nations to secure the desired economic goods. Thus, the logical out-working of envy and socialism is war. In war, economic goods are secured by the more powerful of the two combating parties.

The Soviet battle plan to isolate and neutralize America is really quite simple. Step by step:

1. Neutralize the American military and political presence in the Middle East, and then dominate that area, bringing the control of Middle East oil into the Soviet sphere of influence.

2. Dominate Africa and the strategic metals and minerals which are produced in southern Africa and which are vital to Western civiliza-tion's industrial machine.

3. Dominate the Caribbean and Central America, including Mex-ico, exposing the soft underbelly of the United States, our unguarded southern border.

With Trudeau taking Canada down the rapid road to socialism, the United States would eventually fall like a *"ripe fruit"* into the Soviet sphere of influence. The control of the Middle East, the African conti-nent, particularly southern Africa, and the Caribbean/Central America/Panama Canal areas, with Europe neutralized militarily, isolates the United States from its allies, separates the U.S. from vital oil and strategic mineral resources, puts the Soviet navy in control of the vital shipping lanes of the world, which, very shortly, leads to a collapse and a revolution within the United States. The economically and politically ignorant, spoiled American public, high on drugs, alcohol, good times, debt and professional sports, will throw a massive national temper tantrum, the Russians reason, resulting in a state of anarchy, leading to a dictatorship. Then, the stage will be set for a one world socialistic government, the final stage of the Soviet plan, which has been financed by America's international bankers and supplied by U.S. multinational corporations and U.S. farmers. Are we naive, fools, or co-planners with the Soviets? In any case, we are coming close again to fulfilling the long-held dream of humanistic man—that of one world government/empire. A return to the age of monarchs, of kings and peasants, of lords and serfs, of empires and slaves is on the horizon again.

Egypt, the first world empire, may figuratively rise again. (Holy Moses!) The pyramid, which appears on the U.S. one dollar bill, will again be the international symbol. The pyramid has always been a primary symbol of the occult, tied politically into a one world empire. It is no accident that the pyramid is the symbol of the international banking community. A magazine advertisement for Bankers Trust declared in numerous financial publications recently, *"Historic sym-bol of Bankers Trust—The pyramid atop our Wall Street building."*

Banking originated in occult Babylon which exported it to Egypt. *Pyramiding* investments is always a risky proposition.

Finally, there are some interesting astro/war *("Star Wars")* factors coming into play. Sunspots and solar flares cause changes in the solar magnetic field, which alter the solar winds, which result in the flow of magnetically charged particles sweeping past the earth, interacting with the earth's magnetic field, producing changes in weather patterns and the electronics of the human mind. A REAPER subscriber, who studies these things, wrote :

> *"Notice the sunspot cycle sequences are 11.2 years, 22.2 years, 51.1 years and 179.2 years. The sequence for three of Dewey's war cycles are 11.2 years, 22.2 years and 57 years. Wheeler's 170-year cycle is only 9 years removed from the 179-year sunspot cycle. A correlation between sunspot activity and war? Is it possible that wars occur when sunspot activity is at a minimum? We know there is a correlation between drought, resulting in poor economic activity, and war. The strongest periodic drought cycle has a length of 22.15 years, correlating nicely with the 22.2-year sunspot cycle and the 22.2-year war cycle. A war cycle peaks in/around 1983. The sunspot peak cycle peaked in 1979-80. The drought occurred in 1980. Tough economic times hit in 1981. Sunspots are now on the decline. We could see a sunspot minimum in 1984-86, correlating very closely with the peak of the war cycle in 1983."*

Historically, commodities which experiences bull markets during a time of war are COPPER, COTTON, SILVER, GOLD, SUGAR, CATTLE, and commodities generally, due to the fact that wars are inflationary.

THE MARCH OF THE BARBARIANS

6/18/82

An interesting book in my library is Harold Lamb's THE MARCH OF THE BARBARIANS (1940). It is a fascinating history about a little studied culture. When the word *"barbarian"* is mentioned in a historical context, most minds immediately track to Genghis-Kahn. True, he dominated the Mongol history, as it is recorded. But there is more, so much more to understanding the mind set of the barbarians than can be imagined with just a superficial examination.

Some barbarians stayed in the forests, tending their reindeer herds. Other had herds of horses and lived in the grasslands. These were the steppe dwellers. The isolation from civilization kept these groups barbarians; their wandering made them nomads. They were effectively human animals.

The nomads of the north coated their bodies with grease to keep out the bitter cold. They were rugged, a trait necessary to ensure their survival in their battle against the elements. These barbarians began to raid when the grasses of their steppes failed, forcing them to take from cultivated lands what they needed to survive. Barbarians were hunters and fighters. The cultivators of the soil, men of peace, were no match for the barbarians. With the conquest of the civilized areas, barbarians began to gain security, a never-before-dreamed-of luxury. The civilized, spiritual men fell easy victim to the ruthless, animalistic barbarians.

As our climate again turns harsh, we must wonder if the age-old civilization-altering process of migrations, and the resultant attacks by the barbarians, will fall upon present civilized areas of the world, as marginally civilized men, in marginally civilized areas, yield to their animal instincts. History suggests as much.

With this in mind, this writer noted with considerable concern the way the movie, *Conan, The Barbarian*, captured the fancy of the American public. As advertised, Conan was a *"thief,"* *"warrior,"* *"gladiator,"* and *"king."* And, it seems that the cruelty inflicted upon animals in this movie has pretty much fallen on deaf ears. Heroic, warlike violence has become popular in a vicarious way in our society.

The WASPs (White Anglo-Saxon Protestants) which dominate the U.S. have a very warlike nature. Dr. Iben Browning's studies indicate that U.S. WASPs may be the most violent people to have ever inhabited the face of the earth. There is some basis for this judgment. We are adept at grounding our plowshares into swords. A May, 1982 Gallup poll indicated that Americans are more willing to go to war for their country than are the inhabitants of either Europe or Japan. The United States and *"barbaric"* Russia led the world in arms sales, according to the International Peace Research Institute. In the past three years, the Soviet Union has accounted for 36.5 percent of total weapon sales worldwide; the U.S, 33.6 percent.

During the 1970s, the frustration with inflation led to overt aggression in our society. This frustration has turned inward now to depression, the nation's number one mental illness. This depression may only last for a while, however. Psychologists say the central repression of our age is aggression. Is there a cycle, a human action sequence, from inflationary good times, to depression, to war? Recent psychological research suggests as much. Will the barbaric Soviets, strapped with a deteriorating economy, and persistent, increasing food shortages, decide to revive (continue) their barbaric tradition, in the process kindling, in volcano-like fashion, now dormant aggression of our WASP-dominated culture? Recent psychological research again suggests as much.

Sue Mansfield, in her book THE GESTALTS OF WAR, presents a frightening psychological analysis of how we are primed for war. She sees our society as one frustrated by powerlessness and rage, which will erupt when challenged. Aggression today, according to Mansfield, is converted to guilt and envy, which leads to a masochistic submission to others **or** a sadistic need to punish others. Alarming insight, isn't it? How much has been written recently about our guilt-ridden society? How many volumes have been spewed out concerning the envy which dominates our culture today? While some Americans continue to submit to burdensome over-regulation, other citizens' groups have effectively become vigilantes and tax protestors. War is an appropriate outlet for this aggression. War is a socially acceptable, institutionalized form of aggression, leading to the collective externalization of anger, envy and guilt.

Mansfield believes that wars today are fought out of an insatiable desire for power and goods, in other words, for greed. In a culture such as ours, marked by increasing numbers of lonely, isolated, alienated, economically deprived (or so they believe) individuals, war becomes the magic elixir, a way of externalizing the dominating anger, envy and guilt which was internalized, while gaining the approval of parents. In our materialistic culture, the real personal affection and love which children desire has been replaced by the showering of our youngsters with material goods. Thus, material goods are equated with love and affection. Such love-starved individuals, once adults, can never acquire enough material goods to fill this *"loveless"* vacuum. War thus becomes an avenue for our collectively love-deprived society to further attempt to quench its insatiable desire for *"things."* War also masks our fear and insecurity.

I have often written that war is the ultimate sacrifice (the ultimate tax and tithe) which men are called upon to pay at the altar of government, which plays the role of God. In a sense, war is the ultimate earthly sin, the greatest manifestation of collective human error, which is what sin is—error. Thus, it logically follows, there will be increasing wars as a result of the further separation of a civilization from God. A civilization that sees God as love has less wars. Interesting. The early Christians were hostile to war. Perhaps their God was more of a God of love than the God of the U.S. today—the federal government. Perhaps one of the secrets of avoiding wars is to establish a God of love as ultimate, then provide our children with the personal love they desire and need. It has been conclusively shown that babies die when they do not receive love. Love is basic and impedes aggression, according to respected researcher, Dr. Ashley Montagu. Dr. Montagu stated: *"There is not a single shred of biological evidence to show that man is instinctively aggressive and hostile."* All the while we need to prevent an aggressive centralized government from intervening in the affairs of foreign powers, which inevitably leads to the misery of death and war inflicted upon our young on foreign shores. More emphasis on local militias, civil defense and continental military security would, of course, by contract, be emphasized. But, sadly such is not the case today with our professional warrior class in both the Kremlin and the Pentagon, coupled with the rise of fascination with the heroic warrior, such as *Conan, The Barbarian.*

Like the *Conan* movie, war is an escape. The excitement of battle is more promising than a routine, boring life-style, such as is evident during a depression. Besides, the world owes us one, or so our culture believes. Our pride took it on the chin in Vietnam. And, because Americans worship winners (heroes), dealing with the Vietnam vets has been an unpleasant experience.

In times of war, the government becomes a parent substitute, and accordingly, a source of security for the *"children"* who have not grown up in a nation. Mansfield referred to this as *"cheap grace."* (It seems men will always come up with a blood sacrifice.) Men can attempt to lose themselves, escape from their loneliness, return to the womb (of government), live under the dicates and judgments of the parent (government), receive the judgment of innocence or guilt (depending on whether one wins or loses the war), while the war itself is an effective punishment that reconciles the alienated members of society. Arbitrary group discipline is imposed where self-discipline is lacking. War is the price of personal irresponsibility.

Viewed from these perspectives, war is one of the worst manifestations of a sick society. War is the continuation of political policy by other means, violent, animalistic means. Politics is confiscatory economics; government is an economic parasite.

The free market requires maturity and self-discipline in the character of men who contract, exchanging goods and services in a cooperative manner. War, on the other hand, is the ultimate in conflict. To the degree that war is based on power lust and the desire to obtain economic goods—greed—it is at the other end of the human action spectrum, the unhealthy end, far removed from the cooperation of the free market.

The conclusion drawn from this evidence is apparent; we are headed for a war. It is so easy to see, we have to be blind not to observe it. As if the psychological risks in our own loveless society aren't enough catalysts for war, on the Soviet side of the street, we have the rise of barbaric tendencies, generated by an unloving climate. Can a clash be avoided? Can we defeat the barbarians? Can we turn the hostile tide? The ravings of Al Haig may be far too close to the collective human action which will grip our society in the upcoming years. A massive about face may be the only answer.

A MAD DEFENSE

5/07/82

Great public focus has been brought to bear on U.S. defense spending recently, due to the necessary cuts in the federal budget. Beneficiaries of *"butter"* programs which have been cut are screaming bloody murder for the *"gun"* side of the budget to be slashed also. National defense spending comprises 29 percent of the federal budget. President Reagan's desire to increase defense spending is due to alleged U.S. military inferiority or, to use a bureaucratic term, a *"lack of parity"* with the Soviet Union in military hardware. The U.S.S.R. is said to hold a 4 to 1 nuclear edge over NATO in Europe. The U.S.S.R. has 2,000 naval vessels, compared with 465 in the U.S. fleet. The radar systems which protect our missiles are said to be not only vulnerable, but effectively enemy targets. The NATO allies are said to be overwhelmingly inferior to the Soviet Union in conventional weaponry. Nine out of the 16 U.S. Army divisions are reported unfit for combat. Some two-thirds of the U.S. Navy's operational air squadrons are not ready for combat due to manpower shortages. The Pacific fleet is marginally combat ready. While weapons production costs in this country are accelerating at a 15 to 25 percent pace, the U.S. military infrastructure is eroding. There is a backlog of orders building up because of the large number of small foundries and aluminum forging operations (which make vital metal castings) that have gone out of business in this recession. For all of these reasons and more, President Reagan wants to expand military spending. Meanwhile, due to the projected approximately 50 percent increase in national debt over the next three years, the Pentagon is being asked not only to bite the bullet but to swallow it. (Beyond question, there is incredible waste and excess at the Pentagon.)

In all seriousness, we must question just how strong the Russians are militarily. Given the fact that their economy is in shambles (even when compared to ours), and the reality that 90 to 95 percent of the technology the Russians utilize is either given to them by the West, purchased from the West with American multinational bank financing, or stolen from the West via espionage operations, how can the Russians be militarily stronger? The Soviet Union has been far more

252

humiliated in Afghanistan than the U.S. was in Vietnam. Their break downs in hardware in Afghanistan look like something out of M.A.S.H. Morale is so low among Soviet Union troops that drug abuse and alcoholism are persistent and pervasive problems. Yet, who really knows how strong the Soviet Union is militarily? Can we believe TIME, NEWSWEEK, ABC, NBC, CBS, THE WASHINGTON POST, and/or THE NEW YORK TIMES? The established media has certainly at least appeared to be unreliable, if not deceptive, in previous reporting concerning multinational economic matters. Why should we trust them in military reporting?

Considering the fact that German and American bankers first financed the Russian communist revolution, and that we have continued to do so during this century, makes the question of a Russian military threat against this country at least suspect, unless: 1) Russian military might is for the purpose of intimidating us into submission and/or acceptance of a one world empire. 2) The Russians have, in fact, sacrificed everything for military might.

How is it the Soviets are such a threat in space when they do not even come close to matching our Space Shuttle? How is it the U.S. was unable to recover an astronaut on land (as opposed to water), while the Soviets have always recovered their astronauts on land? A dupe? Is the U.S.S.R. space program a hoax?

The first and primary purpose of a government is to protect its citizens against all enemies, foreign and domestic. Thus it would seem that the primary thrust of a U.S. defense system would include a building up of the Coast Guard, plus aircraft carriers, establishing a reliable radar and fighter/interceptor system, patrolling the Canadian and Mexican borders, establishing an internal militia in each town and city (like Switzerland), and mapping out and implementing a massive national civil defense system, if national defense priorities were properly placed. And yet, these basic national security needs are placed on the back burner. Once these *"basics"* are taken care of, then we could at least look realistically and less fearfully at the military threat posed by the Soviet Union.

The Polish ambassador, who recently defected to Japan, stated that the Soviet Union has used detente to massively build up its strategic forces; that the European nations' defense outlays (NATO) are a joke compared to the Soviet's investment in strategic offensive capability; that the U.S. has never had a firm long-term policy regarding the Soviets; that it is clearly the policy and strategy of the Soviet Union to dominate the West; that all Soviet and Eastern bloc military exercises are offensive in nature; that it's the task of the Polish military to take Denmark in a military conflict with the West and to be a *"second*

wave" behind Soviet forces; and that Europe is now in serious danger
of direct Soviet military attack by conventional means, perhaps involving the use of chemical and biological weapons. (In this writer's
opinion, three areas that definitely are a concern regarding the Soviet
Union's military might are biological and chemical warfare and
sophisticated applications of technology resulting from Tesla's work.)

What about the nature of the Soviet leadership? Is it such that one
should expect military aggression? By any historical standard, the
leadership of the U.S.S.R. has been barbaric. In light of this, the U.S.
policy of MAD (Mutually Assured Destruction) has been nothing
short of insane (mad). But there is a glimmer of hope on the horizon.
On March 16, 1982, Lt. General Daniel O. Graham, U.S. Army
Retired, made a statement to the Senate Armed Services Committee.
General Graham spoke as Director of Project High Frontier.

Project High Frontier, which has received little press, is a privately
funded effort, made up of an impressive group of highly-qualified
scientists, engineers, strategists, economists and management experts.
Their purpose has been to develop a feasible alternative to the current
U.S. and Allied strategic concepts which have been *"stale"* for the last
two decades.

The U.S. has always held the lead over the Soviet Union in technology. In fact, the only way the Soviet Union has kept from being
"blown out" by the U.S. militarily has been by begging, borrowing
and stealing U.S. technology. General Graham's High Frontier program would require only an $800 million commitment in FY 83, a
paltry sum, given present military budgetary considerations. The total
cost for this high technology, High Frontier space-oriented defense
system, is only $24 billion (in constant dollars) over the next five
years, $18 billion of which is military, $6 billion nonmilitary. The
10-year total cost is only $50 billion. General Graham's problem, as
well as the problem of these other patriotic and dedicated scientists of
High Frontier, is how to break the vested self-interest of the
military/industrial complex. It is no accident that Senator Tower of
Texas, Senator Jackson of Washington and Senator Nunn of Georgia,
for example, are all pro-military, even though they don't come close to
agreeing on other issues. They all three come from states where vested
military interests are well entrenched. Eisenhower's warning about the
military/industrial complex comes back to haunt us again.

The High Frontier program does **not** require adding a single nuclear
warhead to the U.S. inventory. There is no way the Soviet Union can
counter High Frontier now by adding more offensive systems. High
Frontier opens up space for industrialization. Just what is High
Frontier?

From a military perspective, High Frontier is a layered defense: two layers in space and one ground based. The first spaceborne system consists of orbiting satellites, armed with non-nuclear space projectiles, capable of attacking Soviet nuclear missiles in the first few vulnerable minutes of their trajectories. The second spaceborne system is designed to intercept, in mid-course, those reentry vehicles which penetrate the first layer. This will probably be much the same as the first layer system, with an improved suite of sensors. It might also incorporate laser or other beam weaponry. These two systems alone, in combination, can reduce the number of Soviet strategic missile warheads reaching their targets by a staggering 95 percent or more.

High Frontier further proposes a ground based point defense system to close the window of vulnerability before the space-based systems are deployed. The purpose of this system, for the next few years, would be to destroy the Soviets' confidence in a first strike against U.S. missile silos.

"Star Wars" technology is with us. Throughout history, nations and armies which have developed superior fighting technology have enjoyed not only a combat advantage, but also a tremendous morale advantage over their enemies. We have nothing to lose and everything to gain by immediately implementing High Frontier's recommendations. Not only does High Frontier's system cost less, solving federal budgetary problems, but it is also our ace in the hole, the one place where we have real advantage—space technology. Will the U.S. general public support such a defense system? Of course. The people would find it exciting. They love space-spent federal dollars. Witness the Space Shuttle. High Frontier would be a basis for hope, something much needed, given today's dismal military and economic outlook.

In January of 1982, I had an interesting discussion with General George Keegan, former head of U.S. Air Force Intelligence. General Keegan enthusiastically endorsed the idea of a space-based laser defense system or a space-based particle beam weapon's system. Keegan, for another, believes that the Soviets have developed an *"electron gun,"* which would neutralize our ICBMs before they could strike Soviet targets. So, assuming the Soviets do have this weapon, we really have no choice but to proceed with the High Frontier program.

Project: Noah's Ark
5/7/82

"Early in 1977, the President of the United States, Mr. Jimmy Carter, announced a few details of a top-secret Pentagon project code-

*named 'Noah's Ark.' It is, supposedly, a system of some 96 'bunkers'
and 'bolt holes' which have been established at various places on the
earth to house approximately 6,500 key officials in case of a nuclear
war.*

*"Many of these 'bolt holes' are underground cities, complete with
streets, sidewalks, lakes, small electric cars, apartments and office
buildings. One such 'city' is carved out of a mountain near
Washington. It is called Mount Weather."* [20]

Observation: Isn't it interesting that the U.S. government has made
preparations for its own civil servants, while the U.S. Civil Defense
system is in shambles. This is another clear example of the historical
truth that governments do not exist for the good of the people. Governments exist for their own good and to rule, not serve.

A Military Ruse?
5/7/82

Reflecting objectively, the purpose of a national defense should be
just that, to defend the people of a given country. Given this observation, it would seem that the United States Department of Defense
would concentrate on such things as civil defense, the National Guard
and local militia, antiballistic missile systems, fighter intercepter aircraft, good radar systems and the like. It becomes readily apparent
that the federal government is paying attention to none of these
things, but instead is concentrating on building an offensive military
machine, as well as one that effectively becomes the world's watchdog. The present federal military policy is, thus, imperialistic.

Given this imperialistic military build-up, which is not in your or my
best interest, nor in the interest of the common man tax-wise, we must
now ask logical questions: *"What is the purpose of this world-wide
military watchdog?" "For what reason exists this aggressive military
machine?" "It can't be to annihilate Red China, can it?"* We're providing loans and military aid to China now. It can't be to destroy the
Soviet Union. We have provided 95 percent of the Soviet Union's
technology and billions of dollars in loans to support that communistic system. And yet, we're told that Chinese and Russian communists are both our ideological and real enemies. How can this be?

Regularly the U.S.D.A. announces sales of U.S. grains—wheat,
corn and soybeans—to both the Soviet Union and China. So, the
respective governments are cooperating in the area of foodstuffs. Are
we feeding our enemy? Are we giving aid and comfort to the enemy?
Apparently not. Then, just what is our military machine for? Why is
the Reagan administration busting the budget, and the country in the

process, for an unconstitutional, illogical, contradictory, offensive military build-up, spending billions for the likes of the MX system and the B1 bomber? Are we fools and/or hypocrites when it comes to military policy? The only other sane alternative answers are that:

1. The Republicans are back to their same old game of supporting the incestuous military/industrial complex domestically and abroad (multi-national debt capitalism).

2. The huge military budget buster will bankrupt the American people, so that they more readily submit to a One World Empire.

3. The U.S. military/industrial complex must be pitted against the Soviet military machine, both of which are financed by the same sources, in a ruse to subjugate the rest of the world to the super-powers, and then convince the American people that a one-world socialistic government is better than mass military annihilation. *"Better Red than dead"* is the argument which has turned the Europeans to pacifists recently. That same game may be tried here soon. All the while, look at all the money being made by the industrial half of the military/industrial complex.

THE 510-YEAR CYCLE

7/2/82

The most awesome, chilling, and yet helpful of all cycles in understanding where we stand in time is the 510-year civilization cycle. For, with the understanding of this half of a millennium cycle, we can see all too clearly how historical events are confirmed in time. History and cycles are *"square."*

This 510-year cycle is little known, and is a topic which is extremely controversial and, thus, is avoided by the academic establishment intellectuals. Only thinkers dedicated to a search for truth in understanding human affairs have dared publish the evidence, frightening conclusions and implications, which can be drawn from studying the 510-year civilization cycle. In addition to this writer's research, the two best sources of information on this long cycle are: The Foundation for the Study of Cycles (124 South Highland Avenue, Pittsburgh, PA 15206) and Brad Steiger's book A ROADMAP OF TIME (Prentice-Hall, Inc., Englewood Cliffs, New Jersey, 1975).

The 510-year cycle is inseparably tied to the Drought Clock, formulated by Dr. Raymond H. Wheeler at the University of Kansas nearly four decades ago.

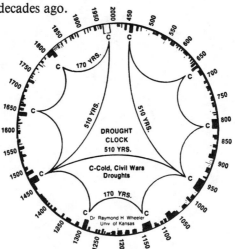

Source - Mainsprings of Civilization - 1945

258

Recall that there are two sides to the economic equation: land and labor. Both must be productive in order for economic prosperity to be pervasive. We have just completed an extended 50-year period of excellent climatic conditions, during which human productivity and creativity have been saddled with the inefficiency of bloated, bureaucratic, central governments, high taxes, inflation, large, international resource consuming military machines, unions, women's and minority's rights, conspicuous consumption, infatuation with leisure time, and all the other superfluous human activities that squander both time and resources. These activities occur only during good climatic times. When the weather turns sour, cold and dry, variable and niggardly, as is increasingly becoming the case, the social worm turns. The human race shakes off its unnecessary, parasitic, spendthrift institutions and activities in order to survive. The *"tar babies"* are cut loose.

At the time of the Maunder Minimum and the Little Ice Age which occurred from 1645-1715, Saturn, Uranus and Neptune were in the same position as they are now. The probability of more cold, severe weather is thus enhanced. The unexpected eruptions of Mt. St. Helens and El Chinchonal in Mexico are troublesome future omens. There were six Richter-6 earthquakes between 1979 and 1981. There were only four between 1950 and 1979. Chinese scientists who have studied these planetary alignments expect the next 25 years to be pocked by major natural disasters and sharp temperature drops in the Northern Hemisphere. Furthermore, until 2030 will be a time of high tidal force, a period when the climate will be unsettled.

The history of the world is a history of wars, of bolts and lurches, of perennial food shortages, pocked by occasional good years. Human ingenuity, under conditions of freedom, has been the shining beacon of progress. Western civilization has concluded such a time cyclically. The bureaucracies have choked out the flame. But, because man is basically an energy machine, he must first and foremost meet his biological needs. When the weather changes and food production becomes more difficult, man's lifestyle changes. As Dr. Raymond H. Wheeler wrote, *" . . . fluctuations in human behavior were associated with fluctuations in world weather."*

We have just entered one of these violent lurches which occurs only every 510-years in human history. It will smash the chains of a world in the grip of the myth that *"government is God."* It will crush the resultant idolatry and dependency which has inhibited man from discovering both moral and scientific laws of the creation, and applying them to his maximum benefit. Necessity is the mother of invention, and we are entering an era of dramatic, necessary change.

It can be impressively argued that all major changes in history have been ultimately caused by science and technology. At least, such have led to many major changes. This is what, in essence, sits on our doorstep. The challenge becomes overwhelming when one realizes that the scientists are pessimistic. We will have to muster all our creativity to survive. And we'll need moral absolutes to prevent abuse of our scientific discoveries. It is now four minutes until midnight on the nuclear war çlock. Respected scientist Isaac Asimov, reflecting on the future, commented,

"I don't think the odds are very good that we can solve our immediate problems. I think the chances that civilization will survive more than another thirty years—that it will still be flourishing in 2010—are less than 50 percent."

The end of the 510-year cycle, historically, has yielded to a Dark Age.

Is there a way of escape? Or must we stand firm and face our problems head-on? Aside from establishing a settlement on a *"journey to the center of the earth,"* or colonizing the moon or Mars, Buck Rogers' style, we must stand and fight. We don't have the capital for such extravagance anyway. We must harness the sun. The physical frontier is gone.

The last frontier was discovered—you guessed it—500 years ago. Columbus discovered America in 1492. Up until that time, mankind lived at basic, subsistence levels. Unlike in our society, entrepreneurs were not widely distributed in the Middle Ages. The elder continent of Western civilization, Europe, became rich following the discoveries of North and South America, Australia, New Zealand and South Africa. These new frontiers allowed the geographic freedom for the individual to flex his muscles and realize self-actualization through assumption of responsibility, drive, motivation and the resulting institutions of capitalism and democracy. Land, labor and energy were cheap. Entrepreneurs were the order of the day.

Earlier, we discussed how science and technology have led to major changes in history. For example, Martin Luther became a historical figure, thanks to the printing press. But science and technology can only deal with energy or matter which is already in existence. As such, science and technology can change and improve form and/or function. This transformation can improve the human condition. But, an easy boon comes only from the discovery of new territory and/or breakthroughs in energy utilization (the sun).

With the discovery of the New World, new energy, new land and fresh resources were added to the human social system. In fact, acreage available for exploitation increased 500 percent and precious metals 1500 percent. Europe grew rich overnight. But now, the geographic frontier has all but disappeared. So, man's ingenuity and creativity must meet the task as never before. But, these attributes are shackled. Conservation, efficiency, productivity and creativity are given lip-service, while taxes, regulations, institutions and inflation are rampant.

The last geographic frontier is dying with the maturing of the Third World. The battle for African and Australian resources speaks to the point that the last primitive areas of the world are being devoured, Antarctica excepted. With the population of the developing world doubling in twenty years, and the population of the globe-at-large doubling in forty years, it becomes obvious that we are being stretched to the limit. And, smooth transitions are the exception, rather than the rule, in history. We see this quite readily in each man's fear of the unknown, manifested by his resistance to change. Politicians and their spawned bureaucracies, thus, are dedicated to status quo-stagnation. It will take a monumental earthquake, figuratively and perhaps literally speaking, to shake things apart so we can build constructively again. Remember, the laws of thermodynamics do not move in an evolutionary direction, but rather in a devolutionary way, retrogressing to disorder and decay. So it is with society, particularly so, when man cuts loose from his spiritual anchor, and his creativity is frustrated, as he slips into the realm of animals.

If our problems are to be solved, Western civilization, the heart of cultural, financial, academic, political and economic world achievement, must lead the way. But, as Peter Oppenheimer, an Oxford economist noted, the Western World is now reacting to events rather than initiating change. This is exactly what historian Arnold Toynbee said would be the case in his massive work, A STUDY OF HISTORY. Societies rise, exist and fall. The key to their flourishing and survival, according to Toynbee, is their successful response to new and different challenges. Challenge and response, challenge and response, said Toynbee, is the life's activity of civilizations. They follow this pattern until they can no longer meet the next challenge. Then they fail. Western civilization is looking down the gun barrel of a number of unmet challenges. We are failing to face reality, and are fleeing to illusion.

One of the main reasons that a response to a challenge which threatens the existence of a civilization is not made, is that road-blocks are erected by tradition and institutions. The civilization becomes frozen, unable to respond, wrapped up by its own bureaucratic red tape and tradition. We see this today in our Congress, hamstrung by nagging special interest groups, while the federal budget runs wild and the Federal Register pumps out 220 pages of new rules and regulations (the law of the land) each and every day. In THE DECLINE OF THE

WEST, historian Oswald Spengler saw this would be the Western dilemma. Civilizations move through the springtime, summertime, autumn and wintertime of their existence. The civilization, at the wintertime of its culture, is in its old age, a time of great world city development, when the culture is frozen. It is unable to respond to its challenges. This is our state of affairs today. On an international level, we have observed our dependence upon imported OPEC oil and imported strategic minerals/metals during the 1970s, both of which are vital to our industrial society and, thus, our way of life. And yet, this resource lifeline of oil and strategic metals and minerals is beyond our control. Our destiny lies in the hands of others. (We are effectively less dependent now because we are in an economic depression.)

A divided Congress is unable to resolve the disputes between producers and consumers in our society, who are split about 50/50.

Our decrepit, antique, ill-equipped and undermanned military, joined by no national civil defense policy, leaves us naked before the most massive conventional and strategic nuclear military build-up in the history of the world—that of the Soviet Union (or so we've been told).

Our financial system, the life's blood of economic exchange, is on the ropes with over $530 billion of loans to Third World developing countries, an amount greater than the capital of the Western international banks—an amount which will never be repaid. The debt owed the West by communists in terms of personal and business debts are nightmares to consider collecting.

The populations of Europe and America are aging. And so, a generation war between the senior citizens and youthful producers is bound to erupt since the actuarial liabilities of the Social Security system are now greater than what everyone in this entire country owns.

In the 1800s, 90 percent of the U.S. population lived in rural areas. Today 98 percent have no involvement with agricultural production. We aren't close to self-sufficiency.

Need we also mention a $1-trillion federal debt which is consuming nearly all the savings and capital generated by the private sector? Or, the fact that interest on the federal debt is now the third largest item in the budget? We're not coming close to meeting our challenges. We're FROZEN!

Mature civilizations are flagged by maximum error in their theoretical, and resulting operational concepts. We see this in our religious/political system where government, the parasite, plays the role of God, the ultimate distortion of reality. We see this in our economic system, where money is created out of thin air, and wealth and power becomes nothing more than a magnetic entry on a computer disc, rather than wheat or gold. We see this in our political system, which assumes that wealth and happiness can be created by passing laws and redistributing wealth from the productive members of society to the drones. We see this in our social system, where envy dominates. We see this in the madness with which our nation has forsaken its first and foremost responsibility: to protect its citizens, via military and militia, from all enemies, foreign and domestic, not to mention a bankrupt justice system. We have witnessed the number of patents issued to U.S. citizens decline sharply. And, we see this decadence in our educational system, which turns out computer-entry specialists who are unable to respond with generalistic wisdom to the problems that plague our institutions. Truly, error has become the American way.

Arnold Toynbee and Ludwig von Mises articulated our state of affairs. Toynbee stated,

"I am not sure whether it is my daughter or my granddaughter who will witness the death of this civilization."

Ludwig von Mises declared,

"I have come to realize that my theories explained the degeneration of a great civilization; they do not prevent it. I set out to be a reformer, but only became the historian of decline."

We have all the characteristics of a mature civilization. This writer has compiled a list of 37 indications of a civilization headed for a fall. A civilization is on the brink when:

1. It is too soft, too luxurious, and too successful, and is, thus, lazy.

2. There is a vast concentration of land holdings by private parties or government, which has a negative effect on both the morale and morals of the people.

3. It fails to adapt to new challenges, whether they be economic, political, social, or climatic conditions.

4. Raw materials are used up at home and have to be imported, but can no longer be afforded.

5. There is a concentration of power and decision making in the hands of a powerful few.

6. The traditional, classic family becomes fractured.

7. There is exploding knowledge and increased complexity that results in each subsequent generation knowing less of the country's total cultural heritage than the generation that went before it.

8. Overwhelming population numbers hinder individual development and achievement.

9. The least capable members of a society outbreed the more capable.

10. Women's and minorities' rights become pervasive issues.

11. Laws strangle the productive members of a society and the judicial system is slow, inefficient and subjective.

12. Belief in the occult increases.

13. Sexual freedom is pervasive.

14. Inflation is rampant.

15. People become disinterested and disenchanted in the political processes.

16. The population's primary focus is on self-gratification and entertainment.

17. World cities arise.

18. Governments and societies emphasize preservation, duplication, security and mass-production.

19. The more capable members of society reject government service for selfish reasons, believing they can maintain their separate self-interests.

20. Drug use and homosexuality become widespread.

21. The tax system becomes brutal and discourages innovation and initiative.

22. Poorly educated members of society take leadership positions in government.

23. The productive population decreases in number due to birth control, abortion, wars, suicide and the like.

24. Crime, immorality and corruption proliferate.

25. Government bureaucracy becomes a barrier between government leaders and the people.

26. The country is flooded with aliens who have no identity nor understanding of the language, culture or history of the nation.

27. The more capable members of society reject military service.

28. Basic industries become controlled by foreign money.

29. More people depend upon government for income than pay taxes.

30. Government fails to unify the conflicting interests of a nation.

31. Religious faith declines.

32. People become passive, rather than active, interested in games, recreation, reading, entertainment and illusion, rather than the real world.

33. Rebelliousness and alienation of youth from older generations is widespread.

34. The lower and middle classes, who are used to getting more each year, are frustrated.

35. A society has a long period of economic growth, followed by a period of slow growth or decline.

36. Those with wealth and power feel guilty and become overly sympathetic to the economic underdogs.

37. An obese, costly, professional military, emotionally detached from the general population, seeks its own self-fulfillment.

Each and every one of these 37 darts hit the target—the United States of America.

We have briefly discussed the 510-year civilization cycle. We've discussed the characteristics of a mature civilization as well as the signs of its decline. Is there a human action progression over the 510-year period? Most certainly. As we run through this human action cycle/progression, just think of the history of this country, the United States of America: Bondage—spiritual faith—great courage—liberty —resources and abundance—selfishness—complacency—apathy— dependency—bondage. Apathy and dependence are the highlights of our civilization now. The 510-year civilization cycle repeats because human nature has not changed. Man follows the same sequence over and over again, if he remains, collectively, a slave to his animal nature.

In the history of this country, men and women in bondage came to these shores. Great spiritual faith characterized the early Pilgrims, the Puritans. Great courage was the hallmark of those who built the nation and ventured west. Liberty, resource and abundance resulted. In this century, selfishness (envy) and complacency set in. Apathy and dependency are now widespread. Bondage waits around the corner. When men value security more than freedom, as we do now, men become slaves waiting for their chains. Freedom is commensurate with responsibility. The security of slavery knows no responsibility.

There is another civilization cycle in terms of land use: 1) Man comes to virgin territory. 2) He chops down the trees. 3)The topsoil is exploited and disappears. 4) The civilization topples and the desert reigns supreme.

This has been the history of Egypt and Ethiopia. Only 4 percent of the trees remain in Ethiopia. Rome cut down all the trees in southern Europe from Spain to Palestine. North Africa's landscape was denuded. On the American continent, where there used to be 18 inches of top-soil, there are now only 8 inches or less. And the drought has been upon us. The trees are gone. The USDA told our farmers several years back to cut down the windbreaks and plant fence-to-fence. So, the topsoil has been exposed to wind erosion and water erosion. It has lost its organic matter, its life, which gives it the ability to withstand the harsh weather. All this is occurring at a time when water is becoming more precious than oil. We use about 400 billion gallons of water a day in the United States and waste 25 percent of that amount. We are under attack by challenges on all sides.

In addition to the fact that Columbus discovered America approximately 500 years ago, the weather changes, the characteristics of a mature civilization, historians' observations, the human action cycle and the land use cycle, just how else do we know that we are at a 500-year turning point? Well, the last great inflation occurred 500 years ago. Spain fell and England came to power. In lockstep, we find that the gold/commodity ratio has recently been at a 500-year extreme. The Reformation, which planted the theological and thus philosophical roots of Western civilization, occurred 500 years ago.

John Calvin was born in 1509. In 1534 he wrote INSTITUTES OF THE CHRISTIAN RELIGION. This marked Calvin as a profound theologian and reformer. John Knox was born in 1505. Knox' religious perspective on civil authority is still quoted in our day. Martin Luther was born in 1483. It was in 1517 that he nailed to the door of the Palast Church the 95 theses against indulgences. Where are these roots now? It was the historian Oswald Spengler in his THE DECLINE OF THE WEST who noted that in the last days of a civilization, humanities (humanism) replace the religious roots of a civilization. Economic activity dominates and economic activity is never founded in a religion or a philosophy. The *"last days"* are a time when the neo-intellectuals attack, condemn and destroy the religious roots of the civilization to such a degree that those who believe in the theology of the *"old days"* are in a distinct, hardly discernible minority.

What a commentary on our time. The massive human action cycle from bondage, to spiritual faith, to bondage, is almost complete. Our spiritual roots have been stripped by the *"intellectuals"* of our time. The creative cry of the responsible individual is lost in the cacophony of sounds emitted by the thousands who march in the ranks of government bureaucracies and corporations, following the pied piper of security to their cages.

Eleven years from now, 1992, will mark the 500th anniversary of Columbus' discovery of America, which triggered the explosive "S"-curve-type growth that established Western civilization. The average life of a nation is only 200 years. The United States just celebrated its 200th anniversary a mere six years ago. Thus, time, historical evidence, statistics, cycles and probabilities are against us.

The Master Mind behind the creation of the Drought Clock and the formulation of the 510-year cycle, Dr. Raymond H. Wheeler, Chairman of the Psychology Department at the University of Kansas, was a man far ahead of his time. Under his instruction more than 200 researchers worked for over twenty years, studying the influences of weather on mankind. Wheeler was not searching for facts that would prove a previously accepted theory. Rather, he was a researcher yearning for truth. Over 3,000 years of weather were evaluated, along with nearly two million pieces of weather information. Over 20,000 pieces of art were studied, as was literature throughout history. In excess of 18,000 battles were examined. All parts of the world were investigated. No stone was left unturned. Wheeler's efforts were comprehensive and exhaustive. Now, exactly what did Dr. Raymond H. Wheeler conclude? Here are his comments:

> *"It seems highly certain that the initiative is again passing from the West to the East for a 500-year period. The present 500-year cycle is due to end around 1980.*
>
> *"The changes that are now taking place will, of necessity, alter many of our patterns of behavior. Our economic system and the world of business are not exempt."*

Dr. Wheeler saw that the time at the end of the 500-year cycle, our time, would be a time evidenced by massive migrations, devastating revolutions and literally the death of the old world and the birth of a new world. Dr. Wheeler expected the death of our world to last until the end of this century, the year 2000. It was his conclusion that at the end of the 500-year cycle is when governments break down and nations collapse, and that there is a wave of international wars which are nation-falling wars. These wars trigger civil strife and revolution. Solzhenitsyn's long-forgotten cry rings true:

> *"We are approaching a major turning point in world history, in the history of civilization."*

Historian Arnold Toynbee confirmed Wheeler in his own way when he wrote:

> *"A Western Time of Trouble, which appears to have begun some time in the 16th century, may be expected to find its end in the 20th century, and this prospect may well make us tremble."*

From the 16th through the 20th Centuries is 500 years.

George E. Mendenhall, Professor of Archeology at the University of Michigan, has confirmed Dr. Wheeler in another way. Dr. Mendenhall discovered that following the 10th generation in every civilization, chaos hits. He commented,

> *"Almost always a combination of the Four Horsemen of the Apocalypse—famine, death, war, pestilence—have caused the destruction. It's our turn now."*

Roberto Vacca in his spine-tingler, THE COMING DARK AGE,

stated,

> *"It seems very likely . . . that the most developed nations are on the way toward breakdown on a large scale. . . ."*

Let's look at some more of Dr. Raymond H. Wheeler's conclusions:

> *"The fifth 500-year cycle since the sixth century B.C. is just now terminating. The end of the cycle is due around 1975 or 1980 in the center of an expected cold-dry period corresponding to the one in the first century A.D. and the one in the tenth century.*
>
> *"Profound revolutions over the whole known world of humanity, regardless of race or culture, have occurred during each of these centuries, often amounting to cultural convulsions."*

Dr. Wheeler went on to state:

> *"Current events show that another world convulsion is occurring second only to (1) the emergence of rational thought in the sixth century B.C., (2) the fall of Rome and other ancient civilizations in the fifth century and the beginning of the medieval world based on feudalism, and (3) the final collapse of the Middle Ages in the fifteenth century. The current convulsion is comparable to the birth of Christianity in the first century and to the birth of the modern nation as a feudal principality in the ninth and tenth centuries."*

There we have it. We now know just where we stand in history. Cycles (time) as well as historical events that confirm are *"square."* We are a facsimile of civilizations which have gone before. We are at a turning point in history, a 500-year turning point.

At this point, we could, and perhaps should, hold a pep rally where we *"laundry list"* all the actions that each of us can and should take to turn things around. But, other writers have ably and capably done this consistently for at least the past three decades. However, their work has been to no avail. Why? It is not because we do not recognize the problems, or have no answers. Rather, it is because our culture is frozen! We are in the wintertime of our civilization. We resist change because we are proud and fear the unknown, and are thus unwilling to give up our comfortable life in order to meet the challenges facing us. In other words, we are dead spiritually. It follows that only a spiritual awakening can turn things around.

I, like you, want to have hope and faith, to believe that we can roll up our sleeves and change things. But, it would be incredibly naive to think that we will be successful, unless we begin with a spiritual rebirth, a massive change of orientation first.

As a student of markets, I have learned that there is no place for false hope in investment decisions. Such only clouds one's judgment and prolongs error. We must ruthlessly discipline ourselves to deal with truths and facts, to coordinate the abstract with the specific, in order to be successful, to be in harmony with reality. It will take an absolute miracle, an overnight religious-type change of mind, to turn this decline around, then leading to reconstruction.

History never repeats itself exactly. It only takes a similar shadow or form. Spengler and the historian, Amaury De Reincourt, recognized that we are at the point in our civilization when we are ripe for a *"man on a white horse,"* a dictator, a caesar, whether a Cromwell or a Hitler. The political cycle of civilization runs from a king (rule by one), to a republic (rule by a few), to a democracy (rule by the many/mob), to anarchy, and back to a king (rule by one). Worldwide humanism, which ultimately leaves each man as his own authority, has brought us to the brink of anarchy. Rule by one is about to follow.

Given the integrated nature of the global economic system, coupled with exploding technology, including genetic engineering, space research, computer innovations and nuclear science, one has to logically conclude that the world would welcome with open arms a *"superman"* who had the intellectual capacity to embrace and apply all the factual knowledge which has been gleaned by our 20th Century intellectual world. A world which focuses on facts, to the exclusion of truth as ours does, is looking for a materialistic savior. Such a *"superman"* would not only be welcomed, cheered and embraced by the whole world, but would also be glorified and worshiped as he solves our problems. The remaining alternatives are another Dark Age or the destruction of the human race. These are unacceptable. Interesting, isn't it? It was Nietzsche, the atheistic, humanistic, German philosopher, who referred to *"superman"* and *"antichrist"* as one and the same. Now, as never before, is the world primed for a macho *"superman."* The stage is set, at the end of the 500-year cycle, for the *"superman"* to be an *"antichrist."* How much better a Cromwell? How much better still a Christian revival?

500 Years Ago

Unless we are astute students of history, we tend to forget what radical changes occurred in human history 500 years ago. The years just preceding and following the year 1500 were marked by men, events and inventions which have had dramatic influences on our lives and culture. A listing of these watershed occurrences, by year, further highlights the importance of the 500-year cycle:

1473   Copernicus was born (died 1543).
1475   Michelangelo was born (died 1564).

1483 Martin Luther was born (died 1546).

1485 The Tudor Dynasty began in England with Henry VII. Wheat prices were very low and a depression occurred.

1487 Civil wars in Japan almost annihilated the peasantry. Shoeblacks challenged the universities in Europe. Migrations of marauding hordes plagued Asia. Bakers defied the cities. Civil wars were severe globally.

1492 Columbus discovered America (West Indies, Watling Island, Cuba and Haiti). Book publishing became a profession. Leonardo da Vinci drew up a flying machine.

1493 Pope Alexander VI divided the New World between Spain and Portugal.

1495 Europe was engulfed by a syphilis epidemic. Leonardo da Vinci completed *"The Last Supper."*

1497 Cabot discovered the east coast of North America. Vasco da Gama rounded the Cape of Good Hope. Michelangelo completed his sculpture *"Bacchus."*

1499 Amerigo Vespucci sailed from Spain to South America and discovered the mouth of the Amazon River.

1500 The first regular postal service was established between Vienna and Brussels. Black-lead pencils were first used in England.

1501 Printing of books and typography expanded by leaps and bounds. Michelangelo completed his sculpture *"David."* Vespucci explored the coast of Brazil.

1503 Leonardo da Vinci completed the *"Mona Lisa."*

1507 Martin Luther was ordained.

1509 John Calvin was born. An earthquake destroyed Constantinople. Cambridge and Oxford were founded.

1512 War broke out between Russia and Poland.

1513 Balboa crossed Panama and discovered the Pacific Ocean. Ponce de Leon discovered the coasts of Florida. The armies of Henry VIII of England and the Emperor of Germany defeated the French at the Battle of Spurs.

1516 Erasmus published the New Testament with both Greek and Latin texts.

1517 Martin Luther nailed his 95 theses on the door of the Palast Church in Wittenberg.

1518 The peace of London was established between France, England, the Emperor Maximilian I, the Pope and Spain.

1519 Magellan sailed around the world. Thomas Gresham, originator of Gresham's Law, founded the Royal Exchange in London. Cortez was received by Montezuma, the Aztec ruler.[21]

William Irwin Thompson made the following statement in his book DARKNESS AND SCATTERED LIGHT:

> *"For 1500 spelled the end of the high Middle Ages, the beginning of the age of exploration, the end of Christendom, and the rise of the modern world system in the new world economy. 1500 was the beginning of the shift from a centripetal, sacred world view to a centrifugal, secular world view; it was the beginning of the shift from Christian to commercial civilization. It was indeed the end of a world."*[22]

The 510-Year Civilization Cycle

Collective Human Action Cycle

Bondage—Spiritual Faith—Great Courage—Liberty—Resources and Abundance—Selfishness—Complacency—Apathy—Dependency—Bondage

Land Cycle

Virgin Territory—Man Chops Down the Trees—
The Topsoil is Exploited and Disappears—The Civilization Topples and Falls—
The Desert Reigns Supreme

Political Cycle

King—Republic—Democracy—Anarchy—King

U.S. WARS SQUARED

New

One of the interesting things about the utilization of the squaring of the price and time forecasting technique is that it integrates the two apparently conflicting theories of time. There are two views of time: 1) time is linear; 2) time is cyclical. Time (history) moves in a straight line with purpose and meaning, with causes producing effects (linear). Time is cyclical and moves in a great eternal circle. Since man returns to the same starting point over and over again, history has no ultimate meaning.

Which view of time is correct? As in so many things, both are true, but neither is individually so. It all boils down to recognizing how linear and cyclical time fit together.

History does have meaning. Civilizations do rise and fall **in line** with cause and effect. Societies do reap what they sow in a linear sense. At the same time, since human nature is a constant, civilizations (men collectively) throughout history tend to repeat themselves in much the same ways. So, there are cycles of civilizations, too.

A man is born, lives, and dies in linear time. During his linear life span, he lives through many yearly cycles, monthly cycles and daily cycles, which are operative until he is called to the grave, the end of linear time.

The sun rises and the sun sets, day after day, month after month, year after year, in a seemingly never ending cycle. But, at some point of time, our sun will burn out, and the cycle of the rising and setting of the sun will cease. Linear time will call the sun's cycle to its conclusion.

Thus, while linear time and cyclical time are integrated and work together, cyclical time is subordinate to linear time. When linear time is up, the cycle ceases. Linear time calls the ultimate shots.

So it is with the squaring of price and time. The very process of squaring (integrating) price and time is the merging of events which take place in history (time). While the squaring of price and time in markets or in history seems to emphasize cycles, which is appropriate since we are focusing in this forecasting technique on a particular point in history, it also ties in superior linear time. For example, to be more specific, in terms of coming full circle (cycle), 360 degrees divided by four gives us 90 degrees—one quarter of a circle, a right angle geometrically, and a quarter of a year. Ninety degrees, a right angle, translated into 90 days, or one-quarter of a year, is the mathematical and geometric fusion of the abstract with the concrete. And, a fascinating part of this technique is that each cyclical turning point, whether it be 90 days, 45 days, 180 days, etc., acts as a **cause** which must be melted in with all the other cyclical turning points which produce the next cyclical turning point—the **effect**. Put more simply still, the strength of each new cyclical turning point must be considered and fused with all preceding cyclical turning points as **causes** which come together to form the next cyclical turning point—the **effect**. Each turning point is a function of all that went before. **Cause** and **effect** is a **linear** concept. So, cyclical time and linear time are in harmony in the squaring of price and time. It is heavenly symmetry.

Since the beginning of the United States, we have entered five declared wars against distinctly recognizable opponents. These wars have for the most part had public backing. The five wars and their dates of commencement and termination are listed as follows:

War of 1812	1812-1815
The Mexican War	1846-1847
The Spanish American War	1898-1898
World War I	1914-1918
World War II	1939-1945

The Korean and Vietnam wars were excluded for historically apparent reasons. Both the war in Korea and the one in Vietnam were undeclared wars, *"police actions,"* U.N. based, and marked by bitter national division over their morality.

The American War for Independence and the U.S. Civil War were, in a practical sense, internal revolutions—Americans vs. Americans. While this was obviously the case in the North versus the South in the U.S. Civil War, it was also the case in the American War for Independence. The 13 American colonies were strongly linked to Great Britain. Many British citizens, who became Americans and lived in the United States, opposed the American War for Independence. Many of those Americans who fought against the *"Crown"* in the American Revolution were originally British citizens, too. Throughout the scope of the American War for Independence, there was considerable strife as to where loyalty belonged.

Now, let's return to U.S wars, squared. Recall that key division points of a circle can be translated into days, months and/or years. One hundred-eighty degrees is one half of a circle and a very important turning point in historical time. Ninety degrees is one-quarter of a circle and a significant turning point (as is 120 degrees of a circle). The number 100 is a number of completion, a number of natural support or resistance. (So is 200.) One hundred divided in half yields 50; 100 divided into quarters yields 25, 50 and 75—all key numerical turning points. The number 144 is 12 squared, a gross. One hundred forty-four was the number of the Master Time and Price calculator developed by W. D. Gann. Something that is *"gross"* is apparent and obvious, beyond question in recognition.

In the squaring of price and time, or events with time, one learns to look for *"clusters."* In technical analysis in a market, one expects support when numerous technical indicators all point to the same price level at the same time. So it is in history, too. In the silver market, for example, if prices are declining, and $5.00 is a historical level of support, and $5.00 is the downside price swing objective, and an uptrend line and a speed resistance line intersect silver prices at $5.00—one takes a good hard look at silver prices when they decline to $5.00. At the $5.00 price level, based upon these confluence of signals, one would expect some support to enter the silver market. A *"cluster"* of indicators has suggested as much.

In terms of U.S. wars squared, we took the beginning date of each of the five wars and added to those dates significant numerical turning points. What resulted was a *"cluster"* of dates between 1988 and 1992. Such a strongly enhanced signal would indicate that the probability of a major declared war by the United States against a national enemy is very likely at that time. Here's how we broke it down:

War of 1812	1812 + 180 = 1992
The Mexican War	1846 + 144 = 1990
The Spanish American War	1898 + 90 = 1988
World War I	1914 + 75 = 1989
World War II	1939 + 50 = 1989

Natural numbers of support and resistance, key division segments of a circle, and the square of 144 all combine to highlight the 1988-1992 period and strengthen the case for this being a time of extreme national danger.

Does this make any sense? Let's take a look. If we have a panic and a crash which triggers a worldwide depression in 1983 (as per our earlier work on the economic squaring of price and time), misery, internal chaos, riots and economic distress which will follow in the ensuing four years (1984-1987) will trigger national breakdown, to be expected in a cold/dry era. Foreign powers will view the United States as being ripe for the picking—to be conquered in a war. The U.S. government, probably dictatorial in nature, will probably see that its only way to maintain power is by uniting the people against a common external enemy. (We have just seen evidence of this Machiavellian technique as recently as the Ayatollah's revolution in Iran, wherein Iranian hatred was externalized toward the United States.)

Is there more confirming evidence? The Mayan study of the sun resulted in the formulation of a 5,124-year cycle of civilization. According to the Maya, 1987 begins the *"hell period"* of our civilization, when earthquakes will literally rip the earth apart. The year 1988 is when some climatologists predict the weather worldwide could go absolutely wild. Is there a correlation, a cause and effect relationship between earthquakes, volcanic activity, erratic and harsh weather, and warfare? Your writer's studies, climatologist Iben Browning's research, and Raymond H. Wheeler's investigations emphatically confirm that such is the case.

In Stan Deyo's book, THE COSMIC CONSPIRACY, he noted that high levels of solar activity correlated with increasing earthquake and volcanic activity and warfare. In 1980, we saw the highest sunspot activity since the early 1600s and, of course, we also experienced the first eruption of a volcano (Mt. St. Helens) in this century, as well as increased earthquakes. And, the war drums have been beating louder. Deyo's conclusions regarding the relationship between increased solar activity, increased volcanic and earthquake activity, and warfare have been confirmed in the Middle East (Iran vs. Iraq). More to our point of study, however, is the fact that Deyo's research into ancient history, correlated with 6,000 years of planetary motion, showed that 49 out of 50 major revolutions and wars (98 percent) in the last 3,500 years **matched to the year** increasing solar activity, earthquakes, and volcanic eruptions. If the Maya are correct about the *"hell period"* of our civilization, which was **based upon their study of the sun,** then what we find, quite alarmingly, is the confirmation of our U.S. war squaring of price and time between 1988 and 1992, dovetailing perfectly with not only the respected Mayan work, but also Deyo's Hewlitt-Packard computer investigations which included some two billion calculations, running a mathematical model of the solar system in reverse for 6,000 years and forward for 1,000 years!

Recall, too, that this war also occurs during the time period when Western civilization is predicted to collapse, according to Raymond H. Wheeler's Drought Clock. The cold/dry era is marked by anarchy, disintegrating governments, economic collapse, piracy and massive migrations. Revolutions and the trend toward decentralization dominate. (Unfortunately, this analysis does not preclude a war in

1983-85.)

In this same vein, it's interesting to note that Robert Prechter, in working with Elliott Wave Theory, is projecting a stock market crash into 1987 that could carry the Dow down to 40. "Forty" on the Dow, for all practical purposes, is the death of the stock market. Prechter is also forecasting $5,040 gold in 1987: *"almost the exact level of a 144× multiple of the original $35 per ounce price! It is worth noting that Elliott considered 144 (the first Fibonacci number which is also a square) as the 'largest number of practical value' when applying the Fibonacci sequence to markets."*

Well, there you have it. The entire grim scenario for the late 1980s. What conclusions can we draw? First of all, although it is not pleasant, it's fair to say that in the late 1980s the weather will be horrible, and accompanied by massive earthquakes and volcanic activity. The probability of war accompanying these earthquakes during our *"hell period"* is 98 percent. And, U.S. wars are squared, too. The organized, sophisticated, mutinational economy, as we know it today, will cease to exist. Anarchy and roving, looting bands will be widespread. Crime will be pervasive. The U.S. government will be so weak that it is questionable whether the nation will be able to survive an all-out war (maybe nuclear) during this time, when our national survival will be at stake.

The division between the WASPs and those who produce, versus the minorities and those who are dependent upon government handouts, will be so great that it is questionable if these divisive groups (which will have been fighting throughout the mid-1980s, beginning with the Panic and Crash of 1983) will be able to pull together to fight a war for national survival.

Taking the two American revolutions, the American War for Independence and the U.S. Civil War, and squaring their termination dates with time brings us to the mid-1980s as a time of renewed civil strife. (American War for Independence—1783 + 200 = 1983; U.S. Civil War—1865 + 120 = 1985.) This civil unrest should occur during the drought following the sunspot peak and should coordinate perfectly with Wheeler's Drought and Civil War Clock.

The Democrats, who should win in a landslide in 1984, as a result of the Panic and Crash of 1983, will cease to exist, as will all other political parties in 1988. The Establishment will collapse.

The old trite expression, *"The bigger they are, the harder they fall,"* has application here. The greater the technological sophistication and thus fragile nature of a life support system, such as upholds this country, the greater the chaos when it collapses. The further removed the people are from providing for their own basics, the greater their pain

U. S. Wars Squared   277

and their readjustment when the fall comes. The pendulum has swung too far in this country. We are out of touch with grassroots reality. All in all, the years between 1987 and 2000 might be the very worst time to live in the United States of America. Stated differently, during this time period, one might be best served by living out of the country.

Joseph Goodavage, a climatologist, has said,

> *"My greatest fear, quite frankly, is the tremendous deprivation, the tremendous ramifications attending the lack of material goods, particularly foodstuffs, must inevitably result in political conflicts that may ultimately, considering the characteristic stupidity of Homo sapiens, result in some kind of a war—a Third World War, perhaps. I've looked very closely for the natural cause of this and the most likely time for this would be 1989. If we are going to have a global conflict, that will occur in 1989, and this is based solely upon my own calculations."*

Is there any way of escape? This writer has found only one. That is, individuals, and then the nation collectively, must first grab hold of the anchor of the personal, sovereign, loving God. Then, cooperative change must come, and come rapidly. The answer is necessarily spiritual. Only a spiritual answer can overcome these strong natural influences to which human *"animals"* are subject.

THE HINCKLEY DECISION: A BLESSING IN DISGUISE

New

The effective acquittal of John Hinckley, Jr. for the attempted assassination of President Reagan has brought into sharp national focus the full ramifications and implications of the injustice and potential anarchy brought about by the evolutionary and humanistic legal system which has captured our society.

Throughout history, the need for law and justice has been fundamental for society. And, down through Christian history, the age-old struggle has not changed. The issue still remains: *"Who makes the laws?" "Who is the ultimate legal authority?" "Who is sovereign?"* Because Christian culture has always seen regeneration in the heart of man as primary and fundamental, leading then to obedience to the laws of God in time, Christian culture established elected government and its courts of law as institutions for the purpose of **implementing** God's laws on earth. Because God was seen as sovereign and ultimate, and government as a servant of the people, government's role was strictly limited. God's law was the absolute standard for justice. Juries applied that standard; courts of law took the particulars of a specific case and determined if mercy was warranted, given the standard. Thus, we had a solid legal system of justice tempered with mercy, where the individual was held accountable. *"Ignorance of the law was no excuse,"* because everyone knew the Biblical law of God. The President was even sworn into office with his hand on the law, Deuteronomy 28.

Furthermore, in Christian culture, it was understood: *"The heart is deceitful above all things, and desperately wicked: who can know it?"* (Jeremiah 17:9) Also, it was clear that the law word of God is *". . . a discerner of the thoughts and intents of the heart."* (Hebrews 4:12) Men, thus, did not trust other men to make laws. Men, in justice, accordingly evalutated and judged the *"facts"* of a case and left the prior establishment of the absolute, abstract, timeless, principled standard of law to God's Word.

Quickly, we see how the tables of justice have been overturned by the competing and antagonistic evolutionary/humanistic legal system of today. If man is an *"animal,"* a product of his evolutionary environment, he is not accountable. How could he be? Accountability is

278

based upon the assumption that man is a free will moral being. There There is no accountability under evolution because there is no morality. Accountability is thus now diffused throughout society into the *"group,"* which makes the ultimate decision maker of good and evil for the group, the government. Government, by default, becomes the sovereign and god of society. Lawyers, accordingly, become *"godlike,"* further accruing power as law making politicians.

In the Hinckley case, the full measure of how our legal system has become alien to our traditional Christian culture became clearly apparent. Instead of the law of a sovereign God ruling supreme in the legal, principled, abstract, timeless realm, and serving as *"the critic of the thoughts and intents of the heart,"* man, instead, usurped that sovereignty (humanism) and attorneys and psychiatrists played the role of God and attempted to discern *"the thoughts and intents"* of Hinckley's heart. Hinckley was not held accountable. He was judged to be insane. Insanity used to be defined as a separation from reality, thus, separation from God and God's laws as the ultimate reality.

As the by-product of the Hinckley decision, the law and sense of justice which resides in the hearts of men in this country were buffeted hard. The injustice and potential lawlessness of our society became a frightening reality. If there is no sovereign God, there is no absolute law, and everything is relative under evolutionary humanism. Thus, everything is permitted and there really is no protection for men.

God's law speaks of mental attitude sins and of sins of both commission and omission. (Sins are, by definition, law breaking.) If I think to myself that I will murder some individual, but do nothing, God alone judges that sin. Man, however, does not judge it. No *"act"* of lawlessness has been committed in time. Only lawless thoughts, in the timeless, abstract realm have occurred. If, on the other hand, I conspire and/or actually kill someone, then I am held accountable and judged under God's law for that lawless act, both by God and by men in a court of law. Men become involved in the judgment process because my lawless act took place in time, in the material realm, where man is accountable and occupies in time. I would have sinned first against God because He is sovereign, and because my thoughts preceded my action.

Men, like God, judge sins of omission, in some cases, in addition to sins of commission. Historically, men have been held accountable for failure to *"stop and render aid,"* in the case of an automobile accident, for example, a sin of omission.

Historically, when men are allowed to play the role of God (humanism), and determine the law, good and evil, right and wrong, then tyranny, injustice, and revolution have been the following results. The

English Civil War of the 1640s was over this very same sovereignty issue. The Puritans and Parliament, spearheaded by Oliver Cromwell, held that *"the people"* governed, with God as the sovereign authority. King Charles I, on the other hand, held that he was sovereign. King Charles I was beheaded after his trial by the people in 1649. The *"divine right of kings"* was chopped off. It was decided that Christ is King and sovereign, not the king of England.

The same issue was substantive in the American War for Independence. Then, the King of England attempted to unlawfully impose his will on the Colonies. The American colonists revolted against the king's unlawful acts, not based in Parliament, and imposed without representation. *"Taxation without representation."*

Again now, today, we are seeing this same old tired sovereignty battle being waged. Haven't we learned this sovereignty lesson the hard way enough times? Do we have to go through another bloody, life and wealth-destroying revolution to again learn what history has taught us time and time again? Gerald Ford wrongfully pardoned Richard Nixon for Watergate. In 1982, the U.S. Supreme Court (THE BRETHREN) ruled by a 5 to 4 decision that presidents of the United States could not be sued (could not be held accountable) for violating an U.S. citizen's constitutional rights while serving as the President. We have come full circle (cycle) back around again to the *"divine rights of kings!"*

Of course, we have not even discussed the travesty of justice resulting from the 200 plus laws a day which go into the Federal Register by edict, which allows all the *"alphabet agencies,"* like the IRS, OSHA, SEC, FTC, USDA and FCC to run unaccountably roughshod over us. *"Taxation without representation?"*

Just how repugnant our present humanistic and evolutionary legal system is to a sovereign God is best demonstrated by the historical fact that He required the ultimate sacrifice of the death of His own son, Jesus Christ, on the cross, in order to satisfy His justice and fulfill His law, so that we could be let off the legal hook and have both eternal life and victory in time.

Restitution, resting in individual accountability, is the basis of God's legal system, which leads to long-term justice and peace in society. In the case of the violation of property rights, restitution of that property, plus penalty, is required. When, in the case of murder, a human life is taken, restitution is also required, the taking of human life from the one who took it by murder (capital punishment). An *"eye for eye, tooth for tooth"* is a principle of restitution, not revenge.

In Christian culture, scriptural true love has always been the keeping of God's law and commandments under grace. Thus, ultimately, Christ's obedience to the law of God on the cross for us was the ulti-

mate act of love by God toward mankind.
The struggle throughout history has not changed. The timeless issue is, *"Will rebellious man strike out on his own, 'do his own thing,' in a pragmatic, animalistic, humanistic, evolutionary, short-term way, and in the process, self-destruct, or will man humbly, beginning at the Cross of Christ, and then in obedience to God's law for his own good, start down the fulfilling road of life, liberty, happiness and prosperity?"* Our society has again reached this sovereignty crossroads. The road marked by *"man's sovereignty"* is the road of death and destruction. The road marked by *"God's sovereignty"* is the road of life, liberty and prosperity—*"Wealth for All."* Which road will we choose?

*   *   *

"Astrology and psychiatry sharing the same couch? Freud probably would turn over in his grave at the thought of it, but a growing number of Philadelphia psychiatrists are referring their clients to a 27-year-old British astologer, whose readings rival the accuracy of their standard psychological testing procedures."

THE EVENING BULLETIN FOCUS
March 7, 1978

*   *   *

"This is what psychiatry is, a faith or religion disguised as medical science. . . . I think psychiatry is essentially a replacement for the preeminence of the Christian religion . . . "

Dr. Thomas Szasz
Professor of Psychiatry
Upstate Medical Center
State University of New York
at Syracuse, in
REVIEW OF THE NEWS
July 14, 1982

THE END OF THE AGE OF SELFISHNESS

New

Fragile technological systems provide for necessities of life and allow us to ignore, if not detest, our neighbors. Practically, we no longer see the importance of the division and specialization of labor, which allows us freedom and the ability to enjoy our elevated life-style. We may acknowledge the point, but we don't truly grasp it. If we did, we would recognize that the very essence of the division and specialization of labor is that we are **dependent** upon other human beings. They are, therefore, important.

Our money has become abstract. This contributes to the problem. If we were on the barter system, we would exchange goods and services and more clearly see, on a day-to-day basis, the importance of others. Even during times of crises, such as floods and tornados, it is outside help (usually from the government) which provides relief. This robs us from establishing mutual interaction and dependency, which in turn would allow us to remain free from the slavery of government. The government has become the cure-all. But around the globe, governments are failing right and left . When the really big crisis hits, whether it be a natural catastrophe, an economic upheaval, or war, government will play the role we have assigned to it. As government plays *"Mr. Fix It,"* in the process it will usurp our freedoms. Consider the following Executive Orders which give the president of this country virtual dictatorial powers. (Source: THE NEW ORDER NEWS-LETTER, P. O. Box 13023, Salem, Oregon 97309.)

> *"A series of Executive Orders signed in February, 1962, gave the President power to place himself in complete control of the nation. He can then administer his power through the ten regions of the United States established for the special purpose of delivering emergency aid and allocating supplies during crisis and disaster situations. Some of the powers available to the President in time of crises or emergency are: Executive Order 10997: Take over all electric power, petroleum, and gas fuels and minerals; Executive Order 10998: Take over all food resources and farms (including farm machinery); Executive Order 10999: Take over all methods of transportation, highways, seaports, etc.; Executive Order 11051: Designate responsibilities of Office of Emergency*

282

Planning, give authorization to put all other Executive Orders into effect in times of increased international tension, or economic or financial crisis; Executive Order 11002: Postmaster General (member of the President's Cabinet) will operate nationwide registration of all persons."

What should we do? What must we do? There are Executive Orders all over the place waiting to enslave us at the first hint of a real crisis. We must become as responsible and self-sufficient as possible, so that we can help in our neighborhood. In times of crisis, the choice will be between neighborhood autonomy and government slavery. This begins with controlling our own economic productivity, the fruits of our labor, our money! This means, after we have paid our taxes, that our money is our own, to be invested and spent as we see fit locally. Avoid established financial institutions. They will loan your money to someone else without your permission, or worse yet, ship it out of the local area. Keep enough cash and survival gold and silver coins for an emergency. Stock up on the necessities. Until we can reform the corrupt financial system so that we will have honest free market money, commodity money, this is the best we can do in the realm of finance. This also means with our affluence we must store up surplus food and medical supplies, as well as water, if appropriate. Extra clothing and bedding, as well as fuel for heating, is likewise important. Friendly relationships with the local community leaders are a must, as well as with the neighborhood. Conversations should be about meaningful subjects (economics, politics, not just the usual superficials—weather and TV). Get to know the editor of the local newspaper and the program director of the local TV and radio stations. They need your expertise and insight. Become involved with your local city council, political caucus leaders and school leaders. One of the fastest growing industries in this country presently is the establishment of private schools. Are you an entrepreneur? Freedom is primarily maintained by sound management of the local family, local church, local school and local government. Last but not least, spend 30 minutes a day in your BIBLE, and spend 30 minutes each week writing your state and national representative and senators. As little as ten letters from the constituency can change the voting inclination of a politician. The spend and elect status quo must be destroyed. The 1980s mark THE turning point for this nation and Western civilization. We must do our part to turn things around. Our children will ask us, *"What did you do to save the country?"* We must answer, *"We took responsibility for all of our human actions."*

CONCLUSION

Religious beliefs are the basis of all following thought and human action. Religion, politics and war all boil down to human action in time, here on earth. Human action is, by definition, economics. The truth or error of religious doctrines is manifested by human action in time. Political human action, which, through legislation, carries out the religious beliefs of a society, is dependent upon its economic base for survival. War is politics by other means; war is violent politics, forceful human action, dependent upon economic financing to achieve a political/economic objective. So, at the root of all human action is economics. Man's basic biological needs—food, clothing, shelter—are primary. Thus, until our economic problem is solved, solutions to all our other problems are at best superficial, and usually detrimentally distracting. But, at the root of the economic problem are religious assumptions about the nature of reality. We must confront religious truth head-on and directly tie it into economics. The first is the ultimate spiritual reality; the second, the ultimate physical reality. In the successful integration of the two lies the hope for man's future.

Economic reality is the reality which none of us can escape. Down through history, as late as the European and Russian experiences of World War II, the Vietnamese/Cambodian tragedies of the 1970s, and the recent revolt in Poland, we find previously good, hardworking, often religious people, forced by dire economic circumstances, cannibalizing and stealing from the dead, devouring their young, and doing such detestable things as selling the bodies of their wives and daughters for sexual favors in return for money to buy bread for the family table. When push comes to shove, a condition which faulty institutions with underlying faulty religious presuppositions inevitably bring about, economic priorities rule the roost. Man, as an animal, is the most dangerous and ruthless of beasts. As it stands now, when the utilities shut down and the food distribution system grinds to a halt, watch out. Man's final option today is to get right religiously, to get involved and assume responsibility in all areas of life, **or** to die in a revolution, in a war or as a slave.

284

The battle historically has always been between slaves and free men. Down through time, men who sought security first and foremost, slaves, have always far and away outnumbered free men. But, it is the free men, when they rise to assume their rightful, responsible roles, who rule. A dedicated 3% can and have changed the course of history.

Slaves are best served by submitting to the authority of free men. Slavery always results in widespread, mass poverty. Besides, the illusion of the false security of slavery in a risk filled world never lasts. Since economic slavery to the economically parasitic state is so widespread today, it should not be unexpected that we are facing and failing to deal with our economic crisis. We are as far removed today from economic reality as we are from spiritual reality.

What we have found, perhaps not surprisingly at the end of our 510-year civilization cycle, is that our culture is frozen into effective personal and institutional inaction. We no longer respond quickly and accurately to the challenges presented by our fast-changing environment. What little is accomplished today is the fleeting byproduct of the few remaining remnants of our previously dynamic Christian culture. We have backed ourselves into the corner of immobility.

Good institutions have progressively become evil as good men have irresponsibly done nothing. The greatest enemy always comes from within, which is our case. Evil is only driven out when good men again assume their rightful, responsible roles. Paradoxically, our technological accomplishments provide us not only with a way of escape, but with the potential of leapfrogging into a glorious future. But, before this can be accomplished, we must renounce the maximum error (sin) which has captured us. There are no new geographical frontiers on this earth. Men have found no inexpensive, satisfactory, long-term answers in their attempted flights into the mystical vacuum of space. Man's last stand must be made here and now on this good earth.

There is a way to escape the ravages and depressing hopelessness of the 510-year civilization cycle. But, it requires a basic religious change, the *"miracle"* of individual regeneration, leading to collective change and restoration. Who knows? Once we embrace the Son, perhaps we will also capture the sun. The first (Son) is the ultimate source of spiritual life; the second (sun), the ultimate source of natural life. When we get our priorities straight, we may find the answer to inexpensive utilization of the greatest and most productive free energy source in the universe—our sun—a breakthrough which would liberate mankind from the drudgery of basic economic production to an extent never before dreamed possible.

On the monetary level, this reconstruction begins by money being created on the local level, by the monetizing of real new wealth, not by credit creation. The ultimate of peaceful economic internationalism comes with international free trade among responsible free men, buying and selling with computer/satellite communication, all made possible by the death of multinational, financial, debt capitalism. Political internationalism, a one world government empire, by contrast, is a disaster waiting to happen.

We have no place left to run, as the Pilgrims did when they courageously journeyed to this country. With the physical frontiers gone, we must now challenge the spiritual high frontier, carrying with us a harnessed and disciplined technological order. Rapidly deteriorating global weather conditions and mounting problems make it imperative that we now shore up the other half of the economic equation, the human side. The welfare state has failed miserably.

There is no greater waste on this earth than the squandering of human potential. But, to truly capture human potential and make it productive and efficient, which is vitally necessary if we are to survive, we must alter and correct our spiritual perceptions about man and the nature of reality. Socialistic education today worldwide has produced miserably inefficient humanoids. In Sweden, the Soviet Union, China, Western Europe and the United States, we find that the result of mass production education, treating people like evolved animals and machines, has resulted in epidemic use of drugs, alcoholism and an infatuation with entertainment and sports, as well as low levels of productivity and high levels of conflict and absenteeism, as mankind rebels against the prostitution of his spiritual nature. The recent technological explosion of inexpensive computers and satellite communications, locked into home TV, has made it possible today, as never before, for the common man to discover and develop his God-given talents. Decentralized, specialized education is a dream that can now be realized, once man again asserts that God, the Master Planner, has a sovereign purpose for the life of each individual. The basics of reading, writing, arithmetic, language, geography, science, government, history, and Christian ethics, once taught and assimilated, can be followed by psychological testing to help the individual discover and pursue his talents, in the best interests of both himself and society long-term. The last thing mankind needs at this point in a challenging history is centralized, bureaucratic, dull, unionized, mass-produced education. Today's educational systems are as destructive to meaningful human progress, as our financial and corporate institutions are to *"Wealth for All,"* as our government is to productive individual freedom, and as our religions are to a joyous, guilt-free, human spirit.

Cycles are basic to the *"natural"* realm. They are part and parcel of the *"natural order,"* in the continual struggle of the *"survival of the fittest.''* Pagan cultures, captured by pagan evolutionary religions, nearly exclusively hold to a primary cyclical view of time. Having all the time in the world, these pagan cultures become accordingly short-term oriented, slaves to nature, because all meaning in life is derived from the present. The future for them is just a warmed-over version of the past, according to their *"great circle"* concept. This not only drops them into the cyclical pattern, characteristic of the *"animal"* realm, but also fits very nicely with evolution. There is a sense of futility which pervades their society, since the *"great circle"* view of life effectively asserts that man never really progresses, and that he can only learn the hard way by repeating his mistakes over and over again, generation after generation. Furthermore, since there is no spiritual anchor with a dominant cyclical perspective, man is unstable and thus *"naturally"* oscillates, just like a cycle. This is the direction in which we are now headed.

By glorious contrast, when men grab hold of the anchor of an absolute, sovereign, loving, personal God who has a linear cause and effect purpose for them in history, men can escape the bloody wheel of the eternal cycle. They are no longer tied to the animal realm primarily, just secondarily. Men can become future oriented and have a real basis for hope and progress. Under the protection of a sovereign, loving personal God, cause and effect (linear) time overrrules cyclical time. Man, a spiritual being with an animal nature, travels the high road and thus leaves the low road of only cycles to animals and the natural order. It is the spiritual nature of man primarily, man's disciplined ability to handle abstract concepts, to think, plan, reason and act in a reality-oriented, linear, cause and effect long-term way, that keeps the animalistic *"law of the jungle"* at abeyance, under authority, and in submission. In this way, real progress is made in human history. And, real progress begins with economic progress, brought about by men of character freely contracting with a long-term view. Economic activity is basic to all following human endeavors.

The human race has progressed where Christian culture has dominated. Christian culture has the potential of literally producing a millennium of prosperity, much preferred to the destruction and dismay which is coming with all the pessimistic propaganda being pumped out at the end of our 510-year civilization cycle, the very occurrence of which is testimony to the fact that we have been captured by our *"animal"* nature, a sad state which a sovereign, personal, loving God never intended. Do we really want to gamble that the dictator arising from the upcoming chaos will be benign? History and present trends projected forward argue against it.

Is the Christian cosmology correct? Is there ultimately a spiritual warfare between a sovereign, loving personal God and his fallen angel, Satan, that involves us? Does Satan, under the pretenses of serving man's best interest short-term, set man up for his ultimate destruction long-term? If so, then the battle between the destruction of our civilization at the end of this 510-year cycle, as opposed to a quantum leap forward into a glorious millennium, does then depend upon each individual's decision regarding spiritual regeneration, leading to Christian reconstruction. Furthermore, it clearly brings into focus the work of Jesus Christ on the cross as the central fact in history, the point where individual spiritual regeneration and personal character development must begin. Reconstruction follows, beginning with the family, carrying over to the local church, local government and local schools, and then to the state and the federal government. Freedom always begins at the bottom and works its way up. The smallest active unit is the individual.

Under Christian cosmology, man is either a slave to God, or a slave to his own sin (animal) nature (which makes him a slave to Satan). Man is predestined/manipulated, by one or the other, by God or Satan. He is never totally autonomous or absolutely free. The beauty of God's system is that man can work his way to a position of maximum freedom, commensurate with the responsibility he successfully assumes. True, he is still ultimately under the authority of a loving, personal, sovereign God, but the greater the degree man assumes responsibility and acts as a good steward, the greater the freedom he has *"earned."* By contrast, under Satan's system, man is offered the *"quick fix,"* the illusion of *"free"* freedom, status, power and wealth short-term. It's a satanic trade-off long-term for slavery, misery, rejection, poverty and death. The latter is effectively what we are beginning to see now, as we reap the results of our evolutionary humanism at the end of this 510-year civilization cycle, as debt capitalism dies.

The power brokers and empire builders of big government, big business, big banking and big religion have had their ego trips short-term. They have held hands with Satan, while ripping us off in the process, made possible in the first place by our irresponsibility. They have skipped along Satan's road to temporal riches and power. But, now it's time for them to pay the satanic piper. The realities of harsh climate, wealth transfer and widespread debt have called their hand. Their *"greatest good for the greatest number"* schemes are being revealed for the lies they are. Those who have been too long involved in all these plans, schemes and conspiracies are facing the horrifying reality that Satan has tricked them. They have sold their birthright for a quick meal. They are realizing the harsh, devastating reality that Satan hates men, all men, including them, to the point that his (Satan's) all-consuming aim is to totally destroy mankind. This is now hitting home with a terrifying fury never before known in human history, as our cosmos crumbles.

Projecting current events to their logical conclusion, we are about to go up in a ball of flames, in a bloody revolution and world war, as the four horsemen of the apocalypse ride from hell. Another equally unsavory alternative is to become submissive slaves under some type of regionalism, catering to a one world imperial order. The only other option begins with massive, individual regeneration, accepting the blood sacrifice of Jesus Christ as the legitimate substitute for the massive blood sacrifices which occur in revolutions, in wars and in slave empires.

A sovereign, loving, personal God, a God of victory, has made it possible for us to snatch victory from Satan when we are facing the jaws of defeat. We have it within our power to quickly establish the true Christian abstract principled base which can turn the marvelous technological and materialistic advances we have made from their present road of cursing to one of tremendous blessing. But, this decision must be made by man individually, leading to collective human action (and restoration). God, the Gentleman, will economically let us reap what we have sowed. There is no escaping short-term pain at this point. But, we can still hold our way of life together and achieve victory long-term. It won't be easy. The empire will strike back. Special interests will not readily give up their filthy lucre, earned by pitting us against each other. And so man, at this critical crossroads in history, will have to choose whom he will serve.

Again, the trick that Satan has used to deceive man consistently down through the ages is his appeal to man's *"animal"* nature—the appeal to man's *"natural"* short-term orientation, his pride, his selfishness, and his irresponsibility. Upon buying Satan's program short-term, man has locked himself into self-destruction long-term. Such destruction inevitably occurs when the economic base of a civilization crumbles, as ours is now doing. Then, the short-term lies are inescapably seen for what they are, when they consume the long-term established economic base of a civilization.

The God of the Bible has been taken far too lightly by 20th Century man. He will not be mocked. Beginning with the Garden of Eden, He based the evidence of both the truth and reality of His harmonized abstract and concrete program for man in the economic realm, the realm of prosperity in time, here on earth, where man's activity triggers his eternal provision as well. Over and over again, throughout the Old and New Testaments, the Bible speaks of spiritual fruits and economic fruits, the key relationship between the two, and Christ—

the first fruits—as the sovereign link. Christians are commanded to bring every thought into captivity to Christ. Christians are called to be stewards, to occupy in time. This is human action. This is also exactly what economics is—human action. These two are inseparable. Satan's deception is to have Christians ignore the economic world. Then man attempts to go direct, to solve his basic economic and following problems all on his own, and to humanistically attempt what Satan attempted on his own and failed, to be as God. This is the essence of evolution and humanism.

Any time man attempts to *"do his own thing"* on his own, he spoils it and the results are long-term failure and self-destruction. Satan's maze leads inevitably to a dead end. Whatever success man enjoys in Satan's system is short-term and due to some application of Biblical law/doctrine/commandments. God's program, by contrast, effectively tells man, *"Look, don't attempt to go it on your own. You have imperfect knowledge and limited time. I have perfect knowledge and infinite time. I am the source of all truth and facts, of everything. Furthermore, I love you. And, because I love you, I had My only Son, Jesus Christ, die for you on the cross to free you from the judgment of My perfect law, under which you were condemned because of your imperfection (sin). Thanks to the substitutionary sacrifice by Jesus Christ on your behalf, you are now 'free' to operate under the freedom and power of My law in time. (Christ eliminated ceremonial law.) This is both in your own best self-interest long-term, your fellow man's best self-interest, and My best self-interest, both in time and eternity. My way makes all things good and profitable—sex, money, commerce, government, etc.—things which Satan has tempted you to use and abuse short-term.*

"You do create your own 'luck' in a sense. The sun shines on the wheat fields of both the good and evil alike. You do reap what you sow. But, I do help My children who help themselves, just like a loving earthly father helps a son who is attempting a task. Jesus has told you, 'Ask, and it shall be given you; seek, and ye shall find; knock, and it shall be opened unto you.' (Luke 11:9) You initiate the effort and I follow up. There is nothing hidden in my program, as is the case in the occult realm. There are only proper and improper uses of My creation, established for your own good long-term.

"You also win with Me long-term because the spiritual high road, based upon principle, is the most edifying and profitable way to reach the same destination sought by the short-term, self-destruct-oriented, humanistic and evolutionary human animals who take the proud, low road. Additionally, because under Me, you are meek in spirit (humble), you are able to listen, learn and respond to your environment

more correctly. Thus, you inherit the earth. In My words, ' . . . seek ye first the kingdom of God; and all these things shall be added unto you.' (Luke 12:31)

"Do not self-destruct. Such is the wasteful, unnecessary end product of Satan's plan for you. The humble, responsible, giving, long-term program I've laid out for you will bring you the life, liberty and happiness you've long desired, as you develop the talents I have given you. I understand your basic economic/biological needs. I also know the only way to maximize their real primary economic fulfillment long-term is by taking the high road, the spiritual road which I have presented to mankind over and over again throughout history. Time and time again Satan has deceived you, using your own people, to lead you away to destruction. Are you going to let it happen again? Jesus has solved the eternal problem. I have sent my Spirit to help you in time. Now, you need to get busy solving the temporal problems, using the principles I've given you in My Bible.

"Look at it this way: The economic prosperity to be reaped generation after generation is the result of individual character, the disciplined, spiritual decision to follow the program I've laid out for you with love. In My words, 'For this is the love of God, that we keep his commandments: and his commandments are not burdensome.' (I John 5:3) Then, technology, savings (capital accumulation), inheritance, real new wealth and contracting in the free market, with the division and specialization of labor, in a decentralized environment, with decentralized government as a helpful servant, will lead to 'Wealth for All.' You see, as a man, as a spiritual being with an animal nature, you maximize your economic prosperity in time by disciplining yourself to follow My laws/doctrines/commandments, for which I also reward you eternally. Self-discipline and self-sacrifice are always spiritual characteristics necessary for progress. Jesus Christ was and is the best example of this. He is the source of eternal life. He is your connection to Me. 'I am come that they might have life, and that they might have it more abundantly.' (Jesus Christ in John 10:10.)

"You are not an evolutionary animal. Animals have no optional self-discipline. Evolutionary humanism is again leading to your destruction, just as surely as it has led to Satan's downfall. The time of harvest is upon us. The time has come to separate the wheat from the tares. 'WEALTH FOR ALL' is yours, if you so choose to again be 'One Nation Under God.' "

APPENDIX
THE CHRISTIAN LIFE (A GRAPHIC PRESENTATION)

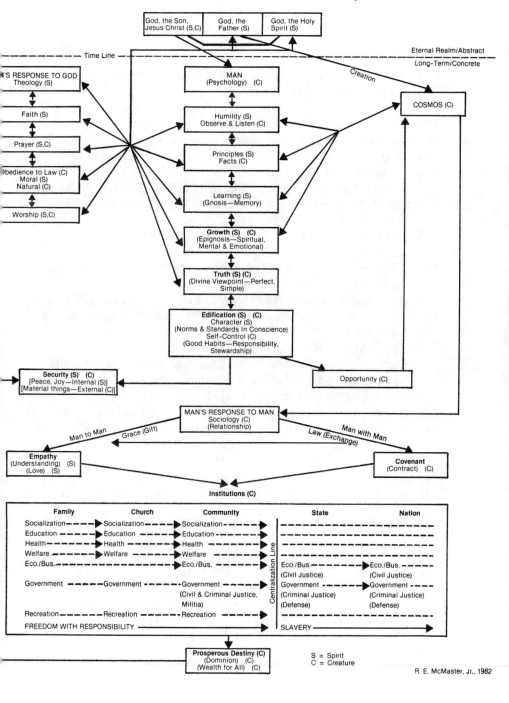

R. E. McMaster, Jr., 1982

NOTES

1. ACRES, U.S.A., P. O. Box 9547, Raytown, Missouri.

2. Associated Press, 50 Rockefeller Plaza, New York, NY.

3. Sam Hedrin, NETWORK, Copyright 1976 by Simoha Productions, Inc., reprinted by permission of Pocket Books, a Simon & Schuster division of Gulf & Western Corporation.

4. Jules Feiffer, Copyright 1975, Used with permission of Universal Press Syndicate, All Rights Reserved.

5. Reprinted by permission of The WALL STREET JOURNAL, Copyright Dow Jones & Company, Inc., 1978, All Rights Reserved.

6. Sam Hedrin, NETWORK, *op. cit.*

7. The WALL STREET JOURNAL, 1981, *op. cit.*

8. Jude Wanniski, Reprinted from the December 7, 1981 issue of BUSINESS WEEK by special permission, © 1981 by McGraw-Hill, Inc., New York, NY. 10020. All rights reserved.

9. Rear Admiral Robert A. Theobald, THE FINAL SECRET OF PEARL HARBOR, permission by Devin Adair Co., Old Greenwich, CT, Copyright 1954.

10. The WALL STREET JOURNAL, 1979, *op. cit.*

11. Smith Hempstone, Article in January 6, 1979, SALT LAKE CITY TRIBUNE, Smith Hempstone, Bethesda, MD.

12. William Irwin Thompson, DARKNESS AND SCATTERED LIGHT, Anchor Books Copyright 1978, Anchor Press, Garden City, NY.

13. Lloyd Demause, "Historical Group Fantasies," THE JOURNAL OF PSYCHOHISTORY, Copyright 1982, The Institute for Psychohistory, 2315 Broadway, New York, NY.

14. *Ibid.*

15. *Ibid.*

16. *Ibid.*

17. *Ibid.*

18. *Ibid.*

19. *Ibid.*

20. Stan Deyo, THE COSMIC CONSPIRACY, P. O. Box 71, Kalamunda, Western Australia, 6906, Australia.

21. THE BOOK OF KEY FACTS, Ballantine Books, New York, 1979, pp. 127-149; and Bernard Grun, THE TIMETABLES OF HISTORY, Simon & Schuster, New York, 1979, pp. 212-240.

22. William Irwin Thompson, *op. cit.*

SELECTED BIBLIOGRAPHY
AND RECOMMENDED
READING LIST

God and His Bible

Bahnsen, Greg L., THEONOMY, Nutley, NJ: Craig Press, 1977.

Lewis, C. S., MERE CHRISTIANITY, New York: MacMillan Publishing Co., 1943.

Rushdoony, Rousas John, INFALLIBILITY: AN INESCAPABLE CONCEPT, Vallecito, CA: Ross House Books, 1978.

_____. THE NECESSITY FOR SYSTEMATIC THEOLOGY, Vallecito, CA: Ross House Books, 1979.

Schaeffer, Francis A., HE IS THERE AND HE IS NOT SILENT, Wheaton, IL: Tyndale House Publishers, 1972.

_____. THE GOD WHO IS THERE, Downers Grove, IL: Inter-Varsity Press, 1968.

Law and Christianity

Ingram, T. Robert, THE WORLD UNDER GOD'S LAW, Houston: St. Thomas Press, 1962.

Rushdoony, Rousas John, LAW AND LIBERTY, Fairfax, VA: Thoburn Press, 1977.

_____. LAW AND SOCIETY, Vallecito, CA: Ross House Books, 1982.

_____. THE INSTITUTES OF BIBLICAL LAW, Nutley, NJ: Presbyterian and Reformed Publishing Co., 1973.

American History and Christianity

Hall, Verna M., THE CHRISTIAN HISTORY OF THE CONSTITUTION OF THE UNITED STATES OF AMERICA, San Francisco: The Foundation for American Christian Education, 1966.

Manuel, David and Marshall, Peter, THE LIGHT AND THE GLORY, Old Tappan, NJ: Power Books, 1977.

The Christian World View: General Philosophy

Campbell, Roderick, ISRAEL AND THE NEW COVENANT, Nutley, NJ: Presbyterian and Reformed Publishing Co., 1954.

Ellul, Jacques, THE ETHICS OF FREEDOM, Grand Rapids: Wm. B. Eerdman's Publishing Co., 1976.

_____. TO WILL & TO DO, Philadelphia: Pilgrim Press, 1969.

Lewis, C. S., THE ABOLITION OF MAN, MacMillan Publishing Co., 1947.

_____. THE WORLD'S LAST NIGHT, New York: Harcourt, Brace, Jovanovich, Inc., 1952.

Machen, J. Gresham, CHRISTIANITY AND LIBERALISM, Grand Rapids: Wm. B. Eerdman's Publishing Co., 1977.

North, Gary, THE DOMINION COVENANT: GENESIS, Tyler, TX: The Institute for Christian Economics, 1982.

Rushdoony, Rousas John, THE FOUNDATIONS OF SOCIAL ORDER, Fairfax, VA: Thoburn Press, 1978.

_____. THE ONE AND THE MANY, Fairfax, VA: Thoburn Press, 1978.

Schaeffer, Francis A., ESCAPE FROM REASON, Downers Grove, IL: Inter-Varsity Press, 1968.

_____. HOW SHOULD WE THEN LIVE?, Old Tappan, NJ: Revell, 1976.

_____. THE CHURCH AT THE END OF THE 20TH CENTURY, Downers Grove, IL: Inter-Varsity Press, 1977.

Education and Christianity

Blumenfeld, Samuel L., IS PUBLIC EDUCATION NECESSARY?, Old Greenwich, CT: The Devin-Adair Co., 1981.

North, Gary, FOUNDATIONS OF CHRISTIAN SCHOLARSHIP, Vallecito, CA: Ross House Books, 1976.

Rushdoony, Rousas John, THE PHILOSOPHY OF THE CHRISTIAN CURRICULUM, Vallecito, CA: Ross House Books, 1981.

Science, Archeology and Christianity

Gish, Duane T., EVOLUTION: THE FOSSILS SAY NO!, San Diego: Creation-Life Publishers, 1973.

Kang, C. H., and Nelson, Ethel R., THE DISCOVERY OF

GENESIS, St. Louis: Concordia, 1979.

McDowell, Josh, EVIDENCE THAT DEMANDS A VERDICT, San Bernardino, CA: Campus Crusade for Christ, Inc., 1972.

Morris, Henry M., MANY INFALLIBLE PROOFS, San Diego: Creation-Life Publishers, 1974.

Wysong, R. L., THE CREATION-EVOLUTION CONTROVERSY, Midland, MI: Inquiry Press, 1976.

Anthropology, Evangelism and Christianity

Richardson, Don, ETERNITY IN THEIR HEARTS, Ventura, CA: Regal Books, 1981.

Turnbull, Colin M., THE MOUNTAIN PEOPLE, New York: Simon & Schuster, 1972.

The Christian World View: Specific Issues

Bahnsen, Greg L., HOMOSEXUALITY: A BIBLICAL VIEW, Grand Rapids: Baker Book House, 1978.

Chilton, David, PRODUCTIVE CHRISTIANS IN AN AGE OF GUILT MANIPULATORS, Tyler, TX: The Institute for Christian Economics, 1981.

Ellul, Jacques, PROPAGANDA, New York: Vintage, 1973.

————. THE BETRAYAL OF THE WEST, New York: The Seabury Press, 1978.

————. THE MEANING OF THE CITY, Grand Rapids: Wm. B. Eerdman's Publishing Co., 1970.

————. THE NEW DEMONS, Oxford: The Seabury Press, 1975.

————. THE POLITICS OF GOD AND THE POLITICS OF MAN, Grand Rapids: Wm. B. Eerdmans Publishing Co., 1972.

————. THE TECHNOLOGICAL SOCIETY, New York: Alfred A. Knopf, Inc., 1964.

Lewis, C. S., MIRACLES, New York: MacMillan Publishing Co., 1947.

————. SURPRISED BY JOY, New York: Harcourt, Brace & World, Inc., 1955.

————. THE FOUR LOVES, New York: Harcourt, Brace, Jovanovich, Inc. 1960.

————. THE PROBLEM OF PAIN, New York: MacMillan Publishing Co., 1962.

MacDonald, Gordon, THE EFFECTIVE FATHER, Wheaton, IL: Tyndale House Publishers, Inc., 1977.

MacPherson, Dave, THE INCREDIBLE COVER-UP, Medford, OR: Alpha Omega Publishing Co., 1975.

Rushdoony, Rousas John, THE ROOTS OF INFLATION, Vallecito, CA: Ross House Books, 1982.

Thieme, Jr., R. B., EDIFICATION COMPLEX OF THE SOUL, Houston: Berachah Tapes and Publications, 1972.

Freedom and Economic Prosperity: The Link Up

Ballve, Faustina, ESSENTIALS OF ECONOMICS, Irvington-on-Hudson, NY: Foundation for Economic Education, 1963.

Friedman, Milton and Rose D., FREE TO CHOOSE, New York: Harcourt, Brace, Jovanovich, 1979.

Hazlitt, Henry, ECONOMICS IN ONE LESSON, New York: Manor Books, Inc., 1962.

North, Gary, AN INTRODUCTION TO CHRISTIAN ECONOMICS, Nutley, NJ: Craig Press, 1974.

Rand, Ayn, CAPITALISM: THE UNKNOWN IDEAL, New York: Signet, 1967.

Roepke, Wilhelm, A HUMANE ECONOMY, Chicago: Henry Regnery Co., 1960.

————. ECONOMICS OF THE FREE SOCIETY, Chicago: Henry Regnery Co., 1963.

————. INTERNATIONAL ORDER AND ECONOMIC INTE-GRATION, Dordrecht, Holland: D. Reidel Publishing Co., 1959.

Rothbard, Murray N., MAN, ECONOMY, STATE, Los Angeles: Nash Publishing, 1970.

Saussy, F. Tupper, THE MIRACLE ON MAIN STREET, Sewanee, TN: Spencer Judd, 1980.

Smith, Adam, THE WEALTH OF NATIONS, New York: E. P. Dutton & Co., 1971 (reprint).

Von Mises, Ludwig, HUMAN ACTION, Chicago: Henry Regnery Co., 1963.

Weaver, Henry Grady, THE MAINSPRING OF HUMAN PROGRESS, Irvington-on-Hudson, New York: Foundation for Economic Education, 1953.

The Cults and Christianity

Lewis, Gordon R., CONFRONTING THE CULTS, Nutley, NJ:

Presbyterian and Reformed Publishing Co., 1966.

Martin, Walter R., THE KINGDOM OF THE CULTS, Minneapolis: Bethany Fellowship, Inc., 1965.

The Occult and Christianity

Koch, Kurt, BETWEEN CHRIST AND SATAN, Grand Rapids: Kregel Publications, 1962.

————. THE DEVIL'S ALPHABET, Grand Rapids: Kregel Publications, 1969.

North, Gary, NONE DARE CALL IT WITCHCRAFT, New Rochelle, NY: Arlington House, 1977.

The Occult, Conspiracy, Political and Financial Connection

Angebert, Jean-Michel, THE OCCULT AND THE THIRD REICH, New York: McGraw-Hill, 1975.

Billington, James H. FIRE IN THE MINDS OF MEN, New York: Basic Books, 1980.

Gunther, Max, WALL STREET AND WITCHCRAFT, New York: Bernard Geis Associates, 1971.

Multinational Debt Capitalism—Finance and Business (General)

Allen, Gary, NONE DARE CALL IT CONSPIRACY, Rossmoor, CA: Concord Press, 1971.

————. THE ROCKEFELLER FILE, Seal Beach, CA: '76 Press, 1976.

Cohen, Jerry S. and Mintz, Morton, AMERICA, INC., New York: Dell Publishing Co., 1971.

Dinsmore, Herman H., THE BLEEDING OF AMERICA, Belmont, MA: Western Islands, 1974.

Griffin, Des, FOURTH REICH OF THE RICH, South Pasadena, CA: Emissary Publications, 1976.

Groseclose, Elgin, AMERICA'S MONEY MACHINE: THE STORY OF THE FEDERAL RESERVE, Westport, CT: Arlington House Publishers, 1966.

Gunther, Max, THE VERY, VERY RICH AND HOW THEY GOT THAT WAY, Chicago: Playboy Press, 1972.

Katz, David M., BANK CONTROL OF LARGE CORPORATIONS IN THE UNITED STATES, Berkeley: University of California Press, 1978.

Labor Party, U.S., DOPE, INC., New York: The New Benjamin Franklin House, 1978.

Morgan, Dan, MERCHANTS OF GRAIN, New York: The Viking Press, 1979.

Ney, Richard, THE WALL STREET JUNGLE, New York: Grove Press, Inc., 1970.

Sampson, Anthony, THE MONEY LENDERS, New York: The Viking Press, 1981.

Sutton, Antony C., THE WAR ON GOLD, Seal Beach, CA: '76 Press, 1977.

Tolf, Robert W., THE RUSSIAN ROCKEFELLERS, Stanford: Hoover Institution Press, 1976.

Multinational Debt Capitalism—Support of Communism

Sutton, Antony C., NATIONAL SUICIDE, New Rochelle, NY: Arlington House, 1973.

_____. TECHNOLOGICAL TREASON, Phoenix: Research Publications, P. O. Box 39026, Phoenix, AZ, 85069, 1982.

The Military/Industrial Complex

Herbert, Anthony B., SOLDIER, New York: Holt, Rinehart and Winston, 1973.

Katz, Howard S., THE WARMONGERS, New York: Books in Focus, 1979.

Sampson, Anthony, THE ARMS BAZAAR, New York: Bantam Books, 1978.

Theobald, Robert A., THE FINAL SECRET OF PEARL HARBOR, Old Greenwich, CT: The Devin-Adair Co., 1954.

Multinational Oil

Blair, John M., THE CONTROL OF OIL, New York: Vintage Books, 1978.

Sampson, Anthony, THE SEVEN SISTERS, Des Plaines, IL: Bantam Books, Inc., 1976.

Stork, Joe, MIDDLE EAST OIL AND THE ENERGY CRISIS, New York: Monthly Review Press, 1975.

Sutton, Antony C., ENERGY: THE CREATED CRISIS, New York: Books in Focus, 1979.

Multinational Debt Capitalism—Political Intrigue and a One World Empire

Griffin, Des, DESCENT INTO SLAVERY, South Pasadena, CA: Emissary Publications, 1980.

Hayek, Friedrick A., THE ROAD TO SERFDOM, Chicago: University of Chicago Press, 1944.

Knupffer, George, THE STRUGGLE FOR WORLD POWER, London: The Plain-Speaker Publishing Co., 1971.

Piekoff, Leonard, THE OMINOUS PARALLELS, New York: Stein and Day, 1982.

Quigley, Carroll, THE ANGLO-AMERICAN ESTABLISHMENT, New York: Books in Focus, 1981.

_____. TRAGEDY AND HOPE, Hollywood: Angriff Press, 1966.

Reisman, George, THE GOVERNMENT AGAINST THE ECONOMY, Ottawa, IL and Thornwood, NY: Caroline House Publishers, Inc., 1979.

Solzhenitsyn, Aleksandr I., THE GULAG ARCHIPELAGO, NY: Harper & Row, 1975.

Somoza, Anastasio, NICARAGUA BETRAYED, Belmont, MA: Western Islands, 1980.

Sutton, Antony C. and Wood, Patrick M., TRILATERALS OVER WASHINGTON, Scottsdale, AZ: The August Corporation, 1978.

_____. WALL STREET AND THE RISE OF HITLER, Seal Beach, CA: '76 Press, 1976.

The Media Whitewash

Cirino, Robert, DON'T BLAME THE PEOPLE, New York: Vintage Books, 1971.

Chayefsky, Paddy, NETWORK, New York: Pocket Books, 1976.

Fishman, Mark, MANUFACTURING THE NEWS, Austin: University of Texas Press, 1980.

Social Control and Society

Huntford, Roland, THE NEW TOTALITARIANS, New York: Stein and Day, 1972.

Rand, Ayn, ATLAS SHRUGGED, New York: Signet, 1957.

Sargant, William, BATTLE FOR THE MIND, New York: Harper & Row, 1957.

Schoeck, Helmut, ENVY, New York: Harcourt, Brace & World, 1966.

Agriculture and Climate

Browning, Iben and Winkless, III, Nels, CLIMATE AND THE AFFAIRS OF MEN, New York: Harper's Magazine Press, 1975.

Carter, Vernon Gill and Dale, Tom, TOPSOIL & CIVILIZATION, Norman, OK: University of Oklahoma Press, 1982.

Walters, Jr., Charles, UNFORGIVEN, Raytown, MO: Acres, U.S.A., Economics Library, 10008 E. 60th Terrace, 1971.

Time and Cyclical Perspectives

Dewey, Edward R., CYCLES, Pittsburgh: Foundation for the Study of Cycles, 1973.

Goodfield, June and Toulmin, Stephen, THE DISCOVERY OF TIME, Chicago: The University of Chicago Press, 1975.

McMaster, Jr., R. E., CYCLES OF WAR, Kalispell, MT: War Cycles Institute, 1977.

Steiger, Brad, A ROADMAP OF TIME, Englewood Cliffs, NJ: Prentice-Hall, Inc., 1975.

Spengler, Oswald, THE DECLINE OF THE WEST, New York: Alfred A. Knopf, 1926.

Technology and Future Potential

Bova, Ben, THE HIGH ROAD, Boston: Houghton Mifflin Co., 1981.

Kahn, Herman, THE NEXT 200 YEARS, New York: Wm. Morrow and Co., 1976.

Norman, Colin, THE GOD THAT LIMPS, New York: W. W. Norton & Co., 1981.

Thompson, William Irwin, DARKNESS AND SCATTERED LIGHT, Garden City, New York: Anchor Press/Doubleday, 1978.

Toffler, Alvin, FUTURE SHOCK, New York: Bantam Books, Inc., 1971.

_____. THE ECO-SPASM REPORT, New York: Bantam Books, Inc., 1975.

Practical Interpersonal Perspectives

Gall, John, SYSTEMANTICS, New York: Pocket Books, 1978.

Hull, Raymond and Peter, Dr. Laurence J., THE PETER PRINCI-PLE, New York: Wm. Morrow and Co., 1969.

Peter, Dr. Laurence J., THE PETER PLAN, New York: Wm. Morrow and Co., 1976.

_____. THE PETER PRESCRIPTION, New York: Bantam Books, 1972.

Schumacher, E. F., SMALL IS BEAUTIFUL, New York: Harper & Row, 1973.

Seabury, David, THE ART OF SELFISHNESS, New York: Pocket Books, 1974.

R. E. McMaster edits a weekly newsletter entitled "THE REAPER."
For more information, please contact:

THE REAPER
P. O. Box 39026
Phoenix, AZ 85069

or call toll-free 1-800-528-0559.